The
Gambia

the Bradt Travel Guide

Philip Briggs
Updated by
Simon Fenton

edition
2

www.bradtguides.com

Bradt Travel Guides Ltd, UK
The Globe Pequot Press Inc, USA

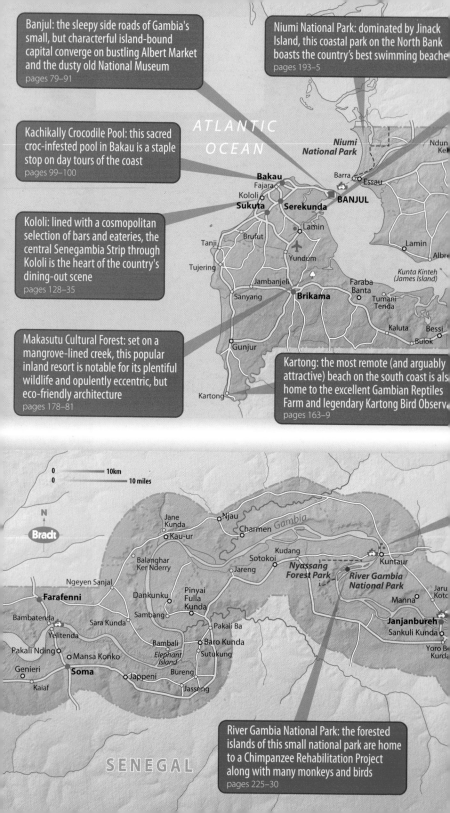

Banjul: the sleepy side roads of Gambia's small, but characterful island-bound capital converge on bustling Albert Market and the dusty old National Museum
pages 79–91

Niumi National Park: dominated by Jinack Island, this coastal park on the North Bank boasts the country's best swimming beache
pages 193–5

Kachikally Crocodile Pool: this sacred croc-infested pool in Bakau is a staple stop on day tours of the coast
pages 99–100

Kololi: lined with a cosmopolitan selection of bars and eateries, the central Senegambia Strip through Kololi is the heart of the country's dining-out scene
pages 128–35

Makasutu Cultural Forest: set on a mangrove-lined creek, this popular inland resort is notable for its plentiful wildlife and opulently eccentric, but eco-friendly architecture
pages 178–81

Kartong: the most remote (and arguably attractive) beach on the south coast is als home to the excellent Gambian Reptiles Farm and legendary Kartong Bird Observ
pages 163–9

ATLANTIC OCEAN

Niumi National Park

Ndun Ke

Bakau
Fajara
Barra · Essau
Kololi
Sukuta · Serekunda · **BANJUL**
Lamin
Tanji · Brufut
Lamin
Yundum
Albr
Tujering
Kunta Kinteh (James Island)
Jambanjeli
Faraba Banta
Sanyang · **Brikama**
Tumani Tenda
Kaluta · Bessi
Bulok
Gunjur

Kartong

River Gambia National Park: the forested islands of this small national park are home to a Chimpanzee Rehabilitation Project along with many monkeys and birds
pages 225–30

0 — 10km
0 — 10 miles

N

Bradt

Jane Kunda · Njau
Charmen · *Gambia*
Kau-ur
Kudang
Balanghar Ker Nderry
Sotokoi · *Nyassang Forest Park* · Kuntaur
Jareng · *River Gambia National Park*
Ngeyen Sanjal
Jaru Kotc
Farafenni · Dankunku · Pinyai Fulla Kunda
Manna
Bambatenda · Sambang
Janjanbureh
Yelitenda · Sara Kunda · Pakali Ba
Sankuli Kunda
Pakali Nding · Mansa Konko · Bambali · Baro Kunda
Yoro B Kurda
Genieri · *Elephant Island* · Sutukung
Soma · Jappeni · Bureng
Kaiaf · Jasseng

SENEGAL

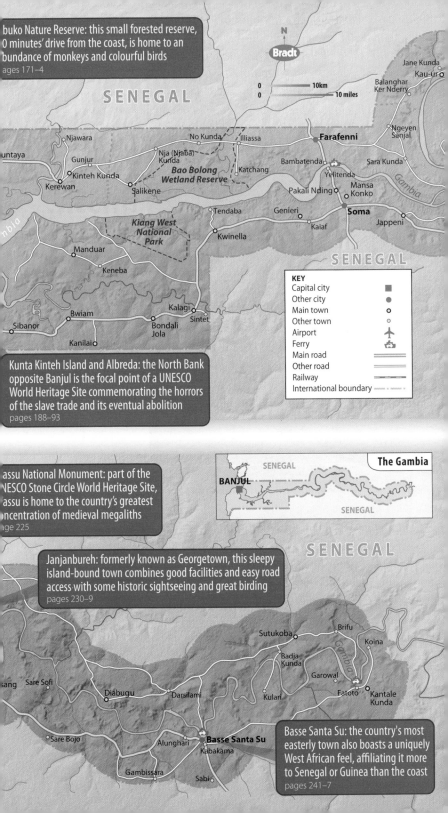

buko Nature Reserve: this small forested reserve, 0 minutes' drive from the coast, is home to an bundance of monkeys and colourful birds
ages 171–4

N

Bradt

SENEGAL

| 0 | | 10km |
| 0 | | 10 miles |

Jane Kunda
Kau-ur

Balanghar
Ker Nderry

Njawara   No Kunda   Illiassa   **Farafenni**

Ngeyen
Sanjal

Gunjur   Nja (Njaba)
Kunda

untaya

Kinteh Kunda   *Bao Bolong*   Katchang   Bambatenda   Sara Kunda
Wetland Reserve

Yelitenda

Kerewan   Salikene   Pakali Nding   Mansa
Konko

nbia   Tendaba   Genieri   **Soma**   Jappeni

Kiang West   Kaiaf
National
Park   Kwinella

Manduar

Keneba

SENEGAL

Kalagi

Bwiam   Sintet

Sibanor   Bondali
Jola

Kanilai

Kunta Kinteh Island and Albreda: the North Bank opposite Banjul is the focal point of a UNESCO World Heritage Site commemorating the horrors of the slave trade and its eventual abolition
pages 188–93

KEY

Capital city	■
Other city	●
Main town	◉
Other town	○
Airport	✈
Ferry	⛴
Main road	
Other road	
Railway	
International boundary	

assu National Monument: part of the
NESCO Stone Circle World Heritage Site,
assu is home to the country's greatest
ncentration of medieval megaliths
age 225

SENEGAL

The Gambia

BANJUL   SENEGAL

SENEGAL

Janjanbureh: formerly known as Georgetown, this sleepy island-bound town combines good facilities and easy road access with some historic sightseeing and great birding
pages 230–9

SENEGAL

Sutukoba   Brifu

Koina

Badja
Kunda

Garowal

sang   Sare Sofi

Diabugu   Darsilami   Kulari   Fatoto   Kantale
Kunda

Sare Bojo   Alunghari   **Basse Santa Su**
Kabakama

Gambissara   Sabi

Basse Santa Su: the country's most easterly town also boasts a uniquely West African feel, affiliating it more to Senegal or Guinea than the coast
pages 241–7

The Gambia

Don't miss...

Wildlife

Wildlife is everywhere in The Gambia, whether it be sparkling dragonflies or colourful butterflies, noisy frogs, scampering lizards or sleepy crocodiles. Pictured here, the endangered Temminck's western red colobus (page 31)

(AVZ) pages 31–44

History

From old-style Creole architecture to mysterious stone circles (such as Wassu, pictured here), Gambia has a varied and fascinating history (t/S) page 225

Beaches

The coastline around Greater Banjul is home to some wonderful beaches. Bakau's beach is the site of a busy fish market

(AVZ) page 99

Birds

The Gambia is a great destination for first-time birders in Africa as birds are a vital part of every habitat; the red-throated bee-eater can be spotted on many river trips

(AVZ) pages 42–4

Culture

The International Roots Festival is a vibrant example of how Gambian heritage and culture is showcased and celebrated

(AVZ) page 17

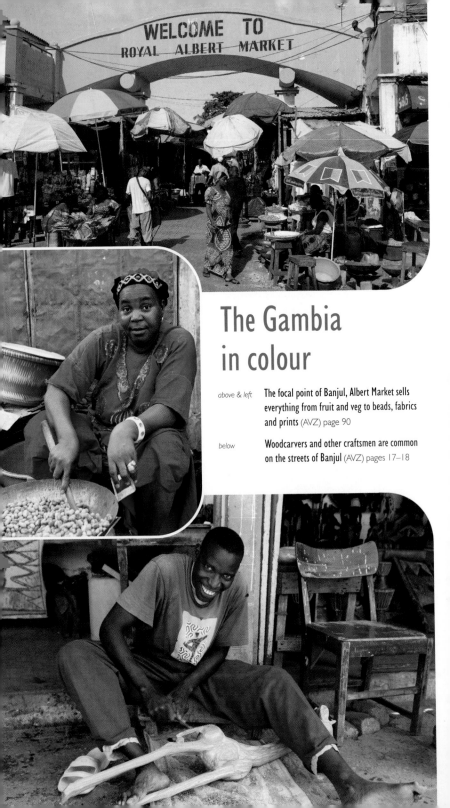

The Gambia in colour

above & left   The focal point of Banjul, Albert Market sells everything from fruit and veg to beads, fabrics and prints (AVZ) page 90

below   Woodcarvers and other craftsmen are common on the streets of Banjul (AVZ) pages 17–18

top   The view over Banjul (AVZ)

above   Towering above the city, Banjul's Arch 22 Monument commemorates the 1994 coup d'état (DC) page 89

right   The small, but pretty, St Mary's Anglican Cathedral (AVZ) page 89

<table>
<tr><td>above left</td><td>Kotu is renowned for offering a great introduction to birdwatching in The Gambia, hosting waders such as the Senegal thick-knee (Burhinus senegalensis) (AVZ) page 122</td></tr>
<tr><td>above right</td><td>Pink-backed pelican (Pelicanus rufescens) in flight in the Bao Bolong Wetland Reserve (AVZ) page 209</td></tr>
<tr><td>left</td><td>Malachite kingfishers are often found near the Kau-ur Swamp (M/S) page 223</td></tr>
<tr><td>below</td><td>The yellow-crowned gonolek (Laniarius barbarus) is considered to be one of the most beautiful birds in The Gambia (AVZ) page 44</td></tr>
</table>

AUTHOR

Philip Briggs (e *philip.briggs@bradtguides.com*) is a travel writer specialising in Africa. Raised in South Africa, where he still lives, Philip first visited East Africa in 1986 and has since spent an average of six months annually exploring the highways and back roads of the continent. His first Bradt Travel Guide, to South Africa, was published in 1991; he has subsequently written Bradt's guides to Tanzania, Uganda, Ethiopia, Malawi, Mozambique, Ghana, East and Southern Africa and Somaliland, and he co-authored the first travel guide to Rwanda. Philip has contributed sections to numerous other books about Africa and he contributes regularly to travel and wildlife magazines specialising in Africa.

UPDATER

Simon Fenton was a travel writer and photographer. After an early career as a biologist, he lived, worked and travelled in Asia for several years before returning to the UK to 'settle down', where he set up the award-winning social enterprise StreetShine. After a perfect storm of events re-ignited his wanderlust, he eventually found himself in Senegal, where he and his Senegalese partner, Khady, built – and run – an eco-guesthouse in Abene, a few miles south of the Gambian border. Simon was a member of a Jola family, a tribe widespread across The Gambia and southern Senegal, meaning that he travelled regularly across the region with a particular interest in documenting the local Jola culture. Tragically, in May 2017, Simon was killed in a car accident in Senegal.

Simon was a contributor to the Bradt guide to Senegal and published two books chronicling his adventures in the country: *Squirting Milk at Chameleons* and *Chasing Hornbills* (see page 255 for more information).

CONTRIBUTORS

Craig Emms and **Linda Barnett** are professional ecologists who lived in The Gambia from 1999 to 2006. During this time they worked with the government in wildlife conservation and were instrumental in the development of a national wildlife conservation organisation called Makasutu Wildlife Trust. As well as undertaking wildlife research and training a great variety of Gambian people at the Darwin Field Station for Biodiversity Research, Training and Education, they co-authored a weekly column called Focus on Wildlife in the Gambian national newspaper *The Daily Observer*, which highlighted the need for wildlife conservation and established an avid readership among Gambians. Craig and Linda now live in England where Craig divides his time between writing novels and ecological consultancy and Linda works in environmental management.

PUBLISHER'S FOREWORD   *Adrian Phillips, Managing Director*

The Gambia has a reputation as a package holiday destination, and as such might seem a little incongruous on the Bradt list. But, while beach resorts abound, this tiny country has a great deal more to offer, including traditional villages and spectacular birdlife. Philip Briggs is Bradt's leading author and arguably the world's best guidebook writer on Africa, and in this book he covers not only the tourist hubs but those isolated spots that will appeal to the independent traveller.

Second edition published January 2018
First edition published October 2014
Bradt Travel Guides Ltd
IDC House, The Vale, Chalfont St Peter, Bucks SL9 9RZ, England
w bradtguides.com
Print edition published in the USA by The Globe Pequot Press Inc,
PO Box 480, Guilford, Connecticut 06437-0480

Text copyright © 2018 Philip Briggs
Maps copyright © 2018 Bradt Travel Guides Ltd; maps include data © OpenStreetMap contributors
Photographs copyright © 2018 Individual photographers (see below)
Project Manager: Laura Pidgley
Cover research: Pepi Bluck, Perfect Picture

ISBN: 978 1 78477 064 8 (print)
e-ISBN: 978 1 78477 525 4 (e-pub)
e-ISBN: 978 1 78477 426 4 (mobi)

British Library Cataloguing in Publication Data
A catalogue record for this book is available from the British Library

Photographs Alamy: Malherbe Marcel (MM/A); Ariadne Van Zandbergen, Africa Image Library (AVZ); AWL Images: Amar Grover (AG/AWL); Dave Coles (DC); Shutterstock: Manja (M/S), trevor kittelty (tk/S); SuperStock (SS)
Front cover Bataleur (AVZ)
Back cover Red colobus monkey (AVZ); Traditional djembe drummer (AVZ)
Title page Fajara beach (SS); Mural depicting a kora player (AVZ); Wassu stone circle (tk/S)

Illustrations Annabel Milne

Maps David McCutcheon FBCart.S; colour base Nick Rowland FRGS

Typeset by Ian Spick, Bradt Travel Guides Ltd
Production managed by Jellyfish Print Solutions; printed in the UK
Digital conversion by w dataworks.co.in

When I first visited The Gambia in 1999, it immediately came across as West Africa's oddest man out. For one thing, this former British colony is a tiny country, the smallest on the African mainland, only 300km long and nowhere more than 50km wide. Linguistically and politically, it is an incongruous Anglophone enclave surrounded on all terrestrial fronts by French-speaking Senegal. Furthermore, where most of West Africa is typically best suited to hardcore independent travel, The Gambia is an altogether more straightforward prospect, with a package-oriented tourist industry focused on the dense cluster of facilities along the Atlantic coastline immediately south of the capital Banjul.

Despite this, The Gambia has always held a special appeal for me. Coming from almost anywhere else in one of the world's toughest travel regions, it feels strikingly approachable, uncomplicated and well organised, partly due to the innate friendliness of its people and partly due to the superior facilities. It is also a very pretty country, dominated by the contrasting waterscapes of the choppy Atlantic Ocean and more serene River Gambia, and literally teeming with colourful tropical birds and monkeys. For those who find the coastal resorts a little too sanitised for their tastes, a quick sojourn upriver – whether for a few hours or weeks – plunges one straight back into the no-frills travel conditions that typified West Africa back in the 1990s.

DEDICATION *By Sean Connolly, author of* Senegal: the Bradt Guide

While travelling in Senegal to research for the first edition of the Bradt Guide, I had the pleasure of meeting Simon Fenton, along with his joyful wife Khady Mané and their irrepressible young boys Gulliver and Alfie. Being two writers with a penchant for West African arcana, we became friends immediately and I wound up spending far longer than I'd planned at their happy homestead in Abéné, Senegal. He was a great friend, gifted author, doting father and a unique inspiration. For all his casual-seeming appearance and attitude, he was a damn hard worker who wrote two enchanting books, built one of the region's most appealing guesthouses and started a family all in a matter of a few years.

Tragically, that all came to an end in May 2017 when Simon passed away in a car accident after completing the research for this guide. Simon and I were comparing notes as he crisscrossed The Gambia and, much like everything else in his life, he gave this project his all, eager to see parts of the country he himself had yet to discover and to reexamine those he'd come to know well. Simon loved The Gambia, Senegal, and the wider region – infectiously so – and he was over the moon to be able to get to share his favourite places with those around him, either by leading tours at The Little Baobab, or now, with the very book you hold in your hands. His irrepressible enthusiasm for West African life, with all its quirks and caprices, is sorely missed by those who had the pleasure of knowing him, and while it's sadly too late to take one of Simon's in-person tours, this book, in to which he so readily threw his heart, is very much the next best thing. You could not be in better hands.

Acknowledgements

PHILIP BRIGGS My first and biggest debt is to Craig Emms and Linda Barnett, authors of an older and highly praised Bradt guide to The Gambia that is long out of print, but that formed the basis for several sections in its current successor, particularly the *Background Information* and *Natural History* chapters.

On the home front, I'm grateful as ever to my wife Ariadne Van Zandbergen for her company on the road and support, and to the usual suspects at Bradt for letting me coerce them into publishing this book and for seeing the manuscript to its publishable conclusion.

On the ground, I am grateful to the support (and in many cases company and/or other input) of several individuals. In no particular order, these are: Mark Thomson of Hidden Africa, Jenny Adams, Joyce Stavroulakis and Dadi Keita of The Gambia Experience, Janis Carter of the Chimpanzee Rehabilitation Project, Barbara Somers and Kawsu Sillah of Kairoh Garden, Devon and Amadou at Jinack Lodge, Marc Van Maldegem of the Kombo Beach Hotel, Geri Mitchell, Maurice Phillips and Matarr Barr at Sandele Eco-Retreat, Misha Freestone of Kololi Beach Club, Martje Hannson of Bokotu Beach Hotel, Cisse Adjaratou, Susan Clifford-Webb and Oliver Webb of Hibiscus House, Fatou Banja of the Laico Atlantic, Lawrence Williams of Makasutu Cultural Forest, Pat Phipps, John Tucker and Colin Cross of the Kartong Bird Observatory.

SIMON FENTON Thanks to Philip Briggs whose masterful previous edition made my work so much easier. I am also indebted to my partner, Khady Mané, who let me disappear for weeks at a time to research this guide as well as having given me many insights in to the local culture, history and traditions. I am grateful to the support on the ground of many individuals: Carlijn Abrahamse of AbCa's Creek Lodge; Dave Adams of Fairplay Gambia; Mustaph Bah; Fouzia Bensouda-Lee of Seashells Restaurant; Lucy Boiang; Ebrima Camara; Colin Cross of Kartong Bird Observatory; Silvia Llopart Gracia of Sambou Kunda; Gill Harvey; Arame Jah; Omar Jammeh; Nikki Lincoln of the Plantation; Oliver Monk; Katie Paine and Ous Jagne of Timbooktoo; Maurice Phillips of Sandele; Sandy Sanyang; David White of Footsteps Eco-Lodge; and Lawrence Williams of Makasutu Cultural Forest.

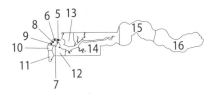

Contents

LIST OF MAPS

Introduction

The Gambia has been called the Gateway to Africa, an assertion with which it is difficult to argue, at least from the perspective of an English-speaker. Closer to Europe than any other Anglophone part of West Africa, this tiny country – the smallest on the African mainland – has become a perennially popular entry point to Africa with sunseekers from Britain and several other northern European countries. During its blissfully sunny dry season, which happens to coincide with the northern midwinter, The Gambia is connected to the UK, and elsewhere in Europe, by a glut of affordable charter flights. And once there, the coastline is dotted with a vast and varied collection of upmarket resort hotels, quirky eco-lodges and grassroots beach camps offering great value for money throughout the spectrum.

Despite its small size, The Gambia offers plenty of variety to tourists. Among the most idiosyncratic legacies of the colonial Scramble for Africa, the country is nowhere more than 50km wide, protruding tendril-like into Francophone Senegal (with which it shares all its terrestrial borders) as it follows the course of the River Gambia inland for 300km. Landscapes and habitats range from lush shady forests festooned with creepers to endless expanses of golden sandy beach, from dry Guinean savannah to bounteous seasonal swamps, from brooding mangrove-lined creeks to the broad expanse of the majestic river that gives the country its name.

While most holidaymakers aggregate at the coastal resorts, others succumb to the down-to-earth allure of the interior, where villages of mud-walled grass-roofed round huts dot the muddy banks of the life-sustaining river. Here, cattle and other livestock wander across pot-holed roads where small-wheeled donkey carts plod lethargically alongside battered old bush taxis. Men sit beneath huge shady trees, brewing pots of green tea, while brightly dressed women walk by, effortlessly carrying bundles or pots on their heads. People follow traditional pursuits, fishing the protein-rich waters of the river, or working the fields using simple hand tools. And while the tropical ambience of Upriver Gambia amounts to more than the sum of its individual attractions, there are highlights aplenty, including the mysterious megaliths of Wassu and the chimps and hippos of River Gambia National Park.

Though beach holidays predominate, The Gambia is also renowned in ornithological circles for providing a superb, and usually affordable, introduction to Africa's rich birdlife. More so than any other African country we know, birds dominate every niche of the Gambian landscape: spectacularly colourful parrots, rollers, bee-eaters and turacos; comical hornbills and decorous crowned cranes; dozens of eagles and other striking raptors; plus a mind-boggling assemblage of marine and other aquatic species. Astonishingly, close on 600 species have been recorded in The Gambia, a country barely half the size of Wales – and fortunately, for first-time visitors to Africa, there's no shortage of knowledgeable local guides to help track down and identify these many avian gems.

In terms of character and facilities, The Gambia is a country of three distinct parts, as reflected in the structure of the regional part of this guidebook, which comprises three well-defined sections. The first and largest of these covers Greater Banjul and Kololi, the country's main package-tourism hub, extending over less than 1% of its area but accounting for perhaps 95% of hotels and other tourist-related facilities. The second section covers the remainder of the coastal belt, an attractive area dotted with low-key eco-lodges and other isolated getaways that cater to a more independent-minded travel market. The final section covers the untrammelled delights of Upriver Gambia, a region that accounts for about 95% of the country's surface area but has very few facilities worth shouting about, making it the ideal African taster for the genuinely adventurous. But rest assured on one thing: whichever part of The Gambia you visit, better still if you expose yourself to all three, it is a wonderfully friendly and enjoyable country; one that has a habit of attracting repeat visitors year after year.

UPDATES WEBSITE

Administered by author Philip Briggs, Bradt's The Gambia update website (w *bradtupdates.com/thegambia*) is an online forum where travellers can post and read the latest travel news, trip reports and factual updates from The Gambia. The website is a free service to readers, or to anybody else who cares to drop by, and travellers to The Gambia and people in the tourist industry are encouraged to use it to share their comments, grumbles, insights, news or other feedback. These can be posted directly on the website, or emailed to Philip (e *philip.briggs@bradtguides.com*).

It's easy to keep up to date with the latest posts by following Philip on Twitter (🐦 *@philipbriggs*) and/or liking his Facebook page (📘 *pb.travel.updates*). You can also add a review of the book to w bradtguides.com or Amazon.

HOW TO USE THIS GUIDE

AUTHORS' FAVOURITES Finding genuinely characterful accommodation or that unmissable off-the-beaten-track café can be difficult, so the author has chosen a few of his favourite places throughout the country to point you in the right direction. These 'authors' favourites' are marked with a ✳.

PRICES With the exception of some upmarket hotels and car-rental agencies, almost every price in The Gambia is quoted in local currency. However, because of the devaluation of many African currencies and a high local inflation rate, we feel that converting dalasi prices to a hard currency equivalent is more likely to produce medium-term guidelines to current prices. We have opted for British pound sterling, and converted 2014 prices at an approximate exchange rate of D60 to the pound.

MAPS
Keys and symbols Maps include alphabetical keys covering the locations of those places to stay, eat or drink that are featured in the guide. Hotels or restaurants that are not listed in the guide (but which might serve as alternative options if required or serve as useful landmarks to aid navigation) are also included on the maps; these are marked with accommodation 🏠, restaurant ✘, bar ♇ or café 🖵 symbols. Note that regional maps may not show all hotels and restaurants in the area: other establishments may be located in towns shown on the map.

Grids and grid references Some maps use gridlines to allow easy location of sites. Map grid references are listed in square brackets after the name of the place or site of interest in the text, with page number followed by grid number, eg: [103 C3].

SEND US YOUR SNAPS!

We'd love to follow your adventures using our *The Gambia* guide – why not send us your photos and stories via Twitter (🐦 *@BradtGuides*) and Instagram (📷 *@bradtguides*) using the hashtag #thegambia. Alternatively, you can upload your photos directly to the gallery on the Gambia destination page via our website (w *bradtguides.com/thegambia*).

Part One

GENERAL INFORMATION

Location West Africa

Neighbouring country Bordered by Senegal on all sides except for its short Atlantic coastline

Size 11,295km^2 (4,361 square miles)

Climate Dry mid-October to early June; rainy mid-June to early October

Status Federal republic

Population 2.11 million (2017 estimate). Annual growth rate of 3%.

Capital Banjul (2017 population, 35,000)

Economy Major earners are agriculture, trade and tourism

GDP US$9.39 billion (2015)

Gross National Income per capita US$1,580 (2014)

Language Official language English. Local languages include Mandinka, Wolof, Jola and Fula

Religion 90% Muslim, 10% Christian, <1% follow traditional religions such as animism

Currency Gambian dalasi (100 bututs per dalasi)

Rate of exchange US$1 = D47; £1 = D62; €1 = D56 (October 2017); for up-to-date rates, go to w xe.com

International telephone code +220

Time GMT

Electricity Three-pin plug, 220–240 volts

Weights and measures Metric and imperial, as in the UK

Public holidays 1 January, 18 February, 1 May, 25 May, 22 July, 15 August, 25 December as well as the movable religious holidays including Koriteh, Tobaski, Milad an-Nabi, Good Friday and Easter Monday

Flag Three horizontal stripes – red, blue and green from top to bottom, each colour separated by a narrow white stripe

National anthem *For The Gambia our Homeland*

National motto 'Progress, Peace and Prosperity'

1

Background Information

By Craig Emms and Linda Barnett, with updates and additions by Philip Briggs and Simon Fenton

FACTS AND FIGURES

LOCATION AND SIZE The Federal Republic of The Gambia lies on the western coast of tropical Africa, at a latitude almost equidistant from the Equator and the Tropic of Cancer. Shaped like a long, crooked finger extending inland from its Atlantic coastline, it is surrounded on all other sides by the much larger French-speaking country of Senegal. It is nowhere more than 48km from north to south (though the coastline, with its bays and promontories, is longer), but it extends inland from west to east for 480km, roughly following the route of the River Gambia. With a total land area of only 11,295km², The Gambia is the smallest country on mainland Africa (the closest contender Swaziland is almost 50% larger). In global terms, it is similar in area to Jamaica or Qatar, about half the size of Wales, and roughly midway between the relatively small US states of Massachusetts and Maryland.

CLIMATE The Gambia has a wonderfully warm climate characterised by a long dry season from mid-October to early June, and a short rainy season from mid-June to early October. July and September are the hottest months, with average daytime maximum temperatures of around 30°C. During this period, frequent and magnificent rainstorms cool everything down for a while, before the humidity shoots up to almost 100%. From December to mid-February the average daytime temperature falls to around 24°C, which is fairly comfortable, especially when coming from a cold wet European or North American winter. After February the days get steadily hotter until the rains come in June. Temperatures are generally slightly lower along the coast, owing to cooling offshore winds, but these figures are only averages, and on some days it can be a lot warmer – in the high 30s or more occasionally in the mid 40s. Average rainfall per year is around 1,020mm, but in the west it can be much higher – up to 1,700mm – while in the drier east it can be as low as 800mm. Over the past 40 years or so, a slight warming in average temperatures and a decrease in rainfall has adversely affected the livelihoods of farmers dependent on rain-fed crops.

THE CAPITAL AND OTHER PRINCIPAL URBAN CENTRES The capital is Banjul (formally Bathurst), a small island-bound city located at the southern tip of the Gambia River Mouth. Unusually for an African city, Banjul has experienced a slight population decrease over recent years, and the current figure of around 32,000 means that while it remains the country's administrative centre, it is by no means the largest town. That accolade belongs to the vast unplanned sprawl of Serekunda (or more accurately Kanifing Municipality), which is more than ten-times larger, with an estimated population of 350,000, and lies on the mainland only 10km to the east of Banjul. Most of the rest of the population is also concentrated on the coastal belt south of the river mouth, where Brikama, Sukuta, Bakau and Gunjur all

CLIMATE CHARTS

Banjul

	J	F	M	A	M	J	J	A	S	O	N	D
max°C	32	33	34	33	32	32	31	30	31	32	32	32
min°C	23	16	17	18	19	20	23	24	23	22	19	17
R mm	1	0	0	0	2	63	235	347	255	5	0	0

Janjanbureh

	J	F	M	A	M	J	J	A	S	O	N	D
max°C	35	37	39	40	39	36	32	31	32	34	36	34
min°C	16	18	20	22	24	24	23	23	23	23	19	16
R mm	0	0	0	1	7	92	195	230	205	65	3	1

Basse Santa Su

	J	F	M	A	M	J	J	A	S	O	N	D
max°C	34	36	38	40	39	36	33	32	32	34	35	34
min°C	15	16	21	24	25	25	23	23	23	23	18	15
R mm	0	5	0	5	20	110	210	252	236	65	5	0

rank along with Banjul and Serekunda among the country's top ten largest towns. Upriver, the largest towns, none with a population much greater than 30,000, are Farafenni, Soma and Basse Santa Su.

ADMINISTRATIVE DIVISIONS The Gambia is divided into six primary administrative sectors, as established under British rule in 1935. These comprise the city of Greater Banjul, which incorporates Serekunda and Bakau, as well as five divisions (officially known as Regions since 2007 but seldom referred to that way). The names of the five divisions are fairly self-explanatory. The Western Division (WD), located entirely south of the River Gambia, comprises the coastal belt south of Greater Banjul as far inland as the Bintang Bolong (whose natural curves form its eastern boundary), with its capital at Brikama. The North Bank Division (NBD) covers the coastal belt north of the River Gambia, inland through the regional capital Kerewan, past Farafenni, to just beyond the town of Ngeyen Sanjal. The Lower River Division (LRD) comprises the South Bank of the river, running east from WD, via the divisional headquarters Mansa Konko and nearby Soma, to just beyond the town of Pakali Ba. The Central River Division (CRD), which covers both sides of the river east of the borders with NBD and LRD, contains the major towns of Kau-ur, Kuntaur and Bansang, but its capital is the small town of Janjanbureh on MacCarthy Island. The Upper River Division (URD) comprises the most easterly part of the country and its capital is Basse Sante Su. Each of the administrative divisions is further split into smaller districts, of which there are now 48. A chief, known as a *seyfo*, heads each of these districts and the chiefs are elected into their position by the village heads, who are known as *alkalos*.

TIME Being almost directly south of Britain, The Gambia is on GMT. Thus British visitors experience no change in time when visiting The Gambia except during the summer months when Britain is on daylight-saving time. The eastern coastline of the USA is 5 hours behind The Gambia, while most of Europe is an hour ahead.

NATIONAL FLAG The national flag of The Gambia is made up of three horizontal stripes – red, blue and green – running from top to bottom. Each of the colours is separated by a narrow white stripe. It was designed by Pa Louis Thomasi and adopted at independence on 16 February 1965. Though not political, it is said that the blue stripe represents the life-sustaining River Gambia, the green symbolises agriculture, the red the sun, and the white stripes the peace that holds the country together.

POPULATION In 1983, the population of The Gambia was 687,817, but this had grown to 2.11 million in 2017, giving an annual growth rate of more than 3%. Much of the increase is due to migration from other strife-torn countries in West Africa, by people looking to settle somewhere more peaceful. However, the fertility rate is also persistently high, estimated to be 4.81 births per woman in 2011. This gives a population density of about 172 people per km², the fourth highest in Africa, after Rwanda, Burundi and Nigeria.

A HISTORICAL BACKGROUND

PREHISTORY There is very little evidence available to tell us when man first settled in West Africa, though it is thought that the earliest settlers were here at least 1.6 million years ago. Before the Stone Age the inhabitants of the region appear to have been nomadic hunter-gatherers who made only temporary settlements before moving on to follow the herds of wild animals that sustained them.

The first actual evidence of people living in the area now called The Gambia comes from Stone Age tools found under the sand dunes at Fajara and Cape Point. These have been dated to around 2000BC. During the Stone Age the lifestyle of the people changed dramatically and they stopped following wild animal herds to settle down and grow vegetable and cereal crops. Cattle were also domesticated during this period. All of this change led to a sudden increase in the size of the human population.

The next major development in West Africa was the coming of the Iron Age (there appears to have been a complete lack of a Bronze Age in the region). The discovery of iron was very significant and heralded the clearance of large areas of forest for agriculture, as iron tools proved to be much more durable than stone tools (and sharper too).

ARABS AND THE BEGINNINGS OF ISLAM Trade became increasingly important for West Africans as the whole structure of society slowly changed. Some people gave up being farmers and herdsmen and branched out into other occupations such as traders, smiths, artisans, artists and administrators. Alongside these, of course, came the first soldiers and rulers. During the 1st century AD, another major event began to change the region. This was the introduction of the camel into North Africa from Arabia. The 'ship of the desert', as camels became known, allowed traders to cross the great Saharan desert for the first time in history. This meant that long trade routes were opened up between West Africa and Europe and Asia, via Arabia. Many goods were then transported north across the Sahara, including gold, ivory and slaves, much of it in return for rock salt imported from the Berber-controlled Saharan salt mines. It appears that by AD500 many settlements were well established in The Gambia. Evidence for their existence is plentiful and can be seen in the form of burial sites, stone circles and shell mounds that are scattered widely across the country.

It was in AD620 that one of the most significant events to shape humankind happened in Arabia. This was the birth of the Islamic religion, founded by the Prophet Muhammad. This new religion proved very popular among Arabs and slowly spread from its birthplace into northwest Africa. At first, Islam was the religion of only the wealthy classes and the rulers but its spread into the general population of West Africa was aided by a group of religious teachers who were called *marabouts*. The marabouts were attached to the chiefs as secretaries to their courts. As a reward for good service many of the marabouts received land from the chiefs and were allowed to found their own villages. These villages had Koranic schools, followed Islamic dietary laws and kept fast during the Holy Month of Ramadan, and soon they became islands of Islam among the traditional beliefs still held by many West Africans.

Another important event now took place, and this was the sudden growth of the slave trade. Up until this point in time most of the slaves taken by the Arab nations came from the Berber people of North Africa. However, the Berbers had also converted to the Islamic religion and it was against Islamic laws for one Muslim to take another as a slave. This meant that a new source of slaves had to be found and eventually a new source was located in sub-Saharan Africa.

THE KINGDOM OF MANDING (MALI) From the 5th century AD, West Africa became divided into several kingdoms. The three main kingdoms up until the 15th century were Ghana, Manding (known as Mali by the Europeans) and Kanem Borno. Present-day Gambia was situated within the Kingdom of Mali, which was itself a sub-state of the vast Kingdom of Ghana, and was known in Baghdad as 'The Land of Gold'. The Kingdom of Mali achieved its own independence in the 13th century under the kingship of Sunjatta Keita, the leader of the Malinké people. By the 14th century, the kingdom had become huge and encompassed all of The Gambia and Senegal in the west and stretched east as far as Nigeria and Niger. At this time trade with the Arab nations reached a peak and Mali became very rich and prosperous. Slaves were traded for salt, which was in short supply in the region, as well as horses and weapons. Huge armies were raised to protect the trade routes and to further extend the kingdom through conquests. Apart from Islam, the Arabs also brought with them books. Many Arabs settled in the region and built mosques, introducing their religion to the lower classes of people until Islam slowly established itself as the main religion. As more West Africans became able to read and write, they were also empowered to increase their trade and therefore their wealth. Thus it was not long before the powers of Europe began to hear of the wealth of West Africa from Arab traders.

The Kingdom of Mali began to subside in the mid 15th century and many people started to move around the sub-region as it disintegrated. The Serer people moved from south of the River Gambia on to the North Bank of the river and created the kingdoms of Siné and Saloum, which remained powerful until the 19th century. A group of Malinké people also migrated south into the valley of the River Gambia, taking Islam with them, where they joined the Jola people, who were already present. These invaders became known as the Mandinka people.

THE KINGDOM OF KAABU The Kingdom of Kaabu started as a westward extension of the Kingdom of Mali, but as the Kingdom of Mali declined the Kaabu kingdom gradually took over the reins of power. Stretching from the River Gambia in the north to Guinea in the south, and ruled by Mandinkas, it was a great centre for trade. However, as time passed, Fula states and kingdoms surrounded Kaabu and many Fulas, who were nomadic pastoralists, migrated on to Mandinka lands, which were fertile and well watered. By the mid 19th century, the Fula formed the largest single ethnic group in the region. However, they were still governed by the Mandinkas, who ruled them with a rod of iron and treated them very harshly. The situation remained the same until after the Soninke–Marabout Wars of the 1880s (page 9) when the marabouts were defeated.

THE ARRIVAL OF EUROPEANS At this time many stories of the untold wealth of West Africa began to reach the ears of the royal houses of Europe. The first nation to strike out for West Africa was Portugal; the Portuguese reached Cape Verde (where the city of Dakar was later built) in 1447. Here, explorers heard about the River Gambia and the gold that was reputed to be found in large quantities along its banks. In 1455, Prince Henry of Portugal sent Luiz de Cadamosto and three ships to search for this river. When they eventually found it they managed to sail only four miles upriver before being attacked by local tribesmen in canoes and forced to give up. The next year they returned again to The Gambia and this time managed to sail 20 miles upriver. Along the way one of their crewmen died and was buried on an island in the river that still retains his name to this day: James Island (also known as St Andrew). The Portuguese eventually achieved a foothold in the country amid other European nations who were also becoming interested in the region. Many trading posts were established along the coast, trading brandy, guns and salt for gold, ivory and leather. The incomers also built forts to protect their trading posts from hostile local inhabitants and from marauding pirates.

Unfortunately for them, the Europeans soon found that the tales of untold wealth in West African gold were vastly exaggerated. They cast about for another source of easily accumulated wealth to be gleaned from these lands and it wasn't long before they realised the vast possibilities of profit that could be gained from the trade in slaves.

THE SLAVE TRADE Slavery had existed in West Africa for many years before the Europeans arrived. Warring tribes had often raided each other's villages and taken prisoners, who were then kept on as slaves. However, unlike the slaves of later years these people were often treated as one of their new master's family and many had a chance to eventually earn their freedom. When the Europeans arrived in West Africa, they were hungry for vast numbers of slaves to work in the cotton fields and plantations of their colonies in the New World. Even so, it was not the Europeans who captured the slaves for this growing trade but the Africans themselves. Many African kings and chiefs soon realised how much wealth they could accumulate from the sale of slaves to the Europeans.

It is interesting to note that in 1620 a British explorer, Captain Richard Jobson, was offered some young women as slaves. He refused, saying that these people were 'of his own shape' and should not be enslaved. He went on to write that the English were a people who did not deal in any such commodities; unfortunately, this noble observation was later proved untrue and England became one of the largest dealers in slaves within West Africa.

As the demand for slaves began to grow, inter-tribal warfare became much more common and attacks on villages more frequent, in order to feed this appetite. Some of the African leaders became very rich by selling their captured enemies into slavery. For the slaves themselves, life was hard and dangerous. Many of them would not survive the voyages taking them to the New World, as the conditions on board the European slave ships were atrocious (it has often been said that a slave-ship could be recognised by its awful smell, even from many miles away). Once they reached their destination, most of the slaves would go on to die within the first three years, and very few of them lived as long as ten years. The slave masters soon realised that it was cheaper to work their slaves to death and replace them with new ones than to treat them well, let them live longer and bear children. Children would have to be fed for years before they became productive workers and were therefore not economically viable. At the height of the slave trade in the 18th century, over 100,000 slaves were transported from Africa every year. Nobody knows for sure the total number of slaves taken from the region in the four centuries of trade. Estimates as high as 50 million have been floated but most historians agree that at least 12 million slaves left the continent between the 15th and 19th centuries.

The Portuguese were the first to develop the slave trade, monopolising it on a massive scale until the mid 16th century, when the English joined in, later followed by the French and the Dutch. The River Gambia became a major route into the interior of West Africa and strategically very important. Over the time of the slave trade there were lots of skirmishes between traders of different nationalities over ownership of the fortified trading stations along the river. Fort James, for example, changed hands eight times in violent clashes over a 60-year period before being finally secured by the British. At around the same time the trading station at nearby Albreda became French-controlled.

The West African kingdoms eventually declined. There followed a period of great instability throughout the region and the balance of power moved to the coastal states. European influence and their introduction of firearms into the region led to even more instability. Islam flourished in the area and the marabouts became very powerful figures among the local people. It was believed that many of the marabouts had divine powers and could communicate directly with Allah. The Fula people were strong believers in the Islamic faith and were widespread throughout the region. Through their influence Islam became the dominant religion.

In the early 19th century, another major event occurred that would change the world: the Industrial Revolution soon took hold of all Europe. Increased mechanisation reduced the need for vast numbers of slaves and increased the need for raw materials and markets for the goods that were being manufactured. Europe gradually came to see the colonies both as sources of raw materials and as markets for manufactured goods; and so the relationship between some Europeans and the West Africans changed accordingly. Slavery was banned by the British in 1807. The Royal Navy became increasingly active in the region, chasing and capturing French slavers and their ships, then releasing the cargoes of slaves and resettling them on to the mainland. The captured slavers were usually hanged. This may make the British seem to be the good guys at this time but such activity appears to have been carried out primarily for economic reasons: the slave trade was damaging the rest of their trading enterprises. The French eventually followed with their own ban on slavery, but not until 1848. Such policies did not put an end to the slave trade, however, which carried on upriver of Albreda and Fort James. The trade was perpetuated mainly by Gambians who had found it very profitable and viewed the change in policy by the Europeans with strong disapproval. In the 1880s, Muslim leaders in The Gambia were still taking slaves and exporting them and it was not until new laws were introduced in the late 1890s that this trade became illegal. Some slavery carried on in The Gambia until at least 1911. However, this should be put into some historical perspective: slavery was not abolished in nearby Mauritania until 1980.

THE COLONIAL PERIOD In 1816, Britain bought the island of Banjul from a local chief, renamed it Bathurst, and built a large fort there to protect their traders and to deny slavers access to the river. Four years later the River Gambia was declared a British Protectorate and in 1826 Fort Bullen was built at Barra Point, on the North Bank of the river mouth opposite Bathurst. In 1828, the British also built another fort upriver at Georgetown (now Janjanbureh). In the early 1830s, there was a short and limited war between the British and the people from the state of Niumi on the North Bank of the river. This resulted in British and French troops retaking Barra Point, which had been captured by the army of Niumi. After a brief and bloody conflict the people of Niumi capitulated to the British.

When the slave trade was officially ended the British and the French found that they needed to establish another source of wealth in West Africa. They decided to introduce groundnuts (peanuts), as there was a huge international market for them. In 1829, large areas along the River Gambia and elsewhere in Senegal were planted with this new crop. However, in the 1870s unforeseen European political and economic events led to increased competition between foreign traders and the growers of groundnuts in West Africa. This poor state of affairs led to the Berlin Conference of 1884–85. At this conference the major European powers split the whole continent of Africa into a number of colonies to be ruled by them. It was at this time that The Gambia became a colony of Great Britain and her boundaries were set into their present-day position. It is said that the borders of The Gambia, which to a great extent follow the twists and curves of the River Gambia, were set by a British gunboat that sailed the length of the river. The gunboat was supposed to have fired its gun both north and south, and the border was placed where the shells landed. However, this is more than likely just a fanciful tale as colonial administrators were known to prefer using rulers and compasses to determine countries' borders; sending a gunboat and using shells would require far too much planning and effort.

THE SONINKE–MARABOUT WARS In the late 19th century the Fula people, led by their marabouts, attempted to overthrow their traditional Mandinka rulers by the use of force. The Fula wanted to extend the Islamic faith to displace the traditional faiths and indifferent Islamic beliefs practised by the Soninke, a Mandinka group to which the local rulers and their courts belonged. This was called a *jihad*, or 'holy war', and the fierce and bloody fighting, especially near Bathurst, became known as the 'Soninke–Marabout Wars'. Eventually the marabouts were overthrown by the colonial powers and the years that followed were peaceful and quiet.

THE WORLD WARS The Gambia became just a small colony, with no inherent wealth in the form of mineral resources, so nobody really knew what to do with it. The main aim of British rule in The Gambia appeared to be to create peace in the area with the minimum of expense. The administration raised enough revenue to run itself but not to provide any social services. Britain's financial policy up to World War II was that its colonies had to be self-supporting, so this resulted in very little attention being paid to the socio-economic development of The Gambia. During World War II the situation improved slightly as Britain assumed direct responsibility for development in its colonies. However, in spite of a few projects that were set up in The Gambia to try and diversify agricultural production, and a few more resources being directed towards health and education in the country, nothing really changed that much. During both World Wars many Gambian soldiers fought on the side of the Allies, as did a lot of other West Africans, and many were killed in action. The brave men who died in the service of their country are remembered in the Fajara War Cemetery (page 110).

INDEPENDENCE It wasn't until the early 1960s that The Gambia again entered the international arena. In 1962, the Gambian parliament – the House of Representatives – was formed. A popular young man by the name of David Jawara, from upcountry, had founded a political party called the People's Progressive Party (PPP) at the start of the decade. This party easily won the elections to form a majority in the House of Representatives. Following this the country gained its independence from British colonial rule in 1965. David Jawara was inaugurated as prime minister, though the Queen of England still remained as titular head of state. One of the first things to change was the name of Bathurst, which reverted to its former name of Banjul. Also around this time Gambia was renamed as *The* Gambia, due in no small part to the fact that it was often getting confused with the African state of Zambia.

From 1965 to 1975, The Gambia prospered. World groundnut prices increased threefold and the tourist industry grew from just 300 visitors during 1966 to over 25,000 ten years later, earning the moniker 'The Smiling Coast of Africa'. Initially most of the tourists came from Sweden, but gradually more and more came from the United Kingdom. It was during this period, in 1970, that The Gambia became a fully fledged independent republic. Prime Minister Jawara became president and also changed his name from David to the local equivalent, Dawda.

However, this high couldn't last forever and groundnut prices began to fall sharply in the late 1970s, making most Gambians worse off than they had been before independence. In 1980, a group of disillusioned soldiers staged a coup, but President Jawara asked for help from the Senegalese and the attempt failed. Later in 1981 there was another coup attempt while Jawara was away in London, and his family were taken as hostages and held prisoner in the Medical Research Council buildings in Fajara. Again the Senegalese army helped, along with special forces soldiers from Britain who secured the release of the president's family, and the coup failed once more. At this time the tourist industry was still growing and became a vital source of income for the Gambian government. Politics became more volatile and support for opposition parties grew, especially the 'Movement for Justice in Africa' (MOJA). Eventually the leaders of MOJA were arrested or were forced into hiding.

In 1982, President Jawara announced that The Gambia and Senegal armed forces would be fully integrated and the Senegambian Coalition came into being. This policy lacked popular support among the Gambian population, especially with the Mandinka who saw the coalition as a takeover bid by the Wolof (who are the predominant ethnic group in Senegal), and tensions flared in the country. However, Jawara won the elections in the same year, and the following elections in 1987, as he still had a large popular backing. Jawara was widely praised for advancing human rights and for his attempts to improve The Gambia's economy, which led to the African Commission on Human and Peoples' Rights (ACHPR) establishing its secretariat in Banjul in 1989.

However, in the late 1980s things went from bad to worse in The Gambia as groundnut prices continued to fall. At the same time the International Monetary

Fund, on whom The Gambia relied heavily, restructured its agricultural subsidies and spending on public services were cut. The remote upcountry areas were hit the hardest and there were cases of malnutrition and even starvation in the poorest areas. There were two more failed coup attempts during this period.

In 1989, relations became strained between Senegal and The Gambia and the coalition was dissolved. Senegal imposed severe border restrictions between the two countries, but by 1991 things had cooled down and a new treaty of friendship and co-operation was signed between the neighbours. In 1992, the PPP was re-elected for its sixth term in power.

THE JAMMEH REGIME Following the re-election, popular support for Jawara began to decline and he started to face growing internal criticism and calls for change, especially for failing to curb corruption and provide basic services. Throughout the early 1990s, civil society groups, university students and working Gambians took to the streets to express their discontent. On 22 July 1994 there was an angry protest by soldiers. This was mostly about their salaries, which were being paid several months late, but also about their poor treatment by Nigerian officers during peacekeeping duties in Liberia and Sierra Leone. Surprisingly this protest turned into yet another coup d'état. This time though, the coup did not fail and Jawara was ousted from power, though he managed to escape to a US warship that happened to be in Banjul Harbour. He was later granted asylum in Senegal. The leader of the successful coup was a young lieutenant in the Gambian army named Yahya Jammeh. A new military government was formed called the Armed Forces Provisional Ruling Council (AFPRC), consisting of several senior military officers as well as civilian ministers from the previous government.

The coup had immediate and serious repercussions for The Gambia. On the advice of the British Foreign and Commonwealth Office (FCO), many thousands of British tourists cancelled reservations and several of the major tour companies halted all flights to The Gambia. The annual number of visitors dropped by over 65% to fewer than 40,000. The USA went one stage further and cut all aid to The Gambia. There was also an exodus of non-government organisations and charities from the country. It was not until March 1995 that the FCO relented and said that travel to The Gambia was safe again. But even then it still took a while for the number of visitors to pick up and the poor 1994–95 tourist season hit the industry very hard, forcing many businesses to close down and lay off workers.

In September 1996, national elections were held and a new constitution was voted in. In the presidential elections Yahya Jammeh won 56% of the vote. Elections for National Assembly Members were held in January 1997, and Jammeh's renamed Alliance for Patriotic Reorientation and Construction (APRC) won 33 of the 45 seats. The president appointed four more members from his party, including the Speaker. In August 1997, the government released several opposition members who had been imprisoned immediately after the coup and granted amnesty to a number of other detainees.

From the mid 1990s, The Gambia enjoyed a high level of political stability, as well as a steady rate of economic growth and huge infrastructural improvements. It also remained a functional democracy, with at least three parties contesting each of the 2001, 2006 and 2011 presidential elections, which returned Jammeh to power with 53%, 67% and 71.5% of the vote respectively. These multi-party elections were widely accepted to be free and fair, though they also attracted some criticism. In 2011, for instance, a fact-finding mission sent by the Economic Community of West African States (ECOWAS) described the pre-electoral landscape as being characterised by 'an unacceptable level of control of the electronic media by the party in power, and an opposition and electorate cowed by repression and intimidation'.

The APRC has displayed strong repressive tendencies, particularly during its second decade of tenure. In 2004, a harsh clampdown on the free press was initiated by the assassination of the respected newspaper editor Deyda Hydara, and the disappearance of the outspoken journalist Ebrima Manneh following his arrest by security police in 2006. A string of alleged human rights abuses include the police killing of a dozen protesters during a student demonstration in 2000, and the abduction and detention of more than 1,000 suspected witches at the instigation of government-sponsored witch-doctors.

The APRC's international reputation has been undermined by its leader's propensity for rhetoric that might generously be described as controversial. In 2007, Jammeh announced that he had discovered a homeopathic HIV/AIDS cure, which he instructed infected followers to take instead of anti-retroviral drugs. In 2008, he launched a crusade against homosexuality with the announcement that the APRC intended to execute all gays and lesbians by implementing laws 'stricter than those in Iran'. In 2010, he described atheists as being 'even below a pig', and a year later he suggested to the BBC that he would 'rule this country for one billion years … if Allah says so'.

Relations with the country's only next-door neighbour reached their nadir in 2005, when an exasperated President Abdoulaye Wade suggested building a tunnel underneath The Gambia following the arrest there of Senegalese solders in transit between Dakar and the Casamance. Neighbourly relations have improved since this jibe. The Gambia managed to wrong-foot the Commonwealth in September 2013, when Jammeh followed the example set by President Mugabe of Zimbabwe ten years earlier by summarily withdrawing his country from what he dismissed as a 'neo-colonial institution'.

Despite this, The Gambia remained a peaceful multi-party democracy with freedom of worship, an unusually stable exchange rate, a relatively lively free-market economy, and an ever-improving infrastructure. New health clinics and hospitals were built on the coast and upcountry, and vastly improved access to schooling under President Jammeh led to an increase of almost 50% in the literacy rate since the mid 1990s.

THE GAMBIA TODAY Things changed, however, in December 2016 when Adama Barrow was elected president of The Gambia with 45.5% of the vote to Jammeh's 36.7%. Despite instantly receiving international recognition, Jammeh refused to acknowledge the results, but was forced to relinquish power after military intervention by ECOWAS states, with the backing of the UN Security Council, while the world looked on. On 21 January 2017, after West African troops rolled in to The Gambia to ensure a peaceful transition, Jammeh relented, going in to exile in Equatorial Guinea. Though Jammeh was reportedly allowed to keep his luxury car collection – to the chagrin of some Gambians – it was, at least, The Gambia's first peaceful transition of power since the country gained independence from the British in 1965. Hundreds of relieved Gambians made the trip back home, some wearing T-shirts bearing the slogan #GambiaHasDecided.

The country is now nearing the point of self-sufficiency when it comes to production of most basic foodstuffs, and though not rich in natural resources it is able to generate foreign currency through the export of groundnuts, mangoes and smoked fish, not to mention the thriving tourist industry. All in all, the future for The Gambia is looking positive.

ECONOMY AND INFRASTRUCTURE

As natural resources are scarce in The Gambia, agriculture has become one of the mainstays of the economy. Nearly 75% of the rural population is employed in agriculture and farming contributes around 23% of the country's gross domestic product (GDP). Production is for two main markets, the first of which is local. Rice, millet, maize, sorghum, findo (a cereal belonging to the grass family), fruits and vegetables are all grown for home consumption. Rice is an important component of the average Gambian's diet. Despite the fact that rice yields have risen dramatically during the last decade and the country is closer to being self-sufficient in rice production, vast amounts are still imported. Food is not in as short supply in The Gambia as it is in many African countries, but agricultural products tend to come in gluts during their growing periods. For example, vast amounts of mangoes are sold everywhere during the rainy season, while at the start of the dry season you see huge piles of watermelons for sale on most street corners.

Groundnuts, cotton and sesame are the principal cash crops. Groundnuts have been the chief cash crop since the British introduced them in 1829 and have remained so even with recent attempts to diversify agriculture. Annual groundnut production is erratic and depends significantly on rainfall. The annual yield for most of the 1960s and 1970s was above 100,000 tonnes, but a strong downward trend was noted in the 1980s and especially the 1990s, reaching a nadir of around 45,000 tonnes in 1996. Post-millennial production has increased again, with several years recording yields of 120,000–150,000 tonnes.

Livestock farming is also an important contributor to GDP. Everywhere you go in The Gambia you will see herds of *ndama* cattle, sheep and goats, most of which are trypano (sleeping sickness) tolerant. Many of these animals are grazed in the bush during the day, where herdsmen stop them from wandering on to farm crops (most of the time), and they are staked out at night. Draught animals such as bullocks, donkeys and horses are also important to rural communities and carts drawn by these animals form the most common transport in such areas.

The Gambia lies within one of the richest fishing zones in the world and the natural productivity of the country's waters is further enhanced by the flow of nutrients from the River Gambia, so it comes as no surprise that fishing is an important industry here. It is estimated around 30,000 tonnes of fish are caught off the coast each year, with the majority of this being taken by fishermen using locally constructed fishing canoes, or *pirogues*, powered by outboard motors. Most of the catch is destined for home consumption as fresh fish, but much is also smoked at special centres along the coast. Fish is one of the main sources of protein in The Gambia. Both frozen and smoked fish are becoming increasingly important in the export market.

Forests are also an important resource in The Gambia, providing fuel, food, medicine and materials for the construction industry. However, unlike fish, which appears to be underexploited at the moment, forests are overexploited and have declined in both quantity and quality over the last few decades. Many people within the country now understand how important forests are, especially in the protection of soil against desiccation and erosion (a problem that is affecting much of the land in The Gambia), as well as for wildlife and recreation.

There is a fair network of roads. In the past, much of it suffered from a lack of maintenance, but this has improved greatly following the recent resurfacing of the South Bank Road all the way east to Basse and the North Bank Road as far as Lamin Koto (Janjanbureh). Most trunk roads west of Brikama are also surfaced, as is the coastal road from Banjul to Kartong near the Senegalese border. Many villages in

1

rural areas can be reached only along sandy dirt tracks. These are fine during the dry season but some of them become impassable during the heavy downpours of the rainy season, for example the road from Kanuma through Niumi National Park towards Jinack Kajata. It is unlikely that many of these roads will be paved in the near future.

While buses and light vehicles now ply most roads in the country, the River Gambia – navigable all the way from the coast to the eastern border with Senegal – is totally underutilised as a transport corridor. Steamers have plied the river in the past and at least one of them has sunk with a terrible loss of life. However, the river appears to be such an outstanding resource that it is really surprising it is not used more.

Industry is not that important to the Gambian economy, comprising about 12% of GDP in 2012 and employing a tiny fraction of the national labour force. The sector can be split into small-, medium- and large-scale industries. Small-scale industries include poultry production, metalworking and welding, repair workshops, and various crafts such as pottery, carving, jewellery making, and tie-dye and batiks. Most of The Gambia's medium- and large-scale industries are involved in fish processing and exportation. Mining for sand and gravel occurs throughout the country, for the most part supplying the local construction industry. Clay is also mined in some areas for use in pottery.

Generating more than 15% of the national GDP, tourism is the largest single industry in The Gambia and dates back to 1964 when Scandinavian tour operators first launched charter flights to the country. Since then the number of tourists has steadily risen, despite a few dips, such as the one experienced after the 1994 coup and, more recently, the Ebola crisis of 2013–16 which, despite not reaching The Gambia, had a knock-on effect for the entire continent, especially the tourist-friendly regions of West Africa. The majority of the tourists are British, but Dutch, Swedish, Germans, French and Danish are also well represented. Nearly 90,000 people are employed by the industry, accounting for about 14% of the workforce, although it has to be said that many of these jobs are insecure, poorly paid, and limited to the tourist season. Many tourists visit The Gambia just for the sun, sea and sand of the Atlantic coast, and are happy to sit on beaches or around hotel swimming pools. However, lots do go on at least one organised trip away from the hotels during their stay. A recent trend, encouraged by the government, has been the creation of more grassroots ecotourism ventures, which generally allow local communities more direct benefits than more conventional tourist models.

PEOPLE AND CULTURE

THE PEOPLE The Gambia is a nation containing a myriad different peoples from all over the world. However, the majority of the country's historical inhabitants are made up of eight different tribes. These are the Mandinka, Wolof, Fula, Jola, Sarahule, Serer, Aku and Manjango. Many recent immigrants from surrounding countries including Senegal, Ghana, Guinea, Guinea-Bissau, Liberia and Sierra Leone have joined them. Many of these immigrants have fled from the civil wars and rebellions plaguing their homelands to seek peaceful co-existence in The Gambia. Mauritanians, intensely proud and dressed in their long, loose, sleeveless robes of blue, run many of the small shops in every village and town that seem to be open all hours. Businessmen from Ghana also run The Gambia's biggest fishery complex at Ghana Town. Alongside these there is also the expat community, which ranges from newly arrived Europeans to second- and third-generation Lebanese, many of whom opted to keep their Gambian passports when they were given a choice of nationalities at the time of independence in 1965.

Although it is not possible to tell the peoples of the different indigenous tribes apart by their appearance, each ethnic group has its own traditions, language and background. Conversely, the small size of the country, generations of intermarriage and the unifying force of Islam have also contributed to a great sharing of cultural heritage among the tribes and peoples of The Gambia.

Mandinka people make up the largest proportion of the Gambian population. Traditionally they were farmers and even today they are engaged in business and farming, especially the production of groundnuts throughout the country.

The **Fula** are also farmers. Traditionally they were mainly cattle herders originating in the area north of the Senegal River, though it is thought by some that they came from much further north than this in earlier times – perhaps even from southern Europe.

The **Wolof** are thought to have originated in southern Mauritania where droughts and raids forced them south into the area north of The Gambia in western Senegal. During the religious wars of the 19th century, the Wolof established themselves in Banjul and on the North Bank of the river as traders and shipbuilders. Nowadays, the Wolof on the North Bank are usually farmers, while those in Banjul are influential in business, commerce and the civil service.

The earliest settlers in the area south of the River Gambia were the **Jola**, who are thought to have migrated from Egypt. They brought palm seed, cotton and rice with them. Nowadays many live near the coastal areas in The Gambia and unlike many of the tribes in the country they have generally retained more of their traditional practices and beliefs, in part because of their independent nature.

The **Sarahule** were rulers and merchants of the Kingdom of Ghana, and thus have a long history in the West African region. Those found in The Gambia arrived during the 19th century as refugees from the religious wars in Senegal. Nowadays many are farmers living along the eastern Gambian border, but remain famous for their gold- and silver-trading activities throughout West and Central Africa.

The **Serer** are among the oldest ethnic group in the Senegambia region, having migrated into the delta regions from north of Senegal. Today they are found mainly along the river mouth, with fishing as their main trade.

The **Aku** played an influential role in Gambian economic and governmental life during the colonial period. They are the descendants of European traders and their African wives, as well as liberated slaves from Sierra Leone. Most are Christian and have European names and continue to figure prominently in Gambian commerce and the civil service.

The **Manjango** are believed to have arrived in the Senegambia region as seasonal migrant workers from Guinea-Bissau. Today their main occupation is tapping the oil palms for wine.

SOCIAL STRUCTURES In the past the tribes of The Gambia organised their society along hierarchical lines with status determined by birth. Marriage between the various classes was uncommon.

The class structure consisted of three broad groups – the freeborn, the artisans and the slaves. At the top were the freeborn who consisted of nobles and commoners. The former were the royal lineages and great warrior families; the latter included farmers, traders and marabouts. Lower down the scale were the artisans who consisted of specialised workers such as blacksmiths, leather workers, woodcarvers and weavers. Although not slaves, the artisan families were attached to the freeborn families in a patron–client relationship.

Musicians were also a lower caste but highly respected. A particular type of musician called a *griot* performed song and poetry, containing stories of a family, village or clan as a form of oral history.

The people of The Gambia today continue to organise their society along hierarchical lines using the same structure as in the past. An individual's roles and behaviour in society are determined by his/her class. However, the inherent respect and reverence shown between the classes is being eroded by urbanisation and the higher level of education received by a higher percentage of the population. Western ideas and moral values are also spreading among the population, especially in the tourist areas where young Gambians are constantly exposed to foreign visitors, but also through television, radio, videos and magazines. Many of the older generation of Gambians fear a moral decline in their teenage sons and daughters.

FESTIVALS AND CEREMONIES During your stay in The Gambia, you are very likely to hear, before you see, a Gambian ceremonial occasion taking place. Festivities such as weddings, naming ceremonies, initiation ceremonies and other special Muslim and Christian festivals are celebrated by lavish feasting, drumming, music and dancing. A village will also celebrate the arrival of a special guest, the event being marked by the dancing of the *kanali* – a group of women dancers.

Festivals and ceremonies are loud and colourful events, with participants having new clothes made and dressing elegantly. Of course they are also costly affairs and so traditionally contributions are made to the host family in the form of money or food. If you are invited to a celebration, you will be expected to bring something. You should also expect to give a present or some money to the griots (musicians and oral historians) that come to these events.

Festivals and ceremonies are very important and much of African life is centred on such events, which help to reinforce the social structure.

Marriage Traditionally, marriages in The Gambia are arranged. However, this practice is less common now in the urban areas. The marriage ceremony itself is the finale of a week's activities, involving the exchange of gifts and visits to relatives. The official ceremony takes place at the mayor's office and is followed by eating and dancing at someone's compound. The procession of cars from the office to the home is marked by much blowing of car horns and shouting, and by the decoration of the bride and groom's car, so much so that it's hard to miss this one!

Initiation ceremony (circumcision) Traditionally, circumcision in many African countries is an event that marks the transition from childhood to adulthood. Boys and girls are circumcised separately in groups, usually between the ages of eight and 12, although it can occur at an earlier age. After the operation, the groups are taken into the bush and taught about their adult responsibilities and rules of behaviour while they are healing. When the children return to their villages, there is much feasting and socialising, and the initiated individuals are given new clothes and decorations by their parents. Special dancing with masquerades, eg: the *kankurang* (a man dressed from head to foot in a costume made of tree bark – there is a life-size model outside the National Museum in Banjul – see page 89) also marks the return of the initiate.

Today in the urban areas, children are circumcised at a hospital or clinic, and the bush school lasts for a shorter period. Female circumcision, or less euphemistically female genital mutilation (FGM), is a controversial subject that receives much attention and discussion in the media at certain times of the year. The practice, though still widely perceived to be an integral aspect of Islamic teaching, causes extreme pain and distress to the individual concerned, and may result in healing problems or even in death caused by infection.

TOSTAN

This regional organisation (w *tostan.org*) empowers African communities to bring about sustainable development and positive social transformation based on respect for human rights. Their mission is that every human being – woman, man and child – has the right to human dignity. 'Tostan' means 'breakthrough' in the Wolof language and the organisation has developed through a reliance on community feedback, respectfully engaging communities by working in their own languages and using traditional methods of learning, allowing communities to fulfil their own potential. Working in The Gambia since 2007, Tostan currently work with 30 communities, specifically focusing on the rights of children and adolescents.

Gamcotrap (w *gamcotrap.gm*) and Tostan (see box, above) are organisations that promote customary health practices among women, while also campaigning and lobbying to dissuade FGM. It is an uphill struggle.

Naming ceremonies One week after a baby is born an important ceremony takes place when the infant is named. An elder, who either shaves the baby's hair or cuts a lock and says a silent prayer, performs this ceremony in the morning (around 10.00). The elder whispers into the infant's ear the name the parents have chosen, which is proclaimed aloud by a griot. While the name is being whispered, a chicken, goat or sheep is slaughtered. A 'charity' of kola nuts, cakes or other special foods is distributed to the guests, and the baby's tuft of hair is buried. Guests bring small gifts for the infant and the griots as well. Later in the day, a meal is prepared followed by drumming and dancing. If you are informed of a naming ceremony, even in casual conversation, this is an invitation to attend. It is an informal invitation, and you will be most welcome.

Muslim and Christian holidays As a predominantly Muslim country, the people of The Gambia celebrate many religious holidays. Observance of these holidays usually involves special prayers and the offering of charity followed by feasting and dancing. They are also occasions for Gambians to dress up and visit friends and relatives. On *Tobaski* day, all heads of families who can afford it slaughter a sheep, goat or cow and divide the meat among friends, relatives and the poor as charity. Christian ceremonies are also observed in The Gambia, particularly in cities where a large proportion of the population is non-Muslim, such as Banjul.

International Roots Festival Partly inspired by the success of Alex Haley's book *Roots*, the inaugural Roots Homecoming Festival was held in May 1996 and, now known as the International Roots Festival, it has since become a biennial week-long event held in May or June of every even year. The festival is a celebration of Gambian culture through music, dance, arts and crafts and also commemorates the enslavement and transportation of millions of Africans to the Americas. Many black people from the USA and Europe participate in the festival – even taking part in traditional ceremonies – and parts of the event are also attended by the President of The Gambia. For more details, see w rootsgambia.gm.

ART Artwork is all around you in The Gambia. Not only in the market stalls, or *bengula* (meeting place), near the hotels or craft markets in Banjul, but also in the metalworkers' yards, and the woodworkers' and tailors' shops along every road.

At the markets you can buy all kinds of woodcarvings, straw and wicker work, leather work, pottery, jewellery, textile work (including weaving) and metalwork. Many of the woodcarvings are finished by the stall owners who sell them, but beware as their colour is a result of staining with shoe polish and will fade with time without constant attention. Having said this, the carvings of African masks, bowls, male and female figures and animals make good purchases and gifts.

The woven cloth you see in the markets represents the most important material in The Gambia in the form of cotton. Cloth is made by '*maabo*', a caste of weavers who traditionally come to The Gambia in the rainy season and produce it on demand for clients. Traditionally these clothes were used for special occasions such as marriage ceremonies, circumcisions and burials. The dyes used for colours in the weaving are made traditionally from natural sources; for example the ironwood tree (*Prosopis africana*) gives a red colour while the mango tree produces black.

Tie-dye and colourful batiks also abound. You will also see clothes that have been crafted in the traditional Gambian style – loose with embroidery – or made on more Western lines. You may want to bring pictures of clothes that you would like made up while staying here. Many of the tailors are able to turn a photograph into a made-to-measure designer dress or suit before your very eyes (or in a week at the most).

Away from the markets, other creative forces are at work. You only have to glance at the metalworkers' yards to see intricate gate designs and the handiwork made from recycled material. Goods range from spoons and ladles through to saucepans, brightly painted metal boxes and candleholders.

MUSIC AND DANCING Drumming is an essential part of West African traditional music, and the music itself is at the heart of the culture. It is through the music that history is passed from generation to generation, social structures are reinforced, and traditional skills are perfected. Particularly in rural areas, the beating of drums is a characteristic Gambian sound, heard on most nights of the week, and often during the day.

Traditional music is performed by a distinct social group of people, the griots, who are minstrels, musicians or praise singers. The local terms are *jali* (Mandinka), *gewel* (Wolof), or *gawlo* (Fula). In this way griots are well respected socially since they act as the historians for West African societies.

Music often accompanies traditional West African dances. The dances depict everyday scenarios including hunting, fishing and working in the fields, and feature

THE GRIOT

When one talks about music in West Africa, one often hears talk of *griots* (pronunciation 'gree-oh'), but the term, derived from the Portuguese for 'troubadour', doesn't even begin to adequately describe the meaning. Not simply musicians, griots are the oral historians and praise singers of societies, descending through families since the times of ancient West African empires. The Mandinka word for griot is 'jeli', which means blood, and you could describe the griot as the lifeblood of a culture. In fact, it is said that when a griot dies, it is as if a library has burned to the ground. In the times before writing, the griot was the only way in which histories of early mankind could be passed along from the elders to younger generations.

My first contact with a griot, at my local mechanic's in Brikama, was less than romantic. While sitting under the mango tree, one of the lads pointed out a house nearby and told me that it belonged to Pa Bobo Jobarteh, one of The Gambia's top *kora* players and a big star. Before long, he came out and started playing the kora, before beckoning me to join him. You could say it's the Gambian equivalent of popping over for tea with Bruce Springsteen, who plays for you while you wait for your car to be serviced. After he'd played a few beautiful songs as his brothers brewed *attaya*, we started chatting.

'I was born into a griot family in Brikama, and I started playing kora at the age of six. When I was 11, I played at WOMAD festival in England, then aged 22, I toured Europe, Asia, Australia and USA. I am good friends with Peter Gabriel and as a boy I played for the Queen, in Buckingham Palace.'

Given the humble surroundings it seems hard to believe, but it's true – I've seen the pictures. As we spoke, Pa Bobo showed me an older CD of his where he's pictured with members of Fairport Convention, recording in an English stately home.

'Historically we griots were the oral historians and custodians of the empire of western Sudan, playing traditional instruments such as the kora, balafon, drums and many more. But our future – the future of the griot – depends on our work being protected and promoted. We have to earn a living to carry on.'

In January 2017, during the height of the troubles after the election, Pa Bobo was forced in to exile in Senegal having released a pro-democracy song that went viral on YouTube. With a €10,000 price on his head, he wasn't taking any chances, but thanks to the power of social media, the griot still managed to sing to thousands and was an influential part of the #GambiaHasDecided movement that eventually propelled President Jammeh out of power and into exile.

Pa Bobo's work is available on iTunes or Bandcamp. If you'd like to stay with Pa Bobo, you can contact him on m 6177550 or via WhatsApp on m 3905045/2099668.

Extract adapted and edited from Chasing Hornbills *by Simon Fenton.*

stories around a wedding or naming ceremony, for example. Traditional beliefs where inanimate objects come to life or spiritual powers enter an animal also find their way into the dances.

Griots play music on a variety of instruments. These include a selection of drums including the *tama*, *sabar*, *mblatt*, *djemba* and *gorong*; stringed instruments range from the single-string plucked lute, or *moolo*, and the *riti riti* or bowed fiddle, to the 21-stringed *kora*; wind instruments include the flute and trumpet, and percussion is represented by the *balafon* (a xylophone made out of hardwood), shake-shake and claves. There is an excellent selection of these instruments, plus more specialised varieties at the Tanje Village Museum (page 156). In addition, most coastal hotels, guesthouses and camps routinely invite local villagers, dancers and musicians to entertain their guests after dinner.

A superb example of recorded Gambian traditional music is the Folkways compilation CD *Gambian Griot Kora Duets*, recorded in 1977 and downloadable legitimately from w emusic.com. It features three eminent kora players including the late Dembo Konte, a world-renowned Brikama-based griot whose other worthwhile releases (many in collaboration with the Senegalese kora-player Kausu Kuyateh) include *Jaliology* (Xenophile, 1999) and *Kairaba Jabi* (Weekend Beatnik, 2004). Other traditional releases worth investigating include *Gambia: Salam – New Kora Music* by Tata Dindin (Network, 2012) and *Kora Music from Gambia* by Jali Nyama Suso (FMP, 2008).

If Gambian music takes your fancy, bear in mind that it cannot be treated in isolation from Senegal and its neighbouring musical powerhouse Mali. The three countries share common musical roots, stemming back several centuries to the ancient Kingdom of Mali, and they've also embraced a similar range of more contemporary sounds, embracing everything from Cuban rumba to reggae to hip-hop. In recorded terms, however, The Gambia's relatively meagre musical output is overshadowed by renowned Senegalese and Malian artists such as Orchestre Baobab, Youssou N'Dour, Ali Farka Toure, Amadou and Mariam, Rokia Traore, Oumou Sangare, Nahawa Doumbia, Fatoumata Diawara, and Sister Fa – among many others whose work is worth exploring.

DRESS AND HAIRSTYLES Much of Gambian dress in urban areas is wonderfully varied and colourful. Traditionally most men prefer to wear a two-piece combination consisting of a *turkia*, a three-quarter-length long-sleeved loose shirt, together with a pair of loose-fitting Arabic-style trousers called *sirwals*. The suit can be made in all types of material, from plain white through to many different batik designs and lacy embroidered material. There seems to be no reluctance on the part of Gambian men to wear bright colours. They will often be dressed in pastels or even bright oranges and yellows.

The most characteristic dress of the women is the *granbuba*. This is a full-length dress which sometimes has a highly embroidered neck. It has simple seams down the sides below large sleeve holes. The dress is worn over a full-length skirt or wrap, either in the same material or a contrasting colour. Women will also wear a matching headdress.

Of course when people are at work, especially during hard manual labour, they will not be wearing fine clothes. Upcountry and in the more rural parts of The Gambia, women in the rice fields and vegetable gardens, and men at work in garages and metal workshops, will be dressed in their work clothes, wearing a wrap and T-shirt and trousers and T-shirt respectively.

The above is a little indication of the traditional dress worn by Gambians. However, like much of the world globalisation is taking place and many young Gambians can be found wearing T-shirts and jeans. Many men also wear woolly hats, especially during the colder months. Lots of young women also dress in very tight dresses and trousers, flouting Muslim tradition. In the office setting, suits and Western-style clothes are often worn. However, Friday normally sees everyone putting on his or her special and traditional clothes to come to work. Public and religious holidays are also a time for Gambians to dress up. If you are out and about travelling the country on such a day, it will seem like a continuous fashion parade along the roads and streets.

Gambian ladies' hairstyles are as varied as their attire. Using hair-straightening lotions, hair extensions, coloured beads and knick-knacks made from plastic, shells and bone, the many different hairstyles are limited only by the imagination. A friend of ours is quite happy to sit for up to 6 hours every week having her hairstyle changed from one elaborate design to another.

SPORTS AND GAMES

WRESTLING This is the oldest sporting activity in the Senegambian region, dating from before the 13th century and probably originating in Mali. Successful wrestlers were and still are seen as extremely important and able men with great innate spiritual and physical powers. Traditionally, the wrestling match is between contestants from two different villages. Each team is called a *kato*. The event is usually marked by a sense of progression with the youngest and least-skilled wrestlers starting first. The entire match builds up towards a climax in which the final bout is between the champions of each team.

As with all Gambian ceremonial occasions, the events are colourful and noisy affairs and music is inseparable from traditional Gambian wrestling. The basic instrument is the drum, with each ethnic group having its own traditional wrestling tunes. Unlike Western wrestling there are no long drawn-out holds and techniques like head, leg or arm locks; simply the first to be knocked down loses.

> After a particularly well-fought fight, friends and well-wishers, especially women, will rush into the arena to press coins into the hands of a favourite contestant and rush out again. Successful wrestlers are believed to possess a superior endowment of spiritual strength, which the Mandinka call *nyamo*.
>
> Extract from *Wrestling in the Gambia* by B K Sidibe and W Galloway

Large numbers of amulets are worn on every part of their body and magic potions are taken to increase their power. Wrestling was once the Gambian national sport. Today it is still popular but has to a large extent been replaced by football. Wrestling is no longer included on the school curriculum so there are fewer people able to take part in the sport. If you wish to watch a wrestling match, they still occur regularly in Serekunda and a few other places throughout the country. The best way to see a contest is to organise a visit through an official guide or a Gambian friend.

FOOTBALL Youngsters can be seen on any open patch of ground or on beaches playing football barefoot, and a few of them have gone on to be international stars in foreign teams. In the evenings you can often see crowds gathered around TV sets by the roads or in bars to watch national and international matches. Occasionally matches also take place at the Independence Stadium in Bakau, where games against neighbouring countries draw large crowds. In 2005, The Gambia hosted the African Under-17 Football Championships, a qualifying competition for the Under-17 World Cup Finals held later that same year. Football fever gripped the nation for a number of weeks and much to the delight of many Gambians resulted in their team qualifying for the finals, held in Peru during September 2005. Excitement levels grew and finally spilled over on 17 September when the minnows of The Gambia took the field to face the might of Brazil. The streets of The Gambia were empty for 90 minutes before delirious fans spilled out of houses, bars and hotels to celebrate the unexpected: The Gambia had beaten Brazil 3–1. Although The Gambia's team did not win the tournament, photographs of the nation's young heroes could be seen hanging in shops and stalls all over the country for many months after the event. Since then, unfortunately, the national football team has continued to fare poorly in major international competitions – indeed, it has yet to qualify for the FIFA World Cup or Africa Cup of Nations – despite a run of good results that led to an all-time best FIFA ranking of 65 in June 2009.

DRAUGHTS AND *WARRI* You may often see small groups of men sitting under trees or in cosy areas around a large board. They will either be playing draughts or the national board game known as *warri*. A typical place to see this is the courtyard of the Serekunda post office. Warri boards can be purchased at many of the craft markets and stalls in the coastal resorts and the stallholder will be only too glad to show you the rules of the game – though they are not simple.

LANGUAGE

English is the official language. The main local languages are Mandinka, Wolof, Jola and Fula, with several others that are less widespread. In practical terms, you will have no problem locating English-speaking people in the western areas and being able to communicate with them. Head further upriver and English-speakers become harder to find. Gambians seem to have a gift for picking up different languages, probably because they live in a highly multi-lingual society. As a result, there are also a few guides, based mostly at the hotels, who can speak passable German, Dutch or French.

RELIGION

Around 90% of the population follows Islam. The remaining 10% are mostly Christian, and there's also a small minority of people (less than 1%) who still believe in traditional forms of religion such as animism. As with most things Gambian, there is a distinct lack of inter-religious animosity within the country. Everyone is free to worship how and who they want, without prejudice, and there is nothing but a healthy curiosity about others' modes of worship and beliefs. Some traditional beliefs are still widely held throughout the population. These include the protective power of *jujus* which are worn by nearly everyone. There are also strong beliefs in the continuing existence of dragons and witches, etc. This may well sound medieval to Westerners but we should remember that we were still burning witches at the stake a few hundred years ago. On the African continent these beliefs are still very potent and are an integral and important part of the way of life – The Gambia is no exception.

Despite the strong Islamic and Christian influence in The Gambia, many practices originating from past traditional beliefs remain. Indeed, much behaviour is still governed by animist beliefs that endow natural objects and phenomena, idols, fetishes and individuals with supernatural forces or the power to protect or to use such forces. Many Gambians, from tiny babies to old citizens, wear amulets, commonly called *jujus* or *gris-gris*, on their body around the waist, neck, arms or legs. The jujus are often leather packets, or cowrie shells, which contain writings from the Koran as a spell, or charm, which is said to protect the wearer. The juju

TRADITIONS AND TABOOS

There are many taboos in Gambian culture. It is widely held, for instance, that if a person dreams of seeing raw fish or a snake, it is a sure sign of pregnancy, or that seeing a shooting star is a portent that a prominent person will die. Another common belief is that anything done on a Saturday will be repeated in the future, for which reason many people avoid visiting the sick and making condolences on this day. It is taboo to buy or sell items like soap, needles or charcoal at night, and it is also forbidden to whistle after dark, since all these things will lead to bad luck. It is also taboo for a widow to go out of her home during her mourning period.

Many animals are believed to have magical or special powers. In rural areas, most people will not kill or eat certain animals because they believe they have some ancestral connection with them. Despite this, many traditional beliefs impact negatively on wildlife. An example is the widespread fear of owls – thought to be transformed wizards and witches whose haunting call announces an impending death – that often results in its subject being killed. By contrast, geckoes and chameleons live charmed lives, in the sense that they are also very widely feared and usually left alone, although this updater's Jola wife once made an offering of her breast to a chameleon in order to protect her newborn baby.

Dragons or *ninki nanka* are the most feared of all animals in The Gambia. They live in remote areas and are usually hostile beasts who are able to kill by merely looking at someone. Fortunately, however, there also exist professional dragon slayers who are immune to such effects, and who for vast sums of money will go and slay dragons. Since no-one else can look at a dragon without dying, clients must rely on the word of the dragon slayer that the deed has been done.

Gambians are also great believers in the sanctity and holy power of certain places. The sacred crocodile pools provide examples, as do the many special sites scattered throughout the country. These sacred sites range from crocodile pools, groves, trees and stone altars through to tombs, burial sites and places where esteemed holy men have prayed. The sanctity of such places is a blessing in disguise as it is prohibited to cut down the trees or otherwise disturb the sites – and so a small part of The Gambia remains untouched.

will have been provided at birth, naming or initiation ceremonies by the local griot, or animist priest. Alternatively, the spell or charm may have been prescribed by a marabout. Gambians consult marabouts for a variety of reasons, but the following are the most common: to protect against evil spirits; to improve one's status; or to remedy a situation.

EDUCATION

Education in The Gambia appears to be the best it has been since independence but there are still big problems to overcome. Most areas of the country now have schools although many teachers are unqualified and poorly paid. Many schools also have a lack of teachers, which means that they have to be run on a shift basis, with one set of pupils being taught in the morning and another set in the afternoon. Even so, many classrooms are very crowded, with high pupil-to-teacher ratios, and have poor resources. The school system is state-run but there are also a number of Islamic schools that are operated in conjunction with the state system by local mosques. Most children in the country get an education up to primary level but then the number falls dramatically for various reasons. Many pupils do not pass their exams and therefore cannot go on to secondary level. Also, many families are so poor that they cannot afford secondary-school fees, school uniforms and books. Many children, especially girls, are also kept out of school to work in the fields or gardens. The literacy rate in The Gambia was just over 37% in 1994, but thanks to improving educational standards, it now stands at slightly more than 50%.

2

Natural History

By Craig Emms and Linda Barnett, with additions and adaptations by Philip Briggs

The Gambia is justifiably proud of its rich natural heritage. This pride is manifested in many different ways, including the Banjul Declaration of 1977, the far-reaching and forward-thinking wildlife law, and the provision of eight protected sites totalling nearly 4.9% of the land area. The Gambia is also meeting its international obligations in preserving the world's biodiversity by being a signatory to many international conventions, including the Convention on Biodiversity.

One of the tools used to prevent overexploitation of wildlife is the Wildlife Act of 1977. In essence the law is fairly simple: in order to safeguard the country's wildlife and natural history, *all* wildlife is protected by law, and anyone who is found hunting, selling, importing or exporting, or keeping wild animals as pets is breaking the law and may be prosecuted, fined and imprisoned. The only exception to this rule is the hunting of a number of species that are considered to be pests. These include warthog, giant pouched rat and francolin. Such hunting is licensed and organised by the Department of Parks and Wildlife Management.

The Gambia is also a signatory to the Convention on International Trade in Endangered Species of Flora and Fauna (CITES). Please remember this if you are offered any live or indeed any part of a *dead* wild animal to buy (eg: a skin, horns or turtle shell). It is illegal to export any of these items from The Gambia, or even to have them in your possession while in the country. If you see an infringement of this law during your visit to The Gambia, *please* inform the Department of Parks and Wildlife Management (\ *4376973;* m *9817559/3917559;* e *info@thegambiawildlife.com;* w *thegambiawildlife.com*). All information received is treated as strictly confidential. You can help to safeguard the wildlife of The Gambia.

GEOLOGY AND GEOGRAPHY

The Gambia is a flat country with a highest point of only 53m above sea level. It lies on a vast plateau of sedimentary sandstone that stretches from Mauritania in the north to Guinea Conakry in the south, and is tilted slightly towards the Atlantic. The main feature of the country is the River Gambia, which enters The Gambia about 680km from its source in the Fouta Djallon Highlands in Guinea. The river flows in a general east–west direction until it empties into the Atlantic Ocean, and cuts a winding, shallow valley for itself through the surrounding sandstones and claystone. The river has also laid down a series of alluvial deposits such as clay and sand which have partly filled this valley. Some of these deposits have been fairly recent in geological time. The river flats are normally separated from the surrounding plateau by a series of low sandstone hills, especially in the east of the country. In some places, though, extensions of the plateau have formed impressive cliffs that overlook the river.

THE COAST For about 40km from the coastline the offshore seas are shallow and lie on the continental shelf, before dropping sharply down into the depths of the ocean. These shallow waters are an important source of fish, not only for people but also for the numerous birds that feed here. Although the seabed is mainly composed of sand, there are also large outcrops of rocks and extensive beds of sea grass that form huge sun-warmed meadows. The sea-grass meadows are grazed by green turtles (*Chelonia mydas*) while dolphins, minke whales (*Balaenoptera acutorostrata*) and Mediterranean monk seals (*Monachus monachus*) hunt the abundant shoals of fish. The coastline of The Gambia consists of a long, recently deposited (in the geological timescale anyway) sandy beach, interrupted in only a few places by low cliffs and associated rock-falls. The top of this beach is clothed with creeping, sand-binding and salt-tolerant plants. Behind the beach is a series of ancient raised beaches. They are generally covered with coastal scrub, a rich habitat of small shrubs and grassland interspersed with taller trees such as baobab (*Adansonia digitata*) and rhun palm (*Borassus aethiopum*). Beyond the scrub most of the coast was once lined with moist coastal forest dominated by tall, thick stands of rhun palms and other salt-tolerant trees. This has now largely disappeared from many parts of the country.

MANGROVES AND *BANTO FAROS* Mangrove swamp, or forest, covers much of the transitional zone between aquatic and terrestrial habitats around the mouth of the River Gambia. It also extends inland along the edges of the river and many of the *bolongs* (creeks), as far as 200km from the sea. There are two main types of mangrove tree. White mangroves colonise dry land edges that are rarely inundated by the tides and are therefore less saline. Red mangroves grow right down into the edge of the sea and are very salt-tolerant. The two types are easy to tell apart as white mangroves poke up aerial roots from below the mud, while red mangroves prop themselves up on curving stilt-like roots. Coastal mangrove forests are fairly low in height, but further upriver they can tower to 20m. Mangroves grow only in tropical and sub-tropical waters and are an endangered habitat throughout the world. One reason for this is that they are often thought of as 'wasteland', and therefore cleared for development. This sometimes has drastic consequences because mangroves form a natural barrier between the sea and low-lying coastal land susceptible to erosion. In fact mangroves actually create dry land by binding mud and sand together. As the mangroves grow they periodically shed their leaves, which gradually builds up the fertility and depth of the soil in which they grow. This continues over hundreds and thousands of years until eventually the swamp becomes dry land. New mangroves grow further out on the edges of the swamp all the time and the process continues. Mangroves are also of enormous benefit in many other ways; for example many of the fish that are caught as adults in offshore waters actually spawn among the roots of mangroves. The swamps also act as a very important nursery for young fish before they head out to the open sea. In addition mangrove swamps are the only source of mangrove oysters (*Grassostrea tulipa*), which are collected and sold by many Gambian women, as well as being a source of timber for firewood and building.

Behind the mangrove swamps you will find the *banto faros*. These are large flat areas of land reclaimed from the sea by the mangroves and then abandoned. Often these flats can be barren, coated in a crystalline layer of salt crusts. In the less saline parts they are covered in thick mats of low-growing succulent plants.

WETLANDS There are many different types of wetland habitats within The Gambia. These range from coastal salt pans, lagoons and marshes, through mangrove swamps, mud flats, saltwater rivers and bolongs, flooded sand mines, animal watering holes, rice fields and permanent freshwater pools lined with reed beds, to vast seasonally flooded marshes. Most of these habitats are extremely rich in crustaceans, annelid worms and molluscs which are harvested by vast numbers of wading birds, especially during the dry season when resident species are supplemented by thousands of migrants from Europe and other areas in the north.

FARMLAND Much of The Gambia is now covered in land managed for agriculture. In the past this was under a rotational regime, where land was traditionally worked every 20 years or so. During the intervening years it was left fallow and covered in regenerating scrub and woodland. Recent rapid population growth means more pressure is being applied to increase crop production to feed people, and some of the agricultural land is now managed on a much shorter rotation, being left fallow for only two or three years in places. Much of this agricultural land is used to grow crops such as sorghum, millet, and especially groundnuts. When the land is cleared for crops, useful trees such as baobab, figs (*Ficus* species), winterthorn (*Faidherbia albida;* previously in the *acacia* genus) and African locust bean (*Parkia biglobosa*) are left intact. After the harvest, the remains of the crops and other vegetables are grazed by herds of cattle and flocks of sheep and goats. During the growing season and into the dry season these animals also range throughout the savannah and woodlands.

SAVANNAH AND THE SAHEL Two types of savannah are found in The Gambia: Guinea savannah and Sudan savannah. In the Western Division (in areas of higher rainfall up to the Bintang Bolong), the type of savannah that is commonly found is called southern Guinea savannah. This type of savannah is made up of a rich mixture of over 50 tree species, which are dense and grow fairly tall. East of the Bintang Bolong, and covering the whole of the North Bank of the River Gambia, Guinea savannah is gradually replaced by Sudan savannah. This type of habitat consists of dry, open woodland with well-spaced trees of moderate height and tall grasses. It occurs frequently on lowland soils and the slopes of low laterite (red clay) hills and ridges, and is characterised by tall red termite mounds that have been formed on the lateritic (approaching the composition of laterite) soils. This woodland is also interspersed with a few taller trees, such as baobab and red-flowered silk-cotton trees (*Bombax costatum*) which are a haven for birds that feed on their nectar-rich, large waxy flowers. In some areas of the Sudan savannah, deeper soils support taller thicker woodland composed of dry-zone mahogany (*Khaya senegalensis*) and African rosewood (*Pterocarpus erinaceus*).

All savannah is subject to bush fires that can occur almost annually in some areas. Some of these are natural fires caused by lightning strikes, etc, but people start many of them, either deliberately or accidentally. These fires change the composition of the savannahs, favouring fire-resistant trees, eliminating species that cannot cope with fires and severely reducing the natural regeneration of the vegetation.

The southward spread of Sahelian savannah, a dry habitat characterised by sparse short grass and scattered shrubs, is expanding through Senegal to The Gambia owing to decreased rainfall and massive deforestation by a timber-hungry population. Already parts of the country north of the River Gambia are showing signs of drying out. It has been noted by a few ornithologists that some birds of the dry Sahel are spreading south into The Gambia too. Only a massive injection of time and effort can possibly hope to stop the Sahel from pushing even further into The Gambia.

GALLERY FOREST To the untrained eye, gallery forest looks much like the rainforest found in other parts of West and Central Africa. However, the two differ in one main respect. Rainforest is fed from rain, while gallery forest is fed from ground water. It doesn't sound an important distinction, and certainly both types of forest are very moist, especially in the rainy season. In fact, it is quite an important variance, as a different range of trees and plants prefer the environmental conditions of gallery rather than rainforest, and vice versa, though there is also a considerable overlap in the plant species that are found in both of these habitats. It is a less important distinction to animals, which tend to be more mobile, and therefore the same, or similar, species are generally found in both. Gallery forests are a natural component of the savannah woodlands and are considered to be the vestiges of the closed, moister forests occurring in southern West Africa. Gallery forest is now a very rare habitat in The Gambia and can be found in only a few places such as Abuko Nature Reserve, Pirang Forest Park and some of the fringes of the freshwater stretches of the River Gambia.

URBAN HABITATS Urban habitats are widespread, though most of the larger urban centres are found in the Western Division. Urban habitats range from the smallest of country villages to the vast sprawl of Serekunda, including everything in between. In some areas these habitats are covered in concrete and tarmac and are devoid of life, except for the usual pest species that can be found anywhere in the world, such as some insects and larger animals, for example rats and mice. Other areas contain large open green areas and many trees, especially mango (*Mangifera indica*). These areas are richer in wildlife, with frogs, toads, lizards, snakes (even large ones like the African rock python, *Python sebae*) and birds making their homes there.

WILDLIFE VIEWING Many people think of West Africa as being relatively poor in wildlife, especially when compared with the great national parks of East Africa. And it is true that the region is now relatively impoverished in terms of glamorous large mammals. All the same, there is wildlife everywhere in The Gambia, whether it be sparkling dragonflies or colourful butterflies, noisy frogs, scampering lizards or sleepy crocodiles. And there are still some large mammals too: hippos, leopards and warthogs, as well as dolphins and a range of monkeys. Furthermore, The Gambia is a well-known hotspot for birdwatchers. Even a simple walk around the grounds of a hotel will reveal numerous firefinches and cordon-bleus, sunbirds and gonoleks, while a week's steady searching could well see you amass over 200 species, depending on how serious you are and how much effort you put in.

Tips for watching wildlife Successful wildlife watching can be quite an art. Its nearest equivalent is probably stalking and hunting food to eat. It is of course more fun to 'shoot' with a camera these days than to shoot with a gun, and much less damaging to the wildlife as well. If you're an outdoor type then most of the following tips will already be well known to you. For people that are less used to the outdoors and to the rigours of watching wildlife, they may seem a little obvious and archaic. But they are well worth following if you don't want to waste your time in fruitless searches for wildlife. The main point is that if you walk slowly and pause often, your chances of spotting something good will be multiplied.

The one thing that you cannot guarantee is luck. Wild animals are unpredictable. You can be in the right place at the right time, with the right clothes and equipment, and follow all the rules for good wildlife stalking, but still not see anything.

Conversely you can walk down a busy main street in a town and see something quite unexpected. Luck is the one thing that we cannot help you with. However, you can help yourself by reading and following the advice below.

The right equipment No special equipment is necessary for watching wildlife although a good set of binoculars can be extremely useful, as getting really close to wild birds and animals is often difficult.

The right clothes It is important to try and blend into your surroundings as much as possible but also to keep cool at the same time. A set of khaki safari-type clothes is a good compromise. Remember it is sensible to wear long trousers in the bush, not only because of the small danger of snakes (trousers will prevent most of them from biting into your leg) but also because of the myriad tiny biting insects such as ants that just love bare flesh. Tuck your trousers into a good pair of light, stout boots and you are almost snake-proof and can walk around without worrying about stepping on something nasty. It will also stop insects from crawling up your legs. A sunhat with a wide brim is a good idea too, not only to protect you from the sun but also to help break up the outline of your head and shoulders (see below).

The right place This is fairly obvious. You cannot expect to see dolphins if you walk through a forest, or warthogs from a boat at sea. Animals all have particular habitats that they adhere to, though there are some species, notably birds, which are far more mobile and can be encountered anywhere. It is not always necessary to go for miles into the bush to spot wildlife. Well-known sites such as Abuko Nature Reserve (pages 171–3) can be excellent for watching animals at close quarters, simply because so many people visit. The animals have become accustomed to visitors and do not run off at the first sight or sound of a human.

The right time This is very important in The Gambia. It gets so hot during the middle of the day that many animals do the sensible thing and have a siesta, normally away from prying eyes. The best times for wildlife watching are from first light to around 11.00, and again from 16.00 to dusk. Of course there are always exceptions. Many butterflies are best seen around midday, and some of the larger animals, especially predators, are best looked for during the first and last few hours of darkness. Take a drive upcountry in the dark and you stand a fair chance of spotting animals dashing across the road that you would not normally see during the daylight. Ask permission at any of the protected areas and they will allow you to walk through in the dark and have a torch-lit safari. It is wise, though, to take a local guide with you – provided you can find one who's not too scared of the dark.

Staying inconspicuous Try and disguise the **shape** of your body, which is a dead giveaway to cautious wildlife, even at a distance. The shape that really gives us away as human is our square shoulders with our head perched on top. Wear a floppy hat or scarf and this will go a long way to breaking up your outline.

It is much harder to see things when they are in deep shadow, so try it yourself and use **shade** to your own advantage. For example walk along a line of trees within their shade while you scan adjacent fields, or sit in shade when you rest. It will give you a much better chance of seeing things before they see you. There is also the added benefit that it is much cooler in shade.

Like shape, the human **silhouette** is instantly recognisable to wild animals, so try to avoid standing on skylines where you stand out like a sore thumb. Remember, too, that you can be silhouetted against other plain objects – for example, ploughed fields or bodies of water.

Wearing clothes or carrying equipment that has a shiny reflective surface is a serious no-no for wildlife watching. The **shine** of such objects can give you away very easily, so go for matt surfaces – and watch those sunglasses.

When searching out mammals, try to walk into the wind so that your **scent** is carried away behind you. This will prevent animals having an advance warning and disappearing before you can see them. Some wildlife, especially mammals, are more reliant on their powerful sense of smell to pick up danger than they are on their other senses. As humans, with our poor sense of smell, we often forget this simple rule.

Fast, sudden **movements** betray your presence, so try to move slowly and deliberately. This also helps by allowing you more time to scan the ground around you for those well-camouflaged and difficult-to-see species, before they burst away in a cloud of noise and dust. One point that is easily overlooked is that moving vegetation is a dead giveaway too, so proceed carefully through tall grass or bushes so that you don't scare everything away. This is perhaps the most important of our tips for watching wildlife.

Wildlife photography

It is difficult to obtain decent wildlife photographs in The Gambia without a good specialist lens, eg: 200mm or 300mm. Having said this, many birds and animals are highly approachable, especially in hotel gardens and around water bodies towards the end of the dry season. The hides at Abuko Nature Reserve (pages 171–3) and the sewage ponds at Kotu (page 123) provide excellent conditions for close-up views of many bird species.

In addition, The Gambia is home to a great variety of plants and insects. Throughout the year both the native flowers and those of the introduced varieties in the hotel grounds can be quite spectacular. However, the first rains result in an explosion of new flowers (eg: the scarlet fireball lilies (*Scadodox multifloris*), which can be seen lining the road leading to the airport terminal), and bright colourful insects, including many butterflies and moths.

Lighting is a critical factor in every type of photography and it is especially true of nature photography. The quality and quantity of light vary enormously during the day in The Gambia. Lighting is at its best in the hours just after dawn and before sunset. At this time it is not too harsh and allows details to be recorded. The light also comes from a lower angle in the sky and helps provide depth to images from the shadows that are created.

If you find yourself taking pictures in the middle of the day, you will see that the natural light becomes very intense, making it impossible to record the detail and contrast of subjects. One way to approach this problem is to use a polarising filter, especially if you are taking pictures of water. The filter removes the unwanted glare from the surface of the water and has the effect of increasing the contrast between any subject and the background.

An overcast cloudy sky will always produce a softer and even lighting, regardless of the time of day. The diffuse light in this situation causes shadows to become indistinct or non-existent, with the result that fine details are revealed.

One more tip is that wildlife photography often requires patience and quite a few hours of sitting or crouching in hot, sticky and cramped conditions. Don't forget to take your insect repellent, sunscreen, hat and plenty of water! And for advice on equipment, see pages 50–2.

PRIMATES At present, five primate species are widespread and relatively common in The Gambia: western red colobus, patas monkey, green (or callithrix) monkey, Guinea baboon and Senegal bushbaby. The first four are fairly easy to see diurnally in the right habitat. The country also supports an introduced population of common chimpanzee, confined to three islands in the River Gambia National Park (pages 225–30), and possibly a relict population of Campbell's monkey.

Temminck's western red colobus (*Procolobus badius temminckii*) This is a large slender leaf-eating monkey with hind legs longer than the arms. The head is small and round, with a short muzzle and flat, broad nose. The upper parts are generally dark grey while the lower limbs and underparts range from rich red to light orange. The face is bluish to black, and the long, tuftless tail is dark, sometimes with an orange tint. As with other colobus monkeys, its thumbs are reduced to mere stumps. It lives in troops of typically around 15–30 individuals, and inhabits various forest and woodland habitats. Despite being found throughout a large area of West Africa, it is disappearing rapidly and listed as endangered, mainly from habitat loss through logging and clearing of forests. Nevertheless, significant populations are present in protected areas such as in Kiang West and the River Gambia National Park, Bijilo Forest Park and Abuko Nature Reserve.

Guinea baboon (*Papio papio*) The largest and most ferocious looking of Gambian monkeys is the Guinea baboon, a West African endemic listed as Near Threatened by the International Union for Conservation of Nature (IUCN) owing to habitat loss within its small range. Grizzled reddish-brown in colour, it has a large dog-like muzzle, and adult males also possess a sharply defined mane and weigh up to 19kg. Baboons are predominantly terrestrial but do visit trees and are quite capable of climbing even smooth palm trunks. They are adaptable feeders, eating most edible plants found in their range, supplemented with small animals ranging from grasshoppers to birds and even young antelopes. Baboons obtain all the water they need to survive from their food and dew, but also like to drink regularly. The Guinea baboon is fairly common upcountry but increasingly scarce along the coast, although it can still be seen in protected areas such as Makasutu Cultural Forest.

Patas monkey (*Erythrocebus patas*) This slender monkey is sandy grey in colour with a russet-red tail, crown and hindquarters, pale facial skin and a dark nose. Males weigh up to 25kg, but females reach a maximum of 14kg. Sometimes dubbed the 'greyhound' of monkeys, it is mainly terrestrial and has long limbs that allow it to travel at up to 50km/h. Widespread and common throughout The Gambia, it inhabits several vegetation types, from open grassland to dry woodland, and is sometimes seen crossing roads upcountry.

Green monkey (*Chlorocebus sabaeus*) A long-legged species associated with forest margins and savannah, the green monkey is grizzled golden-green with off-white underparts, pale grey hands and feet, and a red-tipped tail. The male has a very pale blue scrotum, and can weigh up to 7.5kg. It is adapted to practically all wooded habitats outside of rainforests, but being smaller than a baboon and slower than a patas, it cannot afford to venture as far from the safety of the trees, and is also more dependent on trees for food. Once regarded as a subspecies of the widespread vervet monkey, the green monkey is now considered to be a full species resident only in West Africa. It is the most numerous monkey in The Gambia and can be found throughout the country.

Campbell's mona monkey (*Cercopithecus campbelli*) The Gambian status of this dark, long-tailed, arboreal monkey is uncertain. It once inhabited heavily wooded parts of the country and may still be present in the southwest.

Senegal bushbaby (*Galago senegalensis*) Distantly related to the lemurs of Madagascar, bushbabies or galagos are small primates that emit a scream so loud you'd think it was coming from a chimpanzee or gorilla. The Senegal bushbaby is the only one of around a dozen species that occurs in The Gambia. Nocturnal and quite difficult to find, it can sometimes be picked out by tracing the cry to a tree and shining a torch or spotlight in its general direction to look for the reflection of its large eyes.

CARNIVORES
Spotted hyena (*Crocuta crocuta*) Probably the most common large predator in The Gambia, the spotted hyena has a bulky build, sloping back, brown-spotted coat, powerful jaws, and dog-like expression. Contrary to popular myth, it is not exclusively a scavenger, nor is it hermaphroditic (an ancient belief that stems from the false scrotum and penis covering the female's vagina). Sociable animals, and fascinating to observe, hyenas live in loosely structured clans of about ten, led by females who are stronger and larger than males. It is normally nocturnal and is seldom seen, though its loud, repetitive and reverberating hoot 'whoo-up' carries for up to 5km.

Spotted hyena

Leopard (*Panthera pardus*) This medium to large spotted cat (the largest males grow up to 2m in length and weigh up to 90kg) is solitary and secretive but very habitat-tolerant, typically favouring areas with plenty of cover, such as riverine woodland and rocky slopes. It can occupy territories of 10km² where food is abundant, but territories in The Gambia are much larger than this. It is widespread but adept at remaining concealed in dense vegetation, aided by its beautiful colouring, which also provides a very practical camouflage. As recently as 50 years ago, leopards were so common that they could be watched quite regularly on the outskirts of Banjul. These days they only inhabit very remote areas, such as the national parks.

Leopard

Smaller carnivores Small carnivores are common in the Gambian countryside, but you have to be lucky to see any, as they are elusive and mostly nocturnal. The species recorded so far include **side-striped jackal** (*Canis adustus*) which is widespread, and the **sand fox** (*Vulpes pallida*) which appears to be restricted to the North Bank of the River Gambia. The **African clawless otter** (*Aonyx capensis*) inhabits many wetlands, especially the mangrove creeks, and this is the largest species of otter found in Africa. The black-and-white-striped **zorilla** (*Ictonyx striatus*) is a skunk-like animal that has been rarely recorded in The Gambia, as has the **honey badger** (*Mellivora capensis*), otherwise known as the **ratel**.

African civet

The ratel is a small but ferocious carnivore that is well known because of its habit of raiding bee nests for their honey. The shaggy, dog-like **African civet** (*Civettictis civetta*), with its ornate pattern of blotches, spots and stripes and a boldly marked face, is said to be common. There are three species of **genet** (looking almost like a cross between a spotted cat and a mongoose) which are very good climbers and feed on fruit, insects, snakes, birds and rodents. The **two-spotted palm civet** (*Nandinia binotata*) is a similar-looking animal that has only ever been recorded in Abuko Nature Reserve and Pirang Forest Park in The Gambia. Five species of mongoose are found in The Gambia. These range from the pack-living **banded mongoose** (*Mungos mungo*) which may be seen hunting in the daylight in and around Kiang West National Park, to the nocturnal and very common **marsh mongoose** (*Atilax paludinosus*) which lives a mostly solitary existence. This animal has extremely nimble fingers and survives by capturing crabs at the water's edge. The **African wild cat** (*Felis silvestris lybica*) looks very like a domestic tabby and may be the commonest of the cats in The Gambia. Other species include the rare lynx-like **caracal** (*Caracal caracal*) with a reddish-fawn coat, and the long-legged and beautifully spotted **serval** (*Leptailurus serval*), which are both widespread but uncommon. Identifying any of these species can be difficult.

Banded mongoose

Caracal

UNGULATES

Hippopotamus (*Hippopotamus amphibius*)

The country's largest ungulate can weigh in at up to a staggering 3,200kg, and have a body length of up to 3.5m. Dependent on fresh water, hippos are resident along the River Gambia upstream of Elephant Island, but sometimes come closer to the coast (one was recently observed close to Pirang). A survey by the British Army Ornithological Society in 2003 along the full length of the River Gambia found only 48 hippos. Hippos spend the day submerged in deep water, emerging from the river just before darkness falls to graze on grassland nearby for 4–5 hours before returning to the water to digest the food. There are many existing and potential conflicts between people and hippos, not least of which is that hippos cause considerable damage to agricultural crops on the riverbanks, especially rice fields.

Common warthog (*Phacochoerus africanus*)

Often, but erroneously, referred to as a bushpig, the warthog is a large animal, with males weighing up to 150kg, though females are normally a lot smaller with a maximum weight of 75kg. It is relatively long-legged with prominent curved tusks, and a crest of lank dark hair extending from the crown to the nape of the neck and hanging over the shoulders. The 'warts' are three pairs of thickened pads of skin that protect the jaws, eyes and muzzle. It is widespread and common in wooded, bush and savannah habitats upriver, largely because the majority of the population is Muslim, and therefore does not eat pork. This does not mean to say

Warthog

33

that warthogs live in perfect harmony with people. They can be quite a pest to crop farmers, and are also hunted to provide meat for tourist-oriented restaurants.

Bushbuck (*Tragelaphus scriptus*) This handsome medium-sized antelope has a reddish coat (though mature males become progressively darker with age), with vertical and horizontal white stripes, numerous spots on the haunches, and white markings on the face and ears, above the hooves and under the broad woolly tail. Though common and widespread, it is rather shy and tends to stick to deep cover, where it can remain virtually invisible, announcing its presence only when it bounds off in a blaze of noise and movement, often accompanied by a loud warning bark. The large bushbuck population in Abuko Nature Reserve is relatively accustomed to people and easy to see.

Bushbuck

Maxwell's duiker (*Cephalophus maxwelli*) This tiny antelope is often very hard to spot as it makes its way through the grass and trees. Most sightings are made as it crosses open paths. Again it is very common at Abuko and this is one of the best places to see it. Just over 30cm in height, with a maximum weight of 5.4kg, it is a forest species that lives mainly on fruit but will also eat leaves and shoots, and even ants and other insects. It can often be found following troops of monkeys, waiting for them to drop some half-eaten fruit on the ground.

Sitatunga (*Tragelaphus spekei*) This large but secretive antelope is still present in fair numbers along the banks of the River Gambia. Associated with marshes and other wetland areas rather than forest, it is the world's only aquatic antelope, with widely splayed hoofs and a thick oily coat that repels water. Probably the country's best site for observing sitatunga as they emerge from cover to feed is along the southern bank of the River Gambia in Kiang West National Park.

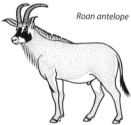
Roan antelope

Roan antelope (*Hippotragus equinus*) This is one of the largest antelopes in Africa and is a very impressive and powerful-looking creature. A male might weigh up to 300kg, with a head and body length of up to 2.4m, and massive arched horns up to 1m long. A herd of these magnificent antelopes frequently wanders into Kiang West National Park from southern Senegal during the wet season.

AARDVARK The aardvark, or ant bear (*Orycteropus afer*), is a strange-looking nocturnal creature that is said to be widespread. It is a large animal with a very long nose, squared-off head and long rabbit-like ears. It spends the day living underground in warrens and even when foraging above ground at night it is very shy, so is seldom spotted. It feeds by digging out colonies of ants and termites and sweeping up the insects into its small mouth with its long, sticky tongue.

BATS Like other mammals, bats (or *tonso* in Mandinka) can regulate their body temperature, and give birth to live

Aardvark

young and suckle them on milk. Unlike other mammals, however, they are able to fly, a unique ability that has led their colonising almost every ecosystem on earth. Indeed, bats account for almost a quarter of the world's 5,000-odd mammal species, and at least 30 species occur in The Gambia, though they have been little studied as yet.

Bats come in two main types: large fruit bats, with wingspans of up to 75cm, and much smaller insect-eating bats. Fruit bats are the more commonly seen, since they roost communally in trees, often in urban areas. They have large eyes and are quite able to see in the dark as they fly from tree to tree, though their sense of smell is also acute and they often use this to locate their food. Fruit bats eat fruit of course, but also pollen and nectar from flowers. The commonest species in The Gambia is probably the **Gambian epauletted fruit bat** (*Epomophorus gambianus*) which can be found just about everywhere.

The insect-eating bats are amazing creatures. Their eyesight is relatively poor but they compensate by using a form of sonar, hearing rather than seeing their surroundings. Depending upon the species in question, they emit short sharp sounds from either their mouths or specially adapted noses. These sounds are sent out in waves around them as they fly, and when these sounds hit an object such as a branch or perhaps a flying insect they bounce back and are picked up by the bats' ears (or their noses in specially adapted species). The sounds are then processed in the bats' brain to produce a 'sound picture' of their environment. These animals are so well adapted that they can detect the location of insects as small as 1mm long, and work out the direction and speed that they are flying. This is even more amazing when you think that they do all of this while they themselves are twisting and turning in very fast flight in complete darkness. These bats are very beneficial to man. They eat vast quantities of insects that are pests to farmers and even the smallest species of bat can eat up to 3,000 mosquitoes per night, helping to keep the numbers of these malaria-carrying insects at manageable levels. Some species have been known to live as long as 30 years.

INSECTIVORES This is a group of small insect-eating mammals that to date have been little studied in The Gambia. The **African four-toed hedgehog** (*Atelerix albiventris*) has been recorded at scattered locations around the country, including in Abuko Nature Reserve). Other species include the **giant shrew** (*Crocidura olivieri*) and the **savannah shrews** (*C. nanilla* and *C. lamottei*).

HARES The **African savannah hare** (*Lepusmicrotis senegalensis*) is a widespread and common species throughout The Gambia. Locals often refer to it as the 'rabbit'. It is generally solitary and nocturnal, living in any area where there is tall grass or scrub.

RODENTS Rodents are a large group of poorly studied animals within The Gambia and contain a variety of species from the very large porcupines to the tiny pygmy mouse (*Mus musculoides*), which weighs 2–3g. One thing that they all have in common is that they eat vegetable matter such as grass, fruits and seeds, and they all have teeth that are constantly growing and therefore need to be kept worn down by gnawing. The **crested porcupine** (*Hystrix cristata*) is widespread but nocturnal and difficult to see, though probably common. Its relative, the **brush-tailed porcupine** (*Atherus africanus*) has only been recorded by the coast at places like Bijilo Forest Park and Abuko Nature Reserve.

On a walk or drive through the countryside you are much more likely to see **squirrels**. Two species, the **striped ground squirrel** (*Xerus erythropus*) and the **Gambian sun squirrel** (*Heliosciurus gambianus*), are particularly common. The former is almost always seen on the ground and can be identified by the white stripe along its flank. The latter is found mainly in trees and has a black-and-white-ringed tail. The **red-legged sun squirrel** (*Heliosciurus rufobrachium*) can also be seen at Abuko Nature Reserve, where it is an uncommon resident of the gallery forest. It is slightly larger than the Gambian sun squirrel and can be identified by its red legs. There are also numerous species of rats, mice and gerbils, including the very common (and edible) **giant pouched rat** (*Cricetomys gambianus*), a completely harmless animal that can weigh up to 1.4kg. This species is grey in colour with a long, naked tail that is white for the last half of its length. This is not really a 'rat', in spite of its English name, but belongs to a very old family of rodents found only in Africa. It has large cheek pouches that it stuffs with food, which it then carries to an underground den to be stored so that it can be eaten at leisure and in relative safety.

DOLPHINS At least two species of dolphin are regularly sighted off the coast – the **Atlantic hump-backed dolphin** (*Sousa teuszii*) and the **bottlenose dolphin** (*Tursiops truncatus*). The bottlenose dolphin is also known to swim upriver as far as Mansa Konko, and is frequently sighted east of the Tanbi wetland complex (south of Banjul) and across the river by Dog Island. It has also been known to enter bolongs in both Niumi and Kiang West national parks.

The bottlenose dolphin can grow up to 3.9m long and weigh anything from 150kg to 650kg. It is a uniform grey colour with an off-white, light grey or pinkish underside. Its main distinguishing features are the prominent dark dorsal fin, and an inquisitive and active nature. It is usually found in groups of up to ten animals but as many as 500 have been seen together offshore. It is highly active at the surface, frequently riding the bow and wake of boats, and sometimes leaping several metres high out of the water. It is a powerful swimmer but dives seldom last longer than 3–4 minutes.

The Atlantic hump-backed dolphin is the smaller of the two species with an adult length of 2–2.5m and a weight of 100–150kg. It is distinguished from the bottlenose by the conspicuous elongated hump in the middle of its back and relatively small dorsal fin on top. The colour is slate-grey on the back and sides, with the underside usually paler. The body may be speckled. It usually swims in groups of three to seven animals, but schools of up to 40 have been sighted off the coast. It appears to prefer shallow coastal and estuarine water less than 20m deep, especially around mangrove swamps. It is often quite difficult to approach and tends to avoid boats by diving and reappearing some distance away in a different location. It surfaces every 40–60 seconds but can stay underwater for several minutes. It seldom rides the bow-waves of boats but is known for co-operating with fishermen by driving fish towards their nets.

Watching dolphins in the wild is one of the ultimate wildlife experiences. Several tour operators and hotels offer dolphin-watching trips on the River Gambia, and they can also sometimes be seen from the deck of the Banjul–Barra ferry.

MANATEE The West African manatee (*Trichechus senegalensis*) is large and cylindrical in shape, reaching a length of up to 3.6m and weighing in at 350–450kg. It has a dark grey wrinkled skin, which is lighter underneath and is almost entirely hairless except for whiskers on its upper lip. Often manatees can look green as the 5cm-thick skin on the back is sometimes covered with a growth of algae. The thick, fleshy upper lip is quite mobile and the head is rounded with very small eyes, no external ears and small round nostrils on the top of the large muzzle. The body tapers into a tail that ends in a rounded fin. The front limbs have evolved into short flippers, each with three rudimentary nails. The hind limbs are no longer outwardly present.

Manatees are entirely aquatic and cannot come out on to land at all. They are superbly adapted to an aquatic existence with nostrils and eyes placed on top of the head so that they can remain almost entirely submerged but still able to breathe and see above the surface. They can dive for up to 15 minutes in an emergency though an ordinary dive lasts between only 1 and 2 minutes. To help them dive their nostrils close with the aid of a valve and oily tear ducts allow them to see under the water. Their normal speed is around 10km/h but when frightened they can swim at considerably faster speeds.

Manatees live mostly in estuaries, coastal lagoons and large rivers and are sometimes encountered in the sea in shallow coastal waters. They are wholly vegetarian, eating a variety of water plants and the leaves of mangroves and other vegetation overhanging the water. They can be found far up the River Gambia, from the mouth to at least as far as Baboon Island. The West African manatee is now considered endangered throughout its range.

REPTILES

Crocodiles Crocodiles have changed very little in the last 65 million years and are perfectly adapted to living in water. Their eyes and nostrils are located on top of the head and they have webbed hind feet. Their nostrils also have watertight valves and there is a flap at the back of the throat, which allows them to feed underwater. Three species are present in The Gambia. Most common is the **West African crocodile** (*Crocodylus suchus*), which was split from the similar-looking but quite distantly related **Nile crocodile** (*C. niloticus*) of eastern and southern Africa in 2011. It can live for up to 100 years in the wild and can attain a length of 6m, with a weight exceeding 1,000kg. The **African slender-snouted crocodile** (*C. cataphractus*) has been recorded occasionally in the vicinity of Georgetown and the River Gambia National Park. The **dwarf crocodile** (*Osteolaemus tetraspis*) is thought to be extinct in The Gambia.

The future of the West African crocodile in The Gambia is almost assured thanks to human intervention. A small population of this species is fully protected in Abuko Nature Reserve. Early in the wet season the crocodiles breed close to the Darwin Field Station in the reserve. Even more significant than the group at Abuko are the populations present at the three sacred crocodile pools. There is one such pool on the North Bank of the River Gambia, at Berending, one in the southern part of the country at Kartung, and the most famous of them all at Kachikally, in Bakau. This last pool, although small, has a large crocodile population. Not only do these pools protect wild populations of this species but they also act as breeding and dispersal centres where excess animals can bolster the wider crocodile population.

Marine turtles These massive shelled reptiles are represented by perhaps five species in Gambian coastal waters. Though they live in the sea, all turtles are tied to land for reproduction and must face many dangers as they haul themselves on to the shore to lay their eggs. In the sea they are powerful and elegant swimmers that cover vast distances during their lifetimes. On shore they are heavy, clumsy creatures that must drag their huge weight through soft sand using only the massive strength of their flippers. Most numerous in Gambian waters, and the only species known for certain to breed on its beaches, is the **green turtle** (*Chelonia mydas*). This is a very large species, up to 1.4m long and 300kg in weight, with a hard smooth shell, a compact and relatively small head, and a tail in both sexes.

Three other species, the **hawksbill** (*Eretmochelys imbricata*), **olive ridley** (*Lepidochelys olivacea*) and **loggerhead** (*Caretta caretta*), are thought to live along the coast but it is unknown whether they use Gambian beaches to breed. The giant **leatherback turtle** (*Dermochelys coriacea*), which can reach a length of 1.8m and an incredible weight of 646kg, is probably by far the scarcest species inhabiting Gambian waters. To date only two specimens have been found on beaches, both dead. This species is easy to identify as it lacks a horny shell, being covered instead with thick, smooth skin that resembles vulcanised rubber. The skin has five long ridges along the back, one each on either side, and five underneath.

LIZARDS These are the most common and familiar reptiles in The Gambia; indeed, there can hardly be a house or compound in the country that does not have a resident gecko or agama. The country's most striking smallish lizard is the **agama**, or **rainbow lizard** (*Agama agama*) which is found almost everywhere in all types of habitat. During the dry season they are generally dull brown in colour, but a month or so before the rains begin the females develop a bright-orange patch along their flank and the males become very gaudy in colour with yellow heads and bright-blue bodies. You can often see the males displaying to one another, with their front feet planted firmly on the ground and their heads bobbing up and down. The agama is active during the day and feeds almost exclusively on termites and ants.

The largest group of lizards in The Gambia is the **geckoes**, and five species have been found here. These common lizards have amazingly adapted feet and eyes. Gecko feet have toe-tips with groups of scales covered in masses of minute hairs that allow them to 'stick' to seemingly smooth surfaces, even glass. The eyes have transparent eyelids that are fused permanently and thus cover the eye with a 'spectacle' that protects it. Geckoes are found in many habitats, but are best known as living in houses where they happily feed on a diet of insects such as cockroaches, mosquitoes, flies and crickets. Geckoes are mainly nocturnal and adapted to living in cooler temperatures than many other lizards. One of the most common species is **Brook's house gecko** (*Hemidactylus brooki angulatus*).

Skinks are another large group of lizards. Four species are found in The Gambia. They look much more like typical lizards than geckoes, are mainly ground-dwelling and are active during the day. They feed almost exclusively on small insects, which they seize in their jaws after a short rush from cover. The **orange-flanked skink** (*Mabuya perrotetii*) and the **brown-flanked skink** (*M. affinis*) both appear to be extremely common and widespread in many different habitats, even in and around urban areas, though the former is normally active only during the wet season. The other two species of skink are much rarer. The **snake-eyed skink** (*Leptosiaphus nimbaense*) has been found only twice in The Gambia. **Armitage's cylindrical skink** (*Chalcides armitagei*) is an uncommon coastal species (see box, page 100).

Chameleons are unmistakable lizards and are famous for their ability to change the colour of their skin to match their background and mood. There are two species of chameleon in The Gambia: *Chamaeleo gracilis* and *C. senegalensis*, which look fairly similar. Chameleons have toes that are bound together and oppose so that they can effectively grip branches. Their tails are prehensile and unlike those of geckoes, agamas and skinks they cannot be shed or regenerated. The eyes of chameleons appear to be placed in turrets and move independently of one another as they search for food. Insects form the main prey of these creatures. These are caught with a telescopic tongue (sometimes longer than the chameleon's body) which can be shot out and has a sticky pad at its tip.

Last but no means least are the **monitor lizards**. There are two species in The Gambia: the **savannah monitor** (*Varanus exanthematicus*) and the **Nile monitor** (*V. niloticus*). The latter is the commonest and also the largest of all the monitor lizards in Africa, reaching a maximum length of 2m. They are powerful-looking animals with well-developed limbs and strong claws. They have a long tail and a long, flexible neck. These lizards are real predators and will eat almost anything from insects to birds and mice. They will also dig up and eat the eggs of turtles and crocodiles and even catch and eat young crocodiles that have just hatched. The Nile monitor is a great swimmer and is therefore usually found in or near water, while the savannah monitor is found in more arid areas, mostly during the wet season.

SNAKES At least 37 species of snake have been identified in The Gambia, though most of these are rarely seen or are confined to certain restricted habitats such as gallery forest. However, some species are widespread and can be found in the bush, woodlands, gardens and wasteland. The snakes that you are most likely to see are the beauty snakes, pythons and cobras. Although feared by people, snakes are not the most dangerous animals in the country. To put it in perspective, many more people die from malaria, which is carried by the humble mosquito.

Only nine Gambian snakes are regarded as being seriously venomous and dangerous to humans. Snakes do not strike at people because they wish to kill them or eat them; they strike because they are stood on by accident or because they are cornered and cannot escape, because they are frightened or because they are protecting their young just as a human mother would protect her children. The ordinary town dweller or visitor is unlikely ever to see a snake, never mind being struck by one. However, if you do see a snake, then do not go near it or attempt to catch it. Back away and leave it in peace and it will do the same to you. Often a snake will see you before you see it and will rapidly slide away in fear.

AMPHIBIANS At least 33 species of amphibian are found in The Gambia, ranging from toads through bullfrogs to reed and tree frogs. The square-marked toad, or **common African toad** (*Bufo regularis*), is probably the most common and regularly encountered. It is a typical large and compact toad with a warty skin. It is dark olive-brown in colour and the skin between the tiny warts on its sides often appears almost black. It is covered by dark patches that are often arranged more or less symmetrically on the back, looking like pairs of dark squares running along either side of the spine – hence one of its English names. In addition, younger animals have a light stripe which runs along the backbone, sometimes yellow in colour, though this often fades in older animals.

This toad is encountered in most types of habitats, including coastal scrub and woodland, forest, farmland, swamps and even in urban areas, especially in the irrigated grounds of hotels and gardens. However, its main natural habitat appears to be Guinea savannah. Toads must keep their skin moist in order to survive. They do this by becoming nocturnal, hiding by day beneath rocks and fallen logs or in holes, and emerging at night to hunt. Their favourite prey appears to be ants but other insects are also eaten, with termites making up a larger proportion of their diet in damper weather. Adult toads make up the diet of a lot of other creatures, including Nile monitors, crocodiles, herons and egrets.

FISH Fish not only play a large role in the ecology of Gambian waters but they are also the mainstay of a thriving local industry. Saltwater fish are common in the shallow seas off the coast. Walk along any beach and you will see dozens of dead fish washed up on the tideline, including stingrays and triggerfish. If you are really interested, a visit to one of the many fishing villages, such as at Tanji, especially when the catches are being brought in, will satisfy even the most ardent of fishwatchers. Commonly caught fish include **bonga** (*Ethmalosa fimbriata*) and **African red snapper** (*Lutjanus agennes*), but even larger species such as sharks are sometimes landed. Along the River Gambia and its bolongs there is a small-scale fishing industry that provides much of the protein needs of the Gambian population. The Gambia is also well known throughout the world for its sports fishing, and indeed some of the largest specimens of freshwater fish ever caught in the world have been hooked here by keen foreign anglers.

Tilapia and **mullets** are perhaps the most common fish in the country. The juveniles of these can be found in vast quantities among the mangroves, which act as a natural nursery. These fish in turn provide food for huge numbers of birds such as herons, egrets, ospreys and fish eagles.

Perhaps the strangest fish of all, and one which you are bound to see wherever there are mangroves, is the **Atlantic mudskipper** (*Periophthalmus papillo*). When the tide is out and the mud is exposed, mudskippers can be seen creeping about using their strong pectoral fins like miniature legs. They are sometimes mistaken for amphibians but they are true fish and have developed their walking ability so well that they can even climb up on to the exposed lower roots of the mangroves.

CRABS The most abundant species of crab in The Gambia is the **West African fiddler crab** (*Uca tangeri*). This species can be seen in huge numbers on the mud alongside mangrove swamps. The males have one small claw and one large claw that they wave around to warn off other males and to attract females. A walk on the beach at night with a torch is the best way to see **African ghost crabs** (*Ocypoda africana*). They inhabit the shoreline and have distinctive eyes on long stalks. They will often scuttle off into the surf and all you can then see is the tops of their eyes looking at you from above the water like miniature periscopes.

INSECTS Of all the creatures inhabiting our world, the insects are by far the most numerous. Science has recognised over one million species so far and there are many, many more that as yet remain undiscovered and undocumented. For this reason it is obviously not possible to write about all of the insects in The Gambia in a short section, so we will give a general account that will hopefully give you an overview of this diverse and fascinating group of animals. We have selected some species which are common and therefore more likely to be seen, and those that are particularly interesting or important to people.

Dragonflies and damselflies These are brightly coloured insects, some quite large, with long transparent wings. They are remarkable fliers, being able to hover with ease and even fly backwards. They live most of their lives as nymphs beneath the surface of ponds, streams and rivers. Dragonflies are voracious predators, both as nymphs and, later, as they emerge, as flying adults. They are very beneficial insects, eating millions of small insects such as mosquitoes each year. Very common species include the **scarlet dragonfly** (*Crocothemis erythraea*), which is bright red, and the **globe skimmer** (*Pantala flavescens*), a dull brown species that can be found almost everywhere in the tropics. An uncommon species in The Gambia is the **emperor dragonfly** (*Anax imperator*). This is a large blue-bodied dragonfly that can also be found in many parts of Europe. Altogether there are over 70 species of dragonfly and damselfly in The Gambia.

Stick insects These lengthy and slender insects have long and very thin legs and antennae. They are coloured brown or green and spend long periods remaining absolutely still, making them very difficult to find as they look just like twigs or sticks. Some species can grow as large as 10–12cm. They are all vegetarian but do not usually occur in large enough numbers to cause damage. They can usually be found hiding among grass stems.

Cockroaches Well known to many of us, cockroaches originate from the tropics, but are now found almost everywhere around the world. Although some species are considered pests because they damage books and clothes and contaminate foodstuffs, many are found only in forests and the bush and cause no harm to man whatsoever.

Mantids These attractive insects always give the impression of being alert and intelligent animals because their long neck allows them to twist their head and follow movement with their eyes, but really they are no more intelligent than other insects. They are beneficial because they prey on many species that are pests. They have well-developed wings and fly mostly at night when they are attracted to lights. Beware: the larger specimens have powerful jaws and can inflict a painful bite. The front legs of mantids are wonderful adaptations for seizing other insects with lightning force before being drawn to the mouth and eaten.

Ants, wasps and bees These are mostly highly social insects, though some species live solitary existences. There are hundreds if not thousands of species in West Africa but some of the most interesting, and in many ways most frightening, are the **army ants**, or **driver ants**. This ant travels in dense columns that may be hundreds of metres long. The workers are all female and blind, with large powerful jaws. The queen is seldom seen but is three or four times the size of the workers and is also blind. There is also a soldier caste with very large-toothed jaws. They all have a powerful bite and once their jaws are locked into position it is very difficult to make them let go. They were once used to suture open wounds by getting them to bite both edges of the wound together, then twisting off their bodies and leaving the head and jaws in place. Their nest is formed in the ground and colonies can contain hundreds of thousands of individuals. Periodically the nests will move, and this is when the ants form a column. Eggs, larvae, pupa and food are carried by the workers who are flanked and protected by the soldiers. If you happen to step on to a column by mistake you will be instantly subjected to numerous painful bites! When a nest has moved the ants then spread out and forage over a wide area. They are mainly carnivorous and have been known to kill and devour animals as large as pythons. Chickens and guineafowl have been stripped to the bone by these ants in hen houses where they cannot escape, and there are stories of tethered horses being eaten in the same way. In contrast, the males are large winged insects that are entirely harmless. They are known as 'sausage ants' and are often attracted to lights in the evening. A good place to see army ants is at Abuko Nature Reserve, where columns are seen frequently crossing the footpaths.

A common feature of the countryside is **termite mounds**. These massive castle-like structures have smooth ventilation shafts that keep the inside of the nest at a constant temperature. They are often used as hiding places by snakes, bats and other animals, so never stick your hand down one! Termites are seldom seen during the day and are mostly small and inoffensive, although they can cause considerable damage to wooden buildings. They are highly social insects with a queen, kings, workers and soldiers. The soldier caste guard the nests and have ferocious bites.

Butterflies The rainy season is undoubtedly the best time to see a huge variety of differently coloured butterflies, of which there are over 170 species in The Gambia, but there are also many that fly during the dry season. Below we have selected two species that can be commonly seen during the whole year and are fairly easy to identify.

The first of these is the extremely common **citrus swallowtail** (*Papilio demodocus*). This species is large, with a wingspan of 7–11cm. It is mainly blackish but also heavily marked and dusted with yellow. There is a yellow band across the hindwing and a similar but broken yellow band on the forewing. On each hindwing there are two large blue, black and orange-marked eyespots. The edges of the hindwings are also scalloped. The citrus swallowtail occurs in open country, cultivated areas, gardens and forest margins. Very commonly found on cultivated and wild citrus trees such as orange, lime, grapefruit and lemon, its caterpillar devours enormous quantities of leaves and is sometimes considered a pest.

The **African tiger** (*Danaus chrysippus*) is another very common butterfly. It is slightly smaller than the citrus swallowtail with a wingspan of around 7–8.5cm. It is an orange-brown butterfly with black borders to the wings and a large triangular black patch on top of the forewings which encloses several white spots. The form of the African tiger found in West Africa also has a large white patch on the hindwings. Both sexes are almost identical but the male has four black spots on the hindwing while the female has only three. This butterfly has a foul taste and is mimicked by the females of other butterflies, which apparently taste better, so that they can escape the hungry attentions of birds and lizards. The African tiger butterfly can be seen flying in many different habitats, including open and bush country, gardens, woodlands and the margins of forests. Its flight is very slow and sailing, giving the impression of being very relaxed. Sometimes you may come across small groups of them in the evening as they prepare to roost together for the night. The caterpillars are very distinctive: smooth and ringed with yellow and black bands.

BIRDS Birds are a major and vital part of every habitat in The Gambia and can be seen just about everywhere. Unlike many of the 'little brown jobs' that can be found in Europe and North America, Gambian birds tend to be more colourful and confiding, therefore making a birdwatching trip to the country a visit to remember. It can also be a great introduction to many species that can be found elsewhere in Africa. Although thousands of birdwatchers visit The Gambia each year, many of them concentrate on the best-known and most easily accessible sites. This means that for the more adventurous there is still a real chance of adding a new species to the country list, as we ourselves have done on several occasions. Almost 600 bird species have been recorded in The Gambia, a phenomenal number considering the small size of the country. Yet there are many reasons why this is so, including the vast array of different habitats, ranging from the coast, through saltwater and freshwater wetlands, Guinea and Sudan savannah, woodlands and forests, to agricultural land, towns and villages. The Gambia is also visited by hundreds of thousands of European birds during the northern winter, as well as by smaller numbers of African birds that migrate from the north and south during the summer.

A visit to each habitat will reveal its own specialised birds. Starting at the coast, there are miles of open, gently sloping sandy beaches where the most common birds are the shoreline waders such as **ruddy turnstone** (*Arenaria interpres*), **sanderling** (*Calidris alba*) and **whimbrel** (*Numenius phaeopus*). These are joined by numbers of **western reef heron** (*Egretta gularis*), **grey heron** (*Ardea cinerea*), **osprey** (*Pandion haliaetus*) and **pied kingfisher** (*Ceryle rudis*). Offshore, and around the scattered fishing centres, **grey-headed gulls** (*Larus cirrocephalus*) are numerous, as are various **terns**. You may be lucky and spot a few **skuas** chasing the other birds and forcing them to drop their hard-earned food, especially around the port at Banjul. Two rarities that are well worth looking out for include the **kelp gull** (*Larus dominicanus*), which was recently found breeding in The Gambia, and **Audouin's gull** (*Larus audouinii*), a bird of global conservation concern which winters in moderate numbers along the coast.

The next major habitat on the coastline is the mangrove forest, which stretches far inland along the course of the River Gambia. A canoe trip along a mangrove-lined bolong is a relaxing and satisfying way to see some serious birds, including **pelicans**, **spoonbills**, **yellow-billed stork** (*Mycteria ibis*) and **goliath heron** (*Ardea goliath*), plus lots of waders, especially at the beginning of the dry season. Others to look out for include **blue-cheeked bee-eater** (*Merops persicus*) and **mouse-brown sunbird** (*Anthreptes gabonicus*). The river itself and its many tributaries are good places to spot the magnificent **African fish eagle** (*Hieraaetus spilogaster*) perched on an overhanging tree. Other wetland habitats are sure to provide you with a good list of spectacular species such as **African darter** (*Anhinga rufa*), **white-faced whistling duck** (*Dendocygna viduata*), **sacred ibis** (*Threskiornis aethiopicus*), **palm-nut vulture** (*Gypohierax angolensis*), **crakes**, **greater painted-snipe** (*Rostratula benghalensis*) and **African jacana** (*Actophilornis africanus*) – the famous **lili-trotter**, to name just a few of the commonest species.

Inland from the coast are the coastal forests, a prime example of which is Bijilo Forest Park, and a few small patches of gallery forest like Abuko Nature Reserve, Pirang Forest Park and the River Gambia National Park. These forests hold small populations of secretive birds such as **grey-headed bristlebill** (*Bleda canicapilla*), **yellowbill** (*Ceuthmochares aereus*), **ahanta francolin** (*Francolinus ahantensis*), **white-spotted flufftail** (*Sarothrura pulchra*), **western bluebill** (*Spermophaga haematina*) and the beautiful **green turaco** (*Tauraco persa*). Walking around the shady footpaths of these forests is like stepping back into primeval times. There are huge buttress-rooted trees and thick tangles of vines and creepers on all sides and the forests echo to the weird calls of birds.

Next we come to the Guinea savannah, which ranges from open areas of grassland through to thickly wooded patches. This is the habitat that once covered huge chunks of the countryside but has gradually been whittled away. Even here, though, you will find spectacular birds such as **bee-eaters**, **green wood-hoopoe** (*Phoeniculus purpureus*), **blue-bellied roller** (*Coaracias cyanogaster*), **barbets**, **African golden oriole** (*Oriolus auratus*) and the dinosaur-like **Abyssinian ground hornbill** (*Bucorvus abyssinicus*) – a huge black bird that stalks through the grass, seldom taking to the air.

Further inland, and also on much of the North Bank of the River Gambia, you will see a gradual transition to Sudan savannah, which is much drier and dominated by massive red termite mounds. Look out for a wide range of birds of prey, especially the large and impressive **martial eagle** (*Polemaetus bellicosus*), plus buntings, coursers and sparrow-weavers. In the far north of the country you can find areas of the dry Sahel, which is encroaching slowly southwards, with its sparse vegetation. Look out here for **northern anteater chats** (*Myrmecocichla aethiops*) which at a distance seem very dark until they open their wings in a short flight and reveal large white wing patches.

Agricultural land ranges from vegetable gardens and dry fields of groundnuts to vast rice fields whose roots and lower stems are perched in shallow water. These are the special domain of the **weavers**, **finches**, **doves** and **glossy starlings**, among others. Where cattle graze you are also bound to find flocks of **cattle egret** (*Bubulcus ibis*) and **black magpie** (*Ptilostomus afer*), stalking around the feet of the cows and darting after insects that have been disturbed. You should also keep a sharp lookout for the **yellow-billed oxpecker** (*Buphagus africanus*) perched on the back of cattle. Here, they provide a good service in picking off ticks and other bothersome parasites.

Surprisingly, one of the best habitats for birds comes from a totally unexpected source. These are the grounds of the many hotels that have sprung up along the coast in recent years. A combination of year-round watering and the planting of exotic flowers in hotel gardens attract many birds to these miniature green oases. These include the **long-tailed glossy starling** (*Lamprotornis caudatus*), **yellow-crowned gonolek** (*Laniarius barbarus*) and many different types of brilliantly coloured **sunbird**. These are considered by some as the most beautiful of all the birds of The Gambia.

THE BANJUL DECLARATION

It is a sobering reflection that in a relatively short period of our history, most of our larger wildlife species have disappeared together with much of our original forest cover. The survival of the wildlife still remaining with us and the setting aside of protected natural habitats for them are concerns for all of us.

It would be tragic if this priceless natural heritage, the product of millions of years of evolution, should be further endangered or lost for want of proper concern. This concern is a duty that we owe to ourselves, to our great African heritage and to the world.

Thus I solemnly declare that my government pledges its untiring efforts to conserve for now and posterity as wide a spectrum as possible of our remaining fauna and flora.

His Excellency the President of the Republic of The Gambia,
Sir Dawda Jawara, 18 February 1977

3

Practical Information

WHEN TO VISIT

The peak tourist season, and the most pleasant time to visit in climatic terms, broadly coincides with the northern-hemisphere winter, ie: late October to April. During these dry months, a high quota of cloudless skies and blazing sunshine is practically guaranteed to those seeking to escape colder and more northerly climes. Other advantages of travel between October and April are that it tends to be cooler and more comfortable at night, there are fewer mosquitoes and other biting insects about, and dirt roads upriver are less likely to be impassable. In addition, plenty of scheduled flights run to The Gambia from the UK (and the rest of Europe) between October and April, so it is often possible to pick up cheap last-minute package deals inclusive of flights and accommodation.

Out of season, May and June are also good for independent travel, with the advantage that the coastal resorts will be much quieter. Over July to September, the average monthly rainfall is above 200mm, and even though much of the rain falls overnight (and the storms can be pretty spectacular), these months are probably best avoided. The rainy season also carries a higher risk of contracting malaria, as mosquitoes tend to be abundant, while the hot and humid conditions can be very uncomfortable at night, particularly upriver where air conditioning and fans are a rare luxury.

For birders, the early dry season, from late October to December, is the optimum time to visit. Following the rains, most wetland habitats will be at their best, attracting huge numbers of passage migrants from Europe, while weavers, bishops and other resident species displaying marked seasonal plumage variations tend to be in full breeding colours. Birding remains rewarding throughout the dry season, as a significant proportion of migrants overwinter in The Gambia, but from February onwards seasonal wetlands tend to have dried up, and there is generally less wildlife around, particularly over May into early June. The beginning of the rainy season is the time when life starts to show itself again: butterflies and dragonflies fill the air, lizards and birds take on their breeding colours, and mango trees attract large numbers of straw-coloured fruit bats. Overall, though, watching the birds and other wildlife in the rainy season becomes difficult because the vegetation is so thick.

TOURIST INFORMATION AND TOUR OPERATORS

The **Gambia Tourist Authority (GTA)** (\ *7946242;* e *info@gtboard.gm;* w *gta.gm*) has a head office in Kotu 500m south of Palma Rima Junction and a smaller office on Senegambia Junction in Kololi. Its website includes several downloadable brochures and other helpful links, as well as a form for submitting queries.

The operators listed below specialise mostly in all-inclusive fly-in packages from the UK or elsewhere. Companies offering domestic excursions from the coast are listed in the introduction to the *Greater Banjul* chapter (page 77).

UK

Birdfinders \+44 (0)1258 839006; e info@ birdfinders.co.uk; w birdfinders.co.uk. Fixed-departure tours to The Gambia with a focus on birding.

Dragoman Overland \+44 (0)1728 861133; e info@dragoman.co.uk; w dragoman.com. Both its Dakar to Freetown & Dakar to Accra overland trips pass through The Gambia.

Explore Worldwide \+44 (0)1252 883689; w explore.co.uk. Offers an adventurous 2-week programme combining Senegal & The Gambia for small groups.

The Gambia Experience \+44 (0)1489 866939; w gambia.co.uk. This supremely knowledgeable outfit, boasting more than 25 years' specialist experience in the country, offers a wide choice of flights & accommodation, including package trips. Though a good port of call for generic beach holidays, it is also the sole or primary booking agent for several top eco-lodges & boutique hotels, & it offers a range of bespoke & fixed-departure birding tours, the latter usually led by Chris Packham or his recommended local guide Malick Suso. It also operates the only year-round scheduled flight from the UK. Check the website for last-minute special offers.

Heatherlea \+44 (0)1479 821248; e info@ heatherlea.co.uk; w heatherlea.co.uk. Fixed-departure ornithological tours to The Gambia.

Intrepid Travel \+44(0)808 274 5111; e ask@ intrepidtravel.com; w intrepidtravel.com. Their 23-day Freetown to Dakar trip includes 4 days in The Gambia.

Limosa Holidays \+44 (0)1692 580623/4; e info@limosaholidays.co.uk; w limosaholidays. co.uk. Specialist birding operator offering twice-yearly tours to The Gambia.

Naturetrek \+44 (0)1962 733051; w naturetrek.co.uk. Fixed-departure guided group tours to The Gambia with an emphasis on birding.

Ornitholidays \+44 (0)1794 519445; e info@ ornitholidays.co.uk; w ornitholidays.co.uk. This 50-year-old company offers dedicated fixed-departure guided birding trips with a good dose of relaxation time thrown in.

Overlanding West Africa \+44 (0)1728 862247; e info@overlandingwestafrica.com; w overlandingwestafrica.com. Independent operator whose overland trip from Dakar to Freetown trip passes through The Gambia.

Sunbird \+44 (0)1767 262522; e sunbird@ sunbirdtours.co.uk; w sunbirdtours.co.uk. Specialists in birding with an 8-day tour in The Gambia.

Serenity Holidays \+44 (0)1489 866939; w serenity.co.uk. Specialise in high-end stays in The Gambia.

Thomas Cook \+44 (0)844 879 8442; w thomascook.com. The biggest supplier of tourists to The Gambia specialises in mid-range to budget package tours catering mainly to the UK & German markets.

US

Access Africa \+1 800 972 5212; e info@ accessafrica.com; w accessafrica.com. Organises a range of tours to West Africa, from festivals & art shows to safaris & historical excursions. Suitable for both twosomes & large groups.

Palace Travel \+1 800 683 7731/215 471 8555; e info@palacetravel.com; w palacetravel.com. Offers a range of tours from 7 to 10 days. Can also be coupled with Senegal.

Spector Travel of Boston \+1 617 351 0111; e africa@spectortravel.com; w spectortravel.com. Offers a 9-day tour through Senegal & The Gambia that showcases their cultural heritage.

WEST AFRICA

African Adventure Tours \+220 4497313; e info@adventuregambia.com; w adventuregambia.com. Based in Fajara, this operator offers a variety of tours including river cruises, 4x4 excursions as well as trips to Senegal.

Bushwhacker Tours m +220 9912891; e info@ bushwhackertours.com; w bushwhackertours. com. Run by expert guide Alieu Bayo, this Banjul-based venture offers fishing trips, 4x4 excursions & combined tours with Senegal.

Gambia River Cruises m +220 7784058/9900231; w gambiarivercruise.com. Based out of Janjanbureh Camp, this small

BIRDING GUIDES

The Gambia is a very popular destination with birdwatchers; so much so that it has developed a significant guiding subculture based solely on avitourism. There must be hundreds of self-professed bird guides who hang around the main ornithological hotspots in Greater Banjul, ranging from bumsters-with-binoculars who would barely know a sparrow from an eagle, to a core of very skilled and dedicated guides who possess great expertise when it comes both to identifying difficult species and locating rarities. The best local birding guides also have a phenomenal talent when it comes to calling up birds, with whistles that mimic the calls of many species. If you want a great example of this, try getting a birding guide to call a pearl-spotted owlet on Fajara Golf Course.

Many hotels now have official birding guides who will take guests out and about. Otherwise, the best place to look for a reliable guide is the Gambia Bird Guides Association next to Kotu Bridge. The guides here can take you around locally but they also arrange trips upcountry in search of special birds, at reasonable but negotiable prices. However, before making any such arrangement, you are strongly advised to rent out the guide locally, by spending an hour or two birding in the vicinity of Kotu Bridge, which is one of the finest ornithological sites along the coast.

company specialises in extended river trips between the coast & MacCarthy Island.
Gambia Tours +220 4462602; e info@gambiatours.gm; w gambiatours.gm; see ad, 2nd colour section. Family-run outfit based in Banjul offering a range of tailor-made tours & excursions, as well as car hire & airport transfers.

Mandinka Tours +223 20729084; e info@mandinkatours.com; w mandinkatours.com. Based in Mali but offering many tours across West Africa, including a 7-day excursion in The Gambia.
ScanTours Gambia e ousmanrambo@gmail.com; w scantoursgambia.gm. Bakau-based outfit with a range of excursions including combined trips to Senegal.

RED TAPE

A valid passport is required, and the expiry date should fall after your scheduled date of arrival in your home country. No visa is required by holders of passports from the UK, or from most member states of the EU, ECOWAS or Commonwealth countries. Other nationalities need a visa, which typically costs around £30 and requires up to five working days to process at any Gambian embassy or consulate, though it may take longer by courier or post. If you are travelling from a country that does not have a Gambian embassy or consulate then you should be able to obtain a visa directly upon landing at Banjul International Airport or at major immigration posts along the border. However, this is not always guaranteed, so safer not to rely on it.

Immigration control at Banjul International Airport will usually stamp your visa or visitors pass for 15 or 21 days, but will grant up to 28 days if you ask. If you want to stay in the country longer, the pass can be extended on a monthly basis for up to three months at the Immigration Department office in central Banjul.

If you are travelling from a country that has yellow fever (most other African countries including Senegal), you may be asked to show a valid yellow fever vaccination certificate, and might theoretically be refused entry if you can't.

A driving licence from any country, so long as one of the languages used is English, is valid for up to three months. For longer stays, an international driver's licence is required.

For security reasons, it's advisable to write up all your important information in a document and email copies to yourself and a few trusted friends or relatives, together with a scan of your passport (which will facilitate getting a quick replacement if it is lost or stolen). Other information you might want to include in this document are your flight details, travel insurance policy details and 24-hour emergency contact number, passport number, details of relatives or friends to be contacted in an emergency, bank and credit-card details, camera and lens serial numbers, etc.

The Gambia maintains an embassy, high commission or consulate in several countries. These include the UK (w *gambiaembassy.org.uk*), the US, Senegal (*11 Rue De Thiong, Dakar;* \+221 821 7230), Belgium/EU (w *gambiaembassybrussels. be*), as well as Austria, Canada, Ghana, Guinea-Bissau, Ivory Coast, Japan, Nigeria, Portugal, Sierra Leone, Sweden and Switzerland.

GETTING THERE AND AWAY

BY AIR Most UK-based tourists visit The Gambia on a package, including flights and accommodation, with The Gambia Experience (w *gambia.co.uk*) or Thomas Cook (w *thomascookairlines.com*), and these companies, which run their own scheduled flights from the UK several times weekly, are also the best source of cheap air tickets from the UK. Coming from the UK or elsewhere in Europe, other charter companies worth checking out in season (October–April) are Condor (w *condor.com*), Corendon Dutch Airlines (w *corendonairlines.nl*), Monarch Airlines (w *monarch.co.uk*), Thomas Cook Scandinavia (w *thomascookairlines. se*), and Transavia (w *transavia.com*). Options are more limited between May and September, but include Brussels Airlines (w *brusselsairlines.com*), Vueling (w *vueling.com*) and Bintercanarias (w *bintercanarias.com*).

Coming from the USA, your options amount to routing through Europe, or catching the Delta (w *delta.com*) flight from New York to Dakar (Senegal), then picking up a regional flight to Banjul with Senegal Airlines (w *senegalairlines.aero*).

From 2018, the easiest way to search for flights to The Gambia will be to use w gambia-flights.com, a new comprehensive flight-comparison site that can show you the cheapest fares available. Using information gathered from a range of sources, you can look in to flight options from any country, city or airport and find prices in several different currencies.

OVERLAND FROM EUROPE To travel overland from Europe, via Morocco, Mauritania and Senegal, is fairly straightforward, provided you have plenty of time and a reliable 4x4 suited to crossing the Sahara. Anybody planning an expedition of this sort is pointed to Siân Pritchard-Jones and Bob Gibbons's dedicated guidebook *Africa Overland*, also published by Bradt (see w bradtguides.com/shop for more details).

SAFETY AND HASSLES

The Gambia is generally a very safe travel destination, certainly in terms of crime and associated issues. Indeed, the biggest concerns for most travellers should be malaria (pages 68–9) and road accidents associated with public transport. It should be pointed out that, as is the case almost anywhere in the world, breaking the law, in particular the usage of illegal drugs (which includes marijuana), could land you in trouble.

CRIME Theft is not a major concern for tourists, but it is worth following a few common-sense rules, as detailed below:

- Most casual thieves operate in busy markets, particularly those in Serekunda and Banjul, as well as in bus stations and the crowded ferry crossings. Keep a close watch on your pockets and possessions in such places, and avoid having valuables or large amounts of money loose in your daypack or pockets.
- Keep all your valuables and the bulk of your money in a hidden money-belt. Never show this money-belt in public. Keep any spare cash you need elsewhere on your person.
- Where the choice exists between carrying valuables on your person or leaving them in a locked room, we would tend to favour the latter option, particularly after dark, but obviously you should use your judgement and be sure the room is absolutely secure. If you do decide to carry large sums of money, or other valuables, with you after dark, then use taxis; don't walk around.
- Leave any jewellery of financial or sentimental value at home.
- Avoid quiet or deserted places, such as unlit alleys by night, or deserted beaches by daylight, particularly if they lie close to or within a major urban area. When in doubt, take a guide, though preferably one who has been recommended to you by your hotel or by other travellers. Known places where muggers occasionally prey on tourists are the beach going south from Bijilo, the beach going north from Calypso Restaurant at Cape Point, and the beach going towards Banjul from Denton Bridge.
- Car break-ins are an occasional problem in built-up areas. A favourite trick is to slash the rubbers holding the windows in place and to remove the glass to get access. Never leave money or valuables in a car unless someone you trust is guarding it.
- If you are carrying expensive gear such as camcorders, cameras, binoculars or telescopes, then keep them out of sight in a rucksack unless you are actually using them. Be extra careful when using them in out-of-the-way and lonely places.
- When swimming, be very careful about leaving your valuables on the beach, as people often get their things stolen while they are splashing about, having fun in the sea. Leave them in a prominent place and keep a sharp eye on them while you are in the water, or better still leave at least one person with them at all times.

If all of this talk of crime is putting you off, bear in mind that violent crime is very rare indeed. You have far more chance of being mugged in New York, London, Berlin, Johannesburg or Sydney than you ever have in Banjul or Bakau. And you are also extremely unlikely to be threatened with a gun of any sort in The Gambia.

If, by some unlucky happenstance, you are robbed in The Gambia, please report it to the police. If you don't report a crime, how are the police to know about it and to do something to stop it happening again? Remember, too, that if you want to claim off your insurance you will need a police crime number. It may take a little time to write a statement, etc, but it's worth the effort.

BRIBERY AND BUREAUCRACY Although bribery and corruption are a fact of life in Gambian business circles, these issues seldom affect tourists directly, so you probably don't need to worry about it! The one exception is at police, military and other roadblocks, where any tourist driving without a valid licence, car insurance, fire extinguisher or warning triangles may be threatened with arrest unless they pay a bribe. You should also be cautious of flashing a camera around in the vicinity of official buildings, bridges, military camps and the like, as the security police might take exception to it, in which case you could well find yourself in for a long and tedious conversation, or worse.

The tendency to portray African bureaucrats as difficult and inefficient in their dealings with tourists is also often overstated. Sure, you come across the odd unhelpful official, but then such is the nature of the beast everywhere in the world. It is worth noting that the treatment you receive from officialdom will be determined partly by your own attitude. Walk into an official encounter with an aggressive, paranoid approach and you are quite likely to kindle the feeling held by many Africans that Europeans are arrogant and offhand in their dealings with other races. Instead, try to be friendly and patient, and accept that the person to whom you are talking may not speak English as fluently as you, or may struggle to follow your accent.

SWIMMING In the wrong conditions, an element of risk is associated with swimming on any beach, even those generally regarded as relatively safe. Swimmers risk being dragged away from shore by riptides, strong undertows and whirlpools, particularly in stormy or windy weather, though it is not always easy to determine the presence of a strong undertow until you are actually in the water. Some tourist beaches in The Gambia display flags indicating whether swimming conditions are safe. Most don't, in which case you should ask local advice before you swim, particularly on quiet beaches where there are no other swimmers about. Weak swimmers should also avoid water deeper than their waist unless they are using some sort of flotation device. If you are caught in a riptide or whirlpool, it is generally advisable not to fight the current by trying to swim directly to shore, but rather to save your strength by floating on your back or swimming parallel to shore until the tide weakens, and only then to try to get back to land.

WOMEN TRAVELLERS As The Gambia is mainly Muslim, it is appropriate that women travellers, particularly, should dress so as not to cause offence (page 51). This is a good idea, not only out of courtesy, but also to avoid the attention of men, which at the coastal resorts can be a big problem. Upcountry you will very rarely have a problem with Gambian men.

Getting hold of tampons or sanitary towels upcountry can be impossible, though it is easy to buy them from any supermarket in the coastal resorts. If you are travelling upcountry it's best to plan ahead and take a supply with you, remembering that when travelling in the tropics it is common for women to have heavier and more irregular periods than they would normally have at home.

GAY TRAVELLERS Any act of homosexuality is criminal in The Gambia. Male offenders currently risk a prison term of up to 14 years, female offenders a term of up to five years. None of which means that homosexuality doesn't exist in The Gambia; only that of necessity it is somewhat clandestine. Also that, setting aside the rights and wrongs of the matter, and at risk of stating the blindingly obvious, this clearly isn't a destination suited to single travellers in search of anything approximating a gay scene, while homosexual couples who do visit the country should exercise maximum discretion.

WHAT TO TAKE

Almost anything you are likely to need can be bought from one of the many markets and supermarkets dotted around Greater Banjul, and even though specialist imported items might be pricier than they are at home, there is no need to arrive laden down with a hoard of inexpensive inessentials. Indeed, for the many visitors who base themselves in a resort hotel and spend most of their time on the beach or by the swimming pool, there's probably no need to pack any more elaborately

The UK's **gov.uk** website (w *gov.uk/guidance/foreign-travel-for-disabled-people*) provides general advice and practical information for travellers with disabilities preparing for overseas travel. **Accessible Journeys** (w *disabilitytravel.com*) is a comprehensive US site written by wheelchair users who have been researching wheelchair-accessible travel full-time since 1985. There are many tips and useful contacts (including lists of travel agents on request) for slow walkers, wheelchair travellers and their families, plus informative articles, including pieces on disabled travelling worldwide. The company also organises group tours. **Global Access News** (w *globalaccessnews.com/index.htm*) provides general travel information, reviews and tips for travelling with a disability. The **Society for Accessible Travel and Hospitality** (w *sath.org*) also provides some general information. To plan a trip to The Gambia, contact specialist UK-based tour operators **Disabled Holidays** (w *disabledholidays.com*).

than one might for a beach holiday in Greece or France. A little more thought and care might be advisable for anybody heading upriver for a few days, but even so, unless you plan on travelling more extensively in West Africa or will be working in a remote part of the country, there's no reason to go overboard on luggage.

CARRYING LUGGAGE For most package tourists, it will matter little whether you bring your luggage in a suitcase, duffel bag or rucksack. If you'll be travelling around a lot, especially on public transport, some type of backpack is strongly advised. Either way, a small daypack will also be useful for carrying water, lunch, field guides, binoculars, etc, on day trips.

CLOTHES Light cotton wear is ideal for the tropical Gambian climate. Depending on how long you'll stay in the country and how static or itinerant you are, that might include two pairs of long trousers and shorts for men or three to four skirts or shorts for women, two swimming costumes, plus as many shirts, socks and underwear as you reckon you will need. A wide-brimmed hat provides good protection against the sun, but even a baseball cap is better than no headgear.

Nights are warm, so one sweater should suffice, supplemented by a light waterproof windbreaker if you travel during the rainy season. Again, depending on your mode of travel and whether you'll be sunning on the beach or birding in the bush, bring at least one solid pair of shoes or boots for walking, and one pair of sandals or other light shoes for casual use. And if your bag starts to become uncomfortably heavy or bulky, bear in mind that any item of clothing that breaks or tears can easily be replaced in Greater Banjul.

Women should also be conscious that The Gambia is predominantly Islamic, and while skimpy swimwear is acceptable beach attire, it would not be at all appropriate anywhere else – keep your shoulders covered and ideally wear a skirt covering the knees if you travel further afield, whether that be to central Banjul, Serekunda Market, fishing villages such as Tanji or Juffureh, or anywhere upriver.

OTHER USEFUL ITEMS The content of this list will depend on what you intend to do on your holiday. A must for most people, even if you are a sun-worshipper, is a good solid, leak-proof **water bottle** to have with you even when just lying on the beach.

Suncream and **insect repellent** are very useful items to carry around (and can easily be bought after you arrive), and a small **medical kit** might be useful (page 68).

If you're a birdwatcher or otherwise interested in wildlife and natural history, then don't forget the **binoculars**, whatever you do. Serious birders will of course need to bring their **telescope** and **tripod**. Another vital piece of equipment if you intend to wander about in the bush unguided is a **GPS device** or **compass**.

For those travelling upcountry, where electricity is erratic, a good **torch** is a must. **Loo paper** cannot always be found when you most need it so carry a roll in your bag. Other sundry items include **tampons** or **sanitary pads**, as they are not always easy to get hold of upcountry.

MONEY

The unit of currency since 1971 is the dalasi (denoted as 'D'), a Wolof word that probably derives from the English word dollar or French *dala* (a type of five-franc coin). It is subdivided into 100 bututs. The dalasi has devalued steadily in recent years, but not as drastically as most African currencies. The rate of exchange in October 2017 stood at US$1 = D47, £1 = D62 and €1 = D56. The highest banknote is D200, which has a value of around £3.50. Other banknotes in circulation are D100, D50, D25, D20, D10 and D5, while coins come in denominations of D1, 50 bututs and 25 bututs. All smaller-value coins have been discontinued.

ORGANISING YOUR FINANCES There are three ways of carrying money: hard currency cash, travellers' cheques, or a debit/credit card. These days, however, travellers' cheques are of practically no use in The Gambia, which means you ideally need to carry an international Visa card supplemented by a stash of hard currency cash.

Unlike in the majority of African countries, the most widely recognised hard currency in The Gambia is the British pound sterling. The US dollar and euro are also accepted at all foreign-exchange outlets, but more obscure currencies might be more difficult to change. The best place to change money is usually private bureaux de change (known locally as forex bureaux), which tend to be more efficient than banks, keep longer hours, and offer a slightly more favourable rate. There are forex bureaux dotted all over Banjul and in major resort areas such as Bakau, Kotu and Kololi, and you also can find one or two in most larger towns

---

PRICES IN THIS BOOK

With the exception of some upmarket hotels and car-rental companies, pretty much every price in The Gambia is quoted in the local currency, and can be paid for that way. Indeed, in many situations, attempting to pay in anything other than dalasi would create complete confusion. In an ideal world, we would follow suit in this book, by quoting all prices in dalasi. Sadly, however, because of the ongoing devaluation of many African currencies, usually compensated for by a high local inflation rate, we feel that aside from basic costs such as entry fees and public transport, converting dalasi prices to a hard currency equivalent is more likely to provide a reliable medium-term guideline to current prices. Aside from hotels that quote prices in euros or US dollars, we have opted for British pound sterling, which is clearly the most widely used hard currency in The Gambia, and converted October 2017 prices at an approximate exchange rate of D60 to the pound.

upriver. Many hotels have foreign-exchange desks, but the rates tend to be poor. Avoid changing money on the street, as it is illegal, and also carries a higher risk of being cheated or robbed.

If you carry a card, make sure it has the Visa or MasterCard insignia, as other brands, including Diners and American Express, are borderline useless in The Gambia. Be aware too that the cards are of use primarily for withdrawing local currency from ATMs. GT Bank, Standard Chartered and Eco Bank accept both Visa and MasterCard. When it comes to direct payments, most larger hotels will accept Visa cards, as will a few tourist-oriented shops and restaurants in Greater Banjul and Kololi, but they are not accepted at smaller outlets and will be practically useless upcountry.

Travellers heading outside of the Greater Banjul area should be aware that ATM distribution around The Gambia is very uneven, and may need to plan accordingly. There are a couple of suitable ATMs at Banjul International Airport, and dozens more are scattered around the capital and resort area as far south as Brusubi Junction and inland to Brikama. By contrast, no operational ATMs can be found in Soma, Janjanbureh or elsewhere along the South Bank between Brikama and Basse (although there is one found in Basse itself), while the only ones on the North Bank are in Farafenni, and the most southerly one on the coast is in the foyer of the Gambia Sheraton. Most ATMs impose a withdrawal limit of D3,000 (about £50), but you can usually do several transactions per banking day, depending on the limit set by your own bank.

A few precautions for those relying primarily on a Visa card for funds. The first is to let your bank know where and when you will be travelling, so they don't become suspicious at a few withdrawals in The Gambia and put a hold on your account. The second is even a valid card might be stolen, swallowed by an ATM, or otherwise rendered useless, so best carry a second card as a back-up, keeping it separate from the rest of your funds. Finally, though credit-/debit-card scams are not commonplace, they have been reported and most usually involve somebody copying a card number and using it to make a fraudulent payment. This sort of thing can largely be avoided by keeping the card out of sight at all times, and by using your card to make a bulk cash withdrawal from an ATM rather than to pay lots of small bills directly.

Carry your hard currency and cards (plus passport and other important documentation) in a money-belt, ideally one that can be hidden beneath your clothing. The money-belt should be made of cotton or another natural fabric, and everything inside it should be wrapped in plastic to protect it against sweat.

Once in The Gambia, try to keep a fair selection of different-sized notes and coins in your pockets, as no-one, anywhere, ever seems to have change for larger notes.

COSTS AND BUDGETING Although The Gambia is not a cheap destination, at least when compared with many parts of Africa, it remains quite inexpensive and very good value in an African context.

So far as travel basics go, accommodation for one or two people will probably average out at around £10 per day if you always go for the cheapest option. You're looking at more like £20–30 per day for a moderate room with air conditioning, and £40–200 or upwards for upmarket comfort.

For food, expect to spend around £5 per head per day if you stick to street food and very cheap restaurants, £10 if you eat once daily in a restaurant, and maybe £20 per day to eat pretty much what you like (excluding really upmarket places). For advice on tipping, see pages 63–4.

Depending on how often and how far you travel, public transport shouldn't average out at more than £1 per day per head, while a charter taxi ride in most towns costs no more than £2.

The main thing you need to add to the above on a daily basis is liquid. Unless you restrict yourself to tap water (not advisable) or the slightly chemical-tasting but perfectly acceptable water in sachets, you'll spend a fair bit of money just keeping your thirst quenched in this hot climate – say £3 per head daily if you stick to bottled water and soft drinks bought in shops, perhaps £10 daily if you add on a couple of beers.

Put this together, and you're looking at a rock-bottom budget of £20/30 daily for one/two people using the cheapest accommodation and avoiding proper restaurants and bars. To travel thriftily but with a bit more freedom and comfort, a budget of around £40/65 for one/two people would be feasible. If you want air-conditioned rooms, two solid meals, and the rest, budget on upwards of £60/100 for one/two people.

The above reckoning excludes one-off expenses such as excursions and guiding fees, factors that tend to create the occasional expensive day, markedly so for those on a tight budget.

GETTING AROUND

MAPS The most reliable country map is the 1:400,000 *MacMillan Gambia Traveller's Map*, which also includes good detail maps of the Atlantic coast and Banjul, which is periodically available to buy on Amazon, but otherwise very expensive through online booksellers. If you can't locate it, the ITMB (1:1,375,000) and Reise Know-How maps to *Senegal & Gambia* are adequate but inevitably dominated by the larger country. Anna's travel map (1:375,000) is made from satellite imagery, and they also do a map of Kanifing municipality (1:24,000), which covers a triangle of Cape Point, Abuko and Bijilo. There is also an *Official Map of Historic and Cultural Sites* produced by the National Centre for Arts & Culture, with inset detail of Banjul. Even the best maps can be quite confusing when it comes to place names, on account of the phonetic spelling in different languages.

AROUND GREATER BANJUL Getting around the Greater Banjul area, and the rest of the southern coastal belt, is very straightforward. Indeed, if you are staying at one of the resort hotels in Bakau, Kotu or Kololi, almost everything you're likely to need on a day-to-day basis – beach, restaurants, supermarkets, bars, and banks – will be within easy walking distance of your hotel. And for day excursions further afield, you have the choice of hiring a taxi, renting a bike, using public transport, or joining an organised excursion set up by a local tour operator or registered guide.

Tourist taxis Two main types of charter taxi operate in Greater Banjul, both on a similar basis to taxi cabs in many Western cities, except that they are unmetered so it is conventional to agree the fare before the journey starts. The more expensive are the specially licensed tourist taxis (usually green with a white diamond on the side) that can be find outside any of the tourist hotels. These are regulated by the Gambia Tourist Authority and should be fully insured. They will run you to any destination, and usually ask a fixed price for a return trip, inclusive of a period of waiting, so may be negotiable for one-way trips or where no waiting is required. The current list of fixed fares is detailed on boards outside most hotels, as well as in the main taxi ranks in the tourist zones.

Shared taxis The preferred option of budget-conscious travellers is shared taxis, which are usually painted bright yellow with green stripes, and tend to be far cheaper than tourist taxis. These unregulated and often uninsured taxis normally ply a set route and pick up passengers along the way for a set fare of usually D8. But they are also quite willing – indeed, usually very eager – to be chartered on a 'town trip', which is where one person hires the whole taxi to wherever they want to go for a negotiable price – typically around £2 per 5km, less than half of what a tourist taxi would ask. These taxis move freely all around Greater Banjul but are not allowed into the Senegambia Strip or Kotu without special permission, so if you are staying in these areas it is best to walk to the junction with Bertil Harding Highway and pick one up there.

Bicycles A rented bicycle is a good way of getting around the hinterland immediately outside Banjul and the resorts, with the great advantage of letting you see the towns and countryside at your own pace. Do be careful when out riding though, as Gambian drivers often pass dangerously close to bicycles or cut them off. Furthermore, many roads are full of pot-holes or have their edges worn unevenly which can force cyclists into the flow of traffic. There are bicycle-hire outlets outside the African Village Hotel and Cape Point Hotel in Bakau, the Badala Park Hotel and Kondo Beach Hotel in Kotu, and the Kairaba Hotel in Kololi. Rates are typically up to D50 per hour for short usage or around D300 per day for longer periods.

Organised day excursions If you're booked into a package hotel for the duration of your stay, an organised day excursion is the easiest way to see something more of the Gambian countryside, especially if time is tighter than money, or independent African travel isn't your thing. A very popular day trip is the full-day Roots Excursion, which runs by boat to the North Bank villages of Albreda and Juffureh, as well as Kunta Kinteh Island, UNESCO World Heritage Sites covered in greater detail on pages 190–2. For birders and wildlife enthusiasts, other worthwhile goals for day excursions include Abuko Nature Reserve (pages 171–3) and Makasutu Cultural Forest (pages 178–81), while beach lovers seeking to fulfil a Robinson Crusoe fantasy are pointed to Jinack Island – often marketed as Treasure or Coconut Island (page 193). Urban adventurers will enjoy a day tour of Banjul city centre and Albert Market, while those seeking something a little more active could join a south-coast excursion embracing a camel safari at Tanji fishing beach and a visit to Tanje Village Museum. For a list of operators in the Greater Banjul area, see page 77.

FURTHER AFIELD Although most visitors to The Gambia never stray far outside the Greater Banjul area, there is a whole country out there to be explored, whether on public transport or on a self-drive basis. Note that there is no rail system in The Gambia, nor any domestic flight network, nor any river transportation (not unless you count the handful of dilapidated ferry services that connect the South and North banks), which means that public transport is all but restricted to the roads.

Public transport Road transport is very cheap (a fiver gets you from one side of the country to the other), but most vehicles are quite rundown, slow, sweaty, crowded and poorly driven. Further details of individual routings are included in the regional chapters of this guide, but generally the best option, at least for the time being, is the recently revived and privatised Gambia Transport Service Company (GTSC). Based in Kanifing (Serekunda), the GTSC operates several scheduled departures daily along the South Bank Road to Soma, Janjanbureh and Basse as well as the North Bank Road between Barra and Lamin Kora, all in relatively new Ashok-Leyland buses with individual seat fans and in some cases air conditioning.

The distinctly inferior alternative to the GTSC buses is the private passenger vehicles known as *gelly-gellys* (minivan size or larger) or shared/bush taxis (saloon cars or station wagons) that cover pretty much every route in the country, offering variable degrees of unreliability and discomfort. The focal point of the passenger vehicle network in the far west is Serekunda, where the two main stations are Westfield Junction (for elsewhere in Greater Banjul and Brikama) and Dippa Kunda (for the south coast). For passenger vehicles from the coast to most

THE BUSH TAXI

I usually turn up sometime before the sun rises for a long trip as it's cooler and I have more chance of bagging the front passenger seat which has some leg room. Otherwise, I'd be stuck in the third row – what would normally be a car boot – where they put a seat for three more people. Once I have my place, it's a waiting game. Prices are set by the government and profit margins are non-existent, so drivers are forced to cram in as many people and as much luggage as possible to ensure they make a few pennies.

I'll usually grab myself a couple of *café toubas*. I'm still not entirely sure what gives this local coffee its distinctive liquorice-like taste, but it's good, if a little too sweet. There's invariably a stall on wheels, where a boy will scoop coffee from a cauldron and then pour it back and forth between two cups, building up a cappuccino froth of impressive heights.

Then there are the urchins: little ragged boys called the *talibe*, often barefoot, faces covered in dust and snot, normally wearing a T-shirt branded with Unicef, Barack Obama 'Time for Change', or these days more commonly #GambiaHasDecided. Groups of them, carrying old tomato purée tins, walk around chanting for spare change. Tragically, they are controlled by gang leaders who will beat them if they don't reach their quota. One modern-day Fagin was charged recently in neighbouring Senegal for beating a boy to death. Years of working with homeless people has led me to believe it's best to give money to an organisation rather than to an individual, but in this case it's hard to resist.

Market stalls sell just about everything, as long as it's cheap and Chinese. Women sell *wanjo*, a Ribena-like drink made from hibiscus, and mangoes from large enamel bowls carried in on their heads. A more modern phenomenon is men selling mobile-phone top-up cards. Small stalls with dubious hygiene standards make omelettes and stick them in rolls with brown lumpy mayonnaise stored in unrefrigerated buckets. Often there's a choice of a spaghetti roll or a macaroni roll, so it's lucky I'm not on the Atkins diet.

Elsewhere, Baye Fall boys with their large turbans, masses of beads and long robes, collect for charity. Goats wander round hoovering up the discarded mango skins and other rubbish. There's a motley collection of bush taxis, buses, trucks and abandoned vehicles that are in a really bad way. On top of all of this are the mad men, the hucksters, the Liberian refugees looking for an English speaker, the baggage handlers and the mass of people seemingly moving all of their worldly possessions.

An edited excerpt from Squirting Milk at Chameleons *by Simon Fenton.*

places further upriver, the main South Bank terminus is Brikama while the sole terminus on the North Bank is Barra.

Car rental Perhaps the most satisfying way to explore The Gambia, though far more costly than using public transport, is in a rented 4x4. Brits should be aware, however, that although it is a former British colony, The Gambia follows the European and American model and drives on the right-hand side of the road. And while the new North Bank and South Bank roads are great, with smooth surfaces that tend to encourage a relatively orderly approach to road usage, all aspirant drivers should be prepared for a somewhat more anarchic environment than the one they are used to.

Driving in The Gambia presents a number of unfamiliar hazards. On older pot-holed roads and dirt roads, vehicles swerve unpredictably to avoid obstacles, and use whichever side of the road they fancy. Especially in the rural areas, dogs and livestock frequently wander into the road, as do children, and even adults, often without looking to see what's coming their way. Then there are the slow-moving donkey-, horse- and bullock-drawn carts, and the bush taxis that swerve madly to avoid colliding with them. Fortunately, outside of Greater Banjul, traffic volumes are low, so driving is not too stressful, especially if you take it slow and easy, and give yourself those vital extra milliseconds to react to the unexpected. Driving at night is best avoided (there are no street lights and many vehicles lack headlights), as is driving in heavy rain.

Another repeat nuisance is the ubiquitous police, immigration, customs and military roadblocks that force drivers to slow down every few kilometres. Usually, you'll be waved on, no problem, but sometimes you'll be stopped and asked to produce your driver's licence and vehicle insurance, and more occasionally your reflector triangle and fire extinguisher. More often than not, this sort of interrogation is quite good natured, and feels more like a pretext for a chat than anything else, but if your papers are not in order, you could be in for a rough ride.

Two reputable car-rental companies are the budget-oriented **AB Rent a Car** (*Palm Rima Junction, Kotu;* ☎ *4460926;* m *7649743/9320776;* e *info@ab.gm;* w *ab.gm*), who offer vehicles from £25 per day, and the newer and more upmarket **Afriq Cars** (*The Village, Kololi;* ☎ *4460086;* m *7700900;* e *info@afriqcars.com;* w *afriqcars.com*), with vehicles from £30.

An alternative to conventional car rental is to strike up a deal for transportation with a taxi driver, ideally one you have used for a few local rides, and with whom you feel comfortable. This will generally work out more cheaply than renting a car, and it shifts the responsibility for driving or dealing with any breakdown or other hassles to somebody experienced in local conditions. A major disadvantage of going this route is that costs (and tensions) can quickly mount if the exact terms are not agreed upfront – for instance, whether the rate includes or excludes the driver's accommodation, food, and other expenses, as well as fuel and any fines imposed at road blocks.

Ferries There are only five places countrywide where motor vehicles can cross between the South and North banks: these are the large but slow ferries connecting Banjul to Barra at the river mouth and Farafenni to Soma on the Trans-Gambia Highway, and the smaller and quicker ferries further east at Janjanbureh, Basse Santa Su and Fatoto.

Organised upriver excursions As is the case with local day trips, most tourists who venture upriver do so as part of an organised overnight excursion, which can be booked through upmarket hotels or any of the operators listed on page 46.

The most popular excursions are one-night trips to Tendaba Camp or Bintang Bolong, which usually incorporate at least one boat trip into the mangroves and creeks that line the main river, or further upriver to Janjanbureh, ideally for at least two nights. For wildlife enthusiasts, arguably the most rewarding trip out of Greater Banjul, doable as a one-night excursion though two nights is better, is to the wonderful camp run by the Chimp Rehabilitation Project in the River Gambia National Park. Few scheduled trips head further upriver than Janjanbureh unless they are continuing into eastern Senegal.

ACCOMMODATION

The coastal resorts of Greater Banjul are dense with accommodation that caters mainly to tourists but ranges in quality from world-class package or boutique hotels, such as the Coral Beach or Ngala Lodge, to scruffy small lodges aimed mainly at backpackers, volunteers and others on a tight budget. Accommodation on the coast north of the River Gambia or south of Tanji tends to consist of modest but pleasant eco-lodges and more basic beach camps catering to those on a low to medium budget, while accommodation upriver is almost all very basic and rundown, the one notable exception being the Chimp Rehabilitation Project Camp in the River Gambia National Park.

Detailed accommodation listings for all towns, resorts and other places of interest can be found in the regional chapters of this guide. Entries are categorised under five main headings: exclusive/luxury, upmarket, mid range, budget and shoestring. Broadly speaking, the **exclusive or luxury** bracket comprises package and boutique hotels that would approach four- or five-star status anywhere in the world. Places listed as **upmarket** would typically be comparable to a three-star hotel in international terms. **Mid-range** hotels are one- or two-star lodgings that don't quite meet international standards, but would still be comfortable enough for most tourists, offering a range of good facilities such as air conditioning (AC), satellite television, en-suite hot showers and toilet. **Budget** accommodation consists mostly of ungraded hotels that definitely don't approach international standards, but are still reasonably comfortable and in many cases have air conditioning and en-suite facilities. **Shoestring** accommodation consists of the cheapest rooms available, and ranges from nice backpacker-type set-ups to genuine dives. This categorisation is not rigid, since it is based on the feel of any given hotel as much as the price, and there are many borderline cases, but it should nevertheless help readers isolate the option best tailored to their budget and taste. Within each category, we have, where appropriate, highlighted any genuine standouts (often but not exclusively owner-managed places with a strong individual character) as an author's pick ✱.

EATING AND DRINKING

Greater Banjul must host at least 100 restaurants catering mainly to tourists, and most international cuisines are represented in resort areas such as Kololi, Kotu and Bakau. Standards are high and prices relatively low. The options upriver are generally limited to hotel restaurants and a few local eateries serving a limited and fairly predictable selection of local dishes. Everywhere in the country, except perhaps the main tourist resorts, a varied selection of street food is sold at kiosks, usually close to the market. Often this consists of sandwiches, made either with airy light French baguettes or with the heavier Gambian *tapalapa*, and filled with mayonnaise, margarine, chocolate spread or a spicy paste made with black-eyed beans. Evening is when *afra* bars, which sell a variety of grilled meat including chicken and beef, come into their own. Throughout the day seasonal fresh fruit, roasted peanuts and cashew nuts, Madeira cake and coconut pieces are readily available to snack on.

Many restaurants have Gambian dishes on their menus, although some may require notice for their preparation. This usually comprises rice or millet served with a spicy fish, meat or chicken stew, which comes in a few main types: *domoda* (groundnut sauce), *yassa* (stewed or marinated in onion and lemon), and *palasas* (a spinach sauce thickened with peanut butter). Another popular choice, known elsewhere in West Africa as jollof rice, *benachin* (literally 'one pot') is a spicy risotto-like Wolof dish made with fish, chicken or beef. Also popular is *superkanja*, a tasty okra soup whose name derives from the Portuguese *supa* (soup) and Mandinka *kanja* (okra). Worth trying too are shrimps fried with garlic in the Gambian style, and Lebanese-style *shawarmas*, comprising thin slices of lamb (or other meats) with salad and hummus in pitta bread.

The usual range of international soft drinks is sold cheaply all over The Gambia, as is the award-winning local lager beer JulBrew. Most restaurants and bars on the coast serve a selection of imported wines and spirits, though this is less common upriver. Despite The Gambia being predominantly Islamic, the vast majority of restaurants serve alcohol, but there are exceptions, particularly in Basse Santa Su. Wanjo is a sweet but refreshing drink made from hibiscus flowers, and ginger and baobab juice are also sometimes available at bars and restaurants. All around the country, you may see men preparing a green tea called *attaya*, which is full of caffeine, and has a strong bitter taste that becomes more refreshing on the third brew (locals tend to drink it with copious amounts of sugar). The preparation of *attaya* takes about an hour and is almost a social ceremony, as the men sit around and chat while the pot is brewing.

PUBLIC HOLIDAYS

In addition to the fixed holidays below, the following variable religious holidays are recognised: Koriteh (Eid al-Fitr), Ashura Day, Laylat al-Qadr, Milad an-Nabi, Tobaski (Eid al-Adha), Good Friday and Easter Monday. Aside from the closure of banks and offices, these holidays have a limited effect on tourists – far less, in fact, than the monthly Operation Clean the Nation (see box, page 60). During the fasting month of Ramadan, however, it is customary to refrain from smoking, eating or drinking in the presence of Muslims between dawn and dusk. All of the large hotels and restaurants remain open during Ramadan, some smaller businesses may open late and close early, and others might not open at all.

1 January	New Year's Day
18 February	Independence Day
1 May	Labour Day
25 May	Africa Day
22 July	Revolution Day
15 August	Assumption of Mary
25 December	Christmas Day

MEDIA AND COMMUNICATIONS

NEWSPAPERS Until relatively recently, the Gambian press was regarded as being largely free from governmental interference, as indicated by its world ranking

CLEAN THE NATION SATURDAY

Initiated by President Jammeh in 2004, Operation Clean The Nation, known locally as Set Settal, is a public programme designed to keep streets and other public areas free of unsightly non-biodegradable litter and organic waste that helps foster disease-carrying bacteria. It is usually enacted on the last Saturday of every month, though it may sometimes be cancelled, or held over to another Saturday, where this date clashes with a public holiday or another important event. It runs from 09.00 to 13.00, with the idea being that everybody chips in to clean up their private compound and/or neighbourhood, though for many it is simply a pretext to take a morning off work or to sleep in. The impact on tourists can be significant. All private and public transport, including taxis, is halted for the morning, which makes it a great time to take a long walk, but can be inconvenient if you plan to do a day trip of any sort, or need to get to the airport (in which case, you or your driver will need to go to the police in advance for special permission, which is usually granted without fuss for any tourist-related reason). Most shops, restaurants and other businesses will be closed too.

of 64 in the 2002 Press Freedom Index (placing it among the top 15 countries in Africa); however, in 2017 its ranking had dropped to 143 out of 180. Since the election of President Barrow, though, there has been a sliver of hope for journalists. The Barrow government seems more willing to let people speak their mind, and has set up a committee to review the draconian media laws of the Jammeh administration. It is yet unclear as to whether any of these will be overturned, and the recent closure of *The Observer* does raise questions over the sincerity of the new government's commitment to press freedom. Despite this, a couple of decent English-language newspapers are produced and sold inexpensively in Banjul, including *The Standard* (**w** *standard.gm/site*) and *The Point* (**w** *thepoint.gm*).

RADIO AND TELEVISION The national television and radio company is the state-run Gambian Radio and Television Service (**w** *grts.gm*), which broadcasts throughout the country. Many hotels and restaurants supplement the rather unexciting state service with a bouquet of international satellite channels provided by the South African company DSTV (**f** *DStvGambia*). Sadly, independent radio stations are now few and far between: the popular Taranga FM was forced to shut down in January 2017 by the Gambian authorities.

POST International post is inexpensive and usually gets to its destination quite quickly during the dry season (when there are regular flights) but more tardily during the rains. Post coming into the country is often delayed, sometimes for months, and unverified stories of registered post being stolen by postal workers abound.

TELEPHONE The telephone system in The Gambia is quite efficient and getting through from overseas can be fairly easy. The international country code is +220, there are no area codes, and all numbers (land or mobile) have seven digits. If you bring an unlocked mobile with you, a local SIM card is very cheap, as is airtime and/or a data bundle. The main providers are Gamtel (**w** *gamtel.gm*), Africell (**w** *www.africell.gm*), Qcell (**w** *qcell.gm*) and Comium (**w** *comium.gm*), all of which have service centres dotted all over Greater Banjul. The first numeral in any seven-digit number will tell you the identity of the provider, as per the table below:

2, 7	Africell
3	Qcell
4, 5	land line (4 on the coast, 5 upriver)
6	land line (around Basse) or Comium
8, 9	Gamtel

INTERNET Greater Banjul has reasonable internet connections. Most hotels have Wi-Fi or some other form of internet access, and there are plenty of cyber cafés around, though these are decreasing in number as more and more locals access the web using mobile phones. If you expect to spend a lot of time online, it will pay to get a local SIM card and data bundle with one of the mobile providers mentioned above (Qcell has the edge when it comes to internet speed on account of its 3G+ GSM network). Upriver, phone signals are patchy and electricity is even more erratic, so that internet access can be problematic even in towns such as Basse or Janjanbureh. If you will only be upriver a couple of days, and can function without internet access, it is easiest just to plan on being offline for that period – and to warn anybody who might otherwise be expecting to hear from you that they won't!

ELECTRICAL DEVICES Electricity is 220–240V. If you intend to operate delicate electrical equipment then you should make sure you use a stabiliser or voltage regulator, as the voltage does tend to fluctuate quite a lot. Adapters are needed for appliances using 110V. A few three-/two-pin adapters could be useful. The power system is pretty dire, and demand often far outreaches the capacity to deliver, so most tourist hotels on the coast operate a standby generator so that they have a guaranteed 24-hour supply. Lodges on the coast south of Tanji are mostly off the grid and tend to operate on solar power, while most upriver lodges and restaurants have a very limited and/or erratic power supply.

INTERACTING WITH GAMBIANS

The Gambia is an amiable and peaceful country full of convivial non-violent people whose approach to life tends to be very laid back – sometimes frustratingly so for Western visitors used to a faster pace of life. Gambians themselves joke about GMT, an acronym not for Greenwich Mean Time but Gambia Maybe Time, and provided you are on holiday, not trying to push through deadlines, this relaxed attitude is part of the country's charm. Unfortunately, however, the innate friendliness of Gambian society is undermined somewhat by a small subset of so-called 'bumsters' who hang around the resort areas of Greater Banjul and habitually hassle any passing tourist, whether it be on the beach, on the street, or in a market. More about bumsters can be found on pages 62–3, but it should be clarified upfront that while they can be extremely annoying, they are not representative of Gambians as a whole, and the whole phenomenon is more or less confined to a few specific resort areas. South of Tanji and upriver of Brikama, first-time visitors to Africa, or at least those with a white skin, may be surprised at the amount of attention they draw by virtue of their conspicuous foreignness – symptoms of which range from having every passing taxi blare its horn at you to being greeted by mobs of exuberant children chanting '*toubab*' (white person) as you walk past. At times, this can be exhausting, but it is essentially just an expression of curiosity and friendliness, and seldom underscored by malice.

ETIQUETTE The Gambia, like any country, has its rules of etiquette, and while allowances will normally be made for tourists, there is some value in ensuring they don't have to be made too frequently.

Greetings are very important in Gambian society. If you need to ask directions, or anything else for that matter, it is considered very rude to blunder straight into interrogative mode without first exchanging greetings – even when shopping. If there is one phrase you should learn, it is the greeting '*Salam malekum*' ('Peace be with you'), the response being '*Malekum salam*' ('Peace returns to you') – a universal Arabic exchange used widely among Gambians. Otherwise, just saying 'Hello' (and where appropriate shaking hands) will do the job.

Because The Gambia is predominantly Islamic, the left hand is traditionally reserved for ablutions. It is thus considered highly insulting (and unhygienic) to use your left hand to pass or receive something, or when shaking hands. If you eat with your fingers, it is customary to use the right hand only. Topless bathing is not acceptable on the beaches or at hotel swimming pools, and elsewhere visitors should be cognisant of conservative Islamic dress codes. Walking around half-dressed, as some tourists insist on doing, is totally inappropriate. Women should ideally wear a loose-fitting summer dress or slacks that that go below the knees, and a top that covers their cleavage and shoulders. Men can get away with wearing shorts but should not walk around topless. Gambians are generally quite tolerant, and they accept that foreigners have different customs, but still it is impolite to go too far in flaunting local dress codes.

When visiting upcountry villages, there are also some forms of etiquette that you should adhere to. One of these is that you should seek out the village *alkalo* and spend a few minutes greeting him before doing whatever it is you came for. It is also a good idea to bring him a small gift, either kola nuts, or a D10 or D25 note will do. This is not only polite but may also be very useful, as the alkalo will know everything that is going on in his village, and may be able to provide guides or translators if you require them. If you are introduced to the Muslim *imam* (holy man) of the village, and asked to enter his home, remember to remove your shoes and hat first, just as you would if entering a mosque.

BUMSTERS The one thing most likely to spoil your holiday in The Gambia is bumsters, the local nickname for a rather parasitic type of young man who habitually latches on to tourists hoping to get something – anything – from the exchange. In the resort areas of Greater Banjul, you'll have only to leave your hotel for a walk and you'll meet at least one bumster. There are a number of classic ways that bumsters approach tourists. Generally they will ask you your name or where you come from, or what hotel you're staying at. More deviously, some might say something like 'Hey, remember me? I work at your hotel', hoping to embarrass tourists into conversation. And whatever the approach, the conversation usually ends up with an offer of guide services, or sex, or drugs, or failing that just a straight request for money. If that doesn't work, most bumsters will shrug it off, but a small minority might become rude and intimidating, accusing their victim of being a racist, in the hope it will shame them into giving him something.

If this is your first trip to The Gambia, don't let bumsters put you off visiting. The Gambia is a wonderful country, full of wonderful people, but it's better to be forewarned and forearmed when it comes to dealing with the one major exception. Most of the time, the best approach to bumsters is to acknowledge their greeting with a cool but friendly 'Hello', without slowing down your pace, or looking like you have any intention of stopping or allowing yourself to be drawn into a conversation. If they persist beyond this, telling them you are busy and/or saying 'maybe later' usually works. But do keep it friendly: swearing at bumsters, or threatening them, tempting though it might be, might be seen as an invitation to hit you with the racist line. If you are a non-confrontational sort of person, another tack would be to hire an official tour guide, who will not only keep bumsters away, but can also help you find out more about The Gambia. Better still, travel upcountry for a few days, away from the tourist areas, to experience The Gambia at its bumster-free best.

PROSTITUTION Prostitution is a low-profile problem in some tourist areas, specifically in a few particular nightclubs and bars in Greater Banjul where single men are likely to be targeted (sometimes even if their partner has just nipped out to the loo). On the whole, though, this must be one of the few countries where the most conspicuous form of sex-for-gain transaction consists of holiday romances between young Adonis-like bumster types, and much older (and generally somewhat less lissom) Western women. Whether this qualifies as prostitution, or borders on it, is a matter of opinion, and doubtless varies from one situation to another. Either way, one thing that you should be aware of if you are seeking some sexual company, be it male or female, is the prevalence of sexually transmitted diseases in the sex trade.

BEGGING Wherever you go in The Gambia, the chances are that someone will ask you for money. This could be a kid walking down the street who will ask for a dalasi, or his mother who will ask for D20. It could be your taxi driver who needs money for repairs to his taxi, or a hotel worker who needs money to fund his education. You will have to decide the merit of each case, but remember that ripping off *toubabs* is a way of life for some Gambians, who are under the impression that everybody living in Europe or North America possesses unlimited wealth. However, we must strongly discourage tourists from handing over money, pens, sweets or other goodies to random children or opportunist beggars. For one, it helps foster a growing culture of dependency on handouts in Africa. It also often entices children living in villages regularly visited by tourists to bunk or abandon their schooling in favour of begging. And more selfishly, it creates a very unpleasant basis for interaction between visitors and locals. If you want to help people in The Gambia, then a far better option is to give money, books, computers or medical supplies to an existing charity or directly to an institution like a village school or clinic. Indeed, many village schools in The Gambia have been built and equipped with money raised by caring Westerners whose actions have genuinely improved lives in a very positive way (see box, page 64).

What might be termed 'real beggars' is a completely different case. Go to any supermarket or restaurant and you are likely to find someone sitting outside and begging for money. Many of these people are mentally or physically disabled, and genuinely in need of help as they cannot find work, or fall back on social security as they might in the West. Just take a moment to watch what Gambians do when they are asked for money. Nine times out of ten they will reach into their pockets and give him or her a dalasi or two. There's no harm in you doing the same.

TIPPING Among locals, tipping in restaurants is not near-obligatory as it is in the USA or many parts of Europe. However, a tip will usually be expected at more touristic restaurants, and it will always be appreciated at local eateries too. If you've enjoyed your meal and the service was good then give a good tip; 10% would be a fair guideline, though with change so often being an issue in The Gambia, just rounding up the bill to an amount that doesn't require change is also often a sensible approach.

The semi-official guides available at most nature reserves and museums generally provide a free service that's included in the entrance fee. A tip is therefore expected, and should be given, assuming that you are happy with the service. It is difficult to give a guideline, as it depends so much on the age, attitude, experience and skill of the guide, but around D50–100 per party per hour or D500–600 for a full day's guiding would feel about right. Skilled birding guides should be paid a little more, as often they have years of experience or training behind them. That said, while it is appropriate to tip genuine guides who have been of real value to you, it is not advisable to tip bumsters or other hangers-on who simply latch on to tourists and try to act like a guide or to make you feel sorry for them.

BARGAINING AND OVERCHARGING Prices in hotels, restaurants, shops, and public transport are generally fixed, and overcharging is too unusual for it to be worth challenging a price unless it is blatantly ridiculous (though many hotels will be open to negotiating a discounted rate, particularly for longer stays). However, tourists must be prepared to bargain over prices in certain circumstances, for instance when chartering private taxis, organising guides, or shopping in markets.

The main instance where bargaining is customary, bordering on essential, is when buying handicrafts. Stall owners will generally quote a price knowing full well

GETTING INVOLVED IN THE GAMBIA

These are just three of the many worthwhile educational charities operating in The Gambia. For a more comprehensive list, see the 'Charity Directory' on The Gambia Experience's website (w *gambia.co.uk/charity*).

AFRIKAYA (e *afrikayathecharity@gmail.com*; w *afrikaya.co.uk*) This UK-based charity was formed in 2007 with the aim to build a nursery school for children who struggled to access education in The Gambia. The charity has succeeded in its goal, and the nursery school in New Yundum near Brikama currently serves 135 children between the ages of three and seven. The school is built around a Kebba tree, which in The Gambia is a symbol of strength, growth and life. They organise various fundraising events in the Wiltshire area, or you can sponsor a child to cover basic costs such as school uniform, reading materials and a healthy lunchtime meal.

FRIENDS OF THE GAMBIA (w *fotga.org.uk*) This UK-registered charity is run by volunteers and works to help the people of The Gambia. It operates a very successful 'adopt a child' scheme (and is always in need of new sponsors to give disadvantaged children the chance of education), provides educational and medical equipment for schools, clinics and hospitals and funds sustainable projects in schools and villages throughout the country.

GOAL FOR THE GAMBIA (e *goalforthegambia@hotmail.co.uk*; w *goal4gambia. org*) A UK-registered charity, GOAL for The Gambia supports education and training opportunities for young people in The Gambia. Currently they sponsor over 300 children from nursery to university in three schools and two nurseries. Sponsorship costs from £5 a month and covers fees, uniforms and books. Additionally, they support school-building projects such as toilets, classroom blocks and new roofs. School visits can be arranged.

they are likely to be bargained down, so it is not necessary to respond aggressively or accusatorially. It is impossible to say by how much you should bargain the initial price down. Some people say that you should offer half the asking price and be prepared to settle at around two-thirds, but many stall owners are more whimsical than such advice allows for. A sensible approach is to ask the price of similar items at a few different stalls before you actually contemplate buying anything.

In fruit and vegetable markets and stalls, bargaining is often the norm, even between locals, and the healthiest approach is to view it as an enjoyable part of the African experience. There will normally be an accepted price band for any particular commodity. To find out what it is, listen to what other people pay and try a few stalls. A ludicrously inflated price will always drop the moment you walk away. When buying fruit and vegetables, a good way to get a feel for the situation is to ask for a bulk discount or a few extra items thrown in. And bear in mind that when somebody is reluctant to bargain, it may be because they asked a fair price in the first place. No matter how tight your budget, most Gambians are much poorer, so don't lose your sense of proportion.

SEND US YOUR SNAPS!

We'd love to follow your adventures using our *The Gambia* guide – why not send us your photos and stories via Twitter (🐦 *@BradtGuides*) and Instagram (📷 *@bradtguides*) using the hashtag #thegambia. Alternatively, you can upload your photos directly to the gallery on the Gambia destination page via our website (w *bradtguides.com/thegambia*).

4

Health

With Dr Felicity Nicholson and Anna Battersby

The Gambia, like most parts of Africa, is home to several tropical diseases unfamiliar to people living in more temperate and sanitary climates. However, with adequate preparation, and a sensible attitude to malaria prevention, the chances of serious mishap are small. To put this in perspective, your greatest concern after malaria should not be the combined exotica of venomous snakes, stampeding wildlife, gun-happy soldiers or the Ebola virus, but something altogether more mundane: a road accident.

Within The Gambia, a range of adequate (but well short of world-class) clinics, hospitals and pharmacies can be found around Banjul, Serekunda and the main resort areas. Most of the larger beach hotels also have their own clinic or a doctor on call. Facilities are far more limited and basic upriver. Wherever you go, however, doctors and pharmacists will generally speak fluent English, and consultation and laboratory fees (in particular malaria tests) are inexpensive by international standards – so if in doubt, seek medical help.

PREPARATIONS

Sensible preparation will go a long way to ensuring your trip goes smoothly. Particularly for first-time visitors to Africa, this includes a visit to a travel clinic to discuss matters such as vaccinations and malaria prevention. A full list of travel clinic websites worldwide is available at w itsm.org, and other useful websites for prospective travellers include w nathnac.org and w netdoctor. co.uk/travel. The Bradt website now carries an African health section (w *bradtguides.com/africahealth*) to help travellers prepare for their African trip, elaborating on the information below, but the following summary points are worth emphasising:

- Don't travel without comprehensive medical **travel insurance** that will fly you home in an emergency.
- Make sure all your **immunisations** are up to date. A yellow fever vaccination is advised to protect you against disease and you may need to show proof of immunisation upon entry if you are entering The Gambia from another yellow fever endemic area. A yellow fever vaccination certificate will then be required on entry. Since July 2016, any yellow fever certificate is considered to last for life if you are over two years of age and/or you are not immunosuppressed at the time of having the vaccine. If either of those criteria applied then revaccination is recommended at ten years. If the vaccine is not suitable for you then you would be wise not to travel, as West Africa has the highest prevalence of yellow fever and there is up to a 50% mortality rate. It's also unwise to travel in the tropics without being up to date on tetanus, polio and diphtheria (now given as

an all-in-one vaccine, Revaxis), hepatitis A and typhoid. Immunisation against rabies, meningitis, hepatitis B, and possibly tuberculosis (TB) may also be recommended.

- The biggest health threat is **malaria**. There is no vaccine against this mosquito-borne disease, but a variety of preventative drugs is available, including mefloquine, atovaquone/proguanil (Malarone) and the antibiotic doxycycline. Malarone and doxycycline need only be started two days before entering The Gambia, but mefloquine should be started two to three weeks before. Doxycycline and mefloquine need to be taken for four weeks after the trip and Malarone for seven days. It is as important to complete the course as it is to take it before and during the trip. The most suitable choice of drug varies depending on the individual and the country they are visiting, so visit your GP or a specialist travel clinic for medical advice. If you will be spending a long time in Africa, and expect to visit remote areas, be aware that no preventative drug is 100% effective, so carry a cure too. It is also worth noting that no homeopathic prophylactic for malaria exists, nor can any traveller acquire effective resistance to malaria. Those who don't make use of preventative drugs risk their life in a manner that is both foolish and unnecessary.

- Though advised for everyone, a **pre-exposure course of rabies vaccination**, involving three doses taken over a minimum of 21 days, is particularly important if you intend to have contact with animals, or are likely to be 24 hours away from medical help. If you have not had this then you will almost certainly need to evacuate for medical treatment, as it is very unlikely that The Gambia will have the necessary treatment.

- Anybody travelling away from major centres should carry a **personal first-aid kit**. Contents might include a good drying antiseptic (eg: iodine or potassium permanganate), Band-Aids, suncream, insect repellent, aspirin or paracetamol, antifungal cream (eg: Canesten), ciprofloxacin or norfloxacin (for severe diarrhoea), antibiotic eye drops, tweezers, condoms or femidoms, a digital thermometer and a needle-and-syringe kit with accompanying letter from a healthcare professional.

- Bring any **drugs or devices relating to known medical conditions** with you. That applies both to those who are on medication prior to departure, and those who are, for instance, allergic to bee stings, or are prone to attacks of asthma. Always check with the country website to identify any restricted medications. Carry a copy of your prescription and a letter from your GP explaining why you need the medication.

- Prolonged immobility on long-haul flights can result in **deep vein thrombosis** (DVT), which can be dangerous if the clot travels to the lungs to cause pulmonary embolus. The risk increases with age, and is higher in obese or pregnant travellers, heavy smokers, those taller than 6ft/1.8m or shorter than 5ft/1.5m, and anybody with a history of clots, recent major operation or varicose veins surgery, cancer, a stroke or heart disease. If any of these criteria apply, consult a doctor before you travel.

COMMON MEDICAL PROBLEMS

MALARIA This potentially fatal disease is widespread in low-lying tropical parts of Africa, a category that includes all of The Gambia, and while the risk of transmission is highest in the rainy season, it is present throughout the year. Since no malaria prophylactic is 100% effective, one should take all reasonable precautions against being bitten by the nocturnal *Anopheles* mosquitoes that transmit the disease (see box, page 71). Malaria usually manifests within two weeks of transmission, but it can be as little as seven days and anything up to a year. Any fever occurring after seven days should be considered as malaria until proven otherwise. Symptoms typically include a rapid rise in temperature (over 38°C), and any combination of a headache, flu-like aches and pains, a general sense of disorientation, and possibly even nausea and diarrhoea. The earlier malaria is detected, the better it usually responds to treatment. So if you display possible symptoms, *get to a doctor or clinic immediately* (in the UK, go to accident and emergency and say that you have been to Africa). A simple test, available at even the most rural clinic in Africa, is usually adequate to determine whether you have malaria. You need three negative tests to be sure it is not the disease. And while experts differ on the question of self-diagnosis and self-treatment, the reality is that if you think you have malaria and are not within easy reach of a doctor, it would be wisest to start treatment.

TRAVELLERS' DIARRHOEA Many visitors to unfamiliar destinations suffer a dose of travellers' diarrhoea, usually as result of imbibing contaminated food or water. Rule one in avoiding diarrhoea and other sanitation-related diseases is to wash your hands regularly, particularly before snacks and meals. As for what food you can safely eat, a useful maxim is: PEEL IT, BOIL IT, COOK IT OR FORGET IT. This means that fruit you have washed and peeled yourself should be safe, as should hot cooked foods. However, raw foods, cold cooked foods, salads, fruit salads prepared by others, ice cream and ice are all risky. It is rarer to get sick from drinking contaminated water but it happens, so stick to bottled water, which is widely available.

If you suffer a bout of diarrhoea, it is dehydration that makes you feel awful, so drink lots of water and other clear fluids. These can be infused with sachets of oral rehydration salts, though any dilute mixture of sugar and salt in water will do you good, for instance a bottled soda with a pinch of salt. If diarrhoea persists beyond a couple of days, it is possible it is a symptom of a more serious sanitation-related illness (typhoid, cholera, hepatitis, dysentery, worms, etc), so get to a doctor. If the diarrhoea is greasy and bulky, and is accompanied by sulphurous (eggy) burps, one likely cause is giardia, which is best treated with tinidazole (four x 500mg in one dose, repeated seven days later if symptoms persist).

BILHARZIA Also known as schistosomiasis, bilharzia is an unpleasant parasitic disease transmitted by freshwater snails most often associated with reedy shores where there is lots of water weed. It cannot be caught in hotel swimming pools or the ocean, but should be assumed to be present in any freshwater river pond, lake or similar habitat, even those advertised as 'bilharzia free'. The most risky shores will be within 200m of villages or other places where infected people use water, wash clothes, etc. Ideally, however, you should avoid swimming in any fresh water other than an artificial pool. If you do swim, you'll reduce the risk by applying DEET insect repellent first, staying in the water for under 10 minutes, and drying off vigorously with a towel. Bilharzia is often asymptomatic in its early stages, but some people experience an intense immune reaction, including fever, cough, abdominal pain and an itching rash, around four to six weeks after infection. Later symptoms vary but often include a general feeling of tiredness and lethargy. Bilharzia is difficult to diagnose, but it can be tested for at specialist travel clinics, ideally at least six weeks after likely exposure. Fortunately, it is easy to treat at present.

MENINGITIS This nasty disease can kill within hours of the appearance of initial symptoms, typically a combination of a blinding headache (light sensitivity), blotchy rash and high fever. Outbreaks tend to be localised and are usually reported in newspapers. Fortunately, immunisation with a conjugate meningitis ACWY vaccine (eg: Menveo, Nimenrix) protects against the most serious bacterial form of meningitis and lasts for five years. Nevertheless, other less serious forms exist which are usually viral, but any severe headache and fever – possibly also symptomatic of typhoid or malaria – should be sufficient cause to visit a doctor immediately.

RABIES This deadly disease can be carried by any mammal and is usually transmitted to humans via a bite or a scratch that breaks the skin. In particular, beware of village dogs and monkeys habituated to people, but assume that *any* mammal that bites or scratches you (or even licks on intact skin) might be rabid even if it looks healthy. First, scrub the wound with soap under a running tap for a good 10–15 minutes, or while pouring water from a jug, then pour on a strong iodine or alcohol solution, which will guard against infections and might reduce the risk of the rabies virus entering the body. Whether or not you underwent pre-exposure vaccination, it is vital to obtain post-exposure prophylaxis as soon as possible after the incident. If you have had three pre-exposure doses of the vaccine then post-exposure treatment is simply two further doses of rabies vaccine given three days apart. However, if you have not had any rabies vaccines before, then you need to have a full course (four to five doses over a month) and you may also need Rabies Immunoglobulin (RIG). This product is unlikely to be available in The Gambia. Evacuate as soon as you can. Death from rabies is probably one of the worst ways to go, and once you show symptoms it is too late to do anything – the mortality rate is 100%.

TETANUS Tetanus is caught through deep dirty wounds, including animal bites, so ensure that such wounds are thoroughly cleaned. Immunisation protects for ten years, provided you don't have an overwhelming number of tetanus bacteria on board. If you haven't had a tetanus shot in ten years, or you are unsure, get a booster immediately.

HIV/AIDS Rates of HIV/AIDS infection are high in most parts of Africa, and other sexually transmitted diseases are rife. Condoms (or femidoms) greatly reduce the risk of transmission.

TICK BITES Ticks in Africa are not the rampant disease transmitters that they are in the Americas, but they may spread tickbite fever along with a few dangerous rarities. They should ideally be removed complete as soon as possible to reduce the chance of infection. The best way to do this is to grasp the tick with your finger nails as close to your body as possible, and pull it away steadily and firmly at right angles to your skin (do not jerk or twist it). If possible douse the wound with alcohol (any spirit will do) or iodine. If you are travelling with small children, remember to check their heads, and particularly behind the ears, for ticks. Spreading redness around the bite and/or fever and/or aching joints after a tick bite imply that you have an infection that requires antibiotic treatment, so seek advice.

SKIN INFECTIONS Any mosquito bite or small nick is an opportunity for a skin infection in warm humid climates, so clean and cover the slightest wound in a good drying antiseptic such as dilute iodine, potassium permanganate or crystal (or gentian) violet. Prickly heat, most likely to be contracted at the humid coast, is a fine pimply rash that can be alleviated by cool showers, dabbing (not rubbing) dry and talc, and sleeping naked under a fan or in an air-conditioned room. Fungal infections also get a hold easily in hot moist climates so wear 100%-cotton socks and underwear and shower frequently.

EYE PROBLEMS Bacterial conjunctivitis (pink eye) is a common infection in Africa, particularly for contact-lens wearers. Symptoms are sore, gritty eyelids that often stick closed in the morning. They will need treatment with antibiotic drops or ointment. Lesser eye irritation should settle with bathing in salt water and keeping the eyes shaded. If an insect flies into your eye, extract it with great care, ensuring you do not crush or damage it, otherwise you may get a nastily inflamed eye from toxins secreted by the creature.

SUNSTROKE AND DEHYDRATION Overexposure to the sun can lead to short-term sunburn or sunstroke, and increases the long-term risk of skin cancer. Wear a T-shirt and waterproof sunscreen when swimming. On safari or walking in the direct sun, cover up with long, loose clothes, wear a hat, and use sunscreen. The glare and the dust can be hard on the eyes, so bring UV-protecting sunglasses. A less direct effect of the tropical heat is dehydration, so drink more fluids than you would at home.

OTHER INSECT-BORNE DISEASES Although malaria is the insect-borne disease that attracts the most attention in Africa, and rightly so, there are others, most too uncommon to be a significant concern to short-stay travellers. These include dengue fever and other arboviruses (spread by day-biting mosquitoes), sleeping sickness (tsetse flies), and river blindness (blackflies). Bearing this in mind, however, it is

AVOIDING MOSQUITO AND INSECT BITES

The *Anopheles* mosquitoes that spread malaria are active at dusk and after dark. Most bites can thus be avoided by covering up at night. This means donning a long-sleeved shirt, trousers and socks from around 30 minutes before dusk until you retire to bed, and applying a DEET-based insect repellent to any exposed flesh. It is best to sleep under a net, or in an air-conditioned room, though burning a mosquito coil and/or sleeping under a fan will also reduce (though not entirely eliminate) bites. Travel clinics usually sell a good range of nets and repellents, as well as Permethrin treatment kits, which will render even the tattiest net a lot more protective, and helps prevents mosquitoes from biting through a net when you roll against it. These measures will also do much to reduce exposure to other nocturnal biters. Bear in mind, too, that most flying insects are attracted to light: leaving a lamp standing near a tent opening or a light on in a poorly screened hotel room will greatly increase the insect presence in your sleeping quarters.

It is also advisable to think about avoiding bites when walking in the countryside by day, especially in wetland habitats, which often teem with diurnal mosquitoes. Wear a long loose shirt and trousers, preferably 100% cotton, as well as proper walking or hiking shoes with heavy socks (the ankle is particularly vulnerable to bites), and apply a DEET-based insect repellent to any exposed skin.

clearly sensible, and makes for a more pleasant trip, to avoid insect bites as far as possible (see box, page 71). Two nasty (though ultimately relatively harmless) flesh-eating insects associated with tropical Africa are *tumbu* or *putsi* flies, which lay eggs, often on drying laundry, that hatch and bury themselves under the skin when they come into contact with humans, and jiggers, which latch on to bare feet and set up home, usually at the side of a toenail, where they cause a painful boil-like swelling. Drying laundry indoors and wearing shoes are the best way to deter this pair of flesh-eaters. Symptoms and treatment of all these afflictions are described in greater detail on Bradt's website (**w** *bradtguides.com/africahealth*).

OTHER SAFETY CONCERNS

WILD ANIMALS Don't confuse habituation with domestication. Most wildlife in Africa is genuinely wild, and widespread species such as hippo or hyena might attack a person given the right set of circumstances. Such attacks are rare, however, and they almost always stem from a combination of poor judgement and poorer luck. A few rules of thumb: never approach potentially dangerous wildlife on foot except in the company of a trustworthy guide; never swim in lakes or rivers without first seeking local advice about the presence of crocodiles or hippos; never get between a hippo and water; and never leave food (particularly meat or fruit) in the tent where you'll sleep.

SNAKE AND OTHER BITES Snakes are very secretive and bites are a genuine rarity, but certain spiders and scorpions can also deliver nasty bites. In all cases, the risk is minimised by wearing closed shoes and trousers when walking in the bush, and watching where you put your hands and feet, especially in rocky areas or when gathering firewood. Only a small fraction of snakebites deliver enough venom to be life-threatening, but it is important to keep the victim calm and inactive, and to seek urgent medical attention.

CAR ACCIDENTS Dangerous driving is probably the biggest threat to life and limb in most parts of Africa. On a self-drive visit, drive defensively, being especially wary of stray livestock, gaping pot-holes, and imbecilic or bullying overtaking manoeuvres. Many vehicles lack headlights and most local drivers are reluctant headlight-users, so avoid driving at night and pull over in heavy storms. On a chauffeured tour, don't be afraid to tell the driver to slow or calm down if you think he is too fast or reckless.

Part Two

GREATER BANJUL AND KOLOLI

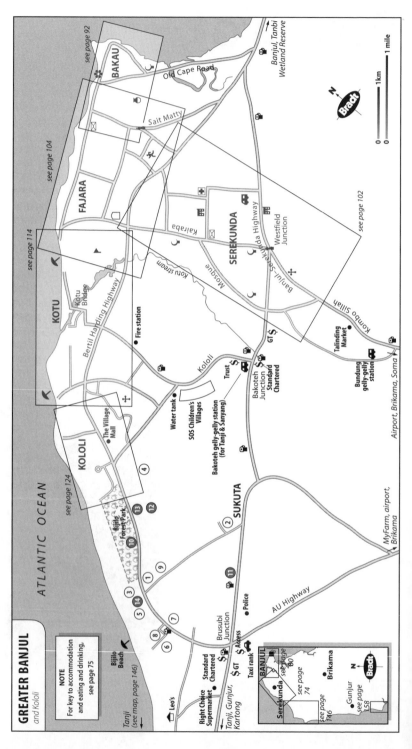

GREATER BANJUL
and Kololi

NOTE
For key to accommodation and eating and drinking, see page 75.

ATLANTIC OCEAN

Tanji (see map, page 146)

Bijilo Beach

Leo's

Right Choice Supermarket

Standard Chartered

Tanji, Gunjur, Kartong

Brusubi Junction

Police

AU Highway

MyFarm, airport, Brikama

SUKUTA

Taxi rank

Bijilo Forest Park

The Village Mall

KOLOLI

see page 124

Water tank

SOS Children's Villages

Bakoteh gelly-gelly station (for Tanji & Sanyang)

Bakoteh Junction

Standard Chartered

Trust

Kololi

Fire station

Bertil Harding Highway

Kotu Bridge

KOTU

see page 114

Kotu stream

FAJARA

see page 104

Kairaba

Sait Matty

Old Cape Road

BAKAU

see page 92

Banjul, Tanbi Wetland Reserve

SEREKUNDA

Mosque

Westfield Junction

Banjul-Serekunda Highway

Kombo Sillah

Talinding Market

Bundung gelly-gelly station

Airport, Brikama, Soma

see page 102

BANJUL

Serekunda

Brikama

Gunjur

see page 74
see page 80
see page 146
see page 158

N

0   1km
0   1 mile

Greater Banjul
and Kololi: An Overview

The Gambia's main population centre, as well as the focal point of its tourist industry, is the administrative region of Greater Banjul and neighbouring suburbs of Kololi, Bijilo and Sukuta. Despite extending over a mere 100km² (less than 1% of the country's surface area), this compact urban conglomeration supports around one-third of the national population, and probably hosts something like 90% of its hotels, restaurants, banks, supermarkets and such – a figure all the more remarkable when you consider that about half the region comprises the more-or-less uninhabitable mangroves and marshes of Tanbi Wetland Reserve.

Administratively, Greater Banjul is divided into two units: the Banjul Local Government Area (LGA) covering the island-bound city centre, and the tenfold-larger Kanifing LGA, accounting for Serekunda and all the beach resorts north of Kololi Point. Officially, Kololi, Bijilo and Sukuta actually lie in Western Region, but in practice they feel like an extension of Greater Banjul the city rather than separate urban entities.

On the ground, Greater Banjul and Kololi are more neatly divided into three broad areas, each with its own distinct character. On the east side of the Tanbi Wetlands, the neat but tiny national capital Banjul, established on the confines of Saint Mary Island in 1816, is the country's administrative centre and a popular goal for day trips with tourists, but seldom used as an overnight base. West of the Tanbi Wetlands, an amorphous, chaotic and rather charmless sprawl of inland suburbs centred on Serekunda has overtaken the capital as the country's main centre of business and commerce. Further west still, following the Atlantic coastline south of the Gambia River Mouth for around 12km, lies resortland: the string of well-developed beachfront suburbs – Cape Point and Bakau, Fajara and Koto, Kololi and Bijilo – that form the heart of The Gambia's package-tourism industry.

In terms of facilities, the coastal strip of Greater Banjul and Kololi, with its plethora of hotels, guesthouses, restaurants, casinos, nightclubs, bars, supermarkets and other shops, can come across much like a European resort annex grafted on to the west coast of Africa. Equally, a definite West African flavour is pervasive everywhere you go; whether it is the hot sun, sandy beaches and palm trees, the bright clothes of the local women, or the plentiful gorgeous birdlife flitting around hotel gardens.

GREATER BANJUL and Kololi
For listings, see pages 135–8, unless otherwise stated

🛏 **Where to stay**
1 Baobab Holiday Resort
2 Camping Sukuta
3 Coco Ocean Resort & Spa
4 Devon Lodge *p131*
5 Kasumai Beach Guest House
6 Lemon Creek Resort
7 Sardinka House
8 Seafront Residence
9 Shelley's

✖ **Where to eat and drink**
10 2 Rays
11 The Blue Kitchen
12 Kaj's Cave
    Kasumai Beach Bar & Restaurant (see 5)
13 Sea Shells
14 Sunbird Beach Bar & Restaurant

And you needn't go far inland to find yourself immersed in an unambiguously African landscape – just take a stroll through the backstreets of Bakau to Kachikally Crocodile Pool, or a shared taxi to the hectic Serekunda market, or a day tour to central Banjul.

One important point to note is that while the coastal resorts of Greater Banjul are a thriving hub of tourist activity during the holiday season (late October to April), they have a definite 'lights off' feel for the remainder of the year. Most hotels and restaurants cut down their services during the off-season, laying off a significant proportion of their staff for the duration, while others close entirely, particularly those owned or managed by expats or foreigners, who may go back to their home countries for a week, or a month, or longer to avoid the rainy season. It's impossible to let you know which places will be closed, or even when, because in many cases this varies year by year, but even at the lowest ebb of tourism, in July and August, there is enough going on that you'll have no problem finding a room, or a meal, or a well-stocked supermarket.

HIGHLIGHTS

Note that most of the sites covered in *Part Three* are easily visited as day trips from the resorts in Greater Banjul – this is a selection of some highlights.

NATIONAL MUSEUM OF THE GAMBIA Housed in the former Bathurst Club, this oft-overlooked enjoyable museum in central Banjul is strong both on local history and on traditional cultures. See page 89.

ALBERT MARKET Handicraft enthusiasts shouldn't miss out on Banjul's historic central market, which is a good place to buy woodcarvings, tie-dyed batik clothing and much else besides. See page 90.

KACHIKALLY CROCODILE POOL Crocodiles so tame you can stroke their backs are the main attraction at this sacred pool in Bakau, though it also hosts a worthwhile museum. See pages 99–100.

BAKAU BOTANICAL GARDEN Almost a century old, this small, low-key and attractively laid-out garden makes for a peaceful retreat from bustling Bakau or Fajara. See page 100.

FAJARA AND KOTU BEACHES Our favourite among several attractive beaches that line the Atlantic coastline of Greater Banjul is the long stretch of white sand connecting Kotu and Fajara. See pages 109 and 113.

FAJARA CLUB The par-69 18-hole course at the Fajara Club is a must for golfers, and the institution also offers several other sports facilities to day members. See pages 109–10.

SEREKUNDA MARKET The country's largest market, set in the heart of Serekunda, might not be for the faint of heart, but it does offer an uncompromising glimpse into the many faces of modern-day Africa. See page 110.

KOTU STREAM A near-mandatory first stop for birders, Kotu Stream regularly yields 50-plus species in an hour or two, and the bridge across it is a good place to hook up with local bird guides. See page 122.

SENEGAMBIA STRIP Love or hate this action-packed street in Kololi, there's no arguing with the abundant choice and overall quality of the dozens of restaurants that line it. See pages 128–35.

BIJILO FOREST PARK Red colobus monkeys, giant monitor lizards and plentiful forest birds are among the attractions of this small pedestrian-friendly reserve only 5 minutes' walk from the Senegambia Strip. See page 138.

GETTING AROUND

Greater Banjul is the most compact part of The Gambia, and the easiest for getting around. There are plenty of tourist taxis available outside all the larger hotels, and a plethora of shared taxis ply all of the main roads and charge a fare of a few dalasi. If in doubt, head for Westfield Junction, which is the main public transport hub in Serekunda, and an easy place to pick up transport to central Banjul, Bakau, Fajara, Kotu and Kololi (as well as to most sites along the Brikama Road).

Day excursions to most sites treated as highlights in this or *Part Three* can be arranged at short notice through a number of local operators, of which African Adventure Tours (**w** *adventuregambia.com*), Arch Tours (**w** *arch-tours. com*), Bushwhacker Tours (**w** *bushwhackertours.com*), The Gambia Experience (**w** *gambia.co.uk*) and West African Tours (**w** *westafricantoursinfo.com*) are recommended. Excursions are also bookable through the activity desks of most of the better hotels, or they can be arranged privately through the National Tour Guide Association kiosks at Senegambia Junction, Palma Rima Junction or Koru Market, or (if birds are your main interest) through any member of the Gambia Bird Guides Association, which is based at Kotu Bridge (page 121).

OTHER PRACTICALITIES

The region covered in this part of the guide breaks up into a number of hotel clusters, each of which is serviced by a selection of restaurants, bars, banks, ATMs, forex bureaux, internet cafés and supermarkets, as well as at least one craft market and taxi park. You are unlikely to need to walk much more than 10 minutes

---

MEDICAL FACILITIES

Most Gambian medical facilities of any quality lie within the area covered in this part of the guide. In case of a problem, however, probably your first course of action should be to visit the clinic in your hotel (assuming it has one), or to ask about the most suitable facility at reception.

Failing that, recommended options include the **Afrimed Clinic and Laboratory** (⚲ *4410685;* **m** *7739415;* **e** *info@africmed-gm.com;* **w** *africmed-gm.com*) recently relocated about 200m along the road leading east from Brusubi turntable, as well as the **Bijilo Medical Centre and Hospital** (**m** *6665555/9980371;* **e** *drmusa@bijilomedical.org;* **w** *www.bijilomedical.org*).

For dental problems, head to the **Smile Dental Clinic** (**m** *3992407/8806177*) in The Village on Kololi. In Serekunda, the **Malak Pharmacy** (*Kairaba Av;* ⚲ *4376087;* **m** *7700719;* **e** *malakpharm@hotmail.com;* ⊕ *09.00–midnight Mon–Sat, 10.00–22.00 Sun*) keeps the longest hours in the country.

from your hotel to locate any of the above facilities. One shop worth singling out is Timbooktoo, in Fajara (page 109), which is the only quality vendor of books anywhere in the country.

EMBASSIES, HIGH COMMISSIONS AND CONSULATES IN THE GAMBIA The vast majority of consular services are in the more fashionable areas of Fajara and Bakau, rather than in Banjul – see w accessgambia.com/information/embassies-in-gambia. html for a full list.

5

Central Banjul

Banjul is the least populous capital city on the African mainland, and probably the most compact, with some 35,000 inhabitants confined to an area of around 3km². Occupying the easternmost quarter of a small island that protrudes hook-like into the southern mouth of the River Gambia, Banjul is lapped by open salt water on three sides, while its southwestern shore is dislocated from the mainland by the maze of mangrove-lined creeks that comprise the Tanbi Wetland Reserve. A solitary road, the Banjul–Serekunda Highway, links the capital to the rest of the country, crossing from the island to the mainland at Denton Bridge some 3km west of the city centre.

Over recent decades, island-bound Banjul has surrendered much of its significance to the nearby mainland, where towns such as Serekunda, Bakau and Brikama now support significantly larger populations. In touristic terms, too, the capital city feels like something of an annex to the coastal resorts that blossom only 10km to its west: a sleepy urban anachronism often visited as a day trip by curious holidaymakers, but seldom viewed as an overnight destination in its own right. And yet Banjul still has many of the trappings of a capital. Most government departments have their headquarters in the city, which is also the site of State House, the administrative centre for the country, and the primary residence of President Barrow.

In its favour, the low-key Gambian capital possesses considerable character. Architecturally, Banjul is a real hodgepodge of old colonial properties, shantytowns and modern office buildings, none more than a few storeys high. And while the overall atmosphere is quite subdued and laidback, certain areas can be very hectic, particularly the stretch of Liberation Avenue that follows the eastern waterfront from Albert Market south to the terminus for the Barra Ferry.

Culturally, Banjul is a melting pot of West African and other cultures. As you walk the streets, you'll see tall blue-robed Mauritanians, Berbers in white flowing *burnouses*, Gambian businessmen in bright tie-dye shirts, and local women adorned in a dazzling array of traditional colours. Many shops are owned by Lebanese expats, who, with their dark glasses, often dress and look like members of the Mafia. There are rastas in brightly coloured woollen hats and T-shirts, and office workers dressed in suits and ties or Western-style skirts and blouses. It is amazing, but typical of The Gambia, that so many different races and cultures live alongside each other.

HISTORY

Little is known about the early history of Banjul. It seems that the earliest Portuguese explorers knew the island as Banjulo, a bastardisation of the Mandinka name for bamboo, which once grew profusely there. The British navigators who followed the Portuguese into the area called the island Combo or Kombo, after an important

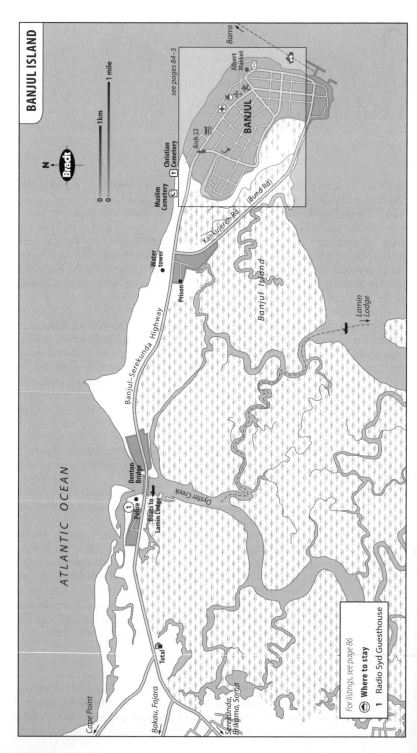

BANJUL ISLAND

N

Bradt

0   1km
0   1 mile

see pages 84–5

ATLANTIC OCEAN

Cape Point

Bakau, Fajara

Serekunda,
Brikama, Soma

Total

Denton
Bridge

Police
Boats to
Lamin Lodge

Oyster Creek

Banjul–Serekunda Highway

Water
tower

Prison

Banjul Island

Lamin
Lodge

Kankujereh Rd

(Bund Rd)

Muslim
Cemetery

Christian
Cemetery

Albert
Market

Arch 22

BANJUL

Barra

For listings, see page 86

Where to stay

1 Radio Syd Guesthouse

kingdom that occupied much of the mainland south of the river mouth. In 1651, the Duke of Courland (present-day Latvia) leased Banjul Island from the King of Kombo and James Island from the King of Barra. But while the Courlanders constructed the first fort on James Island, they appear never to have occupied Banjul, ownership of which eventually defaulted back to the King of Kombo.

Two external events conspired to bring Banjul back into the spotlight in the early 19th century. The first was the formal recognition of the River Gambia as a British possession under the Treaty of Versailles of 1783. The second, in 1807, was the passing of the British Abolition Act, which rendered the slave trade out of Africa wholly unlawful and resulted in the official closure of the River Gambia to any further trade in human booty. Unfortunately, however, this embargo was ignored by ships from anti-abolitionist France and Portugal, and also by the Americans, who had legislated against importing slaves in 1807, but allowed ships to transport them under the Spanish flag.

Initial British naval attempts to prevent slave ships entering the River Gambia enjoyed limited success. So it was that the Governor of Sierra Leone, Sir Charles MacCarthy, sent Captain Alexander Grant to Banjul Island in early 1816 to examine the possibility of setting up an anti-slaving garrison there. Impressed by the island's potential, Grant easily persuaded the King of Kombo, who had shortly before lost several family members to Spanish slavers, to cede the island in return for British protection, along with an annual payment of 103 iron bars. In April 1816, Banjul was formally handed over and renamed St Mary's Island. Three months later, MacCarthy and Grant's plan received written approval from the Earl of Bathurst, after whom the nascent settlement was named.

Captain Grant started work as soon as the treaty had been signed. Acclaimed for his personal energy and vigilance, he was well liked both by the local people and by his own men, who mostly despised the slave trade as much as he did. Construction began with a barracks to house 80 men and the erection of a battery of six 24-pounder guns and two field pieces (still present today in the grounds of State House, but out of bounds to tourists). A defensive trench was dug around the whole site, to help repel potential attacks from certain local chiefs who had profited so much from the slave trade that they violently opposed its abolition. Sir Charles MacCarthy strengthened the garrison by sending more troops from the Royal African Corps. He also stationed a sergeant's guard on James Island to prevent foreign ships from sailing further upriver. Within a few months, the garrison at Bathurst had captured five slave ships as they attempted to sail upriver, a hard and dangerous task given the high stakes involved (anybody found guilty of slave trading was automatically hanged).

Bathurst's growth was encouraged by offering free plots to legitimate merchants, providing that they built substantial brick or stone houses within a stipulated period. By 1818, the island's population stood at around 600, thanks to the relocation of many British merchants formerly operating out of Gorée Island (in present-day Senegal). By 1826, boosted by an influx of Wolof traders from Senegal and freed slaves from Sierra Leone, the non-military population of Bathurst had grown to around 30 Europeans and more than 1,800 Africans.

From hereon, the population continued to grow at a phenomenal rate, and people settled in several distinct communities. Portuguese Town is where the wealthier traders worked and erected their houses. Melville (later Jolof) Town is where the merchants' dependants and servants were housed, along with members of the artisanal class. Soldier Town is where the army was based. The poorest quarter, originally known as Mocam Town, later became Half Die, a graphic reminder that nearly half of its inhabitants died during an outbreak of cholera. These villages were separated originally by strips of cultivated land that eventually disappeared beneath buildings as the population grew, until they all joined up to form one cohesive town covering the entire habitable part of St Mary's Island.

The island may have been the perfect location for an anti-slaving garrison, but in hindsight it had little going for it as a future capital city. Hot, humid, low-lying and surrounded by standing water, it forms a natural breeding ground for tropical diseases such as cholera and malaria, and has also been prone to occasional floods. Furthermore, the geographical constraints imposed by its small size have limited its physical and economic growth to such an extent that it must surely be the only African capital to have experienced a population decline over recent decades (the current population is around 20% lower than the mid 1980s high of 45,000). Nevertheless, Bathurst continued to serve as the Gambian capital after independence in 1965, though both the island and the city officially reverted to their former name of Banjul in 1973.

GETTING THERE AND AWAY

Being small and island-bound, the town of Banjul is not itself a hub of domestic or international transport. All international flights land at Banjul International Airport, which despite its name actually borders the mainland village of Yundum, halfway between Serekunda and Brikama, and is closer by road to the coastal resorts between Cape Point and Tanji than to Banjul. Likewise, the various termini for buses and other public transport running upriver along the South Bank Road are clustered around Serekunda or Brikama, while all transport heading inland along the North Bank Road leaves from Barra, on the opposite side of the river mouth to Banjul. For further details of these connections, see the *Getting there and away* sections in the following chapters.

BY ROAD The only road connection to the capital is the Banjul–Serekunda Highway, which crosses Oyster Creek (the waterway that separates the mainland from the island) at Denton Bridge, which was built in 1986 (the 21st anniversary of Gambian independence) to replace an older namesake. Many hotels and most tour operators based around the coastal resorts offer half-day trips to Banjul City. If you prefer to do your own thing, tourist taxis will readily take you from any resort hotel to anywhere in Banjul, and will wait for you while you do whatever it is you have come for. More affordably, a steady stream of bush taxis connects central Banjul to most other towns and resort areas on the mainland inland of Brikama, and fares are D25 from Serekunda. The bush taxi station for Bakau and Fajara lies on the south side of Independence Drive opposite the National Museum, while the one for Kololi (Senegambia Junction), Serekunda (Westfield Junction) and Brikama is opposite the traffic circle at the junction of Rene Blain Street and Freedom Lane.

BY RIVER The terminal for the motor ferry across the Gambia River Mouth between Banjul and Barra is on the east side of Liberation Avenue about 500m south of Albert Market. The fare is D250 for a normal light vehicle, and D25 for foot passengers. The official crossing times are every 30 minutes or so between 07.00 and 19.00, but the service has deteriorated badly in recent years, so it is likely that you will have quite a wait of a few hours. Unfortunately, the ferry also now carries an FCO safety warning, because of overcrowding, and regular breakdowns that have left it stranded without power during the crossing (a potentially dangerous scenario were it to drift out to sea in rough weather). In addition, though two ferries theoretically carry the workload, one or other of them is often out of commission. However, in May 2017 it was announced that a new ferry, twice the size of the existing ones, will soon start plying this route raising hopes that the crossing will become faster, safer and more efficient.

If you are on foot, and you want to cross to Barra specifically (for instance to visit Juffureh), you can circumvent a lot of hassle by catching one of the regular pirogues that ply the river from Barra to Banjul and vice versa, charging the same fare as the main ferry. Many local people prefer to travel this way as it is quick and cheap, but be aware it can be fairly frightening, if not dangerous, when the river mouth is a little rough, especially when the boat is jam-packed with too many passengers. Plus, there's the indignity of being carried on and off the pirogue on the shoulders of a local lad who'll wade up to his waist to carry you through the water. A far safer option than all these are the Roots Tours to Juffureh, Albreda and James Island offered by most tour operators at the coastal resorts.

ORIENTATION

Banjul is a compact town whose roads are laid out in a grid pattern, making it fairly easy to find your way around. It can be divided into three quite distinct areas, each with its own character. The oldest and most architecturally interesting part of town is the spacious and leafy administrative sector that runs southeast along Independence Drive and Marina Parade from Arch 22 to July 22 Square. Adjacent to this, the main residential area lies to the south of Independence Drive and west of Rene Blain Street. Finally, there is the main commercial centre, a grid of narrow roads running south from July 22 Square and west of Liberation Avenue (the road that links Albert Market and the Barra Ferry terminus).

The main road gateway to Banjul, about 3km east of Denton Bridge, is the prominent Arch 22 Monument. This is where the Banjul–Serekunda Highway becomes Independence Drive, which is arguably the main road on Banjul Island. Unfortunately, although you can travel under Arch 22, it is closed to ordinary traffic (only the president is allowed to drive straight through). If you're driving into town, this means that you have to take the second exit off the traffic circle just before Arch 22, on to Marina Parade, then take a right and then a left to bring you out again on Independence Drive. Better still, if you are heading for the Barra Ferry terminus, it is possible to circumvent most of the busy streets in the city by turning right on to Kankujereh Road about 2km past Denton Bridge and 1km before Arch 22.

Most tourists who visit Banjul consider Albert Market to be the main attraction, especially the craft market. The roads near here, such as Russell Street and Liberation Avenue, are also jam-packed with shops and market stalls, as are the pavements around July 22 Square. Apart from these and the main tourist attractions of the National Museum and Arch 22, though, there's really not a lot more to see. Note that the official road name changes implemented in the 1990s have not been widely adopted by locals, so that most roads effectively have two interchangeable names.

SECURITY

Banjul is a reasonably safe city, even at night, though it would be foolhardy to walk around wearing flash jewellery or carrying more cash than you need. There are a lot of bumsters around, particularly in the vicinity of Albert Market, Arch 22 and the (currently closed) Laico Atlantic Hotel. Usually their motive is no more sinister

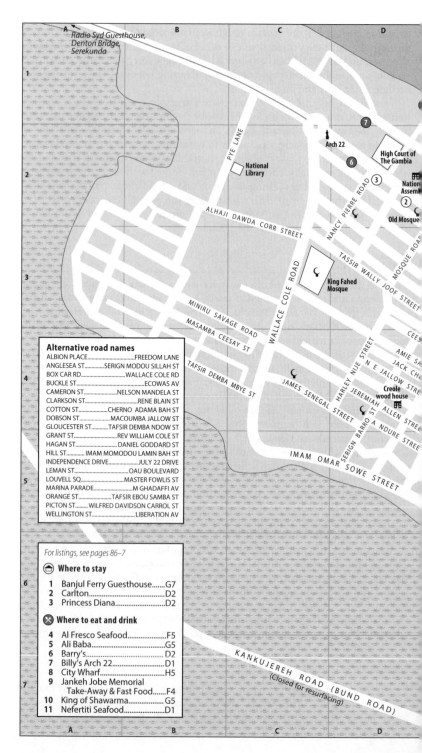

Radio Syd Guesthouse,
Denton Bridge,
Serekunda

PYE LANE

National
Library

Arch 22

High Court of
The Gambia

NANCY PIERRE ROAD

National
Assembly

Old Mosque

ALHAJI DAWDA CORR STREET

WALLACE COLE ROAD

TASSIR WALLY JOOF STREET

MOSQUE ROAD

King Fahed
Mosque

MINIRU SAVAGE ROAD

MASAMBA CEESAY ST

CEES

AMIE SA

JACK CH

N E JALLOW STRE

HARLEY NJIE STREET

Creole
wood house

TAFSIR DEMBA MBYE ST

JAMES SENEGAL STREET

JEREMIAH ALLEN STRE

A NDURE STREE

SERIGN BARRO ST

IMAM OMAR SOWE STREET

Alternative road names

ALBION PLACE..............................FREEDOM LANE
ANGLESEA ST............SERIGN MODOU SILLAH ST
BOX CAR RD.............................WALLACE COLE RD
BUCKLE ST...ECOWAS AV
CAMERON ST.....................NELSON MANDELA ST
CLARKSON ST..............................RENE BLAIN ST
COTTON ST.................CHERNO ADAMA BAH ST
DOBSON ST.............MACOUMBA JALLOW ST
GLOUCESTER ST.......TAFSIR DEMBA NDOW ST
GRANT ST.......................REV WILLIAM COLE ST
HAGAN ST.......................DANIEL GODDARD ST
HILL ST...........IMAM MOMODOU LAMIN BAH ST
INDEPENDENCE DRIVE...................JULY 22 DRIVE
LEMAN ST....................................OAU BOULEVARD
LOUVELL SQ.......................MASTER FOWLIS ST
MARINA PARADE...................M GHADAFFI AV
ORANGE ST...................TAFSIR EBOU SAMBA ST
PICTON ST.........WILFRED DAVIDSON CARROL ST
WELLINGTON ST..............................LIBERATION AV

KANKUJEREH ROAD (BUND ROAD)
(Closed for resurfacing)

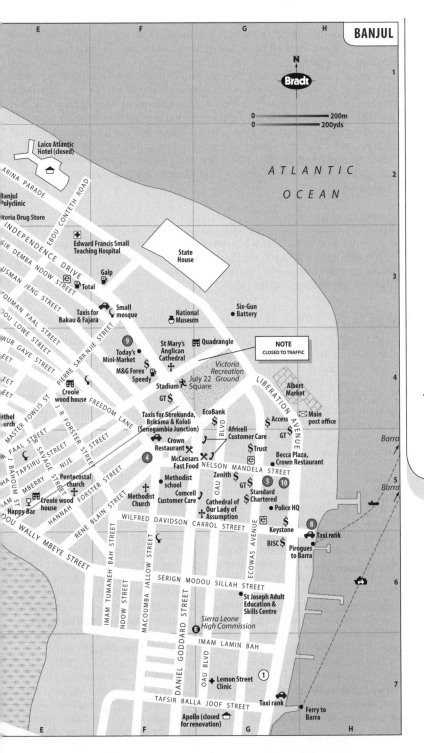

BANJUL

N

Bradt

0 ————— 200m
0 ————— 200yds

Laico Atlantic
Hotel (closed)

ARINA PARADE

EBOU CONTEH ROAD

Banjul
Polyclinic

toria Drug Store

INDEPENDENCE DRIVE

ATLANTIC

OCEAN

SIR DEMBA NDOW STREET

USMAN JENG STREET

Edward Francis Small
Teaching Hospital

State
House

Galp

Total

TOUMAN FAAL STREET

DOU LOWE STREET

Taxis for
Bakau & Fajara

Small
mosque

National
Museum

Six-Gun
Battery

WUR GAVE STREET

PIERRE SARR NJIE STREET

EET

9

Today's
Mini-Market

St Mary's
Anglican
Cathedral

Quadrangle

NOTE
CLOSED TO TRAFFIC

EET

M&G Forex

Victoria
Recreation
Ground

Albert
Market

EET

Speedy

Stadium

July 22
Square

LIBERATION AVENUE

ethel
urch

MASTER FOWLIS ST

Creole
wood house

FREEDOM LANE

J R FORSTER STREET

GT

Main
post office

NIJE STREET

Taxis for Serekunda,
Brikama & Kololi
(Senegambia Junction)

EcoBank

Access

A J FAAL STREET

TAPSIRU STREET

SAVAGE STREET

Crown
Restaurant

BLVD

Africell
Customer Care

GT

Barra

BAHOUM ST

MBERRY

Pentecostal
church

HANNAH FORSTER STREET

McCaesars
Fast Food

NELSON MANDELA STREET

Trust

Becca Plaza,
Crown Restaurant

Barra

IAM ST

Creole wood
house

Methodist
school

Zenith

OAU

GT

5

10

Happy Bar

RENE BLAIN STREET

Methodist
Church

Comcell
Customer Care

Standard
Chartered

DOU WALLY MBEYE STREET

WILFRED DAVIDSON CARROL STREET

Cathedral of
Our Lady of
Assumption

Police HQ

ECOWAS AVENUE

Keystone

Taxi rank

8

IMAM TUMANEH BAH STREET

NDOW STREET

MACOUMBA JALLOW STREET

SERIGN MODOU SILLAH STREET

BISC

Pirogues
to Barra

DANIEL GODDARD STREET

St Joseph Adult
Education &
Skills Centre

Sierra Leone
High Commission

IMAM LAMIN BAH

OAU BLVD

Lemon Street
Clinic

1

TAFSIR BALLA JOOF STREET

Taxi rank

Apollo (closed
for renovation)

Ferry to
Barra

than trying to insinuate themselves into your holiday as a guide or friend, but still it is best to shake them off firmly and politely rather than allowing them to draw you into conversation.

Around Albert Market, there are a few bumsters who work tourists in tag teams. One might, for instance, approach you with some sort of offer or a conversational gambit ('I work at your hotel?' or 'Do you remember me?'), keeping on persistently until the moment you show any sign of irritation or offishness, at which point he'll fling about angry accusations of racism, etc. The second guy then appears, perhaps claiming to be a security guard or a professional guide, and intervenes on your behalf by chasing off the first with a few angry words, hoping that will generate enough trust for you to take him on as a guide or to help negotiate with draft sellers on your behalf.

GETTING AROUND

If you're on foot, you can walk between pretty much anywhere you want in under 30 minutes, especially if you are just visiting the tourist attractions. Alternatively, shared taxis are commonplace and it shouldn't cost you more than D50 to be driven from one side of the city to the other.

WHERE TO STAY

Banjul itself offers a limited selection of accommodation compared with the resorts that line the coast to its west. The one proper tourist hotel, the long-serving Atlantic, has recently closed. Although it is rumoured to be reopening in the future, this was not apparent given its condition during this book's update. Budget travellers are better catered for, with a few acceptable choices that generally feel a lot more down to earth than their counterparts in the nearby resort area. The Apollo Hotel [85 G7], under the same management as the Carlton, was closed for renovations at the time of writing, but expect it to be the top hotel in the budget range once it reopens, hopefully during the lifetime of this guide.

BUDGET

 Radio Syd Guesthouse [map, page 80] (4 rooms) Banjul–Serekunda Highway; 4226490/4228170; m 7678754; e radiosyd1@gmail.com; w gambia-lodge. webs.com. Boasting a breezy beachfront location about 1km west of Arch 22, this whitewashed guesthouse has an improbable back story, being the former headquarters of a Swedish pirate radio station that started life off the waters of Malmö, Sweden, in 1958, relocated to Banjul in the early 1970s, & stopped transmitting in 2001 when its antennae collapsed. Owned & managed by a laid-back Swedish couple, it opened as a low-key guesthouse is 2007, & is now probably the most appealing budget option in the Banjul area, with a lived-in non-institutional vibe & an isolated but convenient location alongside the only bush taxi route between the coastal

resorts & Banjul. It lies right on a beach that's ideal for long walks, as well as an estuary that usually offers safe swimming. The restaurant serves a limited 'catch of the day' type selection to overnight guests, generally for under £4 per plate. The en-suite rooms are nothing flash, but they seem comfortable enough, & come with a fan (but no AC), nets & in some cases self-catering facilities. Not to everybody's taste, perhaps, but great value to those seeking an affordable individualistic beach retreat. *From £12 dbl to £16 for large apt.*

Carlton Hotel [84 D2] (40 rooms) Independence Dr; 4228670/4225549; m 3129942. This stalwart multi-storey hotel a few doors down from the Princess Diana, though comparable in quality to its neighbour, is a little pricier & feels more rundown. Still, it's not bad value, & the en-suite rooms all come with fan or

AC. *£10/12.50 sgl/dbl with fan, £12/15 sgl/dbl with AC.*

🏠 **Princess Diana Hotel** [84 D2] (12 rooms) Independence Dr; 📞 4228715; m 7318265. Probably the pick of the central cheapies, this obtusely named hotel close to Arch 22 seems to have undergone recent renovations, & the clean, tiled en-suite rooms with fan or AC seem pretty good value. *£7.50/8.50 sgl/dbl, £14 dbl with AC.*

SHOESTRING

🏠 **Banjul Ferry Guesthouse** [85 G7] (16 rooms) Liberation Av; m 7272222. A drop in standard from the above, but not so much in price, this useful fallback has a convenient location near the ferry terminal, & quite spacious en-suite rooms with fans. It is also rather rundown & the location is potentially noisy (ask for a room facing away from the street). *£8.50/15 dbl with fan/AC.*

✖ WHERE TO EAT AND DRINK

Since the closure of the Laico Atlantic and Denton Beach Resort, restaurant options are somewhat limited in Banjul. Those listed below are the pick of several similar options dotted around the city.

MID-RANGE

✖ **Al Fresco Seafood Restaurant** [85 F5] Rene Blain St; m 7663564/9900150; 🕐 08.00–late daily. This popular central eatery offers a varied selection of steak, seafood & Gambian dishes. The food is fine but it's quite cramped inside & no alcohol is served. *Mains mostly in the £3–6 range.*

✖ **Billy's Arch 22 Restaurant** [84 D1] Marina Parade; m 3456026/9928918; 🕐 09.00–21.00 (or later if busy) daily. Situated in the shadow of Arch 22, this is a pleasant spot for an alfresco lunch, or for drinks & dinner with the city's best-known landmark lit up in the background. It has indoor & outdoor seating, a full bar, friendly service, & a limited selection of well-prepared prawn, fish & chicken dishes. *Mains in the £3.50–4.50 range, & sandwiches for around £2.*

✖ **Nefertiti Seafood Restaurant** [84 D1] Off Marina Parade; 📞 4222400; m 7776600; 🕐 May & Oct 08.00–17.00 Mon–Sat, Nov–Apr 08.00–midnight Mon–Sat, closed Jun–Sep. The top restaurant in the city centre is this stylish beachfront set-up with colourful indoor & comfortable outdoor seating immediately west of the old Laico Atlantic. It serves a varied selection of tasty Gambian & international dishes, mostly seafood but also ranging from chicken jerk to fillet steak. There's a full bar & free Wi-Fi. *Mains in the £4–5 range, as well as burgers, salads & sandwiches for around £3.*

BUDGET

✖ **Ali Baba Restaurant** [85 G5] Nelson Mandela St; 📞 4224055; 🕐 08.00–19.00 Mon–Sat, 10.00–17.00 Sun. Something of a Banjul institution, this popular fast-food restaurant near the ferry terminal serves typical Lebanese dishes such as *shawarmas* & falafel sandwiches, along with a selection of burgers & Gambian & pasta mains. No alcohol. *Full meals cost around £3 & substantial snacks around £1.50.*

✖ **City Wharf Restaurant** [85 H5] Off Liberation Av; 🕐 07.00–15.00 daily. This waterfront bar near the ferry jetty serves up tasty & affordable fish & chips & soft drinks (but no alcohol) in view of the chaotic boarding procedure of the pirogues to Barra – good value in every sense! *Fish & chips around £1 per plate.*

✖ **King of Shawarma Restaurant** [85 G5] Nelson Mandela St; 📞 4229799; m 7788807; 🕐 09.00–19.00 Mon–Sat. Situated next to Ali Baba's, this is another good Lebanese restaurant serving similar dishes at slightly higher prices. The seafood & juices are recommended. No alcohol. *Around £3.50 mains or £1.50 snacks.*

✖ **Jankeh Jobe Memorial Take-Away & Fast Food** [85 F4] Independence Dr; m 7730553; 🕐 07.00–22.00 Mon–Fri. This eatery opposite the National Museum must be the cleanest in town, & the overhead fans are very welcoming. It's great value too. No alcohol. *Around £1–1.50 for the meal of the day or a sandwich.*

🖥 **Barry's Restaurant** [84 D2] Independence Dr; 🕐 08.00–18.30 daily. Between Arch 22 & the Princess Diana Hotel, this cheerful small café serves a selection of filled baguettes. *Baguettes under £2.*

OTHER PRACTICALITIES

BANKING AND FOREIGN EXCHANGE Banks with ATMs accepting foreign Visa cards include the **EcoBank** [85 G4] on OAU Boulevard, and the **Standard Chartered** [85 G5], **GT** [85 G5] and **Trust Bank** [85 G5] on Ecowas Avenue. There are also a few private forex bureaux dotted around, including **M&G Forex** [85 F4] on Independence Drive and several in the vicinity of Albert Market. Private moneychangers sometimes loiter outside Banjul post office, but they have a reputation for trickery, so are best avoided.

HOSPITAL The country's largest and oldest medical facility, established in 1853, is the **Edward Francis Small (formerly Royal Victoria) Teaching Hospital** [85 E3] (\ 4228224–7) on Independence Drive a block west of the National Museum. It has a casualty department, but for immediate attention it's probably wiser to visit one of the clinics in the Kololi area. The closest thing to a 24-hour pharmacy is the **Victoria Drug Store** [85 E2] on Independence Drive (⊕ *09.00–21.00 Mon–Sat, 10.00–21.00 Sun*).

INTERNET A few internet cafés are dotted around town, and marked on the map, mostly in the vicinity of Albert Market and the Barra Ferry terminus. On the western side of town near Arch 22, the internet café on Independence Drive next to the Carlton Hotel has been recommended.

POST The **main post office** [85 H4] on Liberation Avenue is a convenient place to post home goods bought at the adjacent Albert Market. If you are doing this, it's best to visit the parcel desk to look at the contents and stick on a customs declaration before you finish wrapping it. This way you avoid your parcel being opened later and more roughly by customs officials. For stamp collectors, a special desk sells sets of Gambian stamps.

SHOPPING The **Albert Market** [85 G4] sells everything from vegetables and fruit to beauty products, clothing, shells, beads, fabrics and prints. Situated within the main market, the **Banjul Craft Market** is without a doubt the best place to buy local crafts – musical instruments, batiks, antiques and the usual colourful bracelets and necklaces – in Banjul. The **Kerewan Record Store** next to the entrance is a good place to pick up cassettes and CDs of Gambian and other West African music. Perhaps the best supermarket in town is **Today's Mini-Market** [85 F4] (\ 4201778; ⊕ *09.00–21.00 daily*) on Independence Drive, which stocks a fair selection of wines, spirits and other imported and packaged goods.

WHAT TO SEE AND DO

Banjul is rather short on 'must-see' attractions, the one arguable exception being the worthwhile and well-organised National Museum. However, it is worth dedicating a couple of hours to exploring the town centre, ideally starting in the far west at the distinctive Arch 22 Monument, then following Independence Drive southeast down to the National Museum, possibly diverting north to the waterfront or south into the old residential area, then continuing further southeast via July 22 Square to Albert Market and the bustling stalls and shops that line Liberation Avenue as it runs south to the Barra Ferry terminus.

ARCH 22 MONUMENT [84 C2] (*Independence Drive;* ☉ *08.00–18.00 daily; entrance D50*) Difficult to miss towering as it does above the only road into the city, the imposing but otherwise unimpressive Arch 22 Monument was designed by the Senegalese architect Pierre Goudiaby to commemorate the military coup d'état led by the future President Jammeh on 22 July 1994. Completed and unveiled two years after the event, the triumphal arch stands a full 35m high, comprising two rows of four pillars supporting a triangular roof. Although its neoclassical pretensions seem rather at odds with the surrounding urban environment, the three upper floors – reached by a giddying spiral staircase – contain interesting ethnographic displays on pre-colonial cultures, as well as a small craft shop. If nothing else, the nominal entrance fee is justified by the spectacular views, offered in all directions, across the city rooftops to the river mouth and sea. Photography of the interior is forbidden, but you can photograph the arch from the outside, and it is also permitted to take pictures of the view. The traffic circle below the arch was dominated by a bronze statue of a soldier (who bears a striking resemblance to Jammeh) carrying a baby, but it was removed in May 2017 as it was thought by many to be a glorification of Jammeh.

NATIONAL MUSEUM OF THE GAMBIA [85 F3] (*Independence Drive;* ✆ *4226244;* m *7692772;* e *musmon@qanet.gm;* w *ncac.gm;* ☉ *08.00–18.00 Mon–Thu, 08.00– 13.30 Fri, 08.00–14.00 Sat; entrance D50*) Situated on the north side of Independence Drive, this is the country's premier museum, officially opened by President Jawara in 1985, and housed in an airy wooden-floored building that formerly served as the (whites-only) Bathurst Club. Many of the exhibits are a bit tired-looking, but overall it is a very interesting place to spend an hour or two. Among the more absorbing collections is a varied set of monochrome photographs of Banjul taken in the early 20th century, some fabulous traditional masked dancing kits, displays about the Senegambia Stone Circle sites of Wassu and Ker Batch, Iron-Age societies in the Senegal River region, and the spread of Islam and the marabout tradition. In the pleasant gardens of tamarisk and palm trees, you'll find public toilets, the city's last functional well, a batik stall and a quality silversmith. Still photography is permitted, but not video.

INDEPENDENCE DRIVE AND MARINA PARADE Among the oldest roads in Banjul, these two parallel thoroughfares are lined with several of the city's most interesting 19th-century buildings. These include the **High Court** [84 D2], the **National Assembly** [84 D2], the **Edward Francis Small (formerly Royal Victoria) Teaching Hospital** [85 E3] and various government offices. Also on Marina Parade but sadly off-limits to tourists is **State House** [85 F/G3], a majestic building whose grounds house the Six-Gun Battery raised by Captain Grant in 1816 to prevent slave ships entering the River Gambia (now part of the Kunta Kinteh Island and Related Sites' UNESCO World Heritage Site). Back on Independence Drive, two landmark sites of worship are the **Old Mosque** [84 D2], built in the first half of the 19th century by Bombeh Gaye, and the small but pretty **St Mary's Anglican Cathedral** [85 F4], which was constructed under the name King's Church in 1933. The church courtyard contains a small memorial to five police constables killed in the line of duty in Sankandi in 1900.

SOUTH OF INDEPENDENCE DRIVE One of the oldest parts of Banjul is the residential quarter that runs south from Independence Drive towards the mangroves that form the city's southern boundary. At the west end of this district, on Wallace Cole Road a few hundred metres south of Arch 22, the modernistic **King Fahed**

Mosque [84 C3], built in 1988, is the city's largest and most prominent place of worship, graced by two tall octagonal minarets and with capacity for more 6,000 male and female worshippers. At the other end of the district, on the junction of Macoumba Jallow and Rene Blain streets, a few hundred metres south of July 22 Square, is the oldest surviving place of worship in Banjul: the modest **Methodist (originally Wesleyan) Church** [85 F5] built in 1834. Between the two, the backstreets of this district are dotted with some of the city's finest examples of mid19th-century wooden Creole architecture. Good examples (marked on the map) can be seen next to the Happy Bar on Rev William Cole Street [85 E5], on Pierre Sarr Njie Street [85 E4], and on Sagarr Jobe Street [84 D4].

JULY 22 SQUARE AND SURROUNDS Formerly Independence Square, and before that MacCarthy Square, this is the most central green space in the city centre, a small quadrangle situated at the eastern end of Independence Drive, on the pivot that divides the western administrative region from the southern commercial district. The site of a World War I memorial and a commemorative fountain constructed for the coronation of King George VI in 1937, it is now often used as the site for important ceremonial events, including the opening of the biennial Toots Homecoming Festival. On its western side is the **Quadrangle** [85 G4], or **Government Building**, the oldest building in Banjul, and now housing the **National Archives**. Extended from the original barracks constructed by Captain Grant some 200 years ago, the Quadrangle is topped by a handsome clock tower donated by the Bavreres Company in 1892.

ALBERT MARKET [85 G4] Running south from July 22 Square to the Barra Ferry terminus on Liberation Avenue (formerly Russell and Wellington streets) is the vibrant commercial focal point of Banjul. Its centrepiece is Albert Market, which started life in the mid 19th century and is still going strong today, albeit behind a relatively modern façade constructed after it was razed by a fire in 1988. For curio-hunters, it is the site of the excellent **Banjul Craft Market**, an excellent place to buy everything from sculptures and traditional musical instruments to tie-dyed batik clothing and locally made jewellery. But even if you are not interested in buying, it is a fascinating place to stroll around, with different sections devoted to clothing, fish, meat, fresh produce, fetish stalls and hardware, all of them catering mainly to local buyers rather than tourists.

LIBERATION AVENUE AND HALF DIE South of Albert Market, Liberation Avenue is lined with Lebanese and Mauritanian cloth stores, and the workplace of many local tailors who will convert the raw material to finished clothing for very reasonable prices. Also on this road are several old colonial-era warehouses, most notably the **Maurel and Prom Building**, with its arched double-storey façade. Two blocks inland, on the corner of Daniel Goddard and Wilfred Davidson Carroll streets, the **Cathedral of Our Lady of Assumption** [85 G5], which celebrated its centenary in 2011, is an unusual Catholic building with an adobe exterior supported by heavy buttresses. Nearby at 20 Ecowas Avenue the **St Joseph Adult Education & Skills Centre** [85 G6] (✆ *4228836*) is known for the high-quality handcrafted clothes and other artefacts produced by its female students. Further south, around the Barra Ferry terminus, the old and rundown suburb of Half Die (originally known as Mocam Town but renamed in memory of the many victims of a cholera outbreak in 1869) is the site of some of the city's last remaining Creole-style wood-and-bamboo-weave houses.

TANBI WETLAND RESERVE Established in 2001, this 45km^2 reserve protects the extensive maze of mangroves, open channels, mud banks and other saline wetland habitats that separate Banjul Island from the mainland, running south almost all the way to the small town of Lamin on the Serekunda–Brikama Road. Long known as a birding hotspot, the main road runs adjacent to a large expanse of tidal mud that is exposed at low tide, often giving excellent views of herons, egrets, African spoonbill, pelicans and various waders including pied avocet. It is one of the best sites in The Gambia for rarities, which have in the past included great 'ticks' like saddle-billed stork, European spoonbill and lesser yellowlegs.

A popular access point to the northern wetlands is Kankujereh Road (still widely known by the older name of Bund Road), which skirts the southern fringe of Banjul for about 3km. As of March 2017, though, the road was closed and was still undergoing resurfacing works at the time of writing. For now, access to the wetlands is by boat only, which can be hired from the beach on the north side of the Banjul–Serekunda Highway immediately west of Denton Bridge. Boats can go as far south as Lamin Lodge if you wish, and also offer fishing trips through the mangroves, birding trips or dolphin-spotting excursions in the open sea. Expect to pay around £10–20 per hour, depending on the size and type of boat. Recommended operators include Angling Tours Gambia with skipper Alhagie (m *7799104/3799104;* e *ag_sarr@yahoo.com;* f *anglingtoursgambia*) and Jane's Boats (m *7768074;* e *jane@janesboats.gm;* w *janesboats.gm*), who operate the lazy day cruise through the mangrove creeks that has been popular for nearly 20 years. Book online or via the major tour operators (*£37.50pp for cruise, £28pp for fishing; half price for children, inc some drinks & lunch*).

UPDATES WEBSITE

Go to w bradtupdates.com/thegambia for the latest on-the-ground travel news, trip reports and factual updates. Keep up to date with the latest posts by following Philip on Twitter (*@philipbriggs*) and via Facebook: f fb.me/ pb.travel.updates. And, if you have any comments, queries, grumbles, insights, news or other feedback, you're invited to post them directly on the website, or to email them to Philip (e *philip.briggs@bradtguides.com*) for inclusion.

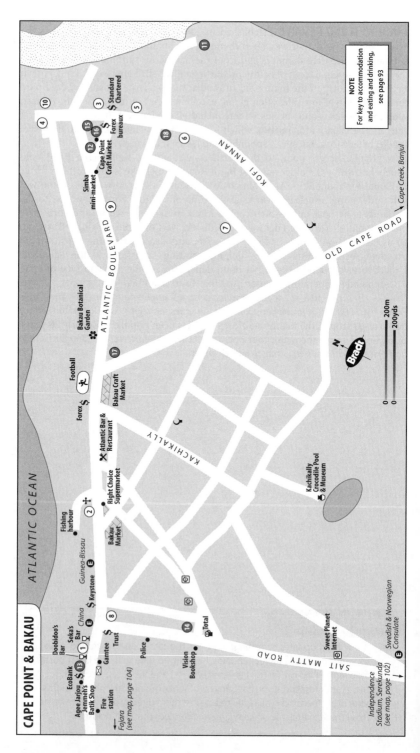

CAPE POINT & BAKAU

ATLANTIC OCEAN

NOTE
For key to accommodation and eating and drinking, see page 93

Standard Chartered

Forex bureaux

Cape Point Craft Market

Simba mini-market

ATLANTIC BOULEVARD

Bakau Botanical Garden

Football

Forex $

Atlantic Bar & Restaurant

Bakau Craft Market

Right Choice Supermarket

Bakau Market

Fishing harbour

KACHIKALLY

Kachikally Crocodile Pool & Museum

OLD CAPE ROAD

→ Cape Creek, Banjul

Doobidoo's Bar

Seka's Bar

China

Keystone

Guinea-Bissau

EcoBank

Agee Jarjou
Jemmeh's Batik Shop

Gamtee Trust

Fire station

Police

Vision Bookshop

Total

Sweet Planet Internet

SAIT MATTY ROAD

Fajara (see map, page 104)

Independence Stadium, Serekunda (see map, page 102)

Swedish & Norwegian Consulate

KOFI ANNAN

Brandt

N

0   200m
0   200yds

92

6

Bakau and Cape Point

The third-largest town in The Gambia, with a population of 75,000, bustling Bakau is perched atop low red cliffs running southwest from Cape Point, the north-facing promontory at the juncture of the Gambia River Mouth and Atlantic coastline. One of the first parts of The Gambia to be developed as a resort area, Cape Point also separates two beaches that could hardly be more different in character. The strip of Atlantic coastline southwest of Cape Point, below the cliffs of Bakau, is essentially a fishing beach, lined with dozens of colourful pirogues, and the site of a chaotic market where the day's catch is gutted and sold. By contrast, the flat sweep of golden sand running southeast of Cape Point ranks among the most attractive swimming beaches in the country, offering distant views to the North Bank on a clear day, and with a relatively quiet and uncrowded feel compared with most other resort areas.

Although a lot of Bakau's seafront has been turned over to residential use, there are also plenty of hotels dotted around, and beach tourism remains arguably the main economic activity today. That said, Bakau is also very much a working town: Atlantic Boulevard, the main thoroughfare, is flanked by the whiffy fishing beach and a large grocery market, while the narrow dusty roads running inland through the old town retain a surprisingly organic and lived-in character. As a result, tourist facilities in Bakau seem to exist in less of an industry bubble (and to be rather less heavily bumstered – see pages 62–3) than their counterparts in, say, Kololi or Kotu.

CAPE POINT & BAKAU
For listings, see pages 94–7

🛏 **Where to stay**
1. African Village
2. Bakau Guesthouse
3. Cape Point
4. Cape Residence Apartments
5. Ocean Bay
6. One World Village Guesthouse
7. Roc Heights Lodge
8. Romana's
9. Smiling Coast
10. Sunbeach

✴ **Where to eat and drink**
Buddha Restaurant & Lounge (see 5)
11. Calypso
12. Fan Fang Chinese
Fisherman's Wharf (see 2)
13. Kunta's Bar & Grill
14. Mac Domoro Cuisine
15. Mr Bass Bendula Garden
16. Rising Sun
17. Saffie J Bar & Restaurant
18. Zaika

HISTORY

Unsurprisingly, the existence of Cape Point was documented by the earliest Portuguese explorers, who christened it Cabo de Santa Maria (a name that later became associated with Banjul Island, known as St Mary's Island in British colonial times). The oldest part of Bakau, Kachikally was most likely founded by the Bojang clan, which has since produced several local Mandinka chiefs (and more recently MPs and other politicians), and which still claims traditional ownership of the sacred crocodile pool in the heart of the old town. Bakau is first name-checked by Lemos Coelho, a Portuguese explorer who landed there in 1669 and noted that it housed a European slave-trading post. Over the subsequent three years, Coelho used the 'very attractive port' as a base for exploring further upriver, and later wrote that if he 'were to return upriver today, he would live nowhere else'. In 1816, Captain Grant, the founder of Banjul, established a sanatorium at Cape Point, close to what is now the British High Commission, and also arranged for a lantern to be hung there at night as a navigational aid. In 1823, Bakau became the site of a primary school founded by the Quaker missionary Hannah Kilhan and two male colleagues. Integrated into the British colony of Gambia in 1888, Bakau was partially destroyed by flooding in 1906. Several old colonial buildings still stand, however, among them the quaint St Peter's Church opposite the market, and several grand clifftop residences.

GETTING THERE AND AWAY

For new arrivals heading to Bakau from Banjul International Airport, it's a drive of around 25km via Serekunda, and taxis to any hotel in the area officially cost around £15, though you may be able to negotiate a better price.

Bakau lies about 13km west of Banjul via the Banjul–Serekunda Highway and the Old Cape Road, a route covered by regular bush taxis, which leave Banjul from the station on Independence Drive opposite the National Museum, and cost around D25. There are also regular shared taxis to Serekunda and Kololi.

Coming to or from Fajara, a steady flow of shared taxis runs along Atlantic Boulevard, the 5km road between the north end of Kairaba Avenue and Cape Point, and they will pick up passengers anywhere *en route*.

The main taxi and public transport rank in Bakau is on Atlantic Boulevard next to the Bakau Guesthouse, but there are also taxi ranks close to the junctions with the Old Cape Road and Sait Matty Road.

 ## WHERE TO STAY *Map, page 92*

The only truly upmarket hotels in Bakau are Ocean Bay and Sunbeach, which rank among the best options in their range anywhere on the coast. A good selection of cheaper options is headed by the self-catering Cape Residence Apartments, while those looking for something more characterful are pointed to the One World Village Guesthouse and very budget-friendly Bakau Guesthouse. Bakau is also home to two long-serving and busy but otherwise rather indifferent package set-ups in the form of the Cape Point and African Village hotels.

EXCLUSIVE

✳ 🏠 **Sunbeach Hotel & Resort** (111 rooms) Kofi Annan St; ☎ 4497190/4496914/4497214; e fom@sunbeachhotelthegambia.com. This sleek, newly reopened resort has a modern North African feel & the smart sgl-storey blocks offer modern rooms with flatscreen TVs, safe, AC, hot shower & verandas offering mostly sea views. The open & spacious grounds host 2 restaurants & 2 swimming pools, while various activities such as beach volleyball, yoga, badminton & games are on offer. Other services include valet, laundry, babysitting & tours. *Contact The Gambia Experience for bookings & rates.*

🏠 **Ocean Bay Hotel & Resort** (195 rooms) Kofi Annan St; ☎ 4494265/4495787; e info@oceanbayhotel.com; w www.oceanbayhotel.com. Among the most appealing large resort hotels in The Gambia, this wheelchair-friendly 5-star complex lies in neat & well-maintained spacious palm-shaded gardens that lead out to a semi-private swimming beach perhaps 300m south of Cape Point. Set in Mediterranean-style dbl-storey blocks with pastel-shaded walls, terracotta tiled floors & tiled roofs, the stylish & reasonably spacious rooms come with king-size or twin bed, dark wood furniture, fan, AC, satellite TV with in-house video channel, private balcony & en-suite hot shower. Other facilities include a large rectangular swimming pool, a choice of 5 indoor & poolside restaurants & bars, 24hr laundry & valet service, tennis courts, watersports, tours, babysitting, foreign exchange & a library. *£84/113 standard sgl/dbl, £102/134 deluxe sgl/dbl, £125/167 premium sgl/dbl, all rates B&B.*

MID-RANGE

✳ ⌂ **Roc Heights Lodge** (22 rooms) Samba Breku Rd; ☏ 4495428/4498301; m 9918727; e enquiries@rocheightslodge. com; w rocheightslodge.com. Compromised only by its suburban location 5–10 mins' walk from the beach, this classy boutique-style lodge is set in luxuriant tropical gardens centred on a recently constructed swimming pool. Notable for its tranquil feel, attentive service, tasteful colonial-style fittings & ethnic décor, it offers accommodation in a variety of dbl or twin rooms with free Wi-Fi, satellite TV, balcony, fan, AC, comfortable sitting area & large en-suite bathrooms. Self-catering apts & penthouse suites (with distant sea views) are also available. There is a stylish restaurant with indoor & garden seating. *US$52.50/72.50 sgl/dbl room, US$55.50/76.50 sgl/ dbl penthouse suite, US$70/93 sgl/dbl apt.*

⌂ **Cape Point Hotel and Restaurant** (75 rooms) Kofi Annan St; ☏ 4494697/4495005; e info@capepointhotel.net; w capepointhotel. net. This family-run hotel lies a few paces' walk from the beach immediately south of Cape Point, & it has good facilities including a swimming pool, children's pool, bar & restaurant. The grounds are small & crowded, making it feel very packaged, & the décor is a little frayed at the edges. The en-suite rooms are reasonably sizeable & come with TV, fridge, bathroom with tub/shower & AC. *£53/66 dbl/apt B&B.*

⌂ **Smiling Coast Hotel** (10 rooms) Atlantic Bd; ☏ 4494653; m 9906956; e contact@smilingcoastguesthouse.com; w smilingcoastguesthouse.com. This friendly dbl-storey guesthouse on the landward side of Atlantic Bd doesn't offer much in the way of character, but the rooms are bright, spacious & clean, & they all come with fan, AC, net, satellite TV, fridge, balcony & en-suite hot shower. A ground-floor restaurant with indoor & outdoor seating serves seafood &

other mains, &there is live music on Sat. *Fair value at £22/33 sgl/dbl B&B, self-catering apt £66.*

BUDGET

✳ ⌂ **One World Village Guesthouse** (7 rooms) Kofi Annan St; m 3080441/3571788/6834569/7358241; e aita@oneworldvillage.eu; w oneworldvillage. eu. Owned & managed by a Gambian–Swedish couple, this refreshingly down-to-earth & funky little guesthouse is set in attractive leafy gardens centred on a circular swimming pool about 500m south of Cape Point & the beach. The standard rooms using shared bath are on the functional side, but very neat & clean, & they come with a fan & netting. There is also 1 larger en-suite room, & 1 mini suite with optional AC. There is no restaurant, but b/fast can be provided at £2.50 per head, while for other meals you can either use the communal self-catering kitchen or head to any of a dozen good eateries within easy walking distance. *£16 dbl with shared bathroom, from £20 en-suite dbl.*

⌂ **African Village Hotel** (73 rooms) Atlantic Bd; ☏ 4495034/4495384; e africanvillagehotel@ yahoo.com; w africanvillagehotel.gm. One of the oldest & most packagey hotels on the Gambian coast, the lively & friendly African Village is looking a little rough at the edges these days, but it remains a popular & good-value choice, not least thanks to its superb location, on a low cliff overlooking the fishing beach, in the heart of Bakau. Facilities include a compact swimming-pool area, a restaurant with a clifftop wooden deck, & a somewhat eroded private beach that offers good swimming tidally. Accommodation is in simply decorated en-suite thatched huts. *£17/25 standard sgl/dbl with fan, £28/45 sgl/dbl with AC & sea view.*

⌂ **Bakau Guesthouse** (29 rooms) Atlantic Bd; m 7701711/9746389; e brian_chico@ live.com; w bakauguesthouse.co.uk. This long-serving & unusually characterful 4-storey hotel opposite Bakau Market is notable above all for the superb views over the fishing beach & harbour offered from the sea-facing rooms & the balcony of the ground-floor Fisherman's Wharf Restaurant (page 96). The rooms are basic & rather timeworn, as might be expected in this price range, but they are still spacious & secure, & come with en-suite hot showers, fans, & in most cases a small private balcony. Overall, an excellent option for budget-conscious travellers. *£13/20 dbl with street/sea view.*

🏠 **Cape Residence Apartments** (12 rooms) Cape Point; m 7665026; e caperesidence@ yahoo.com. Tucked away opposite the Sunbeach Hotel, yet conveniently close to the beach & to several good eateries, this lodge lies in cramped built-up grounds centred on a small but deep circular swimming pool. Aimed mainly at longer stays, it offers accommodation in very spacious & modern apartments, all of which come with AC, well-equipped kitchen with fridge, sitting area with flatscreen TV & small balcony. It has a standby generator & water tank. Very good value. *2- & 4-bed apts starting from £33 with low-season discounts available.*

SHOESTRING
🏠 **Romana's** (12 rooms) Atlantic Bd; 📞 4495127. This scruffy & indifferently managed hotel is adequate if you just need a cheap bed. Rooms have nets & en-suite bathrooms. *£7/10 sgl/dbl.*

✕ WHERE TO EAT AND DRINK *Map, page 92*

When it comes to eating out, you could spend a week in Bakau without repeating a venue. There are restaurants in most of the hotels, but generally the better option is standalone eateries, in particular the cosmopolitan cluster around the Ocean Bay Hotel, which includes the Calypso, Zaika and Mr Bass. For setting and character, the Fisherman's Wharf Restaurant on the ground floor of the Bakau Guesthouse is hard to beat.

UPMARKET
✳✕ **Calypso Restaurant** Off Kofi Annan Rd; m 6920201; ⏰ 09.00–23.00 daily (the bar stays open later at w/ends). Established in 1988, this Bakau institution has an idyllic location on the edge of a large reed-lined pond that supports plentiful crocodiles & waterbirds, & Cape Point Beach extending away to the north. There is the choice of eating in the open-sided thatched main restaurant, in one of the summer houses next to the crocodile pool or beach, or in a wooden treehouse-like construction behind them. It is a popular meeting point for expats on Fri & Sat nights, when there is also often live music. An excellent menu dominated by seafood, steak & pasta dishes is complemented by more affordable snacks & sandwiches. It also has a full bar & tapas menu. Come between 16.00 & 17.00 to see the crocodiles being treated to a fish supper. Overall, a very agreeable lunch spot & great night out, though not the cheapest. *Mains around £10, snacks around £5–6.*

✕ **Fisherman's Wharf Restaurant** Atlantic Bd; 📞 4497460; m 7701711/9844410; w bakauguesthouse.co.uk; ⏰ Nov–Apr noon– late. Also known as La Mer, this ground-floor restaurant stands out for its veranda offering views over the fishing beach & harbour, but also for a bizarrely high-kitsch interior where literally hundreds of traditional African statues, masks & fetishes lurk ghoulishly in the shadows. It boasts a fantastically varied menu, with over 50 seafood dishes ranging from baked mackerel & peri-peri prawns to Moroccan paella, supplemented by a more limited meat & poultry selection. A real one-off, well worth trying at least once during your stay, ideally arriving an hour before sunset to watch the activity on the fishing beach below! *Mains in the £6–10 range.*

MID-RANGE
✳✕ **Mr Bass Bendula Garden** Atlantic Bd; m 7727660; e bendula_garden@yahoo.com; ⏰ 08.00–02.00 daily. A well-known landmark situated opposite the Cape Point Hotel, this vibey rendezvous has the ambience of a street café, with shaded seating spilling out on to the pavement. A varied international menu includes Asian, Mexican & continental dishes, but the main specialities are pizzas, seafood & excellent Gambian staples such as fish with benachin rice. It is particularly popular over weekends, when you can watch live Premier League football accompanied by chilled draught beers. There is also live music on Mon, Wed, Fri & Sat, usually starting at around 21.00. A great place to settle into for a lively evening. *Mains in the £4–6 range.*

✗ Fan Fang Chinese Restaurant Atlantic Bd; ☎ 4497476; m 7361449; ⊕ Dec–Mar 16.00–midnight daily. The only dedicated Chinese eatery in Bakau boasts a central location & a varied menu of pork, chicken, seafood & vegetarian dishes. It is pretty good value but lacking in ambience & the food is only so-so. *Around £4–6 per main inc steamed rice.*

✗ Kunta's Bar & Grill Atlantic Bd; m 7701499; ⊕ 08.00–late daily. Probably the pick of several moderate pavement eateries clustered around the entrance of the African Village Hotel, this place has a pleasant outdoor ambience, cheap beers, & a varied menu concentrating on Chinese, Gambian & seafood dishes. *Mains in the £4–7 range.*

✗ Mac Domoro Cuisine Sait Matty Rd; m 7924096; ⊕ 10.00–02.00 daily. This cheerful & colourful local eatery opposite the police station has coloured décor & serves a varied selection of Gambian & international meat & seafood dishes to an accompaniment of lively African music. *Mains in the £2.50–5 range.*

✗ Zaika Restaurant & Bar Kofi Annan Rd; m 2251004/7079220; ⊕ 16.00–late daily (high season). Formerly the Taj, this is one of the best Indian restaurants anywhere on the coast, with indoor & outdoor seating, a massive menu of dishes including a great vegetarian selection, some Chinese & European favourites as well as a well-stocked bar. Rather low on character but exceptional food. *Expect to pay £4.50–8 per main, inc rice or naan.*

BUDGET

✗ Buddha Restaurant & Lounge Off Kofi Annan Rd; ☎ 4495787; ⊕ Tue–Sun. This smart-looking bar & restaurant at the Ocean Bay Hotel specialises in Asian fusion cuisine, including sushi & tapas, & receives good reviews. *Sushi from £3, tapas from £5.*

✗ Rising Sun Bar & Restaurant Off Atlantic Bd; m 7559192/9900027; ⊕ Nov–Apr 07.00–23.30 daily. This low-key local eatery next to Cape Point Craft focuses on fresh seafood & also has a good vegetarian selection. *Vegetarian dishes around £3, other mains around £5.*

✗ Saffie J Bar & Restaurant Old Cape Rd; m 7395656; ⊕ 10.00–late daily. This relaxed & friendly open-air pavement restaurant opposite Bakau Craft Market might look like little more than a local drinking hole, but it has a long & surprisingly varied menu offering everything from meatballs or beef stroganoff with boiled potatoes to grilled prawns or fish & chips. Down to earth & great value. *Most mains around £4.*

ENTERTAINMENT AND NIGHTLIFE

Most of the restaurants listed above double as bars. Several also host live music at weekends and more occasionally on weekday nights. We recommend Fisherman's Wharf for a central sundowner overlooking the fishing beach and Calypso Restaurant for a more sedate beachfront drink, while Mr Bass Bendula Garden is a good place to enjoy live Premier League football or (later in the evening) live music at weekends.

OTHER PRACTICALITIES

BANKS AND FOREIGN EXCHANGE There are several private **forex bureaux** clustered around the north end of Kofi Annan Road opposite the Cape Point Hotel, and on Atlantic Boulevard opposite the Bakau Craft Market. Local currency can be drawn at the **Standard Chartered** ATM next to the Cape Point Hotel, the ATM outside the **Trust Bank** on the junction of Sait Matty Road and Atlantic Boulevard and at the EcoBank ATM outside the African Village Hotel. Package hotels such as Ocean Bay and Cape Point also have foreign-exchange facilities.

GUIDES If you want an official guide to show you around Bakau or to arrange excursions elsewhere, the local guides association has a kiosk on Kofi Annan Road opposite the Ocean Bay Hotel.

INTERNET If your hotel doesn't offer Wi-Fi or other internet facilities, there are two internet cafés along the back road running northeast from the Total filling station on Sait Matty Road.

SHOPPING For self-caterers, the **central market** in Bakau has a superb selection of fresh fruits and veggies, while the surrounding stalls and small shops stock bread and other locally produced perishables. For imported goods, frozen meat, wines and spirits, and other imported goods, your best bet is the **Right Choice Supermarket** (↖4497156; ◷ 09.00–21.00 daily) next to the market. The **Bakau Craft Market** at the junction of Old Cape Road and Atlantic Boulevard and the **Cape Point Craft Market** behind Mr Bass Bendula Garden both comprise dozens of stalls selling woodcarvings, batik clothes and tablecloths, jewellery and other locally crafted items. Also worth a look, on Atlantic Boulevard a few blocks down from the African Village, is **Agee Jarjou Jemmeh's Batik Shop** (↖4495980) which stocks a wide range of batiks and cloth, including ready-made clothes.

WHAT TO SEE AND DO

The main tourist focal point is the **swimming beach** immediately southeast of Cape Point. If your hotel doesn't offer direct access to this, it can easily be reached along a sandy eastern extension of Atlantic Boulevard north of the Cape Point Hotel. By contrast, the working beach southwest of Cape Point has suffered badly from erosion in recent years, and attempts to reverse its decline have met with limited success, and while swimming is still possible tidally at certain spots, notably below the African Village Hotel, it is wise to ask local advice before you take the plunge. Away from the developed area, a lovely undisturbed beach lined with palms, mangroves and salt marsh runs southeast of the Ocean Bay Hotel and on towards Banjul. Be warned, however, that muggings have been reported from the beach southeast of the Calypso Restaurant, so best not to carry any valuables there, and/ or to walk in a group.

Bakau is a lively, agreeable and often fascinating place to explore on foot, the sporadic attentions of bumsters offering to 'show you the crocodiles' notwithstanding. Well worth a look is the colourful **fresh produce market**, which lies on the landward side of Atlantic Boulevard, and is aimed mainly at locals

---

SACRED CROCODILE POOLS   *By Craig Emms and Linda Barnett*

Three sacred crocodile pools can be found along the Gambian coast. The best-known and most accessible of these is Kachikally in Bakau, but there are also similar pools at Kartong, close to the southern border with Senegal, and at the North Bank village of Berending. People come to these pools from all over The Gambia, even from elsewhere in West Africa, bringing kola nuts for the guardians who will in turn offer up their blessings or prayers. Usually, an elder custodian will bring water from the pool and bless it before the visitors wash in it. The ceremony ends with drumming and dancing, and then the visitor is asked to abstain from unbecoming behaviour. The pools are most often visited by infertile women for curative purposes, but they also attract men wanting to reverse their bad fortune in business or other matters, parents hoping to protect their children during circumcision ceremonies, and wrestlers seeking victory in a competition.

rather than tourists. On the opposite side of the road, easily found by following the fishy smell, a short track curves downhill to the fascinating **Bakau Fishing Centre**, a fishing beach and market that is busiest in the late afternoon but bustles with colourful pirogues and mercantile activity throughout the day. About 1km inland of Atlantic Boulevard, **Bakau Independence Stadium**, built with Chinese assistance in 1983, is the country's premier stage for sporting events and political celebrations, with a capacity of around 30,000.

KACHIKALLY CROCODILE POOL AND MUSEUM
(⏲ *07.00–19.00 daily; a small fee (D50) covers entrance to both the pool & the museum (but you pay extra for an optional guide))* The most popular tourist attraction in Bakau is an ancient freshwater pool situated in the heart of the labyrinthine residential suburb of Kachikally (sometimes spelt Kachikali) about 700m south of Atlantic Boulevard. The pool is under the custody of a chiefly clan called Bojang, whose ancestors reputedly settled in the area around 500 years ago. According to oral tradition, shortly after the Bojang arrived in the area, they were visited by the fertility spirit Kachikally in the form of an apparently distraught elderly woman who pretended that her daughter was drowning in the pool. The family did everything they could to assist Kachikally, who rewarded them by entrusting the pool into their care and asking them to populate it with wildlife. A few weeks later, the family captured and released into the pool a pair of crocodiles which are ancestral to the 80 or so individuals that inhabit it today, and act as intermediaries with the spirit Kachikally. During the rainy season, many of the pool's residents disperse into the surrounding town and countryside, and you hear occasional tales of people waking up to find a young crocodile next to their bed!

Although it is a bit of a tourist trap, the pool is still a popular pilgrimage site for barren women, who come from far and wide to douse themselves in its curative water (any child born after a ritual bathing of this sort is invariably named Kachikally). On a good day you might see more than half-a-dozen crocodiles sunning on the bank, including several 2m-long individuals that are totally habituated to human visitors and even allow themselves to be touched on the back or tail. The largest of these reptilian giants, a 70-year-old 3m-long male named Charlie (reputedly after the first tourist who had the nerve to touch him), seldom makes an appearance these days, though the guides insist he still lives there. The pool itself is often covered in water cabbage, a floating plant that provides shelter for numerous groove-crowned bullfrogs, which form the staple diet of the crocodiles. Be careful close to the water's edge, as crocodiles that seem docile on terra firma might well attack somebody who falls into their watery home.

At the entrance to Kachikally, an informative little museum includes some interesting displays about the history of Bakau and Gambian involvement in World War II. The museum also displays a good collection of African musical instruments, including the harp-like *kora*, a 1.5m-long wooden xylophone, and several tall ceremonial drums, plus a selection of traditional masquerade costumes and masks. The leafy pool grounds also host a surprisingly varied birdlife, with the likes of blue-breasted kingfisher, black-headed paradise flycatcher and yellow-throated leaflove likely to be seen flitting about.

Kachikally Crocodile Pool is poorly signposted, but easily reached from Atlantic Boulevard by following the surfaced Kachikally Road inland from the west side of Bakau Craft Market. Turn left on to a dirt road after about 500m (where Kachikally Road forks sharply to the right) then to the right after another 100m, and you will see the painted entrance in front of you (⊕ *N13 28.627 W16 40.366*). Anyone will

Cape Point is the top locality for one of Africa's most elusive reptiles. This is Armitage's cylindrical skink (*Chalcides armitagei*), which was described by E G Boulenger, the head of reptiles at London Zoo, based on three specimens captured at Cape St Mary by Captain Cecil Armitage during his term as Governor of The Gambia in the 1920s. Unremarkable in appearance, this small skink has transverse stripes across its body, measures up to around 12cm long including its tail, and is one of the few lizards in the region with only three toes on each foot. Neither Boulenger nor Armitage knew anything about the skink's ecology or habitat, and it was long thought to be one of the rarest reptiles in West Africa – indeed, it was not recorded again until 1989, when the Gambian Dwarf Crocodile Project rediscovered it on a narrow belt of coast near Kartong. No further sightings occurred until 2006, when the herpetologists Sébastien and Jean-François Trape collected 13 specimens in the Casamance region of Senegal and another two near the Essoukoudiak River Mouth in Guinea-Bissau. Today, Armitage's cylindrical skink is known from at least ten coastal locales south of the Gambia River Mouth, where it lurks beneath leaf litter and other dead vegetation on dunes and plantations, and the IUCN Red List has downgraded its status from Endangered to Near Threatened.

point you in the right direction, but be warned that any bumster who gets involved in guiding you there will expect a fee.

BAKAU BOTANICAL GARDEN (*Atlantic Bd; ⏱ 09.00–17.00 Mon–Sat; entrance D50*) Established in 1924, this small botanical garden, on the seaward side of Atlantic Boulevard alongside the British High Commissioner's residence, is packed with a wide variety of indigenous and exotic plants, many of which are labelled. A series of winding footpaths, interspersed with benches in shady places, make it a very pleasant place for a morning or afternoon stroll. Considering its small size and urban location, the garden hosts quite a rich birdlife including nesting pairs of hamerkop and a variety of colourful finches and other small passerines.

CAPE CREEK Bisected by the Old Cape Road about 500m south of Bakau, Cape Creek is an extensive saline wetland comprising patches of marsh, mangroves and open water, as well as exposed mud flats at low tide. The area is very good for birds. At low tide, scan the mudflats for waders such as black-winged stilt, Eurasian oystercatcher and common greenshank. It is also worth searching the mud and shrubby vegetation for smaller and more elusive species such as red-billed quelea and various migrant warblers. During the rainy season, you have a good chance of spotting a yellow-crowned bishop performing its strange bumblebee-like display flight in the reedbeds running towards Camaloo Corner (the junction of Atlantic Boulevard and the Banjul–Serekunda Highway).

7

Serekunda, Fajara and Kairaba Avenue

Probably the busiest thoroughfare anywhere on the Gambian coast, the 4km-long Kairaba Avenue connects the inland Westfield Junction (a well-known landmark and transport hub) to the intersection with Atlantic Boulevard 200m from Fajara Beach. Formerly known as Pipeline Road, and still often referred to by that name, Kairaba Avenue was until the early 1970s a rough dirt track flanked for much of its length by working fields and scattered homesteads. Today, it is a wide, straight, built-up and heavily trafficked asphalt road that bisects two substantial but somewhat contrasting settlements: the bustling and chaotic town of Serekunda to the south of the intersection with Bertil Harding Highway, and the leafy coastal residential suburb of Fajara to the north.

Sprawling inland of the coastal resorts, Serekunda is in fact the country's largest and most economically vibrant town, with a population estimated at 350,000, as well as being the most important route crossroads and public transport hub south of the River Gambia. Despite this, it is an oddly amorphous and ill-defined entity. Physically, Serekunda seems to lack clear boundaries, merging almost imperceptibly into the coastal resorts to its northwest and the smaller town of Sukuta to the southwest. Serekunda also lacks a clear political status, often being treated as all-but-synonymous with the Kanifing Municipal Council (a Local Government Area encompassing the entire Greater Banjul Region aside from Banjul Island).

One thing that Serekunda doesn't lack is vitality. Indeed, coming from sedate and orderly Banjul, or from the inherent artificiality of the coastal resorts, Serekunda feels like urban Africa at its most unapologetically raw and energetic. The streets, a seething mass of human enterprise and dodgem traffic, are lined with a hodgepodge of medium-rise office blocks, bright new supermarkets, colonial-era façades and jerry-built tin-roofed homesteads, all crowded together with the absence of design one might expect of a town that has grown enormously, and seemingly without restriction, over the past quarter-century. Everywhere there is noise and colour and movement and crowds of people. And an amazing variety of businesses and shops line the roads: bakeries, metalworkers, welders, car-repair yards, timber merchants, hair salons, spare-part shops ... name it and you can probably find it somewhere in Serekunda.

At the northern end of Kairaba Avenue, past the US Embassy and intersection with Bertil Harding Highway, Serekunda gives way to Fajara, a relatively affluent suburb that runs west from Sait Matty Road to Kotu Stream, along a coastline dominated by low cliffs that slope towards an expansive sandy beach in the west. Fajara, like Serekunda, is not particularly well developed for tourism, boasting only a handful of hotels, but it does house some of the country's finest restaurants, most of them within a block of Kairaba Avenue. Well-known landmarks include the Fajara Military Barracks, the British High Commission, and the Gambian headquarters of

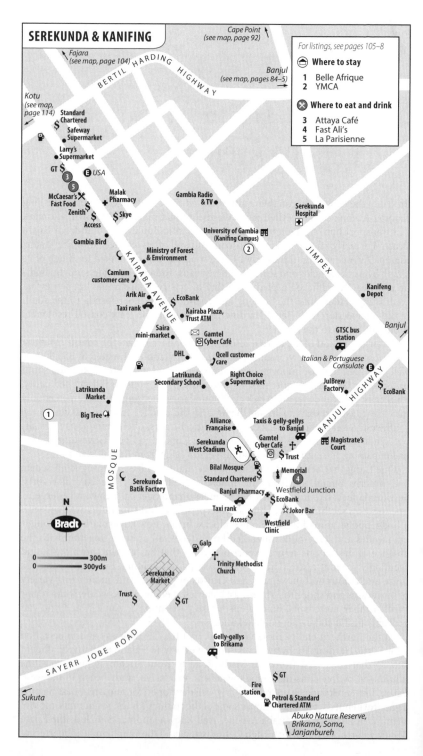

SEREKUNDA & KANIFING

Cape Point
(see map, page 92)

Fajara
(see map, page 104)

BERTIL HARDING HIGHWAY

Banjul
(see map, pages 84–5)

Kotu
(see map, page 114)

Standard
Chartered

Safeway
Supermarket

Larry's
Supermarket

GT

USA

McCaesar's
Fast Food

Zenith

Access

Gambia Bird

Malak
Pharmacy

Skye

Gambia Radio
& TV

Serekunda
Hospital

University of Gambia
(Kanifing Campus)

JIMPEX

Kanifeng
Depot

Ministry of Forest
& Environment

KAIRABA AVENUE

Camium
customer care

Arik Air

Taxi rank

EcoBank

Kairaba Plaza,
Trust ATM

Saira
mini-market

Gamtel
Cyber Café

DHL

Qcell customer
care

GTSC bus
station

Banjul

Italian & Portuguese
Consulate

JulBrew
Factory

EcoBank

Latrikunda
Secondary School

Right Choice
Supermarket

BANJUL HIGHWAY

Latrikunda
Market

Big Tree

Alliance
Française

Taxis & gelly-gellys
to Banjul

Gamtel
Cyber Café

Magistrate's
Court

Serekunda
West Stadium

Trust

MOSQUE

Bilal Mosque

Standard Chartered

Memorial

Serekunda
Batik Factory

Banjul Pharmacy

Westfield Junction

EcoBank

Taxi rank

Jokor Bar

N

Access

Westfield
Clinic

Bradt

0 ————— 300m
0 ————— 300yds

Galp

Trinity Methodist
Church

Serekunda
Market

Trust

GT

Gelly-gellys
to Brikama

SAYERR JOBE ROAD

Sukuta

GT

Fire
station

Petrol & Standard
Chartered ATM

*Abuko Nature Reserve,
Brikama, Soma,
Janjanbureh*

For listings, see pages 105–8

🏠 **Where to stay**

1 Belle Afrique
2 YMCA

✖ **Where to eat and drink**

3 Attaya Café
4 Fast Ali's
5 La Parisienne

the Medical Research Council (a British-funded institution with a high profile in the field of malaria research). The most westerly part of the suburb, bordering Kotu Stream, is given over to the Fajara Club and the 18-hole Fajara Golf Course.

HISTORY

Also spelt Serrekunda, Serekunda is named after Sayerr (or Serre) Jobe, a Wolof marabout who, together with an entourage of relatives and slaves, migrated from the Sine-Saloum region of Senegal to the present-day Gambia in the mid 19th century. Local tradition has it that Sayerr Jobe first settled in the vicinity of Jinack Island, then in Banjul, before relocating to the southern mainland close to the existing village of Sukuta, where he established Serekunda. A successful merchant as well as a respected holy man, Sayerr Jobe is said to have fathered seven sons prior to his death in 1896, when he was buried at Serekunda Cemetery, near what is now the primary school. By the early 1960s, Serekunda had grown to be a small town, but it was only in the post-independence era that it outstripped Banjul as a population and commercial centre, eventually expanding along Kairaba Avenue to merge with Fajara – a posh residential suburb since colonial times – during the economic boom of the 1980s.

ORIENTATION

The four-way intersection at the south end of Kairaba Avenue (✪ N13 26.716 W16 40.486), known as Westfield Junction after a clinic founded there in 1972, is not only the focal point of activity in Serekunda, but also the most important road hub in the whole country. The Banjul–Serekunda Highway runs northeast from Westfield Junction to Banjul. Southeast of Westfield Junction, the Brikama Highway runs past Banjul International Airport and Abuko Nature Reserve to the important junction town of Brikama and the start of the main South Bank Road east to Soma, Janjanbureh and Basse. Southwest of Westfield Junction Sayerr Jobe Road runs right past the covered Serekunda Market, then bisects the inland suburbs of Sukuta and Brusubi, before continuing along the south coast to Brufut, Tanji, Gunjur and Kartong. Then finally there is Kairaba Avenue itself, which runs northwest from Westfield Junction to Fajara, and is flanked by several supermarkets, banks and restaurants, as well as the US Embassy.

GETTING THERE AND AWAY

FAJARA For new arrivals heading to Fajara from Banjul International Airport, it's a drive of around 22km via Serekunda. Taxis between the two officially cost around £15, but you should be able to negotiate a better price. Coming to or from Bakau, a steady flow of shared taxis runs along Atlantic Boulevard between the north end of Kairaba Avenue and Cape Point, and they will pick up passengers anywhere *en route*. A number of shared taxis also run along Kairaba Avenue between Fajara and Serekunda's Westfield Junction (the best place to pick up transport to Banjul), and also the Bertil Harding Highway to Kotu or Kololi (Senegambia Junction) for just D8 per leg.

SEREKUNDA Serekunda is the most important transport hub anywhere on the South Bank, and also the main focal point for public transport around Greater Banjul and along the coast further south.

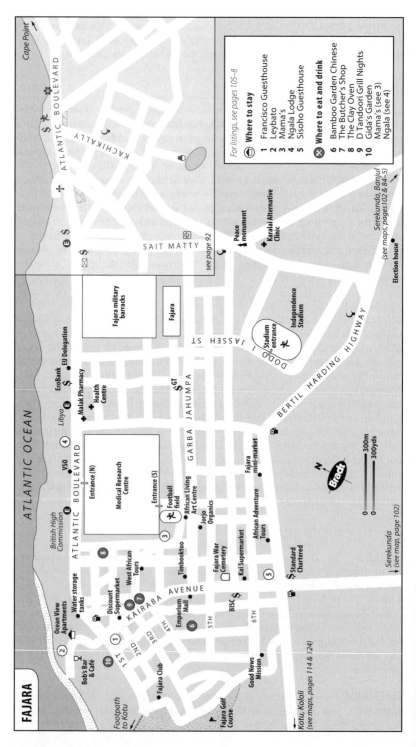

FAJARA

ATLANTIC OCEAN

ATLANTIC BOULEVARD

KACHIKALLY

Cape Point

SAIT MATTY

see page 92

Peace monument

Karalai Alternative Clinic

Fajara military barracks

Fajara

DODO I JASSEH ST

Stadium entrance

Independence Stadium

BERTIL HARDING HIGHWAY

Serekunda, Banjul
(see maps, pages 102 & 84–5)

Election house

EU Delegation

EcoBank

Libya

Malak Pharmacy

Health Centre

GT

GARBA JAHUMPA

Fajara mini-market

VSO

British High Commission

Entrance (N)

Medical Research Centre

Entrance (S)

Football field

African Living Art Centre

Jorjo Organics

African Adventure Tours

Standard Chartered

Serekunda
(see map, page 102)

Ocean View Apartments

Water storage tanks

Discount Supermarket

West African Tours

Timbooktoo

Fajara War Cemetery

Kai Supermarket

KAIRABA AVENUE

Emporium Mall

BISC

Bob's Bar & Café

Fajara Club

Good News Mission

Fajara Golf Course

Footpath to Kotu

Kotu, Kololi
(see maps, pages 114 & 124)

1ST 2ND 3RD 4TH 5TH 6TH

N

0 — 300m
0 — 300yds

Brandt

For listings, see pages 105–8

Where to stay
1 Francisco Guesthouse
2 Leybato
3 Mama's
4 Ngala Lodge
5 Sisoho Guesthouse

Where to eat and drink
6 Bamboo Garden Chinese
7 The Butcher's Shop
8 The Clay Oven
9 D Tandoori Grill Nights
10 Gida's Garden
   Mama's (see 3)
   Ngala (see 4)

AROUND GREATER BANJUL Shared taxis and *gelly-gellys* (private passenger vehicles) to and from Banjul terminate at the southwest end of the Banjul–Serekunda Highway, at a taxi station on the north side of the road close to Westfield Junction (on the Banjul side, they terminate at the station on Rene Blain Street opposite Gamtel House). Public transport to and from the other resorts in Greater Banjul (Fajara, Bakau, Kotu and Kololi) can also be picked up around Westfield Junction, or anywhere along Kairaba Avenue. However, if the prospect of public transport is daunting, or you want to head straight to one of the coastal hotels, it may be easiest just to charter a taxi – they are not expensive and can be found easily at several stands along Kairaba Avenue or in the vicinity of the market.

SOUTH COAST AND BRIKAMA Transport inland to Abuko or Brikama leaves from a small station along Mosque Road about 500m southeast of the junction with Sayerr Jobe Road (✪ *N13 26.133 W16 40.760*). Transport heading to the south-coast towns of Brufut, Tanji, Sanyang, Gunjur and Kartong leaves from Dippa Kunda Taxi Park (✪ *N13 26.032 W16 41.439*), which lies on the north side of Sayerr Jobe Road at Bakoteh Junction (the intersection with Kololi Road) about 1km west of the junction with Mosque Road.

FURTHER AFIELD Situated off Jimpex Road, about 600m northeast of Kairaba Avenue, the recently privatised GTSC's Kanifing Depot (✪ *N13 27.162 W16 40.206*) is the primary departure point for the eight daily GTSC buses that run east along the South Bank Road to Basse via Soma and Janjanbureh. These affordable buses leave roughly once per hour between 06.00 and 12.00, but you are best off trying to catch the express bus, which is only slightly more expensive but a lot faster, and leaves at 08.00 daily. There is no formal system for booking seats in advance, but the GTSC may be prepared to accommodate tourists who want to reserve a seat for the next morning – pop by the office to see what can be done.

If you miss out on the GTSC buses, or opt not to use them, your best bet for gelly-gellys and other transport along the South Bank Road is the hectic main bus station in the town of Brikama, which lies about 23km south of Westfield Junction. Coming from Banjul or Serekunda, you'll find that plenty of shared taxis run back and forth to Brikama all day, leaving Banjul from Rene Blain Road and Serekunda from the south end of Mosque Road. The other place to pick up gelly-gellys and shared taxis upriver is Bundung Taxi Park (✪ *N13 25.126 W16 40.587*), which lies opposite Bundung Police Station 500m northwest of the Brikama Road and 4km south of Westfield Junction. However, while Bundung is significantly closer to Serekunda, it is less convenient to get to than Brikama, and departures inland are less regular.

WHERE TO STAY *Map, page 104, unless otherwise stated*

Accommodation options in Fajara and Serekunda are surprisingly limited, but do include what is arguably the country's premier beachfront boutique hotel in the form of Ngala Lodge, along with a couple of well-established and justifiably popular cheaper options close to Kairaba Avenue, notably the YMCA, which is well positioned for catching public transport upriver from the GTSC bus station.

EXCLUSIVE/LUXURY

✳ 🏠 **Ngala Lodge** (24 suites) 64 Atlantic Bd, Fajara; ☎ 4494045; **e** info@ngalalodge. com; **w** ngalalodge.com. One of the country's most prestigious & luxurious hotels, Ngala Lodge is a sedate, child-free, all-suite retreat set in a converted 1940s ambassadorial residence perched on a low cliff overlooking the beach close to the British High Commission. Each of the suites & semi-suites are individually decorated, but they all share a strong sense of style & fun in the choice of vintage & contemporary artworks from Africa (& further afield), very comfortable furnishings including a king-size bed with walk-in mosquito net, & excellent facilities including AC, fan, minibar & in most cases a private balcony or garden. A separate Manor House comprises 4 suites, a private garden & a sitting area with TV. 6 new Macondo sea-view suites have recently been added, each unique & spacious featuring touches such as private libraries, & 3 have private plunge pools making them among the best rooms in The Gambia. Rooms in the main hotel are centred on the small infinity pool, which leads down to the (exceptional) terrace restaurant, then through lush & shady tropical gardens to the cliff & a short footpath down to a semi-private swimming beach. Other facilities include live music on most nights, free Wi-Fi throughout, an excellent library & book-swap, & excursions to most sites of interest by proper arrangement. The whole experience is enhanced by the dynamic, responsive management & attentive staff. *Book through The Gambia Experience: min 3-night stay £275pp B&B inc transfers.*

MID-RANGE

✳ 🏠 **Leybato Hotel** (19 rooms) Off Atlantic Bd, Fajara; ☎ 4497186; m 9902408; e leybato47@ hotmail.com. Priced at the lower end of this range, this is one of the oldest & best-known establishments in this part of The Gambia, reached along a winding dirt road that extends northward from the junction of Kairaba Av & Atlantic Bd. This sprawling lodge is set among a little oasis of tropical trees & plants at the base of a fairly steep cliff on the eastern verge of Fajara Beach. A popular hangout for expats & volunteers, it has the chilled feel of a superior backpacker hostel, epitomised by the thatched summer huts & hammocks scattered through the shady grounds. The en-suite African-style huts are a bit gloomy inside, but clean enough considering the price, & they come with queen-size bed, net & fan. A restaurant/bar serves inexpensive meals & drinks. Good value. *£25/33 dbl with fan/AC.*

BUDGET

🏠 **Francisco Guesthouse** (11 rooms) Junction of Atlantic Bd & Kairaba Av, Fajara; m 3120519. This long-serving guesthouse lies in small but lushly vegetated grounds only 5 mins' walk from Fajara Beach & is also well positioned for shopping & eating out. Its nicest feature is the jungle-like garden restaurant/bar with large-screen satellite TV. Unfortunately, however, the large carpeted sgl rooms are rather musty & down-at-heel, & seem to have been decorated with a disturbing disregard for aesthetics. Poor value. *From £13 dbl.*

🏠 **Mama's** (8 rooms) 2 blocks east of Kairaba Av, Fajara; ☎ m 7057454; e njies403@yahoo.com; 🔲 mamasrestaurantandguesthousefajara. One of the best & most-established eateries in Fajara now also offers accommodation in cosy, clean, tiled en-suite rooms with dbl bed, fan, satellite TV & hot water. It is a bit of a walk from the beach, but exceptionally good value, with the added advantage of having an excellent restaurant on your doorstep. Volunteering opportunities can be arranged within the local community. *£12pp B&B or £24 for a family room, with AC.*

🏠 **Sisoho Guesthouse** (12 rooms) Kairaba Av, Fajara; ☎ 4497858; m 7700042. Centrally located for eating out, & only 10 mins' walk from the beach, this multi-storey hotel doesn't have too much else going for it, but the clean spacious rooms do come with AC, fan, fridge, TV & hot water. Acceptable. *£15/25 sgl/dbl.*

SHOESTRING

✳ 🏠 **Belle Afrique** [map, page 102] (4 rooms) Kairaba Av; m 07814 366683 (UK, Apr–Oct), 2436456 (Gambia, Nov–Mar); e junbuns@ hotmail.com; 🔲 BelleAfrique13; ⏰ Nov–Apr. Relaxing in the shady garden, it's hard to imagine you are just 15 mins from the heart of Serekunda, with its traffic & lively markets. While not for everyone, this owner-run compound offers a peaceful, relaxed & more authentic experience than that of a resort. The simple rooms have nets, a private veranda & access to a shared bathroom as well as a shared kitchen with cooking facilities, although meals can be arranged for a small extra fee, as can excursions. The owner is also well connected to local musicians & can arrange high-quality lessons for £7–9. *£8 for 1 person, £4 for additional guest sharing the same dbl.*

🏠 **YMCA** [map, page 102] (34 rooms) MDI Rd, Kanifing; 📞 4392647; 📱 3940940/8806451/9824585/2274162; 📧 knmkanteh@ymca.gm or ymca@ymca.gm; 🌐 ymca.gm. Situated around the corner from Serekunda Hospital & about 10 mins' walk north of the GTSC bus station, this clean & well-managed 3-storey hostel is one of the best shoestring–budget options in Greater Banjul. A variety of rooms & small apartments are on offer, all with fan, & substantial discounts are available for longer stays. A restaurant serves meals in the £2–3 range from 09.00 to midnight except Sun. *£7/8.50 sgl/dbl B&B with shared bath.*

🍴 WHERE TO EAT AND DRINK *Map, page 104, unless otherwise stated*

UPMARKET

✳🍴 **Ngala Restaurant** 64 Atlantic Bd; 📞 4496518; 🌐 ngalalodge.com; ⏰ 07.30–10.30 & 12.30–22.00 daily; booking recommended in high season. The small restaurant at Ngala Lodge is one of the most exclusive places to eat in The Gambia, offering the option of sitting in the open-sided interior or on a wide terrace perched on a clifftop overlooking the sea. The emphasis is on seafood, but not exclusively so, & the imaginative fusion menu, prepared by a European chef, is supplemented by several daily specials, depending on the availability of fresh ingredients. Lunch includes a selection of light pasta dishes, while the dinner menu has a strong selection of Thai dishes. The wine list is exceptional too, mostly exclusive to only Ngala, & there is live music most nights. Unlike most other restaurants, there is usually only 1 evening sitting so you can make a whole night of it. *Mains in the £5–8 range (lunch), or £8.50–12 (dinner).*

✳🍴 **Gida's Garden** West of Kairaba Av; 📱 3999756/3709008; 📧 gidas.garden. restaurant@gmail.com; 📘 gidasgarden; ⏰ noon–late Mon–Sat. Popular among expats, this restaurant is set in a side street off Kairaba Av with a relaxed ambience & an emphasis on meat & seafood. There is also a play room for children. *Mains are in the £6–11 range with pasta dishes slightly cheaper at £4–5.*

🍴 **The Butcher's Shop** Kairaba Av; 📞 4495069; 📧 butchers@qanet.gm; 📘 TheButchersShopGambia; ⏰ 08.00–late Mon–Sat. Another perennially popular veteran of the Fajara dining-out scene, this stylish bistro & delicatessen, which opened in 1993, has a varied continental-style menu, with the main emphasis on meat, though vegetarians & fish-eaters will also find plenty to choose from among the salad & pasta dishes. Seating is on a lovely tree-shaded wooden terrace, & it has an excellent wine & dessert menu. *Mains mostly in the £6–8 range.*

🍴 **The Clay Oven** 1 block south of Atlantic Bd; 📞 4496600/4496978; 📱 7973737; 📧 vimal@theclayoven.gm; 🌐 theclayoven.gm; ⏰ noon–15.00 & 19.00–midnight daily. Widely regarded to be the country's best Indian restaurant, the Clay Oven has been under the same hands-on owner-management team since it first opened its doors at Cape Point in 1991. Now situated on a back road in Fajara, it offers garden or AC indoor seating & an extensive menu of oven-baked tandoor dishes & curries, as well as a varied Chinese selection, with sizzler evening on Tue. Vegetarians are well catered for, the bar is well stocked, & there's free Wi-Fi too. *Expect to pay around £6–10 for a main inc rice or naan.*

MID-RANGE

🍴 **Bamboo Garden Chinese Restaurant** 6th Rd, off Kairaba Av; 📞 4494213; 📱 7888312; ⏰ 16.30–23.30 daily. This well-established Chinese restaurant a short walk west of Kairaba Av has a pleasant garden & serves a good range of meat & vegetarian dishes at reasonable prices, as well as excellent king prawns. *Mains with rice around £4–7.*

🍴 **Mama's Restaurant** 2 blocks east of Kairaba Av; 📱 9929606; ⏰ 08.00–midnight Tue–Sun. This long-serving but recently relocated owner-managed restaurant is a favourite among expats for its good down-to-earth food, reasonable prices & relaxed garden ambience, with live music every Thu. The main menu features a cosmopolitan selection of meat, seafood & vegetarian dishes, many with an Italian twist, & there is also an affordable 'menu of the day' (soup & main) available from 11.00 to 18.00. Also worth a mention is the seafood buffet on Fri evenings & roast pork buffet on Sun evenings. Another speciality is fondue, which must be ordered 2–3 days in advance. *The menu of the day costs £4,* *mains are in the £3.50–6.50 range & buffets/ fondues are around £8.50pp.*

BUDGET

✗ **D Tandoori Grill Nights** Kairaba Av; m 3906789. Previously Koko Curry & slightly more downmarket than its predecessor, this Indian focuses on take-away options, serving tandoori wraps & basic curries to go. *Meals in the £2.50–5 range.*

✗ **Fast Ali's** [map, page 102] Westfield Junction; m 9911229. Probably the best of this row of fast-food joints selling Lebanese snacks & pizzas. No alcohol. *Meals in the £2–5 range.*

☕ **Attaya Café** [map, page 102] Kairaba Av; m 7333344; 🅵 attayacafe; ⏲ 08.30–22.00 daily.

Opposite the US Embassy, this little café serves a range of coffees, juices, cakes & sandwiches. There's free Wi-Fi & a book corner with an eclectic selection of Gambian & international novels.

☕ **La Parisienne** [map, page 102] Kairaba Av; m 7660676; ⏲ 07.00–midnight daily. Established in 1996 & occupying a prime location opposite the US Embassy, this excellent café has the choice of indoor seating with blasting AC, or outdoor seating on a wide veranda. A good spot for b/fast or a between-meals snack, it serves a delicious selection of inexpensive pastries, croissants, sandwiches, homemade ice cream & light meals, as well as excellent coffee. It is all very reasonably priced, & there's free Wi-Fi too.

ENTERTAINMENT AND NIGHTLIFE

✴️♀ **Bob's Bar & Cafe** [map, page 104] Off Atlantic Bd; m 9045291/7259047. This locally run bar is on the sandy track leading over a ridge towards the Leybato Hotel & is a fantastic spot to enjoy the local rasta vibes. Enjoy a cold beer in the brightly painted roundhouse or the small garden courtyard while listening to reggae. Bob can rustle up meals on demand & can also organise drumming lessons. He's also a skilled hat maker, & displays his wares around the bar.

☆ **Jokor Bar** [map, page 106] Westfield Junction; ☏ 4375690; m 7713091. Primarily a nightclub & occasional live music venue, this Serekunda institution, on the south side of Westfield Junction, also serves decent inexpensive food in the courtyard garden. The nightlife doesn't really get going until around 23.00, so it is normally quiet in the early evening.

OTHER PRACTICALITIES

BANKING AND FOREIGN EXCHANGE Serekunda is serviced by the largest concentration of banks in the country. These include branches of **Standard Chartered Bank**, **Access Bank** and **EcoBank** on Kairaba Avenue, as well as an EcoBank on the Banjul–Serekunda Highway opposite the JulBrew Factory, and a **Trust Bank** on Mosque Road opposite Serekunda Market. All these banks have ATMs, and there is also a standalone Standard Chartered ATM at the filling station about 1km along the Brikama Road.

If you are staying in **Fajara**, the closest banks with an ATM, depending on exactly where you are, would be the **Standard Chartered Bank** at the junction of Kairaba Avenue and Bertil Harding Highway, or the **EcoBank** on Atlantic Boulevard about 300m east of Ngala Lodge. For private foreign-exchange facilities, there are a few **forex bureaux** around Serekunda Market, but this is quite a busy area so you're better off changing large sums at one of the **forex bureaux** in Kololi, Kotu or central Banjul.

INTERNET The **Gamtel Cyber Café** about halfway along Kairaba Avenue is probably the best in the country, charging around D20 per hour for use of one of the ten computers. In addition to keeping long hours (⏲ *07.00–22.00 daily*), it also has air conditioning and a fast connection. A second Gamtel Cyber Café, almost as good, can be found at the south end of Kairaba Avenue just before Westfield Junction.

There are other cyber cafés but they are mostly slower and smaller. There's also free Wi-Fi if you eat or drink at the La Parisienne or Attaya Café.

MEDICAL Though not exactly operating to Western standards, the **Westfield Clinic** (*Westfield Junction*; ☎ *4392213/4393523*) is one of the best equipped in the country. The well-regarded **Malak Pharmacy** (*Kairaba Av*; ☎ *4376087*; m *7700719*; e *malakpharm@hotmail.com*; ⊕ *08.30–midnight daily*) near the US Embassy is the closest thing in the country to a 24-hour pharmacy.

SHOPPING In addition to the chaotic but compelling **Serekunda Market**, Serekunda is endowed with many good supermarkets, most of them concentrated along the north end of Kairaba Avenue near the US Embassy and Fajara. Perhaps the best stocked is the **Safeway Supermarket**, which also keeps quite long opening hours (⊕ *09.00–20.00 Mon–Sat, 10.00–20.00 Sun*). One shop that warrants a special mention is:

Timbooktoo Garba Jahumpa Rd; ☎ 4494345/6; e timbooktoo@qanet.gm; w timbooktoo.co.uk; ⊕ 10.00–19.00 Mon–Fri (closed 13.00–15.00 on Fri), 10.00–20.00 Sat; see ad, page 112. Far & away the best bookshop in The Gambia, Timbooktoo spreads across 2 storeys & stocks an excellent range of reference books about the country (& West Africa in general), as well as current & classic English-language fiction, popular non-fiction, textbooks, guidebooks, field guides, maps, newspapers & local/world music CDs. It also has a selection of secondhand novels.

WHAT TO SEE AND DO

FAJARA BEACH Fajara feels more suburban than resort-like, and most of its coastline is hemmed in by low cliffs and cut off from public access by private properties. The main exception is in the far west, where the cliffs give way to the open swathes of sand that comprise the popular Fajara and Kotu beaches. This lovely beach can be accessed either by following the footpath to Kotu that runs along the northern boundary of the golf course and Fajara Waterfront (a massive residential development that was under construction in 2017), or else by taking the dirt road that runs from the north end of Kairaba Avenue to the Leybato Hotel.

FAJARA CLUB (✪ *N13 28.013 W16 41.847*; m *7053821*; e *baxnja@yahoo.com*; 🅵 *TheFajaraClub*; ⊕ *08.00–sunset daily*) An offshoot of the colonial Bathurst Club, established in the 1930s and originally housed in what is now the National Museum, the Fajara Club was renamed and relocated to its present-day location between Kairaba Avenue and Kotu Stream at some point in the mid 1970s. Its main point of interest is the 18-hole par-69 golf course, which opened in 1973 to replace an older course at Denton Bridge near to Banjul. An unusual feature of the course, attributed to the sandy soil on which it stands, and the seasonally dry climate, is that instead of the usual greens, it has 'browns' which need to be tidied up by brown-sweepers between games. Other facilities include a swimming pool, tennis and squash courts, full-size billiards table, a reasonably priced restaurant serving decent pub grub, and a lively bar dominated by a large-screen TV that draws big crowds for major international sporting events.

The Fajara Golf Course is also renowned as a very good birding spot. There is a range of habitats from open areas to coastal scrub and a few tangled patches of woodland. The course also lies alongside part of Kotu Stream and holds lots of different birds, with black-headed plover and wattled plover on the open areas,

Senegal coucal and African silverbill among the scrub, and pearl-spotted owlet in the taller trees. The black-shouldered kite is one of several birds of prey sometimes seen flying over the course.

The Fajara Club is a members-only institution, but visitors are welcome to take out temporary membership. For golfers, this works out at £30 per person per round, inclusive of green fee, club hire, balls, caddy, brown-sweeper and mat, with a discount if you have your own clubs. Note that a quite strict golfing dress code is maintained: no denim, and all shirts must have a collar and sleeves. For other facilities, you are looking at around £3.50 per person per day for use of any of the following: swimming pool, tennis or squash courts, or billiards table. Access to the bar and restaurant costs around £1.50, though it is included in all the above fees.

FAJARA WAR CEMETERY Maintained by the Commonwealth War Graves Commission (w *cwgc.org*), this military cemetery on the east side of Kairaba Avenue contains the graves of 203 soldiers, mostly Gambian and British in origin, who died in combat in World War II, when Banjul (then Bathurst) was an important Allied naval base. In keeping with the racist attitudes that informed European colonialism, the graves are segregated into clusters, some exclusively for soldiers of indigenous Gambian origin, others reserved for combatants of European descent. All but four of the combatants are identified by name, and there are ten non-war service burials and three war graves of non-Commonwealth nationalities. The cemetery also contains the Royal West African Frontier Forces (RWAFF) Memorial Tablet, which commemorates another 33 Gambians who died in service but whose last resting place is either unknown or cannot be maintained.

AFRICAN LIVING ART CENTRE (*Garba Jahumpa Rd;* m *7066607/7449090;* ☺ *noon–18.00 daily; entrance free*) Owned and managed by an extraordinary Gambian hairstylist and beautician who learned his craft in the fashion and beauty houses of New York, the African Living Art Centre is an eclectic and idiosyncratic set-up that operates primarily as an upmarket salon and 'beauty sanctuary' specialising in hairdressing, massage, chiropractic treatments, manicures, pedicures, facials, bodywork, makeovers, bridals and wedding planning. It also incorporates an art gallery, where textiles, masks, beads and statues can be bought, and occasional exhibitions are regularly held. The highly rated restaurant and bar, which specialises in international fusion cuisine, was closed at the time of writing but was due to reopen sometime in 2017, and the management still offers private catering and florist services by prior arrangement.

SEREKUNDA MARKET If you want a taste of unadorned modern-day Africa, try a visit to Serekunda Market, on the corner of Sayerr Jobe and Mosque roads. This is a hive of activity and you can buy anything from traditional African clothes to Western platform shoes, from rolls of sticky tape to music CDs or cassettes, or from traditional medicines to gleaming new imported tools. It is crowded and noisy and sometimes smelly (especially near the stalls that sell spice), so it can be a real culture shock to Westerners used to pushing a shopping trolley along sanitised aisles in a spotlessly clean supermarket. This is a good safe place to meet ordinary Gambians and see what their world is really like, but do keep your valuables tucked away and a wary eye open for pickpockets. If you are at all nervous about visiting the market, take an official guide or a Gambian friend with you. They'll look out for you and show you around.

THE 'BIG TREE' AND SEREKUNDA BATIK FACTORY Situated close to each other along Mosque Road in the area known as Dippa Kunda, these two attractions are well worth combining with a visit to the nearby Serekunda Market. The more

PAPER RECYCLING SKILLS PROJECT   *By George Riegg, General Manager*

Established in 2001 as the first paper mill in The Gambia, the Paper Recycling Skills Project (PRSP) (m *7707090/7748058;* e *icecool@qanet.gm;* PaperRecyclingGambia) is a registered non-profit organisation based in Fajikunda, about 3km south of Westfield Junction off the Brikama Road. In its early days, the PRSP introduced the traditional craft of papermaking to The Gambia, allowing it to recycle used paper and other waste materials into handcrafted value-added products. All profits from the sale of the various products were invested into supporting education either by distributing free learning materials to needy students (over 45,000 exercise books plus pens, pencils and reading books) or by providing training and teaching assistance in environmental-awareness building through lectures, workshops and community outreach programmes.

After moving to the PRSP Craft Village compound in Fajikunda in 2007, the organisation developed new programmes to expand its positive impact on the environment and in the community. It developed a technique to turn freely available waste materials (such as paper, grasses, leaves, sawdust and other biomass) into fuel briquettes to be used for cooking instead of firewood or charcoal. It has also helped develop a cleaner-burning fuel-efficient domestic stove which can use the briquettes (as well as wood and charcoal), saving the user up to two-thirds of normal fuel expenditure. These initiatives are creating economic and health benefits for the community, while the reduced need for wood and charcoal saves many trees in a country with an ever-depleting forest cover. An 18-month project during 2011/12 firmly established PRSP as the country's foremost 'Biomass Recycling Research and Training Centre', and it now trains community groups to replicate the technology elsewhere in the country.

Since 2012, the PRSP compound has been turned into a 'walk-the-talk' showpiece for sustainable living and a balanced ecosystem, demonstrating that living in harmony with the environment brings many benefits. More than 80 trees representing 30-plus species have been planted alongside 60 other types of plants (flowers, shrubs, herbs and vegetables) to create a diverse mini ecosystem using permaculture techniques. Recycled tyres, old bricks and other waste materials have been used for the hard landscaping. Compost toilets provide nutrition for the plants and reduce waste. Grey water is used for the gardens, and a small solar installation provides electricity. A tree nursery has been established to provide seedlings of fruit-bearing trees free to the community.

The Craft Village also is home to the 'Greenie' movement, which links together environmental initiatives in schools and communities with various private, corporate and institutional partners. The 'Greenie' mascot is a little doll used to promote environmental activities understandably through media such as school books, posters, leaflets and training guides. Environmental awareness is a complex issue, and by personalising it 'Greenie' helps to communicate positive messages to children and adults alike. True to the 'Greenie' motto 'together we CAN do it', the PRSP team warmly welcomes visitors interested in real sustainable community action.

interesting for craft hunters is the batik factory (\ 4392258), started by the late Mussu Kebba Drammeh, where you can see the tie-dye process in action, from the design, waxing and boiling to the finished product, and also buy batiks at source. To get there from the direction of the market, follow Mosque Road north for around 1km, then turn to the right, and you should see it on the right side of the road behind a woodcarving factory. If in doubt, ask directions, as the place is well known locally, or call for directions as you get close. Far more easily located is the 'Big Tree', a massive silk cotton tree on the west side of Mosque Road about 500m past the batik factory next to Latrikunda Market.

ALLIANCE FRANÇAISE (*Kairaba Av;* \ *4375418;* e *info@afbanjul.org;* w *afbanjul. org;* ◼ *AllianceFrancaiseBanjul*) Serekunda's Alliance Française de Banjul is a French cultural centre whose primary purpose is to hold French classes, exhibitions and shows. Its website is a good place to check out not only what is happening at the centre itself, but also what's happening culturally in the rest of the country.

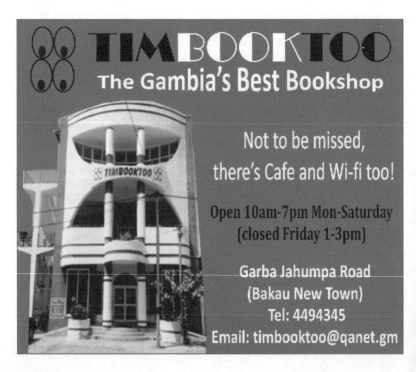

8

Kotu and Palma Rima

Ranking second only to nearby Kololi as the most developed resort area along the Gambian coast, Kotu lies on a wide sandy beach that runs southwest from Fajara for about 2km. The area is bisected by and named after Kotu Stream, a small mangrove-lined waterway which, despite its relatively small catchment area of around 60km^2, can lay claim to being the busiest birdwatching site in the country. Indeed, Kotu Bridge, which crosses the stream about 400m upriver of its mouth, and whose north bank houses the official Gambia Bird Guides Association kiosk, has become such a popular rendezvous for avitourists that on a busy day it can look a bit like a binocular salesmen's convention!

Although Kotu is a popular and recommended base for birdwatchers, the area is also well suited to more conventional beach tourism, being rather more hassle-free than its counterpart at Kololi, and endowed with several good package hotels, as well as dozens of restaurants, beach bars and other tourist facilities. The main cluster of development, generally referred to as Kotu, flanks a short strip of surfaced road that runs from the north bank of Kotu Stream to Kotu Beach. About 1.5km west of the stream lies a secondary cluster of developments generally known as Palma Rima (after the well-known resort hotel that lies at the junction with the Bertil Harding Highway). These two built-up areas are separated from each other by a largely uninhabited area of coastal marsh that runs west from Kotu Stream and can be explored from the pedestrian-friendly 1km Kotu Cycle Path.

GETTING THERE AND AWAY

Coming directly from Banjul International Airport, it's a drive of around 22km to Kotu via Yundum and Sukuta. The official charge for taxis is around £15, but you may be able to negotiate a better price.

Heading to Fajara or Bakau, the easiest option (at least from Kotu itself) is to walk along the footpath that runs uphill from the east of the beach to the cul-de-sac at the west of Atlantic Boulevard, from where a steady flow of shared taxis runs past the north end of Kairaba Avenue to Cape Point.

The most direct connection between Kotu and Palma Rima is the Kotu Cycle Path, which can be walked in about 10–15 minutes. To travel between them by car, you need to head back south to the Bertil Harding Highway, a drive of around 4km.

Kotu lies about 16km west of Banjul via the Banjul–Serekunda Highway and Bertil Harding Highway. Catch one of the regular bush taxis to Kololi (Senegambia) that leave Banjul from the station on Rene Blain Street opposite Gamtel House, ask to be dropped at Kotu Police Station (for Kotu) or Palma Rima, then walk or catch a taxi.

Taxis to pretty much anywhere you want can be picked up on the main strip through Kotu, where the main taxi stand is tucked away opposite the Bungalow

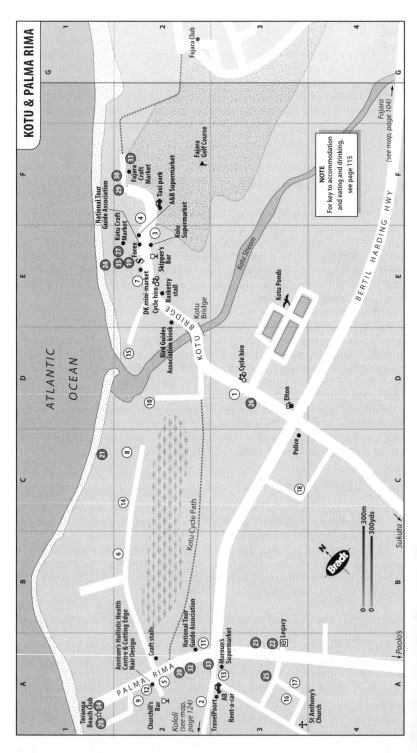

KOTU & PALMA RIMA

ATLANTIC OCEAN

PALMA RIMA

Teranga Beach Club

Churchill's Bar

Anntom's Hollistic Health Centre & Cutting Edge Hair Design

Craft stalls

National Tour Guide Association

Kololi
(see map, page 124)

TravelPoort

A&B Rent-a-car

Maroun's Supermarket

Legacy

St Anthony's Church

National Tour Guide Association

Kotu Craft Market

Forex

DK mini-market

Cycle hire

Basketry stall

Bird Guides Association kiosk

KOTU BRIDGE

Kotu Bridge

Skipper's Bar

Kolu Supermarket

A&B Supermarket

Taxi park

Fajara Craft Market

Fajara Golf Course

Fajara Club

Cycle hire

Elton

Police

Kotu Stream

Kotu Ponds

BERTIL HARDING HWY

Kotu Cycle Path

→ Fajara
(see map, page 104)

Paolo's

Sukuta →

NOTE
For key to accommodation and eating and drinking, see page 115

N
Bradt

0 — 300m
0 — 300yds

Beach Hotel. However, since they are official tourist taxis, they tend to be quite expensive. A cheaper option is to walk up to the junction with Bertil Harding Highway and pick up a shared or private taxi there.

↑ WHERE TO STAY

UPMARKET

⌂ **Flourish Wellness Resort** [114 B2] (40 rooms) Kotu Beach; ✆ 4464704; e info@ flourishresorts.com. This Nigerian-run resort consists of attractive bright green 2-storey European-style houses based around a large lagoon pool, set back a short distance from the beach. The resort is run as a haven of tranquillity with an Ayurveda spa, yoga, meditation, hydrotherapy, massage, natural body treatments, anti-ageing programmes and nutritional analysis. In addition, there are lawn tennis courts, beach volleyball, child-care facilities, a children's playground & Wi-Fi throughout. The rooms are well equipped with modern facilities including AC & hot water, although are slightly characterless. There are 4 bars & the restaurant serves excellent European & African dishes. *Suites are priced according to location: from £60/75 sgl/dbl to £140/165 sgl/dbl on the beach, all rates B&B.*

⌂ **Kombo Beach Hotel** [114 E2] (258 rooms) Kotu Beach; ✆ 4465466–8; e info@ kombobeachhotel.gm; w www.kombobeachhotel. gm. The largest, busiest & smartest of the package hotels in Kotu, Kombo Beach can come across as a little impersonal, which is understandable given its size, but it has a great beachfront location, good service & a vast swimming pool, beach bar, Wi-Fi (at a cost), clinic, gift shop, good spa & salon, well-stocked book swap, & sports such as table tennis, tennis, volleyball, billiards, darts, archery & an outdoor gym. The en-suite rooms all come with fan or AC, satellite TV, fridge, hot shower or tub & balcony or terrace. It also provides a busy entertainment programme & plenty of good in-house dining options, though the location also lends itself to culinary exploration further afield. *From £60/80 standard sgl/dbl, £75/90 sgl/dbl with AC, £85/105 superior sgl/dbl, £95/115 premium sgl/ dbl, all rates B&B.*

MID-RANGE

❋ ⌂ **Luigi's Apartments** [114 A2] (33 rooms) Palma Rima Rd; m 9908218; e info@ luigis.gm; w luigis.gm. Situated in Palma Rima 200m from the beach, this smart & reasonably priced owner-managed lodge is justifiably one of the most popular in The Gambia. A variety of spacious & immaculately clean en-suite rooms & apts is available, all with stylish modern furniture, funky décor, AC, free Wi-Fi, flatscreen TV & DVD player, room safe & tea/coffee. Self-catering apts also have private balconies & a well-equipped kitchen. The courtyard swimming pool area has deckchairs (but is rather lacking in shade or character) & 24hr electricity is supplied by a generator. A hidden garden around the back contains an attractive lily pond hosting geese & peacocks. There's also an excellent Italian restaurant (page 118) on the ground floor, & plenty of other good eating options within easy walking distance. *From £25/40 standard sgl/dbl B&B, from £55 dbl suites & self-catering apts. Weekly rates are slightly cheaper.*

✳ 🏠 **Sand Beach Holiday Resort** [114 C2] (30 rooms) Point Zone Kotu; ☎ 4464734; e infosbhrgambia@gmail.com. This new resort is about 500m along the road from Palma Rima towards Kotu. Attractive, brightly coloured houses surround a large pool set back a short distance from the beach, & although the space is quite wide & open, trees have been planted & shaded sun loungers are available. The bar/restaurant is in a uniquely shaped thatched *bantaba* & there is also a spa, resident doctor, hair salon & business centre. Each room has an en-suite wet room, AC & modern facilities including satellite TV, Wi-Fi & a fridge. *Good value, with prices starting from €35 for a standard dbl through to €100 for a dbl bungalow, all rates B&B.*

🏠 **Bakotu Hotel** [114 E2] (88 rooms) Kotu Stream Rd; ☎ 4465555; e bookings@bakotuhotel.com; w bakotuhotel.com. This medium-sized family-run hotel on the landward side of the main strip is perhaps the best of the cheaper package options in Kotu. It has also long been a popular choice with birdwatchers thanks to its leafy gardens & short nature walk leading to a well-positioned private viewing platform overlooking Kotu Stream. It is only a couple of mins' walk from Kotu Beach, & has an agreeable swimming-pool area with sun terrace. The en-suite rooms are simply but tastefully furnished, although facilities such as safe, fridge, fan & AC are by request only. A more recent addition is the separate annex of apts, complete with en-suite bathrooms, kitchenette, living area & private terrace overlooking the Kotu Stream. Other facilities include an on-site mini market, 2 good restaurants, a bar & evening entertainment. *Rates on application, but between £25 & £65 depending on room & length of stay.*

🏠 **Bungalow Beach Hotel** [114 F2] (110 rooms) Kotu Stream Rd; ☎ 4465288/4465623; e info@bbhotel.gm. Set in large gardens in the heart of Kotu, this is one of the better & more popular package hotels, although rather institutional in appearance & feeling slightly rundown, but with a great beachfront location & good facilities including a swimming pool, children's pool, playgrounds, beach bar, restaurant, souvenir shop, spa, cyber café, mini market & evening entertainment (in winter but not summer). The large en-suite apts are laid out in characterless 2-storey blocks & come with twin or dbl bed, kitchenette, fridge & private balcony. *£25 for standard dbl or £50 for a dbl apt.*

🏠 **Calabash Residence** [114 A2] (15 rooms) Palma Rima Rd; ☎ 4462293; m 7776600; e info@calabashresidence.gm; w calabashresidence.gm. Located a few doors up from Luigi's, this agreeable complex offers accommodation in modern spacious studios or 1- or 2-bedroom apts distinguished by their warm earth colours & above-average facilities. Each bedroom is en suite with combined tub/shower & queen-size or dbl bed, & the 1-bedroom apts also have a large open-plan sitting area with satellite TV & well-equipped kitchen. There's AC & free Wi-Fi throughout the apts, the good Terrace Bar & Restaurant (page 120) downstairs, & plenty of other decent eateries close by. The swimming pool is in a pretty tropical garden with attractive thatched umbrellas & palm trees to provide shade. *£45 dbl studio, £60/85 1-/2-bedroom apt.*

🏠 **Palma Rima Hotel** [114 A2] (170 rooms) Palma Rima Rd; ☎ 4463380/1; e smartlinepalmarimahotel@hotmail.com; w palmarimahotel.com. Large, impersonal & difficult to love, this stalwart hotel on the junction of Bertil Harding Highway & Palma Rima Rd does have a few redeeming features – in particular the sprawling palm-strewn grounds, centred on what is reputedly the largest pool in the country – but the distance from the beach & rather rundown feel all count against it. The standard accommodation, set in institutional 3-storey blocks, is quite musty & has no AC. Far better are the sgl-storey bungalow rooms with large, airy whitewashed interiors with optional AC, satellite TV, cane & bamboo furnishing, & private balcony. *£30/40 sgl/dbl standard room, £35/50 sgl/dbl bungalow, all rates B&B.*

🏠 **Riyan Apartments** [114 A3] (19 rooms) Bertil Harding Highway; ✆ 4463734; e riyanapartments@gmail.com. Though it isn't very convenient for the beach, this apt complex on the junction of Palma Rima Rd seems like a pretty classy set-up, centred on a courtyard swimming pool shaded by palms with bar. The spacious & modern apts all come with a proper kitchen, a comfortable sitting area with satellite TV, dark-wood furnishing, private balcony, & 1 or 2 bedrooms with twin or dbl beds & nets. AC runs on a metering system that might set you back around £3 daily. *€38/65 sgl/dbl, with attractive discounts for low season or longer stays.*

🏠 **Sunset Beach Hotel** [114 D2] (97 rooms) Kotu Stream Rd; ✆ 4463876/4466397; e info@ sunsetbeachhotel.gm; w sunsetbeachhotel.gm. This friendly, unpretentious & well-managed package hotel combines an attractive beachfront location on the east shore of Kotu Stream Mouth with good facilities including a pleasant swimming-pool area, free Wi-Fi, mini market, beauty salon & live music most nights. The spacious standard rooms come with twin/dbl bed & have tiled floor, bright modern décor, AC, satellite TV & en-suite hot shower. Junior suites also have a sitting area & kitchen. One of the better-value options in this range; however, beach erosion is becoming a problem & access to the beach now requires a walk across a sandbag bridge. *£43/53/72 for sgl/dbl/trpl with AC, £53/67/90 for sgl/dbl/trpl suite, all rates B&B. Good low-season discounts available.*

🏠 **Wavecrest Apartments** [114 C3] (8 apts) ✆ 4406979; e wavecrest@gamnet.gm; w wavecrest-gambia.com. Although set away from the beach, these bright, fully serviced apts offer some of the best self-catering accommodation in The Gambia. The 1- & 2-bed apts come with AC, Wi-Fi, LCD TV, king-size bed & fully equipped kitchen, & the rooftop restaurant, serving European & African dishes, is a pleasant spot to enjoy a cold drink at sunset. *£40/47 dbl room only/B&B, with discounts in low season.*

BUDGET

✳ 🏠 **Kunta Kinteh Apartments** [114 C2] (21 bungalows) m 7791278/3992964; e info@ kuntakinteh.com; w kuntakinteh.com. Accessed via a 1km dirt track running east from Palma Rima Rd opposite Luigi's, this complex next to the beach

restaurant of the same name offers self-catering accommodation in 2-bedroom bungalows scattered along the beach immediately west of the Kotu Mouth. All apts come with dbl beds, well-equipped kitchens, sitting rooms with satellite TV, clean bathrooms & private balcony. There's free Wi-Fi & if you choose not to self-cater you can eat at the neighbouring beach restaurant (page 119). There is a hair salon that also offers beauty treatments, a craft shop & a tailor that can knock up local attire. Several sports such as football, beach volleyball & fishing can be organised. It mainly deals in stays of a week or more, but will also do short stays if apts are available; either way it ranks as one of the best deals along the coast. *£250/week up to 2 people & an extra £50pp thereafter. Extra £35/week charge for AC. Price inc airport transfers if required.*

🏠 **Badala Park Hotel** [114 D3] (202 rooms) Kotu Stream Rd; ✆ 4460400/1; e badalaparkhotel@gmail.com; w badalaparkhotel.com. Another hotel best approached with muted expectations, Badala Park lacks a beachfront location & the dbl-storey blocks feel even more cramped & rundown than the Palm Beach. The rooms are quite gloomy & musty, & look like they were furnished by a decorator who learned their trade in a 1950s British boarding house. More alluring facilities include a large swimming pool with children's area amid a garden with a nice jungle feel, bar, snack bar, restaurants, shop & satellite TV in a public area. Local entertainment is laid on most evenings during the tourist season. *£26/35 sgl/dbl with fan, £36/45 sgl/ dbl with AC, all rates B&B.*

🏠 **Bakadaji Hotel** [114 A2] (17 rooms) Bertil Harding Highway; m 7441888; e bakadaji@gamtel.gm or kawsun@yahoo. com. Situated on the north side of Palma Rima Junction, 5 mins' walk from the beach through the back gate, this place appeals to wildlife enthusiasts on a budget because of the leafy grounds teeming with monkeys & birds. Less inspiring is the timeworn accommodation, which consists of a block of dbl rooms with fan & fridge, or freestanding bungalows with 2 dbl bedrooms, kitchens & a sitting area. There is also an inexpensive on-site restaurant & bar. Still, it's fair value. *£16.50 dbl, £25 for bungalow sleeping up to 4, all rates B&B.*

🏠 **Palm Beach Hotel** [114 D2] (160 rooms) Off Kotu Stream Rd; m 2211938;

e palmbeachhotel@hotmail.com;
w palmbeachgambia.com. About the cheapest package hotel on this part of the coast, the Palm Beach has in its favour a wonderful isolated beachfront location on the west bank of the Kotu Stream Mouth, & the en-suite rooms with satellite TV, wooden furnishings & AC are very reasonably priced. It is rather more difficult to enthuse about the tacky décor & rather rundown & cramped feel of the dbl-storey blocks, unless you are a fan of concrete dolphin statues. Facilities include a restaurant, swimming-pool area & beach seating. With realistic expectations, it seems pretty good value. *£26.50/29.50/39 standard sgl/dbl/trpl, sea-views rooms from £45, all rates B&B.*

SHOESTRING

🏠 **Teranga Suites** [114 A3] (18 rooms/ 8 apts) ☎ 4461961; m 7337048; e terangasuites@ gmail.com; w terangasuites.com. Set in the backroads south of Palma Rima Junction, about 1km from the beach, this owner-managed dbl-storey lodge offers accommodation in clean en-suite rooms with fan & AC, although the place is starting to look a little rundown. Facilities include a swimming pool & bar, & there are plenty of restaurants within easy walking distance. They also own a block of 8 apts just around the corner, behind the Teranga restaurant, which is in better condition. Apts have kitchen, living room, hot water, TV & AC. Fairly good value. *£12/15/25 sgl/ dbl/trpl rooms, £15 apts.*

🏠 **Timbuktu Guesthouse** [114 A3] (14 rooms) ☎ 4464314; m 2505295; e tumbuktuu_1@yahoo.com. Situated in the backstreets opposite Teranga Suites, this is a good-value dbl-storey guesthouse offering accommodation in en-suite dbl rooms with satellite TV, Wi-Fi, fridge, hot water & use of shared kitchen. *£12/17 dbl with fan/AC.*

✖ WHERE TO EAT AND DRINK

There are dozens of eateries dotted around Kotu and Palma Rima, and most of the hotels also have restaurants. The following is a selective mix of well-established favourites and some interesting new places.

UPMARKET

✱✖ **Barista Beach Bar** [114 C1] m 7537916; f baristabeach; ⊕ 08.00–midnight daily. Possibly one of the loveliest of the many beach bars & restaurants along the coast between Cape Point & Brufut, this Dutch-owned place is like a little slice of quirky Europe on a quiet stretch of white sandy beach. 4-poster beds draped with linens & with thatched roofs provide rest points for beach lovers, while a whitewashed bright & breezy restaurant, complete with a stand-up piano & other odds & ends serves European favourites, seafood, steaks & Gambian dishes. There is a massage studio attached & a BBQ every Fri. *Meals in the £5–8 range, BBQ £8.50.*

✱✖ **Luigi's Pizza & Pasta House** [114 A2] Palma Rima Rd; m 7102102/8905055; w luigis. gm; ⊕ 08.00–16.00 & 18.00–23.30 daily. With its airy high-ceilinged interior & pleasant terrace, this genuine Italian restaurant is something of a Gambian institution, & widely regarded to serve the best pizzas around, along with various pasta & seafood dishes, & cheaper salads & baked potatoes with toppings. It has a fully stocked bar

& also serves killer coffee. *Most mains are in the £5–6 range.*

✱✖ **Samba's Kitchen** [114 A2] Palma Rima Rd; m 9884620/7139744; e samba.trawally@gmail. com; ⊕ 09.00–23.45 daily. Under joint British–Gambian owner-management, this restaurant at the south end of Palma Rima Rd receives plenty of good feedback. It's a multi-faceted set-up with relaxed outdoor seating on the terrace or in the courtyard, a more formal indoor dining area, & a separate sports bar with large-screen TVs, pool tables & darts. The award-winning Gambian chef is something of a celebrity & the well-crafted menu includes a varied selection of attractively presented meat & seafood dishes, as well as salads, sandwiches & other light meals. It caters for vegetarians & vegans, & will also cook fishermen's catches by request. Live music on Fri nights & all-you-can-eat buffet roast Sun lunch. *Mains in the £7.50–9 range, Sun buffet £7.50.*

✖ **Come Inn** [114 A3] Kololi Rd; m 7049210; f ComeInnGambia; ⊕ 10.00–02.00. Just opposite the Palma Rima Junction, this would be the pick of the several bars & restaurants around this area for ambience. Fenced off from the road, a path leads through a shady tropical garden into an attractive seating area with a thatched bar. Wi-Fi is available as well as the usual menu, albeit at slightly higher prices. *Most mains £6–10.*

✗ JD's Bar and Restaurant [114 D3] Kotu Stream Rd; **m** 7993430; **e** Sgreggans@aol.com; ⏱ Nov–Feb 08.00–02.00 daily. Set in large leafy gardens close to the junction with Bertil Harding Highway, this lively bar & restaurant has a great sound system with regular live music, large screen for Premier League football & other major sports events & plenty of outdoor seating. The speciality is Brazilian steak served in a variety of styles, but it is also very good for seafood. *Most mains are in the £5–7 range.*

✗ Shiraz Restaurant [114 A2] Palma Rima Rd; **m** 7670000/7700010; ⏱ 09.00–late daily in season, 19.00–23.00 out of season. Situated close to the junction with Bertil Harding Highway, this is one of the country's top Lebanese restaurants, with indoor & outdoor seating, & a tasty selection of Mediterranean-style grills, shawarmas & mezze dishes. Unlike many Lebanese restaurants, alcohol is served. *Mains around £6–8, though cheaper snacks are also available.*

MID-RANGE

✻✗ Kunta Kinteh Beach Restaurant [114 C2] **m** 9901283/9907294; **w** kuntakinteh.com; ⏱ 08.30–midnight daily. Boasting a great beachfront location in the shade of a grove of coconut trees along a dirt road running east from Palma Rima Rd, this popular place offers the option of sitting indoors or on an umbrella-shaded terrace. The à la carte menu is dominated by seafood, steak & chicken dishes in a variety of international styles, & it also does a beach BBQ buffet on Sun. It also has free sun loungers, plus entertainment on Tue, including acrobats & fire eaters. *Mains around £3.50–4.50, sandwiches & snacks around £2.50, buffet £6 pp.*

✻✗ Mosiah's Jamaican Bar & Restaurant [114 E2] Kotu Craft Market; **m** 2446930; **f** MosiahsBar; ⏱ Oct–Apr 08.00–late daily. This new funky-looking restaurant in Kotu Craft Market is already winning rave reviews for its take on Jamaican classics fused with Gambian & European favourites. You can either sit on the veranda among the hustle & bustle of the market or relax upstairs & watch the the action

from above. For meat eaters, the goat curry is a must. A delivery service is also available. *Most mains are around £5, while their signature goat curry is £8.50.*

✻✗ Sailor's Bar & Restaurant [114 F2] Kotu Beach; **m** 7732388/7774064; **e** sailor.beach@ hotmail.com; ⏱ 08.00–23.00 or later daily. Situated at the far eastern end of the road along Kotu Beach, this long-serving restaurant is one of the most consistent in the area. The funky interior is adorned with African artworks, & there's also a breezy terrace sitting area & a thatched stilted wooden platform on the beach. The focus of the dinner menu is seafood, with specialities such as paella (for 2), grilled prawns & fish, but there are also plenty of meat & chicken dishes. Light meals & sandwiches are served during the day. *Light meals around £4.50, mains £5–9.*

✻✗ Solomon's Fish Hut [114 A1] Palma Rima Rd; **m** 7630007/9941031; ⏱ 08.00–23.00 daily. One of the country's longest-serving beach bars, Solomon's is set in a large hut-like building with matted roof at the north end of Palma Rima Rd. It serves excellent fish, prawns & other seafood, with fish & chips in foil being the speciality, & also rents out sunbeds for a nominal daily fee. *Mains in the £5–6 range.*

✻✗ Tandoor [114 E2] Kotu Craft Market; ☎ 42211803; **m** 2637711; **f** Tandoor.Gambia; ⏱ Oct–Mar 16.00–23.00 daily. This superb outdoor Indian restaurant fills up early at the height of the season, & little wonder when it is so reasonably priced. Tandoor dishes such as fish or chicken tikka are particularly recommended, but it also does a good line in curries, with vegetarians being well catered for. There's inexpensive house wine & draught beer too, & an excellent traditional kora player most nights. *Expect to pay around £5 per head for mains with rice or naan bread.*

✗ Ali Baba Pizza [114 E2] Kotu Craft Market; **m** 7112618; ⏱ Oct–Mar 17.00–23.00 daily. Situated right next to the superior Tandoor, the relaxed outdoor eatery serves good pizzas & pasta dishes, along with a selection of tasty Gambian dishes. *Mains in the £4.50–6.50 range.*

✗ Cafe Denmark [114 A3] Kololi Rd; ☎ 4464950; **m** 9983590; ⏱ 08.00–late. A popular haunt for expats, locals & tourists, with a large terraced area just off the road, this serves typical Gambian & European dishes as well as a few Danish specials. There is also live music at 21.00 every Wed & Sun. *Mains £3.50–8.*

✕ Domino's Beach Bar [114 E1] Kotu Beach; m 3688104/7090356; ⏰ 24hrs. Situated on the beachward side of Kotu Craft Market, this popular beach bar serves surprisingly pricey drinks & a selection of quite affordable meals including pizzas, sandwiches, burgers & Gambian dishes. There's free sunbeds for diners, drumming & a campfire on Mon night, & live music on Sat night. *Meals in the £4–7 range.*

✕ New Bailey Beach Bar & Restaurant [114 A1] Palma Rima Rd; m 3770503/7362918; ⏰ 08.00–late daily. This well-established beach bar next to Solomon's has a pool table, sunbeds to rent for a nominal fee & a varied menu with specialities including grilled tiger prawns in garlic butter & T-bone steak. There's a beach BBQ on Tue nights & reggae party on Sun. *Mains in the £3.50–7 range, BBQ £5pp.*

✕ Ningke Nangka Bar & Restaurant [114 F2] m 7915622; ⏰ 07.00–midnight daily. This large 3-storey building houses a bar, restaurant & beach area with sunbeds, named after a dragon well known in Gambian legends. They serve the usual European & Gambian staples as well as providing low-key entertainment during the evenings in tourist season. The friendliness of the staff & management more than makes up for the lack of character. *Mains in the £5–8 range.*

✕ Paradise Beach Bar & Restaurant [114 F2] Kotu Beach; m 7306700; e papadawda@ yahoo.com; ⏰ 09.00–22.00 or later daily. This affordable beach restaurant makes the most of its great location, with plenty of outdoor seating & sunbeds for diners, & it also has a good menu of tasty Gambian & Western dishes, including a popular all-day b/fast & excellent benachin rice. The traditional BBQ buffet with live music on Sun is particularly recommended. *Mains in the £4–7.50 range, buffet £5.50pp.*

✕ Patta Patta Restaurant & Bar [114 A2] Palma Rima Rd; m 2547435; ⏰ 08.00–late daily, Thu–Sat in low season. This relaxed & popular owner-managed restaurant has an outdoor setting next to Luigi's & a varied menu with plenty of seafood options, as well as Gambian dishes. There's a buffet on Thu, karaoke on Sun, & live local music from 22.00 on Thu, Fri & Sat. There are also 10 small but clean rooms (*£17 dbl*) behind the bar. *Mains are mostly around £5–7.*

✕ Terrace Bar & Restaurant [114 A2] Palma Rima Rd; ☎ 4462293; ⏰ 07.00–23.00 daily. Situated below Calabash Residence, this aptly named restaurant is set on a wide terrace with comfortable seating & fans overhead. It specialises in Gambian dishes, but also has a good selection of seafood & salads. *Mains are mostly in the £4–6 range.*

BUDGET

✻✕ Ice Queen Plaza [114 A3] m 7778384. This low-key place is probably the pick of the local places to eat in the sandy streets around the Teranga Suites & Timbuktu Guesthouse. Serving Gambian food, English b/fasts, salads, burgers, seafood & afra in a courtyard just off the street, it's very good value. *Most mains less than £5.*

✻✕ Paolo's Restaurant, Pizza & Bar [114 A4] Bertil Harding Highway; m 7447164; ⨍ PaolosRestaurantItalianPizzeria. This place arguably serves the best pizzas in The Gambia, cooked in an authentic wood stove. A delivery service is also available. *Pizzas from £3.50.*

✕ Amigo's Resto-Ba [114 A2] Palma Rima Rd; m 7912872; ⏰ 08.00–midnight daily in season. Despite the Spanish name, this is primarily an Asian eatery, with an extensive menu of tandoor, curry & Chinese dishes supplemented by a few continental staples. There's a full bar & terrace seating under umbrellas. *Mains in the £4–5 range.*

ENTERTAINMENT AND NIGHTLIFE

As is the case elsewhere on the Gambian coast, the line between bars and restaurants is often quite blurred. Several of the places listed on pages 118–20, including any of the beach restaurants, are good for a few drinks, while the likes of Samba's Kitchen, Cafe Denmark, JD's and Patta Patta have live music several nights of the week. More dedicated nightspots include the following.

♀ Churchill's Bar [114 A2] Palma Rima Beach; **m** 3146047; ⊕ 08.00–02.00 daily. Tucked away between Luigi's & Calabash Residence, this well-established & well-stocked drinking hole serves cheap draught beer & affordable pub-grub in an atmosphere strongly reminiscent of a British 'local'.

☆ Ningke Nangka [114 F2] **m** 7915622; ⊕ 07.00–midnight. This large bar & restaurant complex on the beach also has a nightclub.

☆ Teranga Beach Club [114 A1] Palma Rima Beach; **m** 7412159; ⊕ 20.00–late Tue–Sun. This vast open-air complex at the beach end of Palma Rima Rd had clearly suffered a bit of structural damage before this guide was researched, but it still hosts discos & more occasionally live music over weekends during high season. The proprietor, Abdel Kabirr, had some hits in Europe in the 90s & is in the process of setting up a 60s-style R&B band.

OTHER PRACTICALITIES

BANKS AND FOREIGN EXCHANGE Several private **forex bureaux** can be found within 100m or so of Kotu Craft Market at the east end of Kotu Stream Road. A little surprisingly, there are no banks or ATMs in Kotu or Palma Rima; the closest are on Bertil Harding Highway, either to the west around Kololi's Senegambia Junction, or to the east at the junction with Kairaba Avenue.

BICYCLE HIRE Two cycle-rental stands can be found along Kotu Stream Road: one opposite the Kombo Beach Hotel [114 E2] and the other opposite Badala Park [114 D3]. Rates are under £1 per hour for short usage or £5 per day for longer periods.

GUIDES The **Gambia Bird Guides Association**, which includes around 75 official bird guides, is based in a summer house on the west side of Kotu Stream Road immediately north of the bridge [114 E2]. Its members guide locally but can also arrange guided day trips to birding sites elsewhere on the coast, and longer trips upriver to Tendaba, Janjanbureh and even into Senegalese sites such as Niokolo-Koba and Djoudj national parks. Unfortunately there is no official website or other contact details for the association, but you will reliably find at least half-a-dozen guides in attendance at any time between 07.00 and 19.00. The guides are all competent and many are very knowledgeable indeed. Expect to pay around £10 per person for a 2-hour guided bird walk around Kotu Stream and Ponds, which is also a good way to feel out whether you would like a guide for trips further afield.

The **National Tour Guide Association** (**m** *9173332/9997711*) has two offices in the area: one at the entrance to Kotu Craft Market [114 E2] and the other at Palma Rima Junction next to the Palma Rima Hotel [114 A2]. This association was created in 1997 and all its guides have official status and are government-trained. They can guide to most sites in and around the Gambian coast (though you are better taking a dedicated bird guide for ornithological sites) and also set up visits to wrestling competitions and other local activities. Guide fees are around £8.50 per party for a half-day tour and £17 for a full day.

HEALTH AND BEAUTY Several of the smarter hotels, such as Kombo Beach and Bakotu, have spas and beauty salons attached. In Palma Rima, **Anntom's Holistic Health and Fitness Centre** [114 A2] (**m** *3413784*; ⊕ *08.00–22.00 daily*) has a good gym (with weight-training machines, treadmill, etc) and also offers treatments such as massages, manicures, pedicures and reflexology. Next door, **Cutting Edge Hair Design** [114 A2] (**m** *7369711/7878854*) has stylists with experience of both African and European hair.

Kotu and Palma Rima OTHER PRACTICALITIES

8

INTERNET Most of the better package hotels have free or paid Wi-Fi. If yours doesn't, try the public internet café in the Bungalow Beach Hotel or **Legacy Internet** [114 A3] 300m south of Palma Rima Junction.

SHOPPING For handicrafts and other souvenirs, the largest and best stocked of three markets in the area is **Kotu Craft Market** [114 E2], which lies on the beach side of Kotu Stream Road opposite the Bakotu Hotel. It is rivalled in scope by **Fajara Craft Market** [114 F2], which lies about 5 minutes' walk further east just before Sailor's Bar and Restaurant, and a smaller cluster of stalls in Palma Rima along the dirt road running east from opposite Luigi's. Most of the larger hotels also have gift shops selling a more limited selection of local handicrafts at fixed prices.

For grocery shopping, the best-stocked option is the superb **Maroun's Supermarket** [114 A3] (**m** *7732631;* ⊕ *08.45–22.00 Mon–Sat, 10.00–22.00 Sun*), which lies on the south side of Bertil Harding Highway diagonally opposite the Palma Rima Hotel, and incorporates a good butchery, delicatessen and wines and spirits section. Several lesser but still quite well-stocked **mini markets** lie along the eastern end of Kotu Stream Road, within 100m or so of Kotu Craft Market, while the fresh produce market next to Fajara Craft Market is recommended for fruit and veggies.

WHAT TO SEE AND DO

The main attraction at Kotu and Palma Rima is the beach, which, despite being bisected by the Kotu Stream Mouth, is now probably the best along the developed part of the Gambian coast, being less affected by erosion than its counterparts at Kololi and Bakau. The main clusters of beach developments are in Kotu immediately east of Kotu Market, and at the north end of Palma Rima Road, and both sites are serviced by several beach bars and restaurants (many of which are listed individually earlier in this chapter) serving food and chilled drinks, and renting out sunbeds for a nominal fee.

KOTU STREAM [114 D2–G4] Kotu is renowned in ornithological circles for offering a great introduction to birdwatching in The Gambia, and a good deal of this is due to the presence of Kotu Stream, which is most easily accessed where it passes beneath the road at Kotu Bridge before it empties into the sea. International birdwatchers have been visiting this site for decades now, and even though the surrounding areas have become more urbanised, it still retains a good number of birds. Indeed, accompanied by a knowledgeable guide (and several are available at the Bird Guides Association kiosk north of the bridge), it should be possible for an Africa novice to clock up around 40–50 species in a 2–4-hour walk, while those more experienced in African conditions might be looking at closer to 70. Especially at low tide, the mangrove-lined mud flats host plenty of waders and herons, including greater painted-snipe, pied avocet, whimbrel, spur-winged plover and Senegal thick-knee, while half-a-dozen kingfisher species range from the very common pied to the more elusive giant kingfisher. The site is also good for osprey and for several species associated more with woodland and thicket, including the eagerly sought oriole warbler, African silverbill and various bee-eaters.

KOTU CYCLE PATH [114 A–D2] Another famous birding site that has an amazing array of birds along its length, and has provided many thousands of birders with new species for their life lists, is the 1.2km cycle path that runs between Kotu Stream and

Palma Rima roads. The selection of birds here depends quite a lot on season, and how marshy conditions are, but among the more common aquatic species likely to be seen are white-faced whistling duck, African jacana, African spoonbill, squacco heron and black egret (also called the umbrella bird, for its habit of fishing with its wings ballooned outwards to form a shaded canopy). The sedge and reed beds here can be good for warblers, finches, widow birds and the localised red-billed quelea, while a notable grassland species is the yellow-throated longclaw, which often performs conspicuous aerial displays in breeding season. At dusk, this can be a good place to see the spectacular standard-winged and long-tailed nightjars.

KOTU PONDS [114 D–E3] A third key birding site is the so-called Kotu Ponds, which in fact comprise a trio of flooded sewage pits reached via a short dirt road opposite Badala Park Hotel. The pits are separated from the road by about 50m of open woodland that often hosts interesting species such as blue-bellied roller, yellow-crowned gonolek and various babblers. An amazing range of waterbirds can sometimes be seen in the ponds, and the best thing is that they allow you to get fairly close. Among the hundreds of waders that might congregate around the pool margins, look out for black-winged stilt, common greenshank, wood sandpiper and spur-winged plover. There is also often a large flock of white-faced whistling duck, plus grey-headed gull, white-winged black tern and various kingfishers. Rarities here have included red-necked phalarope and one of the few recent sightings of tufted duck in The Gambia. Be warned that the sewage ponds are a working environment and trucks come regularly to empty their loads of liquid waste, so you have to be a bit careful when walking around. You may be asked a nominal fee for entry, and though this is not official, doing so will encourage the workers to keep the place good for birds.

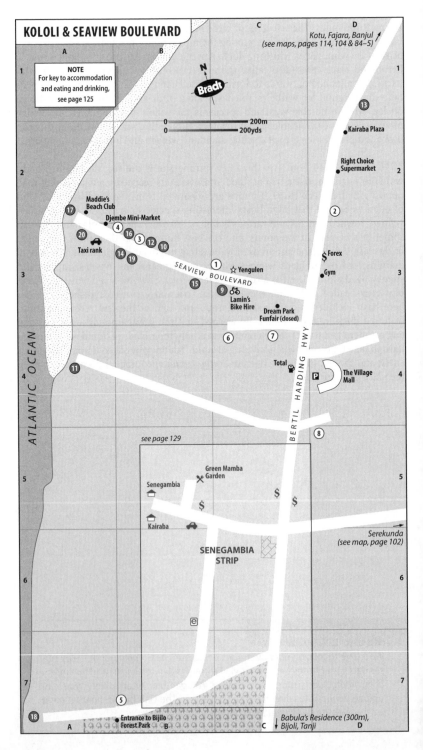

KOLOLI & SEAVIEW BOULEVARD

NOTE
For key to accommodation
and eating and drinking,
see page 125

Kotu, Fajara, Banjul
(see maps, pages 114, 104 & 84–5)

Kairaba Plaza

Right Choice
Supermarket

Maddie's
Beach Club

Djembe Mini-Market

Taxi rank

Forex

Gym

SEAVIEW BOULEVARD

☆ Yengulen

Lamin's
Bike Hire

Dream Park
Funfair (closed)

Total

BERTIL HARDING HWY

The Village
Mall

ATLANTIC OCEAN

see page 129

Green Mamba
Garden

Senegambia

Kairaba

Serekunda
(see map, page 102)

SENEGAMBIA
STRIP

Entrance to Bijilo
Forest Park

Babula's Residence (300m),
Bijoli, Tanji

9

Kololi and Environs

There's nowhere else in West Africa quite like Kololi. Situated on the Atlantic coastline 15km west of Banjul, this once unremarkable small Gambian village, having first been exposed to tourism in the 1970s, today forms the hub of the country's booming package resort industry. Here, within an area of about 2km², you'll find a couple-of-dozen hotels, including such venerable landmarks as the Kairaba and Senegambia, along with a cosmopolitan and seemingly inexhaustible selection of restaurants and bars, and other tourist facilities such as nightclubs, supermarkets, banks and craft markets. Kololi is also, you'll quickly notice, a major stomping ground for bumsters, whose attentions might be daunting on initial exposure, though mostly they're quite innocuous and quickly lose interest in familiar faces.

The main touristic focal point in Kololi is the tight cluster of hotels and restaurants that runs west from Senegambia Junction (on Bertil Harding Highway) to the Senegambia Hotel and Kololi Beach Club. This area is most often referred to simply as 'Senegambia', or 'The Strip', and almost every visitor to The Gambia ends up here at some point, for a meal, or a drink, or a night out. Other important tourist centres are Seaview Boulevard, a few hundred metres north of Senegambia Junction, and a more dispersed group of hotels dotted around Bijilo to the south. The main attraction of this area is emphatically the beach, followed by the busy and wonderfully varied restaurant scene. However, it also boasts one genuinely worthwhile attraction for wildlife enthusiasts in the form of Bijilo Forest Reserve, a patch of bird- and monkey-rich coastal woodland running along the beach between Kololi and Bijilo.

NORTHERN KOLOLI

Although tourism in Kololi traditionally centres on the bunched cluster of restaurants and other facilities immediately west of Senegambia Junction, recent years have witnessed the blossoming of two new important focal points a short distance further north. The first of these, situated on the east side of Bertil Harding Highway about 600m north of Senegambia Junction, is The Village, a modern shopping mall housing a supermarket, several boutique shops and a handful of restaurants. The second, and more important, is an 800m-long road, sometimes referred to as Seaview Boulevard, which runs west from Bertil Harding Highway to the beachfront Djembe Beach Resort and Poco Loco Bar.

GETTING THERE AND AWAY Coming from Senegambia Junction, it's less than 10 minutes' walk to The Village and perhaps 20 minutes to Seaview Boulevard. From further afield, any shared taxi or other public transport heading along Bertil Harding Highway can drop you right outside The Village or at the junction for Seaview Boulevard. Otherwise, catch a taxi, and pick up another when you are ready to leave (there's a busy rank opposite the Djembe Beach Resort).

WHERE TO STAY

Upmarket

Djembe Beach Resort [124 B3] (84 rooms) Seaview Bd; 2026200; m 7783814; e info@djemberesort.com; w djemberesort.com. Previously the Sunswing, this relatively new hotel is set in large well-manicured grounds centred on a swimming pool & opening directly on to the swimming beach at the end of Seaview Bd. Spacious standard rooms come with queen-size (or 2 ¾) beds, satellite TV, AC & balcony, & there are also 1- or 2-bedroom bungalows with a well-equipped kitchen (fridge, microwave, oven & all the standard utensils), sitting room & en-suite bathroom with combination shower/tub. There are plenty of restaurants within 200m of the hotel & facilities include free Wi-Fi throughout. Definitely one of the better hotels in its price range. *From £50/65 for a standard sgl/dbl, £91.50 for a 1-bed villa, all rates B&B.*

Mid-range

✳ Djeliba Hotel [124 B3] (83 rooms) Seaview Bd; m 7324228/7004498; e reservations@djelibahotel.com or info@djelibahotel.com; w djelibahotel.com. Liberally adorned with traditional African artworks, this funky modern hotel comes across as refreshingly contemporary by comparison with most competitors in this price range. The most spacious accommodation is in the main block above reception, but all rooms come with dark-wood furniture, brightly coloured fabrics, fridge, fan, AC, balcony & en-suite bathroom with extractor. The beach is only 3 mins' walk away, & the well-tended grounds have an agreeable swimming-pool area, spa, restaurant & bar. Good value. *Standard sgl/dbl €45/55, en-suite sgl/dbl €55/70, apt €90 (sleeps up to 3), all rates B&B.*

Seaview Gardens Hotel [124 C4] (78 rooms) 4466660–2; m 3510071/6741012; e reservations@seaviewgardenshotel.gm; w seaviewgardenshotel.gm. Situated along a cul-de-sac running off Bertil Harding Highway parallel to & about 150m south of Seaview Bd, this quite classy but disingenuously named hotel lies about 10 mins' walk from the sea & has no garden worth talking about. The spacious & airy en-suite rooms are in dbl-storey Mediterranean-style blocks & come with satellite TV, AC & free Wi-Fi. Good value. *From US$45/60/100 for deluxe room/suite/villa, all rates B&B.*

Budget

Bamboo Garden Hotel [124 C3] (22 rooms) Seaview Bd; 2128232/3432226; e reservations@bamboohotel.gm; w bamboohotel.gm. Although quite compact, this is a good-value option with friendly & welcoming staff, only 5 mins' or so walk from the beach. The round houses are smart with bamboo trimmings & surround a pool & bar area with attractive gardens. *£30/33 standard sgl/dbl, £37/41 sgl/dbl apt, all rates B&B.*

Dandimayo Apartments [124 D2] (12 rooms) Bertil Harding Hwy; m 7898321; e terrymaher1967@gmail.com. Set back just off the highway, these apt blocks surround a swimming pool just behind a large bar/restaurant area that serves English favourites including a Sun roast. The rooms are perfectly acceptable, if slightly garishly decorated & come with AC, safe & fridge. *£25 for apt inc English b/fast.*

Paradise Suites Hotel [124 C4] (53 rooms) 4466264/4463439; e info@paradisesuites.gm; w paradisesuites.gm. This rather rundown hotel next to the Seaview lies in uninspiring grounds with a very small swimming-pool area, but it's only 5 mins' walk from the beach (through a gate at the back) & even closer to the restaurants & other amenities at The Village. The en-suite rooms are nothing to shout about, but they do have AC, queen-size bed, plenty of cupboard space, satellite TV & sizeable bathroom with tub. With realistic expectations, it's fair value. *£30/33 sgl/dbl, £53 for a villa.*

WHERE TO EAT AND DRINK A row of perhaps a dozen restaurants runs along the north side of Seaview Boulevard and includes several affordable options specialising in West African cuisine, although as elsewhere, there is a fair turnover with places coming and going each season. The Village Mall also boasts a few eateries, with a stand-out for wine-lovers being the aptly named The Vineyard, while the excellent patisserie Caramel will delight those seeking a fresh coffee fix.

Upmarket

✷ ✖ **The Vineyard** [124 D4] 1st floor, The Village Mall; m 3311111/2; e vineyard. gambia@gmail.com; ⊕ noon–23.00 Mon–Sat, 17.00–23.00 Sun. This owner-managed restaurant has an attractive modern interior with light-wood furnishing, a large-screen TV for sports events, free Wi-Fi, & the choice of airy indoor or terrace seating. An interesting international menu focuses on Indian cuisine, complemented by a lengthy cocktail & wine list, with most being sold by the glass. *Mains are mostly in the £6–8 range.*

Mid-range

✷ ✖ **Manos Mediterranean Restaurant** [124 B3] Seaview Bd; m 7888758/7822267; ⊕ 11.00–23.00 daily, 16.00–23.00 off season. This Mediterranean restaurant offers an original menu with a focus on Greek & Turkish cuisines. Run by a Dutch–Gambian couple, one of whom was behind the designs at Poco Loco & the Djeliba Hotel, it's no surprise that the décor is as exquisitely tasteful as the food itself. Attached is a VIP membership bar offering private booths, & there's AC & top-end spirits not readily available elsewhere. Wi-Fi is available in season & there is live music on Wed & Sat. *Mains in the £5.50–8 range or their speciality mixed grills around £12 for 2.*

✷ ✖ **Poco Loco** [124 A2] Seaview Bd; m 7881177; e pocoloco.gambia@gambia.com; w pocolocogambia.com; ⊕ 10.00–late daily. Set on a solid wooden deck at the beach end of Seaview Bd, this brightly coloured dbl-storey beach bar scores highly on ambience & location, but is let down by the indifferent service. A good cocktail menu is complemented by an eclectic selection of local & continental seafood & other dishes. There's an upstairs sunset deck with bean bags, plus a beach area with sunbeds. *Mains mostly in the £3.50–6 range.*

✖ **D'Nubian Seafood Garden** [124 B3] Bertil Harding Hwy; m 7709622; ⊕ 09.00–01.00 daily. Focused mainly on fresh seafood, accompanied by a choice of 7 tasty sauces, this relatively smart eatery also offers a selection of Gambian dishes. *Mains in the £5.50–6.50 range.*

✖ **Muna's Bar & Restaurant** [124 B3] Seaview Bd; m 2653944/2653977; ⊕ 08.00–midnight daily. With seating on the airy terrace or in the sports-bar-like interior (complete with free Wi-Fi & large-screen TV), this is a popular hangout during live football matches. It has an unusually varied menu including seafood, curries, wrapped baguettes & pan-African dishes, spanning the continent from the Cape to Morocco, which can be explored in the Taste of Africa sampler. *Mains in the £4–8 range.*

✖ **Tapaloca** [124 B3] Seaview Bd; m 7969601; ⏺ tapaloca96spanishfood; ⊕ 17.00–23.00. Authentic Spanish food served by friendly staff. Tuck in to paella, Iberian ham, & tapas & Spanish wines from their nice terrace & watch the world pass by. *Plates £2.50–9.*

✖ **Woodies** [124 A3] Seaview Bd; m 2134456; ⏺ Woodiesthegambia; ⊕ 08.00–late. This attractive & popular Dutch-run bar/restaurant has a wooden decking veranda, big-screen TV for sporting events & a full menu of Dutch snacks, European favourites & Gambian dishes. *Mains in the £5–11 range.*

Budget

✖ **Afra FM** [124 C3] Seaview Bd; m 2361100/3981452; ⊕ 08.00–02.00 Mon–Fri, 24hrs Sat, This restaurant specialises in African BBQ, known in The Gambia as afra, & fish, chicken, lamb & beef is available. *£1.50–4 depending on the type of meat or fish.*

✗ Buka African Kitchen [124 B3] Seaview Bd; m 7444676; e bukagambia@yahoo.com; ◷ 10.00–02.00 Sun–Thu, 10.00–04.00 Fri/Sat. With long hours that make it a good spot for a last round, this unpretentious Nigerian-owned restaurant also serves a varied selection of dishes from all around West Africa. *Mains mostly in the £3.50–7 range.*

✗ Haggler [124 H1] Bertil Harding Hwy; m 7797025. Popular with expats, this serves traditional British pub favourites alongside pasta & paninis. There is a pool table, large outdoor terrace or indoor seating area & big-screen TV for sporting events. Great value. *£3–3.50 for most mains.*

✗ Marjatta & Adams [124 B3] Seaview Bd; m 7211119; f marjattaadamsrestaurantbar; ◷ 08.00–late. As well as serving the usual Senegambian menu, this restaurant offers plates of local Gambian food at local prices, served on its large outdoor terrace. *Gambian plates £1.70, other mains £3–5.*

✳ ⏛ Caramel [124 D4] Ground floor, Village Mall; m 7709622/7952666; e caramel@mail. gm; ◷ 07.00–22.00 Mon–Sat, 08.30–22.00 Sun. This funky patisserie is a fantastic spot for a fresh coffee, b/fast, toasted sandwich, filled baguette or ice cream, & it also serves a tempting selection of pastries, cakes & other freshly baked goodies. You can eat inside or on the terrace, & there's free Wi-Fi.

ENTERTAINMENT AND NIGHTLIFE The flashy **Yengulen** [124 C3] (previously Duplex Night Club) on Seaview Boulevard (m 9962222/7592325; *over-21s only*) is one of the most popular in the country. The nicest spot for an outdoor drink is probably beachfront Poco Loco, which faces west to catch the sunset and usually hosts live music over weekends. More sedately, most of the restaurants along Seaview Boulevard have agreeable terraces that stay open until well after midnight.

SHOPPING The country's largest structure of its type, **The Village Mall** [124 D4] is a horseshoe-shaped double-storey construction on the east side of Bertil Harding Highway and is home to several trendy clothes shops, a few restaurants, a car-rental company and a dental clinic. It also incorporates the superior ground-floor **Xpress Supermarket** (m 6688001; ◷ 09.30–22.00 Mon–Sat, 10.00–21.30 Sun), which stocks a comprehensive selection of imported goodies, and has a good butcher, fresh produce, delicatessen and wine sections. Less well stocked but more convenient for those staying at the far end of Seaview Boulevard is the small **Djembe Mini-Market** [124 A2] next to the Djembe Beach Resort.

ACTIVITIES The main centre of tourist activity in North Kololi is the hotel swimming pools and, of course, the beach in front of the Djembe Beach Resort and Poco Loco, which is far more alluring than its eroded counterpart at the end of the Senegambia Strip. The only bespoke tourist attraction in the area, situated directly opposite The Village, is Dream Park, a family-oriented amusement park that opened in 2007 but looked very closed at the time of writing. Whether it will open again is anybody's guess. Lamin's Bike Hire [124 C3] (m 3412338) operates opposite the Blue Angel restaurant on Seaview Boulevard with bikes available at £3.50/5 for a half/full day.

THE 'SENEGAMBIA' STRIP

Ubiquitously referred to as Senegambia after the iconic 350-room hotel that dominates its beachfront, the touristic heart of Kololi consists of a J-shaped kilometre of road lined with dozens of restaurants, bars and other tourist facilities. Ironically, however, while this part of Kololi is easily the busiest resort along the Gambian coast, the main beach leaves much to be desired by comparison with most

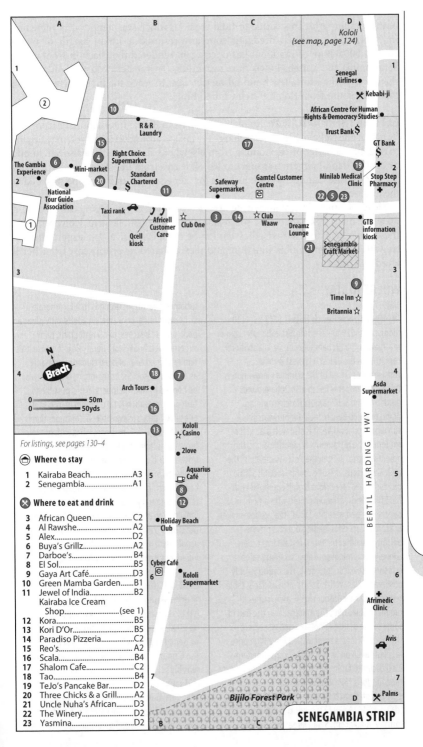

SENEGAMBIA STRIP

For listings, see pages 130–4

🏠 Where to stay

| 1 | Kairaba Beach | A3 |
| 2 | Senegambia | A1 |

✖ Where to eat and drink

3	African Queen	C2
4	Al Rawshe	A2
5	Alex	D2
6	Buya's Grillz	A2
7	Darboe's	B4
8	El Sol	B5
9	Gaya Art Café	D3
10	Green Mamba Garden	B1
11	Jewel of India	B2
	Kairaba Ice Cream Shop	(see 1)
12	Kora	B5
13	Kori D'Or	B5
14	Paradiso Pizzeria	C2
15	Reo's	A2
16	Scala	B4
17	Shalom Cafe	C2
18	Tao	B4
19	TeJo's Pancake Bar	D2
20	Three Chicks & a Grill	A2
21	Uncle Nuha's African	D3
22	The Winery	D2
23	Yasmina	D2

of its counterparts. This is due to tidal erosion, which was temporarily remedied in 2004, when a Dutch dredging company restored a 1.5km length of beach using 1,000,000m³ of sand, but has once again rendered the beach in front of the Senegambia and Kairaba hotels close to sandless. Fortunately, you need only follow the curve of the J for a few hundred metres west to reach the more pristine beach that runs south from Kololi Beach Club to Bijilo.

GETTING THERE AND AWAY Kololi lies 20km from Banjul International Airport via Yundum and Sukuta. The official charge for taxis is around £15, but you may be able to negotiate a better price. Coming from elsewhere, for instance Fajara, Serekunda or central Banjul (where transport to Kololi leaves from the station on Rene Blain Street opposite Gamtel House), just ask for 'Senegambia' and you'll be dropped at the junction.

Heading out from Kololi, private taxis to wherever you are going can be picked up at the main taxi park on the south side of the Senegambia Strip. However, since these are official tourist taxis, they tend to be quite expensive. A cheaper option is to walk up to Senegambia Junction, and pick a shared or private taxi from Bertil Harding Highway.

WHERE TO STAY
Upmarket
Kairaba Beach Hotel [129 A3] (160 rooms) 4462940–2; e info@kairabahotel.com or reservations@kairabahotel.com; w kairabahotel.com. One of the oldest, classiest & most consistently praised of The Gambia's larger hotels, this 5-star property lies in lush 20ha grounds bordering the Senegambia Hotel & running down to Kololi Beach. Ideal for birdwatchers & sun worshippers alike, it is also well placed for exploring the restaurants & nightlife along the adjoining strip. Built in the Portuguese style, the neat & spacious en-suite rooms, though a little old-fashioned, are bright & well equipped with quality fittings. All rooms come with a twin or queen-size bed, satellite TV, AC, tea-/coffee-maker & a large glass door leading out to a private balcony. Facilities include 6 restaurants & bars, a lovely swimming-pool area, a beauty salon, a gift shop, an excursions desk, the country's only observatory, as well as sports such as darts, table tennis, squash, outdoor chess, lawn games & mountain-bike hire. The Kairaba lacks the flair of some of the boutique hotels listed elsewhere in this book, & rooms come with quite a high price tag, but taken on its own rather corporate terms, it's difficult to fault. *£85/101/116 standard/deluxe/superior dbl, £132 suite, all rates B&B.*

Kololi Beach Resort [124 B7] 4464897, (UK) +44 1624 610223; e bookings@kololi.com; w kololi.com. Set in large, quiet & well-groomed beachfront grounds that incorporate a large swimming-pool area, an adults-only plunge pool, private beaches, bar & restaurant, mini supermarket, book-swap library & golf course, this family-owned & -managed club runs primarily as a private resort for its members, but it can also be booked by non-members, & it is possible to turn up at reception & take a room on the spot or a villa if they are available. Accommodation is in large, airy 1- & 2-bedroom villas with modern furnishings, fully fitted kitchen, fan & AC, & private patio or balcony. Other positives are the hands-on management, direct access to a good beach, plentiful monkeys & birdlife (thanks partly to its location right opposite Bijilo Forest Park) & proximity to the many restaurants & bars along the strip. *1-/2-bed villas from £100/night for 2–6 people, with reductions available out of season. Introductory rates are also available.*

Mid-range
Senegambia Hotel [129 A1] (351 rooms) 4462717/4461889; m 2000348; e info@senegambiahotel.com; w senegambiahotel.com. The largest hotel in The Gambia, the iconic Senegambia has been a sensibly priced & thoroughly reliable all-round mid-range option since it opened in the early 1980s. Its most attractive feature is the luxuriant 10ha beachfront garden, whose lush tropical vegetation, filled with interesting nooks &

crannies, supports plenty of wildlife, including giant monitor lizards, playful green monkeys & an alluring selection of woodland birds (notably the likes of oriole warbler & black-headed gonolek). There is even a special 'vulture feeding' event, which takes place at around 11.00 daily, & attracts dozens (sometimes hundreds) of these large scavenging birds. Other facilities include a pleasant swimming-pool area, a beach bar, a well-stocked gift shop, tailors, a unisex hairdressing salon, several restaurants, as well as tennis, squash, table tennis, volleyball, minigolf & archery. It is close to dozens of bars & restaurants, but there's also a wide range of in-house evening entertainment, including stage shows, African cabaret nights & a weekly BBQ. The rooms are in 2-storey buildings dotted around the gardens, & they all have AC, fan, satellite TV, safe, en-suite bath or shower, & private balcony or patio. Overall, it has a lot more character than most package hotels, & it's an excellent central choice for birders or families with mixed interests. *From £58/70 sgl/dbl B&B.*

Budget

🏠 **Babula's Residence** [124 C7] (15 rooms) 📞 4461041; m 6788969/7788969; e info@babula.info. Set in the backroads of Kerr Serign about 500m southeast of Senegambia Junction, this unpretentious owner-managed complex offers accommodation in a hodgepodge of pleasant but shabbily furnished 1-, 2- & 3-bedroom apartments, all with nets, fans,

kitchenette & en-suite tub or shower. A funky little ground-floor café serves adequate & affordable meals. It seems like an agreeable & reasonably priced set-up, despite being a bit of a walk from the beach. *£13.50/16.50/18.50pp for 1-/2-/3-bed apt.*

🏠 **Devon Lodge** [map, page 74] (8 apts); m 7076017/7736750; e devonlodgegambia@ gmail.com; w devonlodgegambia.com. Run by an English–Gambian couple, this is one of the most highly rated lodges in the region, providing the opportunity to gain a real insight into life in The Gambia. Fully serviced self-catering apts come with dbl/twin bed, en-suite shower, well-equipped kitchen, open-plan living area, satellite TV & private veranda overlooking the well-tended gardens. There's free Wi-Fi, & the hosts are happy to organise shopping or take-away services. The apts occupy a peaceful location close to Bijilo Forest Park, away from the buzz of the main strip but still within walking distance of the main cluster of restaurants. *£30/night or £200/week, or £20/night in low season.*

🏠 **Sky Guesthouse** [124 D5] (8 rooms) Off Bertil Harding Hwy; m 3700701; 🇫 SkyMotel. Set back just off the highway between The Village & Senegambia, this is a great budget choice for those wishing to sample the local restaurants & nightlife, less than 1km from the beach. Rooms are newly painted, come with ceiling fans, en suites with hot water & nets. Good value. *£12.50/16 standard dbl or with kitchen, discounts available in low season.*

🍴 **WHERE TO EAT AND DRINK** The best part of 50 restaurants are clustered within 5 minutes' walk of Senegambia Junction. Most international cuisines are well represented, and standards are pretty high. The listings below are therefore quite selective, pulling out a few well-established favourites, along with some newer places that offer exceptional value or an unusual menu or ambience. But don't be afraid to explore further – there are plenty of other choices and the healthy competition level tends to weed out any real duds sharpish.

Upmarket

☀️🍴 **Gaya Art Café** [129 D3] Bertil Harding Hwy; 📞 4464022; e info@gaya-artcafe.com; w gaya-artcafe.com; ⏰ Jul–Oct 12.00–19.30, Nov–Jun noon–midnight Mon–Sat. Situated on Bertil Harding Hwy between the Senegambia Craft Market & somewhat less sophisticated bars, this reinvigorating & charming Mediterranean-style café with free Wi-Fi justifiably bills itself as an oasis of calm amid the hustle & bustle of

the Senegambia area. A varied & imaginative Greek-influenced menu, with plenty of vegetarian options, includes salads, wraps & tapas. It also offers a good choice of cocktails (with Happy Hour on Thu), smoothies & afternoon teas, all served among beautiful & delicate artefacts in the delightfully chilled climate. *Mains in the £7–12 range, wraps & tapas in the £4–5 range.*

☀️🍴 **Green Mamba Garden** [129 B1] m 6662622/7811118;

e tony@greenmambagarden.com;
w greenmambarestaurant.com; ⏰ 19.00–23.00
daily. Tucked away on an inauspicious alley running
north past the Senegambia Hotel, this lovely
garden bar & restaurant has a lively but peaceful
atmosphere (at least when the nearby hotel
standby generator is standing by), a good cocktail
& wine list, & exceptional food. The speciality is
the Mongolian grill (allowing you to select from
dozens of raw ingredients to make your own fresh
stir-fry). *Grill £6.50 for 1 round or £8.50 for as many
as you like. It also has a varied selection of à la carte
grills in the £7.50–10 range.*

⚹ ✗ **Reo's** [129 A2] Off Senegambia Rd;
🔲 reosbarandrestaurant; ⏰ 07.30–00.30 Sun–
Thu, noon–02.00 Fri–Sat. This new modern bar
& restaurant is rapidly gaining a reputation for the
quality of its food & has possibly the best burger
in The Gambia as well as steaks, seafood, Italian
dishes & other favourites. Either sit inside with AC
& flatscreen TV for sporting events or under the
fan on the balcony outside. Spend enough time
drinking their wonderful cocktails and you may
even see monkeys from the nearby Bijilo Forest.
Most mains in the £5–13 range.

⚹ ✗ **Scala Restaurant** [129 B4] 📞 4460813;
e scala@qanet.gm; ⏰ 18.30–23.30 daily.
Established back in the 1980s, this Danish-owned
& -managed restaurant has long been highly
rated for its ambience, service, quality food &
reasonable prices. The emphasis is on continental
fine dining, & the menu, though not extensive,
includes an imaginative selection of fish, seafood &
meat dishes. There's also usually live West African
music at a comfortable volume. *Mains mostly in the
£7–12 range.*

✗ **African Queen Restaurant** [129 C2]
m 7569236; ⏰ 08.30–midnight daily. If the
pushy waiters touting at the entrance don't put
you off, this well-established restaurant is perhaps
the pick of a bunch of similar semi-outdoor set-
ups lining the southeast side of the strip. Serves a
range of seafood, grills & sizzlers, including some
superb peri-peri prawns. *Most dishes cost around
£6–8 while the house specialities – lobster, various
sizzlers & spicy Kalahari hotpots – are around
£10–13.*

✗ **Kori D'Or** [129 B5] **m** 7193239; ⏰ 08.00–
midnight daily. Notable for its striking orange &
yellow décor, this stylish bistro, with both indoor
& outdoor seating & an attractive bantaba bar, has

an interesting menu of continental & fusion dishes
alongside meat & Italian options, as well as a super
tantalising dessert menu, although it can be a little
hit & miss. *Mains in the £7–15 range.*

Mid-range

⚹ ✗ **Kora Bar & Restaurant** [129 B5]
📞 4462727; **m** 6660006/7074444; **e** info@
thekorarestaurant.com; **w** thekorarestaurant.
com; ⏰ Nov–Mar 18.00–late daily. Another
well-established favourite, the Kora has plenty
of ambience, whether you eat on the terrace or
the wooden-floored interior. The main focus is
seafood (the mixed platter for 2 is good value at
£15 if you're hungry) but it also serves good grilled
chicken & a varied vegetarian selection. *Mains
mostly in the £5–7.50 range.*

✗ **Al Rawshe Restaurant** [129 A2]
m 7722821; ⏰ noon–midnight daily. This
excellent Lebanese restaurant with indoor &
outdoor seating places a strong emphasis on
seafood. Specials include a grilled 'catch of the
day' for 2 (£11.50), a Lebanese-style Fri buffet
(£6.50pp), & a good meze selection.

✗ **Cabana's Beach Bar & Restaurant** [124
A4] Kololi Beach; **m** 2222282;
🔲 CabanasBeachBarandRestaurant; ⏰ 09.00–
midnight. The pick of a couple of beach bars
just to the north of the Senegambia Hotel, this
dark modern bar opens out on to a light-filled
glassed-off terrace, which is good for windy days,
that overlooks the beach, where sunbeds with
umbrellas are available. The service is great, there
is Wi-Fi throughout & the menu offers the usual
European & Gambian suspects. *Most mains are in
the £5–10 range.*

✗ **Darboe's Bar & Restaurant** [129 B4]
m 7816814/7596661; ⏰ 09.00–01.00 daily.
Thanks to its large-screen TVs, this cheerful
locally owned eatery is often packed during key
Premier League football matches & other major
sports events. But the long hours (& free Wi-Fi)
ensure that it is also a great spot for English-style
b/fast, a lunchtime sandwich or burger, a tasty
Gambian dinner dish such as chicken yassa, afra
or domada, or a night out watching (occasional)
live music. *Mains are around £5, while sizzlers are
£7–12.*

✗ **El Sol** [129 B5] **m** 6320000; **w** elsolgambia.
com; ⏰ 16.00–22.30 daily. Choose between a
tastefully decorated AC interior or the veranda to

enjoy Mexican classics such as nachos & burritos, as well as burgers, steak, chicken dishes & tapas. There are also sumptuous desserts & an extensive cocktail list – passion-fruit mojito, anyone? *Mains in the £7–8 range, tapas £3.50–5.*

✗ **Jewel of India** [129 B2]
m 7443895/7641297; ⏰ 18.00–23.00 daily. The best Indian in Kololi, this long-serving restaurant has an extensive menu that includes curries, tandoor grills & filling biryani dishes. Vegetarians are well catered for here. *Most mains are in the £5–7 range & Sat is buffet night.*

✗ **Paradiso Pizzeria** [129 C2] ✆ 4462177; ⏰ 10.00–23.00 daily. This local joint looks a little shabby from the outside but the food is excellent, especially the huge choice of different pizzas (cooked while you wait), which you can eat inside or take away. Service is variable & can be quite poor when it is very busy, but it's very affordable. *£3.50–6.50 for regular pizzas.*

✗ **Tao Restaurant** [129 B4] ✆ 4461191; ⏰ 18.00–23.00 daily. Now more than 15 years old, this veteran Thai restaurant serves good spicy food, & is also known for its friendly & efficient service. The Thu buffet is recommended if you're hungry. *Most mains are around £5–7.*

✗ **TeJo's Pancake Bar** [129 D2] m 2271970; w tejospannenkoekenbar.jimdo.com; ⏰ 10.00–23.00 daily. Just around the corner from Senegambia at the end of the strip of restaurants from Yasmina's, this Dutch-run restaurant & bar specialises in pancakes but also serves a range of desserts, including Dutch apple pie. *£5–7.50.*

✗ **Three Chicks & a Grill** [129 A2] m 2323333; ⏰ 16.00–23.00 daily. Colourful, relaxed café with a lovely brightly painted patio decked in pretty fairy lights & relaxed bamboo furniture. Friendly staff serve some of the juiciest burgers in the country, as well as delicious wings, freshly cooked fish & steaks. *Mains in the £6.50–8.50 range, snacks £4.50.*

✗ **The Winery** [129 D2] ✆ 2713577; ⏰ 10.00–02.00 daily. Another new restaurant offering Spanish fare, including tapas & an extensive wine list. The attractive wood-lined bar & inside area extends out like a veranda towards the street. *£8.50–11 for mains, tapas £4–5.*

✗ **Yasmina** [129 D2] m 7100008; ⏰ 09.00–midnight daily. Situated right on Senegambia Junction, this informal terrace restaurant is the busiest & among the best of several mid-range

Lebanese eateries in the vicinity, offering a selection of Mediterranean & Gambian dishes. *Mains in the £5–6 range.*

Budget
✴ ✗ **Buya's Grillz** [129 A2] Senegambia Hwy; ✆ 4466721; m 9956891/2099609; f buyasgrillz; ⏰ 09.00–04.00 daily. Opposite the Senegambia, this locally run grill bar looks set to provide snacks & fast food for the late-night crowd, serving Gambian plates, afra, steak, seafood & pizza. No alcohol. Great value. *Gambian dishes £1.50, other dishes £2–5.*

✴ ✗ **Kairaba Ice Cream Shop** [129 A3] ✆ 4462940; ⏰ 09.00–midnight daily. Situated just outside the entrance to the eponymous hotel, this very agreeable fan-chilled delicatessen serves freshly brewed coffee, fruit juices, imported ice cream, waffles & pancakes, as well as a selection of savoury-filled paninis. *Paninis around £5, waffles/pancakes under £3.*

✴ ✗ **Uncle Nuha's African Restaurant** [129 D3] ⏰ 08.00–20.00. The only place on the strip catering to a predominantly Gambian clientele, this sweaty hole-in-the-wall next to the market serves large carbo-loaded platefuls of whatever local dish(es) they've conjured up that day. No nonsense. No alcohol. Great value. *Mains around £1–3.*

✗ **Alex Restaurant** [129 D2] m 7844910/7826322; e alexbergeijk@gmail.com; ⏰ 08.00–late daily. Despite a certain lack of character, this place is popular for expats & tourists alike, perhaps due to the wide range of reasonably priced dishes, friendly service, draught beer, happy hour & a Wi-Fi connection. There's a pool table inside, although most eating & drinking takes place on the outdoor terrace. *Dutch snacks from £1–4, mains in the £5–6.50 range.*

✗ **Shalom Cafe** [129 C2] m 2572285; ⏰ 11.00–19.00 Mon–Sat. This little mint-green café serves a selection of homemade cakes & snacks. There's a book-swap service, & they also sell hand-woven baskets & other items made locally in the community.

✗ **Swiss Tavern** [124 A7] m 9147949/2012121/3734085; e swisstavern@hotmail.com; f swisstaverngambia; ⏰ 09.30–midnight daily. Situated on the pretty beach between Kololi Beach Club & Bijilo Forest Park, this locally owned beach bar has comfortable seating in thatched summer houses & serves a selection of Gambian & seafood dishes, as well as slightly cheaper sandwiches & snacks either in the beach bantabas or the veranda of the bar building itself. Wi-Fi is available. *Mains around £5.*

ENTERTAINMENT AND NIGHTLIFE The Senegambia Strip lies at the epicentre of The Gambia's limited nightlife scene. A handful of dedicated nightspots includes **Dreamz Lounge** (m *7777814;* f *dreamzlounge*) and **Club Waaw** (m *7784662*), both of which are on the first floor of the row of buildings that also includes the African Queen [129 C2]. Just round the corner on Senegambia Highway are a string of bars and clubs including **Time Inn** [129 D3] (m *2327579;* f *CaribeCanarias*) and **Britannia** [129 D3] (m *7684293*). Between them, they are usually open every night, starting at around 22.00 and staying open until the early morning or when the last guest leaves. All are pretty much out-and-out pickup joints, frequented by large numbers of prostitutes, bumsters and other potential hangers-on, and theft is also an occasional problem.

For a more wholesome night out, many of the restaurants listed above (and some that aren't) double as terrace bars, staying open until midnight or later, and it is really just a case of picking whichever one takes your fancy and pulling up a seat. Among the best spots for live music are **Club One** [129 B2] (*next to African Queen;* m *7823620; starting at 23.00 most nights*) and more occasionally **Darboe's Bar & Restaurant** (page 132). The rather dour **Kololi Casino** [129 B5], a few doors up from the Kora Restaurant, closed abruptly following President Jammeh's gambling ban and whether this and other casinos will reopen under Barrow remains to be seen.

OTHER PRACTICALITIES

Banks and foreign exchange The most convenient bank and ATM for visitors is the **Standard Chartered Bank** [129 B2] on the main strip opposite the main taxi rank. There are also **Trust** and **GT** banks [129 D2], both with ATMs outside, on opposite sides of Bertil Harding Highway about 100m north of Senegambia Junction. In addition, there must be a dozen private **forex bureaux** along the strip and the side road to Kololi Beach Club, all offering similar rates. It can be worth shopping around, though be warned that it will be difficult to shake off the attentions of any bumster who notices you leaving a forex bureau without having changed any money.

Guided excursions Several agencies offer day trips to sites such as Banjul City, Abuko Nature Reserve and Makasutu Cultural Forest, as well as dolphin-watching trips, 'Roots Excursions' to Albreda, Juffureh and Kunta Kinteh (James) Island, and excursions to most other sites west of Serekunda and Brikama. Established agencies include the upmarket and highly regarded **The Gambia Experience** (w *gambia.co.uk*), which has an office in the Senegambia Hotel [129 A2], and the more budget-oriented **Arch Tours** [129 B4] (*next to Sarges Hotel;* m *9906890;* w *arch-tours.com*), and **Bushwhacker Tours** (*Senegambia Strip;* m *7062502/9912891;* w *bushwhackertours.com*). Trips can also be arranged through the official government-trained guides at the National Tour Guide Association shelter in the middle of the traffic circle in front of the Senegambia Hotel [129 A2]. Guide fees are around £8.50 per party for a half-day tour and £17 for a full day.

Health and beauty The best options are the hairdressing and beauty salons in the Kairaba, Sarges and Senegambia hotels.

Internet There is an internet café at the **Gamtel Customer Centre** [129 C2], and most hotels and restaurants now also have Wi-Fi, among them the Gaya Art Café,

Darboe's Bar & Restaurant, and Caramel in The Village. To install a local SIM card in your (unlocked) tablet, phone or modem, and set up a local data bundle for internet usage, just pop into the **Africell Customer Care** office [129 B2] or **Qcell** kiosk [129 B2] next to the main taxi park.

Laundry If your hotel can't do your laundry, your best option is **R & R Laundry** [129 B1] (m *497480;* ⊕ *09.00–19.00 Mon–Sat*) opposite Shalom Cafe.

Shopping The Village Mall, 500m north of Senegambia Junction, houses the best supermarket in the vicinity and a selection of other shops catering mainly to tourists and wealthier locals (page 128). Several smaller but reasonably well-stocked grocery shops can also be found along the strip, the best being the **Right Choice Supermarket** [129 B2] (m *7940525;* ⊕ *09.00–22.00 daily*) next to the Standard Chartered Bank. Others include the **Safeway Supermarket** [129 C2] and an anonymous **mini market** [129 A2] on the main circle next to the entrance of the Senegambia Hotel.

Situated on the southwest side of Senegambia Junction, the **Senegambia Craft Market** [129 D3] incorporates around 50 stalls selling a wide variety of local and traditional craft items and clothes. Other good handicraft outlets include the gift shops in the Senegambia and Kairaba hotels.

Tourist information The **Gambian Tourist Board (GTB)** maintains an office on Senegambia Junction next to the craft market [129 D2], but it seldom seems to be manned.

BIJILO AND SUKUTA

Though it lies only 2km southwest of Kololi (from which it is separated by the small Bijilo Forest Park), low-key Bijilo is strikingly different in feel, with beach activity being centred on a wide sandy shore that is relatively quiet and bumster-free. Until recently, Bijilo was almost completely ignored by the tourist industry, but today it houses several newish package hotels, most of which lie on or very close to the beach. In a sense, Bijilo as it stands represents a kind of best-of-both-worlds scenario, as there's little of the hustle and bustle associated with all the other resorts to its northeast, yet it is literally just a 5-minute taxi ride to the cluster of restaurants and late-night scene at nearby Kololi. Immediately inland of Bijilo, Sukuta is a small town best known to overland travellers as the site of the legendary Camping Sukuta (page 136).

GETTING THERE AND AWAY Bijilo flanks the Bertil Harding Highway about 2km southwest of Kololi *en route* to Brusubi Junction, the traffic circle at the four-way junction with Sayerr Jobe Road (to Serekunda), the AU Highway (to Banjul International Airport and Brikama), and Coastal Road (which runs south to the Senegalese border via Brufut, Tanji, Gunjur and Kartong). The hotels in Bijilo all lie within around 200m of Bertil Harding Highway, so are readily accessible on shared taxis or other public transport between Bakau or Kololi and Brusubi Junction. Coming to or from the airport, you will need to take a private taxi, which costs around £15.

WHERE TO STAY *Map, page 74*
Exclusive
✳ 🏠 **Coco Ocean Resort & Spa** (89 rooms)
Bertil Harding Hwy, Bijilo; 📞 4466500; e info@

cocoocean.com; w cocoocean.com. Arguably the most stylish large hotel in the country, the 5-star Coco Ocean sprawls across expansive

& well-tended gardens, with some resident monkeys, down to a long attractive white-sanded swimming beach decked out with shaded sunbeds. Reminiscent of North Africa or the Swahili Coast, the innovative architecture makes extensive use of arches & domes, contrasting whitewashed walls with contemporary bright colours. Accommodation is in a variety of light, airy & attractively decorated high-ceilinged suites & houses, all of which come with AC, fan, satellite TV, writing desk & large en-suite bathroom, & the costlier units also have verandas, sitting rooms & private plunge pools. Facilities include 1 Thai & 2 fine-dining restaurants, a world-class spa, 3 swimming pools, Wi-Fi & 24hr room service. *£103.20/120.40/146.20 junior/ superior/deluxe room, £331.10 beach house & just £1,720 for the Presidential Villa. All rates B&B, HB option available.*

Upmarket

🏠 **Seafront Residence** (20 rooms) Bijilo Beach, behind the filling station; 📞 4463147; m 7019000; e info@seafront.gm; w seafront. gm. This Mediterranean-style all-apt complex, which opened in 2012, has a large & attractive freeform swimming pool, & is less than 5 mins' walk from Bijilo Beach. Though rather lacking in character, the apts are spacious & modern, & consist of 1 or 2 bedrooms with king-size bed & net, a sitting room with satellite TV, a well-equipped modern kitchen, & a bathroom with combined tub/shower. Good value. *From £73/91 sgl/dbl 1-bedroom apt, £128/146 sgl/dbl 2-bedroom apt, all rates B&B.*

Mid-range

🏠 **Baobab Holiday Resort** (42 rooms) Bertil Harding Highway, Bijilo; m 7053394/9905787/8905832; e baobabbookings@hotmail.com; w baobabresort. net. Very popular with Dutch package tourists, this compact & unpretentious resort lies opposite the Coco Ocean, about 10 mins' walk from the beach. The neat, clean en-suite rooms, in colourful dbl-storey blocks centred on a welcoming figure-of-8 swimming pool, all come with queen-size bed, Wi-Fi, fan, satellite TV, hot shower, & private terrace, with optional AC & fridge. There are also apts with a sitting & dining room. Facilities include a good restaurant & spa. Exceptional value. *£25/33 sgl/dbl, £42/50 sgl/dbl deluxe, all rates B&B.*

🏠 **Kasumai Beach Guest House** (6 rooms) Off Senegambia Hwy; m 2762280; e office@ kasumaibeach.com; w kasumaibeach.com. This Austrian-run guesthouse offers comfortable rooms right on the beach, next to the popular beach bar of the same name. Rooms include Wi-Fi, flatscreen satellite TV, AC & free access to sunbeds. A new 12-room boutique hotel was under construction as this book was researched, so check the website for details. *£30/35 sgl/dbl without AC, £35/40 sgl/ dbl with AC.*

🏠 **Lemon Creek Resort** (56 rooms) Off Bertil Harding Hwy, Bijilo; m 6611700/6611800; e lemon.creek.hotel@gmail.com; w lemoncreek. net. Dutch-owned & -managed, & built in Spanish colonial style, this small hotel slots somewhere between the package & boutique ends of the markets. The sizeable & tastefully decorated rooms are arranged in dbl-storey blocks & all contain a wooden 4-poster queen-size bed with net, fan, AC, satellite TV, safe & private balcony. The large grounds are bisected by a small stream, with the swimming-pool area on the opposite side to the rooms. The property leads to a semi-private swimming beach enclosed by natural vegetation & boasting a small but pretty lagoon. Overall, a clear standout in this price range. Good value. *£42/50 sgl/dbl, £82 suite, with substantial discounts May– Sep, all rates B&B.*

Budget & camping

✳️ 🏠 **Camping Sukuta** 500m north of Sayerr Jobe Rd, Sukuta; m 9917786; e campingsukutagambia@yahoo.de; w campingsukuta.com. Something of an overlanders' institution, this German-owned & -managed lodge & campsite in Sukuta has long been the place to stock up, rest up & trade knowledge & experiences with drivers coming in the opposite direction. Efficiency, comfort & friendliness are the bywords of this camp, which lies in well-tended & tidy gardens & has a good book swap & library, a decent restaurant/bar , a small shop that sells essential vehicle spares & a selection of groceries, a self-catering kitchen, & Wi-Fi for around £2.50 per day. Accommodation is clean, well maintained & comes with a fan. *€10/14 sgl/dbl, €17/19.50 sgl/ dbl with en suite, €26 house with AC, safe, veranda, €3.80 camping plus €1.20–2.50 per vehicle.*

✻ 🏠 **Sardinka House** (6 rooms) Off Bertil Harding Hwy, Bijilo; m 7860005; e sardinkahouse@yahoo.com; ⨍ Sardinka Guest House. Run by a long-term resident British couple, this friendly family-oriented place centres around a pool surrounded by palms & a relaxing bantaba, where you can enjoy some of the coldest drinks in The Gambia, sunbeds, a craft shop & library. All rooms either have, or have access to, fully equipped kitchens as well as TVs, fans, & 2 have AC. There is a solar back-up system so you won't notice power cuts. Although self-catering, a meal will be provided on the day of arrival & there's generally a weekly culinary event such as BBQ or curry night. You are welcome to join fishing excursions, the only fee being a contribution to petrol costs. *£25 per room with discounts for long-term stays.*

🏠 **Shelley's** (24 rooms) Off Bertil Harding Hwy; m 2547385; e shelleysgambia@outlook. com; w shelleysingambia.com. Close to the Bijilo Medical Centre, this new Welsh-run guesthouse is centred on a large swimming pool. The rooms are spotlessly clean & modernly decorated & there are family rooms available, as well as 2 apts. There is a bar/restaurant serving snacks & simple home-cooked meals with a large TV & pool table, as well as a small gym. Good value. *£12pp room only, £15pp B&B.*

🍴 WHERE TO EAT AND DRINK *Map, page 74*

✻ 🍴 **The Blue Kitchen** m 9804961; ⨍ bluekitchengambia; ⏱ 09.00–23.30 daily. Part of a German NGO where a percentage of all profits are fed back into local community projects, this bar & restaurant serves excellent food in lovely surroundings. Either sit inside the main restaurant/bar area where a huge flat-screen TV broadcasts major sporting events, or for more tranquil surroundings, sit in the gardens backing on to a local woman's vegetable garden, small children's playground & craft shop. Choose from Gambian or European food, roast on a Sun & Fri night buffet for £7.

✻ 🍴 **Kaj's Cave** m 2304950; e heffas@ hotmail.com; ⏱ noon–midnight daily. Tucked away in the sandy backstreets of Kerr Serign, this little gem has been serving local expats in the know for the past couple of years. It's under 10 mins' walk from the Senegambia Hwy at 2 Rays, turning inland. There's a new menu every day along with regular mainstays such as homemade burgers with bacon & cheese & fish & chips. Dishes include European classics as well as interesting fusions of local products such as butter fish in a creamy bacon sauce. The bar attracts a regular crowd & beers are cold to the point of nearly freezing. Excellent value where food is as good as any top restaurant. *Most mains £3.50 or less.*

✻ 🍴 **Sea Shells** Senegambia Hwy; m 7760070/7428820; e fuzzfuzz@hotmail.com; ⨍ seashellsgambia; ⏱ 10.30–late Mon–Sat. One of the finest restaurants in The Gambia, this Moroccan-run place, as the name implies, serves fresh local seafood (the house speciality is lobster thermidor) but also fine meat dishes such as chateaubriand. The setting is warm & intimate & service is impeccable & friendly. Additionally, the pastry chef makes exquisite cakes, cheesecakes (including their famous Nutella cheesecake) & some of the best bread in the country. There's also an excellent wine list. *Mains in the £8–12 range, lobster thermidor £20.*

✻ 🍴 **Sunbird Beach Bar & Restaurant** Bijilo Beach; ☎ 4464594; m 9901914/7770127; e gibousagnia@yahoo.com; ⏱ 09.00–late. Another strong contender for Gambia's best beach bar. Setting this one aside from the competition is the lovely green lawn shaded by palms, running down a slope towards the wide open sands of the beach. There's a choice of seating at tables or sunbeds with thatched umbrellas, & the friendly waiting staff will bring snacks such as sandwiches or European/ Gambian mains to your relaxation point of choice. To find it, take the first right heading south from Coco Ocean Hotel on the Senegambia Hwy.

🍴 **2 Rays** m 2344460/234; ⏱ 08.00–late daily. This food enterprise was founded by 2 brothers who both have over 15 years' experience working in the restaurant business. They serve a fabulous range of international favourites including fillet steak, meatballs, fajitas, burgers, & various pizzas & pastas, plus a variety of cocktails. There's an attached bakery, & they also offer catering services for weddings & birthdays.

🍴 **Kasumai Beach Bar & Restaurant** Off Senegambia Hwy; m 2762280; e office@ kasumaibeach.com; w kasumaibeach.com; ⏱ 09.00–22.00 daily. Next door to Sunbird Beach Bar, this also offers sunbeds & a restaurant serving continental food, fresh seafood, Gambian dishes & a decent wine list. The gardens are a lovely place to enjoy a drink & free Wi-Fi is provided. There are several events each week including live music on Sun, salsa & a fire & culture night. A massage service is also available. *Mains around £5.*

WHAT TO SEE AND DO Inland from the beach, Bijilo is a primarily residential area with few sights as such, although MyFarm offers a fascinating insight for anyone interested in local eco-farming techniques and products.

Bijilo Forest Park (⏲ *07.00–18.00 daily; entrance D150, children under 12 free*) Protecting 51.3ha of coastal forest and scrub overlooking the beach running south from Kololi Beach Club, the Bijilo Forest Park, created in 1982, ranks among the best-preserved habitats of its type in the country, yet it lies within easy walking distance of the Senegambia Strip and associated hotels. For most visitors, its main attraction is the opportunity to get close to free-ranging but very habituated populations of three primate species: the widespread and easily seen green monkey, the slightly shyer and more localised red colobus, and the seldom-seen patas monkey. Other mammals include Gambian sun squirrels, which are frequently spotted in the trees, and striped ground squirrels which you can see on the forest floor. In addition, Bijilo supports one-third of all the butterfly species recorded in the country, a variety of lizards including Nile monitor, agama and brown-flanked skink, and more than 130 bird species, including three types of bee-eater, red-necked falcon, stone partridge, and rarities such as Ahanta francolin and western bluebill.

In early 2017, a section of the forest near the entrance was chopped down as the new Barrow government came into power. Perhaps taking advantage of the political confusion, there was short-sighted talk of a new hotel development. However, a protest was quickly organised via social media and within days the work halted, seemingly for good, thankfully before too much damage could be done.

The entrance to the reserve lies opposite Bijilo Beach Club, only 5–10 minutes' walk from most hotels and restaurants along the Senegambia Strip. Here, you need to pay the entrance fee and pick up the more-or-less mandatory guide, a service included in the entrance fee, though a tip is expected. From the gate, a network of nature trails, comprising around 5km of well-marked and maintained footpaths, leads around the reserve. The paths are divided into colour-coded circular routes, so that you can choose how far and in what direction you want to walk. Most of it is fairly level, though there are a few steeper parts with rough steps. Another straight path which runs through the forest and scrub near to the beach is known as 'the ornithological path', since it affords excellent opportunities to view many of the park's birds. Overall, Bijilo Forest Park is a wonderful example of how the Gambian coastline once looked and is well worth a visit at any time of the year. If you are staying outside Kololi, most hotels and operators arrange visits, or you can just ask a taxi to drop you at the entrance – there will always be taxis waiting outside when you are finished.

MyFarm (*Nema Kunku, near Sukuta;* m *7121212;* e *myfarm@gambiastartup.com;* w *gambiastartup.com;* ⏲ *daily*) With the strap line 'Helping the community to help itself', this 1ha farm was set up by the NGO Africa Startup (Gambia) as a training and education centre for young Gambians, offering an 'educational journey from seed to business', learning through play and practical activities. MyFarm aims to demonstrate best practice in horticultural techniques, adding value to local produce and creating an entrepreneurial spirit. Their guiding principle is environmental protection, showcasing appropriate sustainable alternative technology and they aim to become self-sustaining through various income-generating activities including the sale of high-quality local produce and beauty products, some of which are available at Timbooktoo bookshop (page 109). Check their website for volunteering opportunities.

THE GAMBIA ONLINE

For additional online content, articles, photos and more on The Gambia, why not visit **w** bradtguides.com/thegambia.

Part Three

THE COASTAL BELT

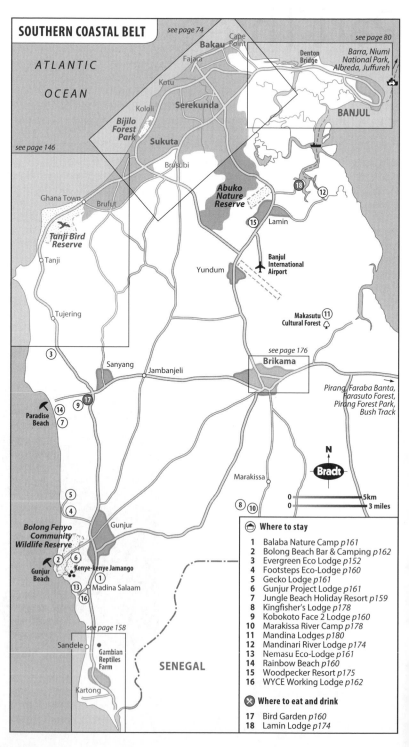

ATLANTIC

OCEAN

see page 74

Cape
Point

Bakau

Fajara

see page 80

Denton
Bridge

Barra, Niumi
National Park,
Albreda, Juffureh

Kotu

Kololi

Serekunda

BANJUL

Bijilo
Forest
Park

Sukuta

see page 146

Brusubi

Ghana Town

Brufut

Abuko
Nature
Reserve

18

12

15   Lamin

Tanji Bird
Reserve

Tanji

Banjul
International
Airport

Yundum

Tujering

Makasutu   11
Cultural Forest

3

Sanyang   Jambanjeli

see page 176

Brikama

Pirang, Faraba Banta,
Farasuto Forest,
Pirang Forest Park,
Bush Track

14
Paradise
Beach   7

9   17

N

Bradt

5

4

Bolong Fenyo
Community
Wildlife Reserve

Gunjur

Marakissa

8   10

0   5km
0   3 miles

2

Gunjur
Beach

Kenye-kenye Jamango

13   Madina Salaam
16
1

see page 158

Sandele

Gambian
Reptiles
Farm

SENEGAL

Kartong

🛏 **Where to stay**

1   Balaba Nature Camp *p161*
2   Bolong Beach Bar & Camping *p162*
3   Evergreen Eco Lodge *p152*
4   Footsteps Eco-Lodge *p160*
5   Gecko Lodge *p161*
6   Gunjur Project Lodge *p161*
7   Jungle Beach Holiday Resort *p159*
8   Kingfisher's Lodge *p178*
9   Koboloto Face 2 Lodge *p160*
10 Marakissa River Camp *p178*
11 Mandina Lodges *p180*
12 Mandinari River Lodge *p174*
13 Nemasu Eco-Lodge *p161*
14 Rainbow Beach *p160*
15 Woodpecker Resort *p175*
16 WYCE Working Lodge *p162*

✖ **Where to eat and drink**

17 Bird Garden *p160*
18 Lamin Lodge *p174*

The Coastal Belt: An Overview

It's tempting to introduce the Atlantic coastline north and south of Greater Banjul as the Very Best of The Gambia, or something similarly hyperbolic. True, there are a great many more tourist amenities, of an overall higher standard, packed into the confines of Greater Banjul and Kololi. Conversely, when it comes to free-spirited exploration, nowhere on the coast can offer an adventure comparable to heading upriver into the largely undeveloped and off-the-beaten-track interior.

Nevertheless, the coastline south of Greater Banjul could in particular be seen as offering the best of both worlds. Coming from the city, it feels refreshingly rustic and unaffected, dotted as it is with a few small fishing villages whose organic appearance blends in with the lush nature reserves and swathes of farmland that separate them. Easy to get around, the south is liberally dotted with a collection of low-key and sensibly priced eco-lodges and beach camps whose down-to-earth ethos is the very antithesis of the packaged hotels of Greater Banjul. Not least, the actual beaches are, for the most part, quite splendid – long swathes of white sand shaded by swaying palms and largely free of unsightly developments.

Even more remote and undeveloped is the northern coastline protected in Niumi National Park. Accessible from Greater Banjul only by ferry or by private boat transfer, this short stretch of coast lies almost entirely on Jinack Island (separated from the mainland by a narrow creek), where a handful of tiny villages nestle alongside a few unabashedly rustic beach camps, and one of the finest swimming beaches in the country.

The coastal belt covered in the subsequent chapters also incorporates some inland or riverside sites commonly visited as a day trip out of Greater Banjul. On the North Bank, several riverine locales collectively inscribed as the 'Kunta Kinteh Island and Related Sites' UNESCO World Heritage Site' are the goal of the popular Roots excursions from the resorts. On the South Bank, the road to Brikama, the country's second-largest town, offers access to the wonderful Abuko Nature Reserve, Makasutu Cultural Forest and Brikama Craft Market – as well as Banjul International Airport, the point of entry for all fly-in tourists to The Gambia.

HIGHLIGHTS

TANJI BIRD RESERVE The recently opened eco-lodge in this community-owned reserve seems set to become a favourite of birders. Equally tantalising are day trips to the bird-rich Bijol Islands and a walking trail to Tanji Bridge. See pages 150–2.

TANJI This down-to-earth village, among the largest on the south coast, is renowned for its fascinating artisanal fishing beach and private village museum, as well as offering enjoyable camel safaris. See pages 152–7.

TUJERING BEACH South of Tanji, this ranks among the country's most beautiful and safest swimming beaches, with the bonus of offering good birding, not to mention tasty food at a locally run beach bar. See page 156.

KARTONG BIRD OBSERVATORY Well established as a ringing centre, this excellent facility overlooking a community wetland reserve is the best starting point for exploring a corner of the country famed for throwing up avian rarities and new records. See pages 167–8.

ALLAHEIN RIVER It's possible to cross this river to Senegal and visit villages of the Casamance region, at what must be one of the most beautiful border crossings in Africa. Alternatively, hang out in one of the riverside bars with an international view. See page 168.

GAMBIAN REPTILES FARM At once a rehabilitation, breeding and community education facility, this herpetological centre outside Kartong is a great place to see (and learn about) snakes, tortoises, lizards and crocodiles at close quarters. See pages 168–9.

ABUKO NATURE RESERVE The Gambia's largest surviving tract of Upper Guinean Forest supports a wonderful variety of birds (270 species recorded in 1km^2) and small mammals such as monkeys and antelope. See pages 171–3.

BRIKAMA CRAFT MARKET For serious handicraft buyers, this well-organised market near Brikama is the best place in the country to pick up quality work at source. See pages 177–8.

MAKASUTU CULTURAL FOREST Enjoyable day tours, night extravaganzas and extended stays at the architecturally flamboyant Mandina Lodges are offered at this owner-managed private reserve – the most westerly site to possess a genuinely 'upriver' feel. See pages 178–81.

ALBREDA, JUFFUREH AND KUNTA KINTEH (JAMES) ISLAND This trio of slave-trade-related historic sites, collectively inscribed as a UNESCO World Heritage Site, is the target of the popular Roots excursions to the North Bank and Fort James. See pages 190–2.

JINACK ISLAND Comprising the entire Atlantic coastline north of the river mouth, budget-friendly Jinack is both the centrepiece of Niumi National Park and the country's ultimate 'desert island fantasy' destination. See pages 193–5.

GETTING AROUND

A network of good surfaced roads connects the main towns and villages in this region. The most important of these, both running in a broadly north to south direction, are the South Coast Road from Greater Banjul and Kololi to Kartong via Brusubi Junction, Tanji, Sanyang and Gunjur, and the Brikama Highway (effectively the start of the South Bank Road) between Serekunda and Brikama via Abuko, Lamin and Banjul International Airport. Connecting these two trunk roads in a broadly west to east direction are the surfaced roads between Brusubi Junction and Banjul International Airport, between Sanyang and Brikama, and between Gunjur and Brikama.

The area is serviced by plenty of gelly-gellys and shared taxis. Coming from Greater Banjul, the main terminus for transport along the South Coast Road is Dippa Kunda Station in Serekunda, though you should also be able to pick up something at Brusubi Junction. Heading to Brikama and sites *en route*, transport can be picked up at a station on Mosque Road about 200m north of Serekunda Market, or at Westfield Junction. Day excursions to most sites in the region can also be arranged through hotel activities desks, local tour operators or private guides.

OTHER PRACTICALITIES

There is quite plentiful **accommodation**, but it is more spaced out and very different in style from the clustered package hotels that dominate in Greater Banjul. It includes some of the country's finest boutique lodges and hotels, mostly dotted around Brufut, along with a succession of fine beachfront eco-lodges (typically with solar power, borehole water and compost toilets) south of Brufut, and plenty of low-key budget beach and other camps throughout. With the exception of the boutique hotels around Brufut, rooms with air conditioning are a rarity, thanks partially to the lack of grid power, and some places don't even have fans.

Standalone **restaurants** are few and far between, since most people tend to eat at their hotel or camp. There are a few **banks** with **ATMs** in Brikama, and on the road back towards Serekunda, as well as at Barra (the North Bank ferry terminus opposite Banjul). There are no banks or ATMs elsewhere north of the river (not in Niumi National Park, Albreda or Juffureh) and the most southerly ATM on the coast is in the lobby of Brufut's top hotel, the Coral Beach. Internet access is patchy. A few of the better hotels have Wi-Fi, but there are no internet cafés (except in Brikama) and even mobile access can be problematic on the coast north of Barra and south of Brufut.

FOLLOW US

Use #**TheGambia** to share your adventures using this guide with us – we'd love to hear from you.

- ⓕ BradtTravelGuides
- 🐦 @BradtGuides & @philipbriggs
- 📷 @bradtguides
- ⓟ bradtguides

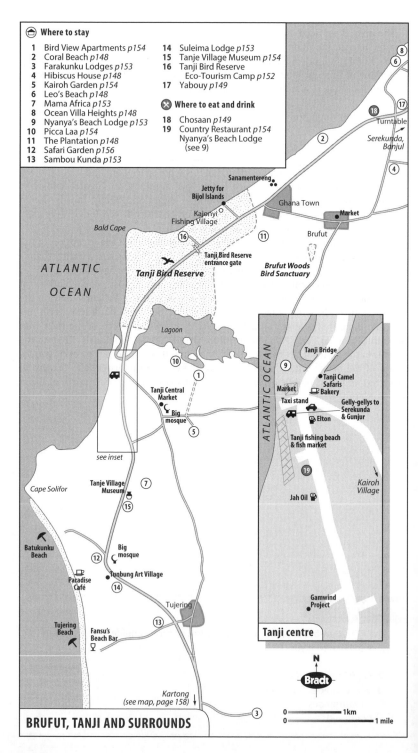

⬯ Where to stay

1 Bird View Apartments *p154*
2 Coral Beach *p148*
3 Farakunku Lodges *p153*
4 Hibiscus House *p148*
5 Kairoh Garden *p154*
6 Leo's Beach *p148*
7 Mama Africa *p153*
8 Ocean Villa Heights *p148*
9 Nyanya's Beach Lodge *p153*
10 Picca Laa *p154*
11 The Plantation *p148*
12 Safari Garden *p156*
13 Sambou Kunda *p153*
14 Suleima Lodge *p153*
15 Tanje Village Museum *p154*
16 Tanji Bird Reserve
      Eco-Tourism Camp *p152*
17 Yabouy *p149*

⊗ Where to eat and drink

18 Chosaan *p149*
19 Country Restaurant *p154*
      Nyanya's Beach Lodge
      (see 9)

Sanamentereng

Jetty for
Bijol Islands

Kajonyi
Fishing Village

Ghana Town

Market

Bald Cape

Brufut

16

11

Tanji Bird Reserve
entrance gate

Brufut Woods
Bird Sanctuary

ATLANTIC

OCEAN

Tanji Bird Reserve

Lagoon

10

1

Tanji Central
Market

Big
mosque

5

see inset

Cape Solifor

Tanje Village
Museum

7

15

Batukunku
Beach

12

Big
mosque

Paradise
Café

14

Tunbung Art Village

Tujering

Tujering
Beach

Fansu's
Beach Bar

13

Serekunda,
Banjul

18

Turntable

17

4

2

ATLANTIC OCEAN

Tanji Bridge

9

Tanji Camel
Safaris

Market   Bakery

Taxi stand

Elton

Gelly-gellys to
Serekunda
& Gunjur

Tanji fishing beach
& fish market

19

*Kairoh
Village*

Jah Oil

Gamwind
Project

Tanji centre

N

Bradt

*Kartong
(see map, page 158)*

3

0   1km
0   1 mile

BRUFUT, TANJI AND SURROUNDS

10

Brufut, Tanji and Surrounds

Past Kololi and Bijilo, the Gambian coastline curves in a southwesterly direction for about 8km to Bald Cape, before veering sharply southward to Cape Solifor, the country's most westerly landfall, another 5km further south. Within this relatively short stretch of Atlantic frontage, the coast undergoes a dramatic change in character, as the built-up resorts north of Bijilo give way to the residential suburbia of Brufut and then the more rustic open shoreline and fishing villages typical of the south coast. Further south, Tanji Bird Reserve, which incorporates Bald Cape, is one of the country's most rewarding ornithological sites, and a near-essential day trip for keen birdwatchers. The village of Tanji, on the reserve's southern border, is another popular tourist attraction, thanks to its bustling fishing beach and well-constructed private museum to its south. For those who prefer to base themselves away from the main resorts, the area also boasts some good accommodation options, ranging from the upmarket Coral Beach Hotel and a couple of sumptuous boutique hotels in Brufut to a very reasonably priced eco-lodge in Tanji Bird Reserve.

BRUFUT

This town of around 10,000 people feels somewhat transitional between Greater Banjul and the small villages and wilder beaches that characterise the south coast, coming across like a semi-rusticated southern outpost of the sprawling city with which it intergrades. Traditionally, Brufut is primarily a residential area, and even today it couldn't be described as resort-like in the manner of, say, Kololi or Kotu. But it also houses a trio of relatively new and alluring upmarket hotels, most notably the five-star Coral Beach Hotel, and a couple of more boutique-like properties in the form of Leo's Beach Hotel and Hibiscus House. On the southwestern border of Brufut, the small village of Ghana Town was founded by Ghanaian fishermen, who catch and smoke fish for export to their home country.

GETTING THERE AND AWAY Brufut flanks the main Coastal Road for a distance of about 4km south of Brusubi Junction, the landmark traffic circle at the four-way intersection with Sayerr Jobe Road (from Serekunda), Bertil Harding Highway (from Kololi and Bijilo), and the AU Highway (from Banjul International Airport and Brikama). Its hotels are all quite well signposted if you are in a private vehicle, but Leo's Beach Hotel and Hibiscus House are both fairly isolated and best reached from the airport (or elsewhere) in a private taxi, which should cost about £15. Most people heading to the Coral Beach Hotel will presumably also use a private taxi, but this hotel could easily be reached on any public transport running from Serekunda to Tanji. If you are heading to Brufut Woods, you could catch a shared taxi or gelly-gelly to the central market area of Brufut, and walk from there.

WHERE TO STAY *Map, page 146*
Exclusive/luxury
❋ ⌂ **Leo's Beach Hotel & Restaurant**
(6 rooms) Brufut Heights; m 7212830; e info@
leosgambia.com; w leos.gm. Opened in 2013,
this absolutely stunning boutique hotel, owned
& managed by a flexible, efficient & enthusiastic
Austrian couple, has quickly gained an enviable
reputation for its food, service & quality
accommodation. Set on a low cliff, it is centred on
a large swimming pool in neat gardens that lead
to a footpath running down to a beautiful secluded
beach. The large en-suite rooms, which combine
clean contemporary lines with quality imported
fittings & stylish local rosewood furniture & décor,
mostly have a sea view & all come with AC, fan,
satellite TV, iPod deck, minibar, coffee-making
facilities, hot water & even a mobile phone loaded
with local numbers for your personal use. A 20kW
photovoltaic solar-energy system provides enough
electricity to cover all its power demands. An
added attraction, well worth the excursion even if
you are staying elsewhere, is the breezy poolside
restaurant, which specialises in simple but
delicious Mediterranean-style seafood. Not cheap,
but still excellent value for money. *£104–120 dbl
B&B for low or high season*.

Upmarket
⌂ **Coral Beach Hotel** (194 rooms)
Brufut Heights; ☎ 4410889; e reservations@
gambiacoralbeach.com; w gambiacoralbeach.
com. Formerly the Sheraton Gambia Hotel, this
isolated resort at Brufut Heights vies with Coco
Ocean as the country's most impressive & stylish
large hotel. Set on a steep slope running down to
an idyllic park-like swimming pool area & private
beach, it has a contemporary feel, dominated
by curvaceous Sahelian-influenced architecture,
earthy colours & walls hung with bright African
artworks. The en-suite rooms & suites are
surprisingly nondescript, at least in comparison
with the dramatic exteriors, but very comfortable
& well equipped, coming with twin ¾ beds or
1 queen-size bed, AC, fan, satellite TV & private
terrace. Facilities include 2 restaurants (with fresh
seafood being a speciality), gym, spa, business
centre, the only lifts in The Gambia, & free Wi-Fi
& ATM in the lobby. Rates depend on season,
availability & room type. *Prices start at around £75
for dbl B&B*.

❋ ⌂ **Hibiscus House** (10 rooms)
Brufut; m 7982929, (UK) (0)7427 688277;
e info@hibiscushousegambia.com;
w hibiscushousegambia.com. The backstreets
of Brufut might not seem like the most obvious
location for one of The Gambia's top boutique
hotels, but it is where you will find Hibiscus
House, nestled unobtrusively among low-rise
local compounds & fantastically bumpy dirt roads.
Set in a mango-shaded compound rattling with
birdlife & dominated by a sparkling swimming
pool, this hotel is notable for its hands-on & very
accommodating British owner-managers, sociable
atmosphere & welcoming staff, all of which ensure
plenty of repeat business. The spacious individually
styled rooms are simply but tastefully decorated,
with twin or queen-size bed, fans & en-suite hot
shower, & there are also 2 apts that share a second
pool. Although it is 2km from the sea, the hotel has
the advantage of a bumster-free village setting
away from the main tourist areas. For those who
want a break from the in-house pool, the hotel
can arrange trusted local taxis to take you to
various isolated beaches further south, as well as
expeditions further afield. Facilities include free
Wi-Fi, a good restaurant & bar, & a lounge with
plenty of board games & a well-stocked book swap
& library. *£76 dbl Garden Room, £98 dbl Casuarina
Deluxe room, min stay 3 nights, all rates B&B*.

Mid-range
⌂ **Ocean Villa Heights** (7 rooms) Brufut
Heights; m 2487430; e info@oceanvillaheights.
com; w oceanvillaheights.com; see ad, 2nd colour
section & page 157. Situated upon a clifftop
overlooking a deserted beach, Ocean Villa Heights
is a British-run boutique hotel complete with an
iconic red telephone box at the entrance. Rooms
are modern & comfortable, all with AC & en suites
with hot water. A restaurant serves both Gambian &
European dishes in the £5–8 range. The hotel offers
sea fishing, birdwatching & other tours, or you can
simply relax on the sun terrace by the pool. *From
around £35 dbl B&B*.
⌂ **The Plantation** (8 rooms) Brufut;
m 2222660; e nikki@theplantationgambia.
com; w theplantationgambia.com. While this
British-run guesthouse in the sandy streets on the
outskirts of Brufut may feel remote, it's ideally
placed for exploring village life, the nearby bush

& wide empty beaches, all just a 20-min drive from the main coastal resorts. From the highway, follow the signs along a bush route on the left just before the police checkpoint as you leave the outer suburbs of Brufut towards Tanji. The traditional palm leaf-roofed round houses are comfortable & tastefully decorated, with solar power, fans & en suites with hot water. The bar attracts local expats & tasty food is on offer, with traditional Gambian dishes, European favourites & a Fri night BBQ. Tours can be arranged with local people & owner Nikki also provides hairdressing services & other beauty treatments. *£25/35/45 sgl/dbl/trpl B&B, with low-season discounts available.*

🏠 **Yabouy** (3 rooms) Ocean Rd, Brusubi; m 6727273/7727272/3727273/9904990; e chaamidaa@gmail.com. As well as running a popular cooking school (see below), Ida hosts guests in her beautiful house. The homestay is on the highway heading west towards Tanji & in close proximity to the shops & bars of the turntable area as well as the beaches of Brufut Heights. There are 3 rooms: 1 suitable for a family with an en-suite bathroom & 2 dbls with a shared bathroom. The rooms are spotlessly clean, tastefully decorated with African artwork & equipped with fan, nets & Wi-Fi. Outside is a lovely shady courtyard in which to relax. *£30pp B&B.*

🍴 WHERE TO EAT AND DRINK *Map, page 146*

🍴 **Chosaan** Ocean Rd, Brusubi; ✪ N13 24.144 W16 44.230; m 7506995. Probably the pick of several roadside bar-restaurants catering to locals, expats & tourists along the road heading west from Brusubi turntable, not least as it's the only one offering Wi-Fi & live music every night. Food is reasonably priced & the large tiled veranda is a great spot to spend an evening. *Mains in the £3.50–4.50 range.*

OTHER PRACTICALITIES

Banks and foreign exchange There are several banks with ATMs in the area, including **Standard Chartered Bank** and **EcoBank**, as well as several private **forex bureaux** around the turntable and the first 100m or so of Ocean Road heading west. Beware that the turntable garage is a well-known haunt of pickpockets.

Health and beauty The best options are the hairdressing and beauty salons at The Plantation or Coral Beach Hotel.

Shopping There are several mini-markets catering to expats, tourists and wealthier locals in the immediate vicinity of the turntable.

WHAT TO SEE AND DO Because Brufut marks the transition between the developed coast north of Bijilo and the more rustic south coast, it makes a useful base for exploring in either direction. The hectic Senegambia Strip, with its dozens of restaurants and nightspots, is only about 6km to the northeast (a 20-minute taxi ride), while Tanji Bird Reserve and fishing beach are only a few kilometres to the south, as are the lovely beaches at Batukunku and Tujering.

Yabouy Cooking School (m *6727273/7727272/3727273/9904990*; e *chaamidaa@ gmail.com*; ⏲ *Sep–May*) Legendary local Ida Cham (owner of Yabouy guesthouse, see above) has created an experience that is, for many, the highlight of their Gambian holiday. The only home-cooking class available to date in The Gambia, a day's cooking with Ida in her Brufut home is not a simple case of spending the day in her kitchen. First off, you'll dress up in African clothes – brightly patterned shirts for the men and dresses and head scarves for the ladies. Next up, you travel together to nearby Tanji market, a sensory overload in itself, where Ida will guide you through the various stalls to buy fish, vegetables and other ingredients. Her emphasis is on healthy choices and she's well versed in catering for vegetarians or those with specific dietary requirements. After returning and preparing the meal as a group, you will eat African style, communally if you dare, and then relax to play local games and share cultural values. The day lasts from 09.00 until 14.00 and is £45 per person, which includes a transfer to and from your hotel.

Ida is expanding her enterprise to include a supper club (Come dine with Ida), where she serves a home-cooked evening meal, served against the backdrop of kora and storytelling (⊕ *19.00–22.00; £28pp inc hotel transfer*). She has also developed a community-based tourism initiative for larger groups (up to 50) that offers visits to a living museum on the beach at Kartong, 45 minutes' drive down the coast.

Brufut Woods Bird Sanctuary This wedge-shaped community-organised sanctuary, which lies about 2km inland from the Tanji Bird Reserve, is an initiative of the West African Birds Study Association (WABSA), an organisation formed in 1994 by a group of local youths and bird guides dedicated to preserving the country's flora and fauna. Protecting around 1km² of well-preserved coastal woodland immediately south of Brufut, this dry scrubby forest, serviced by a good network of footpaths, is regarded as perhaps the best site for woodland birding this side of Abuko, though species seen here tend to be associated with more open canopies. Among the more interesting birds regularly observed are African pied hornbill, striped kingfisher, green turaco, Vieillot's barbet, swallow-tailed bee-eater, mottled spinetail, red-shouldered cuckoo-shrike, yellow-bellied hyliota, red-bellied paradise flycatcher and western violet-backed sunbird. It is also often a rewarding site for raptors such as lizard buzzard, dark chanting goshawk, Gabar goshawk, African harrier-hawk, long crested eagle, palmnut vulture and lanner falcon. A local guide nicknamed Doctor Owl is well known for his ability to locate nocturnal species such as Verreaux's eagle-owl, white-faced scops owl and long-tailed nightjar.

To get there, catch a shared taxi or other public transport to Brufut, request to be dropped at the central market, then ask for directions to the reserve entrance and ticket office, which is on the west side of the Madiana Road about 800m south of the town centre. All the birding guides based at Kotu Bridge know the site and can guide you there. There's no official entry fee, but a D50 tip would be appreciated.

Sanamentereng Just a short walk south of the Coral Beach Hotel is this sacred site, best visited with a local guide. Located in a clearing in the clifftop, this baobab tree and simple hut attracts Muslims from all over The Gambia in search of good fortune or health. There's a stone at the base of the hut for offerings, while the well at the bottom of the cliff is said to contain special water that can help women overcome infertility.

TANJI BIRD RESERVE

Established in 1993, the 6km² Tanji Bird Reserve (m *9816799/2064997;* e *info@ thegambiawildlife.com;* w *thegambiawildlife.com;* ⊕ *daily; entrance D35pp*) protects most of the 4km coastline between the Coral Beach Hotel and the mouth of the Tanji (or Karinti) River on its southern border. It incorporates Cape Bald, a lateritic peninsula that resurfaces about 1.5km from the mainland to form the Bijol Archipelago, the country's only offshore islands, and also protected within the reserve. Although not exactly historical in a conventional sense, the coast protected by Tanji Bird Reserve was first documented in 1456 by the pioneering Portuguese explorer Luiz de Cadamosto, who encountered dangerous breakers around Cape

above   A museum display at the Ker Batch National Monument, one of four UNESCO-inscribed stone circles in Senegambia (AVZ) pages 223–4

right   A mural in the National Museum of Albreda, one of several harrowing displays depicting the West African slave trade (AVZ) page 190

below right The ruins of Fort James form the most important relict of the slave trade in northern Gambia (AVZ) page 192

below left The Fajara War Cemetery contains the graves of 203 soldiers, both Gambian and British, who died in World War II (AVZ) page 110

left   Fine examples of Creole architecture are found right across The Gambia, such as here in Janjanbureh (AVZ)

below left   A bride in Soma wearing a traditional outfit (AVZ)

below right   The Gambia is a nation of different peoples, made up of eight distinct ethnic groups — this woman is a member of the Wolof (AVZ) pages 14–15

bottom   A fish market on the beach in Tanji (AVZ) page 155

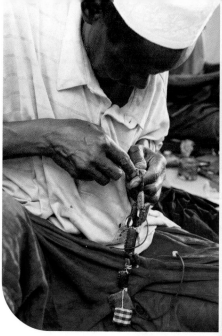

above left &
above right

Arts and crafts are all around you in The Gambia, not only in the market stalls, but also in the metalworkers' yards and the woodworkers' shops (AVZ) pages 17–18

right

Drumming is an essential part of African music and, particularly in rural areas, the beating of drums is a typical Gambian sound (AVZ) page 18

below

Inspired by Alex Haley's *Roots*, the International Roots Festival is a celebration of Gambian culture (AVZ) page 17

*above &
below*

The central feature of
the country is the River
Gambia, bisecting the
North and South banks
(AVZ) and
(AG/AWL) page 25

left

The cliffs which
dominate the coastline
around Fajara give
way to open swathes of
sand that makes up the
gorgeous Fajara beach
(SS) page 109

above   Within the Makatusu Cultural
         Forest and set alongside the
         mangrove-lined Mandina Creek,
         Mandina Lodges is home to both
         plentiful birdlife and a peaceful
         bush atmosphere (AVZ) page 180

right   The Bijilo Forest Park is one of the
         best-preserved habitats of its type
         in the country, home to a dense
         population of red colobus and the
         more elusive patas monkey
         (AVZ) page 138

below   The sandy beach, dotted with palm
         trees, is Kololi's main attraction
         (AVZ) page 125

Ocean Villa Heights Hotel

'A small boutique hotel with a big personality'

With European standard comfort and luxury, we have a room to suit your taste and budget. Most come with stunning sea views and air conditioning, and there's an on-site bar and restaurant and massage treatments. Welcoming guests all year round. You will find us where warm welcome meets the cool Atlantic breeze.

Telephone: +220 2487430 or +220 3777663
what app, viber
Email: info@oceanvillaheights.com
www.oceanvillaheights.com

Bald while sailing between the mouths of the rivers Gambia and Casamance, and also reported the presence of an unnamed river there.

Despite its small area, Tanji Bird Reserve encompasses a wide range of habitat types, including sandy beaches, tidal lagoons, mangrove swamps, barren flats, coastal scrub and dry savannah woodland. More than 260 bird species, including 34 birds of prey, have been recorded, with the greatest diversity being noted in early and late winter, when many Palaearctic passage migrants stop by. Of the rarities, it is worth looking out for white-fronted plover, Audouin's gull and kelp gull on the beach. Other interesting marine birds include ruddy turnstone, slender-billed gull, and half-a-dozen tern species. Inland you may be lucky and find red-billed quelea or yellow-breasted apalis alongside more typical woodland and grassland species. The Bijol Islands are an important breeding site for several species. A large breeding colony of royal terns can be found on the smaller of the two islands, along with lesser numbers of Caspian tern, grey-headed gull and western reef heron. Up to 700 roosting pelicans are present over June to August, and smaller numbers can be seen throughout the year.

Tanji Reserve is not just good for birds. Green turtles nest on the Bijol Islands and along the beach on the mainland part of the reserve, especially over June to October. The mammals present in the reserve include western red colobus, green and patas monkeys, various genets, African civet, spotted hyena, crested porcupine and bushbuck. There are also snakes such as pythons, cobras and puff adders, though of course you will be extremely lucky (or unlucky, depending on your view) to see any of these. There is also a good selection of butterflies and dragonflies at Tanji. In the sea just off the reserve a number of marine mammals have been spotted, including minke whale, Atlantic hump-backed dolphin, bottlenose dolphin and the extremely rare monk seal.

The main activity in the reserve is **bird walks**, which can be undertaken with or without a guide (*D400/hour*), as you choose. You are free to explore anywhere on foot, but an excellent introductory trail leads from the eco-lodge and park headquarters to Tanji Bridge, which crosses the lagoon formed by the Tanji River as it empties into the ocean immediately north of Tanji village. It takes about 45 minutes to walk this, but if you are looking at birds, it might well take 2 or more hours. The other main activity is morning **boat trips** to see the stunning birdlife on the Bijol Islands, which can be arranged through the lodge and cost D750 per person (minimum group size of five). The boat trips run from September to December daily, but only go once weekly over the breeding season of January to August, to avoid overly disturbing the birds.

GETTING THERE AND AWAY Tanji Bird Reserve is bisected by the main coastal road between Brufut and Tanji. There are two main access points from this road. The first, coming from the north, is Kajonyi Fishing Village (⊕ *N13 23.076 W16 46.501*), the official launch site for boats to the Bijol Islands, which lies about 200m north of the main road along a dirt track signposted to the right about 2km past the Coral Beach Hotel and 500m past the Ghana Town junction for Brufut. Less than 1km past this, the main entrance gate and eco-lodge site (about 500m from the main road) are also signposted to the right (⊕ *for junction N13 22.777 W16 46.839*).

In a private taxi, either of these access points is around 20–30 minutes' drive from the main coastal resorts further north. Alternatively, the regular gelly-gellys that leave from Dippa Kunda taxi park (Bakoteh Junction) for Tanji can drop you at either of the access points by request.

WHERE TO STAY AND EAT *Map, page 146*

✳ ⌂ Tanji Bird Reserve Eco-Tourism Camp (8 rooms) **m** 7288221/9924160; **e** ecocamptanjibirdreserve@yahoo.com. Opened in Nov 2013, this eco-lodge, set above the beach on a low ridge overlooking a small waterhole that attracts plenty of birds & other wildlife, is an ideal base for budget-conscious nature lovers & birdwatchers seeking an alternative to the package hotels further north. It also has good eco-credentials, being part of a project to help local people derive meaningful income from what was community land before it became a reserve, & profits are split between local communities & the agencies responsible for reserve management.

The accommodation, in semi-detached bungalows with high domed roofs designed for natural ventilation, is built with eco-friendly mud bricks & relies solely on solar power (with inverters for storage when there's no sun) & borehole water. The brightly decorated rooms have tiled flooring, fridge, twin beds with wooden net frames, en-suite cold shower, standing fan & private balcony. Day visitors are welcome to make use of the attractive outdoor restaurant, which has seating in summer houses, & serves seafood & Gambian dishes in the £6–7.50 range, along with the usual bottled drinks & seasonal fresh fruit juice. *£30 dbl B&B.*

TANJI AND AROUND

Immediately south of the bridge across the Tanji River Mouth, the main South Coast Road bisects Tanji (also sometimes spelt Tanje or Tanjeh), a busy seafront town of around 6,000 inhabitants that stretches inland for about 1km to a central square flanked by a market and a large mosque. The busiest fishing and fish-smoking centre along the Gambian coast, Tanji makes for a popular day trip out of the coastal resorts further north, though its wide sandy beach – lined with pirogues and strewn with dead fish and offal – feels more like an extension of the market than it does a viable swimming venue. In addition to offering a fascinating glimpse into the everyday workings of a traditional fishing beach and market, Tanji is well known for the popular camelback excursions offered by Tanji Camel Safaris (pages 155–6).

GETTING THERE AND AWAY The town is bisected by the main road along the south coast and easily reached by shared taxi or gelly-gelly from Dippa Kunda taxi park in Serekunda or Brusubi Junction south of Bijilo. The fare is less than D50. It is also easy enough to pick up transport on to Gunjur, Kartong and other destinations further south.

⌂ WHERE TO STAY *Map, page 146, unless otherwise stated*

Most people visit Tanji as a day trip, often in conjunction with the neighbouring bird reserve, but there are a couple of affordable lodges scattered in and around town.

Upmarket

✳ ⌂ Evergreen Eco Lodge [map, page 142] (5 rooms) ⊕ N13 17.248 W16 47.325; **m** 7021151, (UK) (0)7954 583517; **e** evergreengam@gmail.com; **w** evergreen-lodgesgambia.com; see ad, page 157. Tucked away in the bush just south of Tujering, Evergreen Eco Lodge lies in a beautiful garden about 25 mins' walk from the quiet expanse of a deserted beach. There are 4 spacious & tastefully decorated roundhouses complete with king-size beds, wet rooms & porches as well as a luxury house

with its own patio, all built using local materials & according to sustainable eco-principles. The restaurant serves freshly cooked meals of the day, fusing African & international cuisines. Bicycles & fishing gear are available for hire & holistic massage therapies & yoga workshops are available. Additionally, the lodge supports several local projects including beekeeping & moringa (a tropical tree that provides many nutritional & health benefits) production, & products are available to purchase. The lodge is signposted on the right-hand side of the highway as you leave Tujering heading southwards. Warmly recommended for anyone seeking a quiet eco-retreat. *£65/75 sgl/dbl roundhouse, £85 for the dbl luxury house, all rates HB with reductions for groups or long-term stays.*

☀ 🏠 Farakunku Lodges (4 rooms) ⊕ N13 18.148 W16 46.620; **m** 7260669; **e** heather-moses@farakunku-lodges.com; **w** farakunku-lodges.com. Situated inland of the main coastal road near the village of Farakunku, which lies about 7km south of Tanji & 2km past Tujering, this small lodge comes across as a true labour of love, thanks to the enthusiastic & eco-conscious British–Gambian owner-managers, who live on site & are very attuned to the interests & requirements of birdwatchers, their main clientele. The compact but well-tended grounds are alive with birds, as is a newly added tree sanctuary with bird pool in a separate compound a minute's walk away. The spacious & well-ventilated octagonal lodges have high wooden ceilings, screened windows, tiled floors, ceiling fan, cane furniture, king-size beds with walk-in nets, a secure lock-up dressing room for cameras & other costly birding gear, & en-suite hot shower. Facilities include a small but welcome plunge pool, bicycle hire (*£6/day*) & a restaurant serving a set 3-course meal that can cater for pretty much any special culinary requirements with advance notice. An integrated solar system powers the entire site. 3 excellent bird guides are permanently employed at the lodge, which lies in an area of woodland that supports excellent avian variety. The lodge can also be used as the base for a full week-long birding package visiting different sites every day, while non-birders are catered for by day excursions to the lovely beaches at nearby Tujering & Batukunku. One of our top recommendations for bird enthusiasts anywhere in The Gambia. Very fair value, too. *£67/80 sgl/dbl HB.*

☀ 🏠 Mama Africa (8 rooms) ⊕ N13 20.465 W16 47.511; **m** 7178711; **e** berndax@aol.com; **w** mama-africa-gambia.org. Following its destruction upon the orders of the former president, Mama Africa has been rebuilt & relocated to a large plot of land towards the cliffs on the right just past Tanji village, from where it is signposted. Internationally acclaimed Gambian artist Isha Fofana & her German husband have lovingly created this lodge, & the roundhouses surround a garden studded with wood carvings. Each house is a work of art in itself & the spacious

solar-powered rooms are beautifully decorated & have king-size beds, wet rooms & fans. The restaurant serves Afro–European fusion food with vegetables, including chard, beetroot & others not normally grown in The Gambia, plucked straight from the adjacent gardens, which guests are welcome to visit. The cultural centre, complete with displays of local art & outside stage with bar/restaurant for musical & theatrical performances, was being completed when we visited & should be open by the time this book is published. *Around £85 per room HB.*

🏠 Suleima Lodge (7 rooms) **m** 3905079/9905079; **e** suleimalodge@yahoo.com. Situated between the villages of Batakunku & Tujering, this lodge lies in large forested gardens centred on a 33m-long pool only 10 mins from a quiet beach. Accommodation is in solar-powered suites whose Sahelian-influenced architecture has an earthy, organic feel. The surrounding area is good for birdwatching & fishing, & the lodge also offers several excursions further afield. *Rates start at £85 per room or £120 for the executive suite, both B&B. HB & FB options are also available.*

Budget

☀ 🏠 Sambou Kunda (4 rooms) ⊕ N13 19.018 W16 47.496; **m** 7533097/7533085; **e** samboukunda@gmail.com. Set in a forested area just 10 mins' walk from the beach, this is a new & outstanding-value Gambian–Spanish lodge. Built with compressed earth blocks, local materials & according to eco-principles, the very large spacious rooms have en-suite wet room & a mezzanine level with an additional bed. Delicious Spanish & African meals are served in the large thatched bantaba for around £5–6. The owners also offer tailor-made trips in The Gambia, Senegal & Conakry in Guinea, specialising in off-the-beaten-track places that most operators don't reach. Profits from tourism help support a local school that teaches solar installation to young women from the surrounding villages, aiming to provide education, generate jobs, train entrepreneurs & empower women. *From around £12 B&B.*

🏠 Nyanya's Beach Lodge (5 rooms) ☏ 4414021; **m** 6895072; **e** info@nyanyas-beach-lodge.com; **w** nyanyas-beach-lodge.com. The most central option in Tanji has a great location in large overgrown grounds overlooking the lagoon mouth between the bridge, the beach & the village. Accommodation is in simple but clean & brightly decorated round huts with dbl bed, net, en-suite cold shower & standing fan by request. The restaurant & bar, set on a wooden deck offering a view over the lagoon, serves fresh fish dishes for around £4–6. The only drawback is that it may be quite smelly if the wind is blowing in from the nearby fishing beach. *£15/25 sgl/dbl.*

Picca Laa (10 rooms) m 2369014; e book@ piccalaa.co.uk; w piccalaa.co.uk. Set in large forested grounds just 10 mins from the beach, this eco-friendly lodge, managed by Tanji locals, is a great option in this range. Brightly coloured solar-powered roundhouses are simple but clean & come with dbl or twin beds & en-suite bathroom with cold shower, although their eco-principles mean there is no AC. Complimentary drinks are offered on arrival, & tasty Gambian evening meals, made using vegetables grown onsite, are served for around £7. Biding tours to Tanji & other nearby reserves are offered with local guide Laibo Manneh, late-night excursions to Kololi can be arranged, & bikes can also be hired if you fancy a leisurely cycle along the beach. *£20pp B&B.*

Shoestring

✳ 🏠 Bird View Apartments (4 rooms) ✪ N13 21.260 W16 47.139; m 7685455; e info@ discover-gambia.com; w discover-gambia.com. This rustic camp near the bird reserve is situated in a lovingly tended tropical jungle garden near the bird reserve on the edge of Tanji village & just 1.5km from the beach. The lodge is run by a Gambian–German couple who are knowledgeable about the local area as well as keen fans of African music & drumming in general. There are 3 rooms with shared bathrooms & 1 with en suite as well as a kitchen, as there is no restaurant. Groups can rent all of the accommodation for a reduced rate. *£10/12 dbl for shared bathroom/en suite.*

✳ 🏠 Tanje Village Museum (9 rooms) m 9926618/7057045; e abdoulie.bayo@ yahoo.com. The forested grounds of this popular museum provide a tranquil retreat with traditional Mandinka-style roundhouses available in which to stay, providing a unique guesthouse experience. The simple huts with en-suite bathrooms have dbl or twin beds with nets & cold showers. The restaurant serves Gambian & European food as well as the usual bottled drinks. *£10pp B&B.*

🏠 Kairoh Garden (18 rooms) ✪ N13 20.900 W16 47.027; m 9993526; e information@ kairohgarden.com; w kairohgarden.com. Set in massive orchard-like grounds with permaculture gardens teeming with birdlife in the semi-rural backroads east of central Tanji, this welcoming Dutch–Gambian owner-managed lodge helps to fund the Kairoh Garden Foundation, which supports the education of around 100 orphans & other disadvantaged local children. It is set back about 2km from the beach & consciously chooses to offer its guests an integrated & down-to-earth African village experience rather than a resort-like atmosphere. Accommodation is basic but clean & well ventilated, with a choice of bright en-suite rooms or dingier rooms with shared showers, all with nets & private balconies, but no AC or fan. It mostly uses solar power (though there is a back-up generator), & facilities include a restaurant serving set meals for around £2/4/5 b/fast/lunch/ dinner, & a relaxed bantaba set below mango trees hung with hammocks. Tours can be arranged around The Gambia, & they have a second **Kairoh Garden Lodge** in Kuntaur near the River Gambia National Park (page 225). The management can also put together programmes for professionals such as nurses & teachers to meet their Gambian counterparts working in local communities all over The Gambia & Senegal. *£9pp with shared bath, £11 en suite.*

✖ WHERE TO EAT AND DRINK *Map, page 146*

The best options are the hotels. For affordable central fish meals, **Nyanya's Beach Lodge** has a great location, but allow time for preparation. The pick of the bespoke eateries, all of which are pretty low-key, is the **Country Restaurant** on the main road.

WHAT TO SEE AND DO In addition to the sites listed below, Tanji Bird Reserve (pages 150–2) is easily visited from Tanji, since the entrance gate lies only 3km back along the road to Brufut.

Tanji fishing beach This is the largest of the series of small artisanal fishing centres that stretch south along the coast south of Brufut. As such, it is a fascinating place, and particularly suited to photographers with lots of opportunity for action shots (though locals may object to close-ups). The first thing you'll notice upon entering this or any other fishing beach will be the sometimes overwhelming smell, followed by the collection of brightly painted wooden pirogues anchored just offshore or pulled up high on to the beach. These local canoes vary in size from small one-man jobs to large boats that have crews of half-a-dozen or so and which include shelters for the sailors. You may even see a few boats under construction on the beach, and it is fascinating to see how they are put together using methods that have changed little over generations. Many of the larger boats are not Gambian and are crewed by a whole range of nationalities from Senegalese right through to people based as far away as Ghana.

Most of the fishing that takes place from these pirogues uses traditional methods. Gill nets are used to catch small quantities of fish, which are then landed on the beach and sold to local traders, who in turn sell it to the coastal communities. Many fish are also sun-dried or smoked in huts by the beach. If you walk around and show an interest, most people will be pleased to show you how the process works. Unfortunately, while smoking fish is an excellent way to preserve them, it is also heavy on firewood, with the result that huge areas of coastal forest and scrub around Tanji have been chopped down. The recent construction of an ice plant to freeze fish can only help in curbing the deforestation.

If you keep your eyes open as you walk along the beach among the pirogues you will see all sorts of discarded marine life, from crabs to the severed heads of hammerhead sharks. Two things that you shouldn't see are dolphins and marine turtles, which are legally protected in The Gambia. There are, and always will be, accidents where these species are caught and drowned in fishing nets, and of course there are also unscrupulous people who will break the law, but on the whole local fishermen do avoid beaching dolphins and turtles.

Boat trips If you are feeling adventurous, you might like to go out on a short trip on a pirogue or even accompany the crew while they are fishing. This will cost you, of course, but fishing is a hard life and not well paid, so the crew will welcome the additional income. There are no fixed prices as not many tourists are brave enough to do this, so you will have to negotiate. A trip like this can be very exciting as you crash out through the surf. You may feel a little unsafe in some of the pirogues, which seem to roll about too much or leak in water just a little too fast, but don't be overly worried. Remember that these fishermen have to go out every day in these same boats, no matter what the conditions are like, and most of them are very good at what they do. Do remember to watch your camera gear or binoculars, as they are extremely likely to get wet, especially during setting off and landing. We suggest you keep them safely wrapped up in plastic bags during these parts of your trip or, better still, don't take them with you at all. Once salt water gets into your camera or binoculars they corrode very fast and are more or less ruined!

Camel safaris Unique in The Gambia, Tanji Camel Safaris (m *7711609*; ⊕ *08.00–18.00 daily; D75 to take photos of the camels*) is prominently signposted on the left-hand side of the road, just after Tanji Bridge as you enter the town from the north. It has ten camels (most of them imported from Senegal), which it uses to take tourists on camelback rides on the beach, giving a great vantage point for viewing the hustle and bustle of the fishing village. Half- or full-hour options are available, and cost

£10 for 30 minutes. There is a bantaba that sells drinks and a small shop that stocks souvenirs, but for meals you need to head to Nyanya's (pages 153–4) directly opposite.

Tanje Village Museum (⊕ *N13 20.326 W16 47.807*; m *9926618/7057045*; e *abdoulie.bayo@yahoo.com*; ⊕ *08.00–17.00 daily; entrance D240 with discounts for Gambians & children, inclusive of optional guide*) Owned in the 1990s by Abdoulie Bayo, former curator of Banjul's National Museum, the excellent Tanje Village Museum is very popular with tourists and is also used extensively by local school groups for educational purposes. It lies about 1km south of town on the landward side of the main coastal road. It is divided into several parts, most impressively perhaps a life-size replica of a traditional Mandinka compound showing various types of huts and their uses, and the museum also hosts traditional craftsmen such as a blacksmith, weaver and kora player. There is a building with various displays on Gambian culture and musical instruments, as well as an informative display on the wildlife of The Gambia (the latter put together by Craig Emms and Linda Barnett, the authors of the original Bradt Guide). The short nature trail through the grounds includes a selection of labelled trees, and a trail guide can be bought with information on the traditional medicinal uses of 30 species. Set aside 45–60 minutes for the full guided tour. At the end of your exploration of the museum you'll find welcome shade in the bantaba, where a selection of cold drinks and food is for sale. The forested museum grounds provide a tranquil retreat and offer unique Mandinka-style roundhouses in which to stay (page 154).

Batukunku Beach Two of the loveliest beaches in The Gambia lie on the coast immediately south of Cape Solifor, the country's most westerly point. Coming from the north, the first and less developed of these is Batukunku, whose wide sandy beach is set in a shallow bay protected by a small rocky peninsula about 1km south of Cape Solifor. To get there, follow the main coastal road south past Tanje Village Museum for about 1km until you reach Batukunku village. Here, you need to turn right into a road that angles sharply back from the junction next to **Safari Garden Restaurant** (⊕ *N13 19.661 W16 48.022; map, page 146*), then continue driving for another 1km, turning left through a partly derelict wall, before you come to the beach itself. The beach has a reputation for being very safe in terms of both security and swimming. The **Paradise Cafe** (m *7724788*) beach shack is staffed by friendly guys who will prepare simple dishes such as freshly caught fish, chicken and chips or rice for around £5.

Tujering Beach About 2km south of Batukunku Beach as the crow flies, the long sandy beach at Tujering is just as beautiful, but boasts better facilities in the form of **Fansu's Beach Bar** (m *6442623/7791039*), a comfortable and likeable place to sit over a few drinks or a meal (the catch of the day costs around £5; lobster and prawns are pricier). Swimming is normally safe, but check with Fansu's before you take the plunge. You can drive to within about 200m of the beach, after which you need to walk through sandy dunes surrounding a reed-fringed lagoon that often offers rewarding birding. The beach lies about 1.5km west of the main coastal road; to get there drive south past Batukunku for another 2km or so until you reach the village of Tujering, where you need to turn right on to a dirt road at a junction immediately north of the signpost for the Tujering Viscera EcoBank (⊕ *N13 18.792 W16 47.304*).

Tunbung Art Village (*Tujering*; ⊕ *N13 19.512 W16 47.741*; m *9982102/9827255*; e *info@tunbungartvillage.gm*; w *tunbungartvillage.gm*) The quirky and wonderful

Tunbung Art Village is a ragged assembly of skewed huts, wildly painted walls and random sculptures that peer out behind walls and from treetops. It's the creative universe of Etu Ndow, a renowned Gambian artist who sadly died in 2014, but his nephew Abdoulie continues to keep the memory of his uncle alive. Workshops are available (*around £40 for a half-day workshop for 2*) in screen printing, painting and crafts using natural materials. The studio is in the forested grounds of the family compound and there's a permanent exhibition of Etu's work.

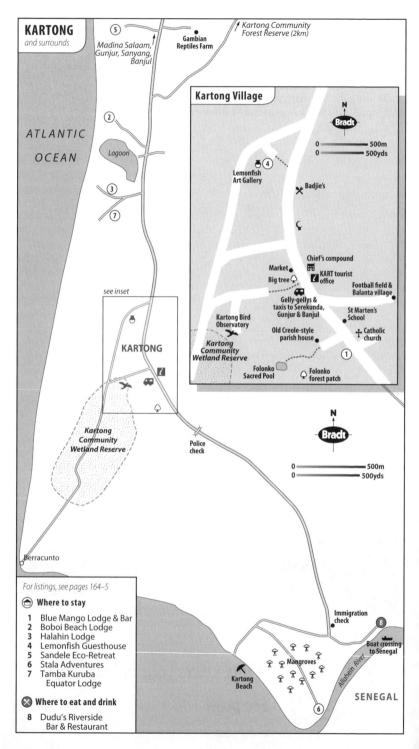

KARTONG
and surrounds

Madina Salaam,
Gunjur, Sanyang,
Banjul

⑤

● Gambian
Reptiles Farm

↗ Kartong Community
Forest Reserve (2km)

ATLANTIC

OCEAN

②

Lagoon

③

⑦

see inset

KARTONG

*Kartong
Community
Wetland Reserve*

Berracunto

Kartong Village

N

Bradt

0 ————— 500m
0 ————— 500yds

Lemonfish
Art Gallery ④

✕ Badjie's

Chief's compound

Market ●
Big tree 🌳

KART tourist
office

Football field &
Balanta village

Gelly-gellys &
taxis to Serekunda,
Gunjur & Banjul

St Marten's
School

✝ Catholic
church

Kartong Bird
Observatory ✕

Old Creole-style
parish house ●

①

*Kartong
Community
Wetland Reserve*

Folonko
Sacred Pool

Folonko
forest patch

N

Bradt

0 ————— 500m
0 ————— 500yds

Police
check ☓

Immigration
check

⑧

Boat crossing
to Senegal

Allahein River

Mangroves

Kartong
Beach

SENEGAL

⑥

For listings, see pages 164–5

🏠 Where to stay

1 Blue Mango Lodge & Bar
2 Boboi Beach Lodge
3 Halahin Lodge
4 Lemonfish Guesthouse
5 Sandele Eco-Retreat
6 Stala Adventures
7 Tamba Kuruba
  Equator Lodge

✕ Where to eat and drink

8 Dudu's Riverside
  Bar & Restaurant

11

South to Kartong

The least-developed and arguably most attractive part of the Gambian coast runs south from Tanji for about 30km to Kartong and the Allahein River on the border with Senegal. There used to be three main clusters of accommodation in the area, but sadly the most northerly of these, around Sanyang, disappeared under government bulldozers in mid 2013. The other main clusters are around Gunjur and Madina Salaam, about 10km further south, and towards the Senegalese border, where Kartong is also emerging as a particularly rewarding destination for nature-lovers along the Gambian coast, thanks to its attractive beach and riverine scenery, well-managed reptile park, and a cluster of good birdwatching sites.

SANYANG

Located about halfway between Tanji and Gunjur, this junction town of around 6,000 inhabitants lies 4km inland of the long stretch of palm-fringed white sand referred to by Gambian operators as Paradise Beach. Sadly, however, most of the low-key beach camps and restaurants that lined Sanyang Beach were bulldozed to the ground in May 2013. The official reason for this presidentially sanctioned demolition job is that these camps (many more than a decade old) encroached on to government land. But local consensus seems to be that the purge was essentially a clean-up operation linked to the mooted development of an upmarket residential complex on Sanyang Beach. However, with the downfall of the Jammeh regime, some beach bars are now re-establishing themselves and hopefully this means there will be more places springing up over the next couple of years.

GETTING THERE AND AWAY Regular gelly-gellys to Sanyang town leave from the Dippa Kunda taxi park in Serekunda and cost around D11. There is also plenty of transport connecting Sanyang to other towns along the main road between Brufut and Kartong, as well as along the 13km road east to Brikama, giving quick and easy access to the airport. Regular shared taxis used to connect Sanyang town to the beach, but these are no longer so frequent owing to the lack of custom.

South to Kartong   SANYANG

11

WHERE TO STAY AND EAT   *Map, page 142*

☀ 🏠 **Jungle Beach Holiday Resort** (10 rooms) Paradise Beach; m 9986143; e info@ junglebeach-resort.com; w junglebeach-resort. com. A friendly beach bar & restaurant that escaped Jammeh's purge of 2013, this resort has a lovely ambience, although a little quieter than its neighbours. There's a large bar containing books, Wi-Fi & a coconut tree grove that provides shade for the sunbeds on this idyllic beach. Reasonably priced Gambian & European meals are available & local musicians put on regular *djembe* performances. Basic rooms are available with nets & fans. *£20/£28 sgl/dbl B&B, HB an additional £10.*

159

🏠 **Kobokoto Face 2 Lodge** (20 rooms) m 7377474; e kobokotolodge@gmail.com. A survivor of the recent accommodation purge is this lodge situated about 1.5km from Sanyang Junction & 2.5km before the beach, which was being renovated by its new friendly Moroccan owners as research for this guide was undertaken. Accommodation is in cool & spacious twin or dbl en-suite thatched huts, & there are also family bungalows sleeping 3. A restaurant serves Moroccan & European cuisine including pizza in the £3.50–4.50 range. The large grounds, planted with mango & various indigenous trees, should attract plenty of birds. Drumming lessons available & they intend to give performances. It's an agreeable enough set-up, but lacks the beachside location of most other accommodation on the south coast. *£27.50 dbl.*

🏠 **Rainbow Beach** (15 rooms) Paradise Beach; m 7158487; e jawlajj@yahoo.com; w rainbow.gm. Next door to Jungle Beach, this has a slightly more package-holiday feel. There is a restaurant, beach bar & a spa offering massage & beauty treatments. In season, there is traditional wrestling on the beach every Sun at 16.00. Basic rooms have en-suite bathrooms, nets & fans. *£10/room.*

✖ **Bird Garden Restaurant** m 3608647; ⊕ Nov–May. Just off the highway, this restaurant has a pleasant shaded eating area serving delicious food, including Gambian, Italian & other European dishes & Indian curries. There is Wi-Fi & an eclectic library, & next door is a carpentry workshop that trains local young people & produces the furniture you will be sitting upon. *Mains in the £5–7 range.*

WHAT TO SEE AND DO Slightly quieter and more easily accessible than both Tanji and Gunjur, Sanyang's fishing village is very picturesque with colourful pirogues lining the beach. It's is a popular spot for musicians and many drumming courses and performances are available to see and experience: just ask at any of the beach bars. Since 2013, the four-day Sanyang International Cultural Festival has taken place, usually during the final week of January, with contemporary and traditional world music, cultural dance, a tourism fair, African cuisine, kids games, arts and crafts and organised tours to historic places and sacred shrines. Some of the money generated goes to helping local children and improving school facilities.

GUNJUR AND MADINA SALAAM

Despite being the largest town on the south coast, Gunjur still supports a relatively modest population of around 18,000, most of whom live close to the landlocked town centre, which is notable for its busy market, but is otherwise of limited interest to travellers. About 2km west of the town centre lies the small but vibrant Gunjur artisanal fishing beach and nearby Bolong Fenyo Community Reserve, the latter a good site for birdwatching. A similar distance south of town, tiny Madina Salaam (literally 'Village of Peace'), also known as Gunjur Madina, is the site of a few pleasant but low-key lodges situated on or close to the beach.

GETTING THERE AND AWAY Gelly-gellys to Gunjur go along the coast from Dippa Kunda taxi park in Serekunda or inland from Brikama, and cost around D20. However, if you want to stay at any of the lodges around Madina Salaam, you are best off catching a vehicle heading on to Kartong and dropping off there. There is also a fair amount of transport connecting Gunjur to other towns along the south coast.

WHERE TO STAY AND EAT *Map, page 142*
Mid-range
✴ 🏠 **Footsteps Eco-Lodge**
(9 rooms) m 7700125/7732060;

w footstepsinthegambia.com. Set on a large permaculture-based stand overseen by the hands-on British owner-managers & their friendly

& enthusiastic staff, this perennially popular eco-lodge northwest of Gunjur grows all its own fruits & vegetables, runs entirely on solar power & borehole water, & boasts a unique freshwater swimming pool that relies on natural filtration as opposed to chemicals. Accommodation is in brightly painted & airy domed huts with 1 dbl & 1 sgl bed & en-suite shower & odourless compost toilet, solar fans & there are also 2 larger 2-bedroom log cabins & a 2-bedroom house set in the vegetable patch a short distance from the main gardens. There's plenty of birdlife in the gardens, & it's about 25 mins' walk to the beach along a well-defined bush path. The restaurant serves a selection of tasty light lunches in the £3.50–5 range, as well as a set 3-course dinner for around £6.50–10, with all dishes using fresh homegrown & locally sourced ingredients. Fishing trips & other excursions can be arranged by the management. Free airport transfers are included in stays of 7 days of longer. It lies about 1.5km west of the main South Coast Rd, about 2km north of Gunjur, & the junction is clearly signposted. *Roundhouses £45/30/20 1/2/3 people B&B, cabins £75, Sunbird House £90, with low-season discounts.*

🏠 **Gecko Lodge** (5 bungalows) 📞 (Italy) +39 334 5957519; m 2288274; e olicz@hotmail.com; w gecko-lodge.com. Situated about 1km from Footsteps, this shady & peaceful owner-managed boutique retreat consists of 5 comfortable & tastefully decorated en-suite dbl bungalows with king-size or twin beds. There is also a stylish & airy communal sitting area whose décor & architecture show a fusion of Mediterranean & African influences, a mixture also reflected in a menu dominated by Italian & Gambian dishes. It is perhaps 15 mins' walk from the beach, & a variety of excursions can be arranged. *£45pp HB.*

🏠 **Nemasu Eco-Lodge** (6 rooms) m 3686127/7427774; e hotelnemasu@gmail. com; w hotelnemasu.com. Under US–Australian management, this small & beautifully sited solar-powered camp is set in a grove of tall swaying palms right above the beach, about 1km & well signposted from Madina Salaam, & has a very peaceful & relaxing atmosphere. There's a range of accommodation options, including spacious en-suite roundhouses, slightly newer bungalows with ocean views, a secluded Shell House with a monkey family for neighbours & a private safari

tent in the nearby forest. Meals, mostly fresh fish & seafood, are in the £4–5 range, & are served in an open-sided beach restaurant & bar. *Roundhouses £45 dbl, dome house £35 dbl, rooms with shared bathroom £20/30 sgl/dbl, Shell House £70, ocean front rooms £60/70 dbl/trpl, safari tent £45 dbl, £10pp camping, all rates B&B, with discounts in low season. HB & FB available.*

Budget

🏠 **Balaba Nature Camp** (10 rooms) m 9919012; e balabacamp@icloud.com; w balabacamp.co.uk. This long-serving locally run lodge, set in a large compound in an area of relatively pristine Guinea savannah woodland near Madina Salaam, is about 700m from the main coastal road along an unsigned track that runs inland almost opposite the turn-off for WYCE. Accommodation, built in the local style, is in sgl, dbl or twin rooms or round huts, with mosquito nets & kerosene lamps, using shared showers & toilets. The surrounding woodland holds wildlife such as monkeys, monitor lizards & bushbuck, & a list of birds seen by previous visitors exceeds 500 species & includes many rarities. A range of activities is available by request, & the camp can also run excursions to most sites of interest within day-tripping distance. Alternatively, you can walk to the beach, about 20 mins from the camp, & catch some sun. *Slightly overpriced at £40 FB, with reductions available for HB.*

🏠 **Gunjur Project Lodge** (8 rooms) m 3145757/9922674; e info@thegunjurprojectgambia.com; w thegunjurprojectgambia.net. Owned & managed by a British family involved in several local community projects, this lodge lies about 2km southwest of Gunjur close to the fishing beach & affiliated Bolong Fenyo Community Reserve. It started life as a base for (mostly British & Dutch) school & youth groups coming to The Gambia to work on community projects, but ordinary tourists are also welcome, with the option of being involved in these projects if they so choose. The lodge is set in a spacious neat solar-powered compound with a small sparkling swimming pool, Wi-Fi & a shaded restaurant serving burgers & filled baguettes in the £3–4 range & a cosmopolitan selection of mains for around £5–6. The tiled rooms are on the small side but bright, airy & spotlessly clean, & come with dbl or twin bed, net, en-suite shower & private balcony, but no fan or AC. It is less than 1km from the beach & Bolong Fenyo. *£30/35/40 sgl/dbl/trpl B&B.*

🏠 **WYCE Working Lodge** (10 rooms) ➘ (UK) +44 1922 663014; **m** 6727808/3709183; **e** admin@wyce.org.uk; **w** wyce.org.uk. Operated by the British-based Gambia-registered WYCE (short for Wonder Years Centre of Excellence), this is emphatically a working lodge aimed at volunteers (skilled or unskilled) willing to spend anything from a few days to several months working on local community projects, though passing travellers are also welcome, especially those willing to get involved in their work. The charity is dedicated to working with the Gambian government & local communities to make The Gambia a 'wealthier & healthier place for everyone' through the provision of a first-class education & healthcare system, & as such it is involved in the funding & running of a local school & clinic, &

other skill-based projects ranging from beekeeping to candle-making. Basic but very clean rooms have twin beds, nets & en-suite shower & flush toilet. Meals are served in a relaxed communal area with an outdoorsy feel & a good stock of books & board games. Rates are inclusive of laundry & all meals. *£39.30pp FB, if staying for 7 nights airport transfers inc.*

Shoestring
🏠 **Bolong Beach Bar & Camping**
m 3059670/7100892. A basic camp set by the bolong just off the beach with stunning views. Basic facilities are offset by the friendliness & enthusiasm of Lamin & Bunja who can provide simple local meals & offers drum & dance lessons. There are plans to build some basic roundhouses. To reach the camp, turn right at the beach past the fishing boats, & it is set in the forest to your right, just before Sankule's bar. *£6.50pp HB.*

WHAT TO SEE AND DO
Gunjur Beach Less than 1km west of the Gunjur Project Lodge, this working fishing beach, though neither so chaotic nor so large as its counterpart at Tanji, is a good place to watch colourful pirogues land with the day's catch and distribute them to traders on the shore. There's a Japanese-built ice plant in the small beachfront village, which is also known as Kajabang, and several smoking houses run inland along the main road. Protected by a natural rock reef a few hundred metres offshore, the beach running north from the village is usually fine for swimming (safest, though, to ask first), and Sankule Beach Bar (⊕ *Nov–Apr*) about 300m to the north offers comfortable seating, cold drinks and a limited selection of inexpensive seafood meals.

Gunjur Village Museum (**m** 6436637; **e** *lamin@gunjurmuseum.com;* **w** *gunjurmuseum.com; entrance D100*) Clearly signposted from the Gunjur–Brikama intersection and run by the cheerful and highly knowledgeable Lamin Bojang, this little museum showcases natural, cultural and historical artefacts from all over The Gambia. Lamin is also a bird and wildlife guide, with a particular interest in medicinal plants, and offers nature walks in the surrounding forest.

Bolong Fenyo Community Wildlife Reserve (**m** *3453232;* **w** *thegambiawildlife. com; entrance D50, optional guides (who know the birds well) can be hired for around D150*) Situated immediately inland of Gunjur Beach, Bolong Fenyo was the first community conservation project established in The Gambia, formally gazetted in 2008. Operated by the Gunjur Environmental Protection and Development Group (GEPADG), it extends over 3km^2 of savannah and wetland habitats, including the eponymous freshwater lagoon and around 400m of coastline, and protects a range of small mammals including bushbuck, red-flanked duiker, red colobus and green monkey, as well as a resident crocodile population. The main attraction is birds, of which around 150 species have been recorded, including osprey, African jacana, black crake, grey-headed kingfisher, red-bellied paradise flycatcher, green crombec and many marine birds typical of The Gambia. The entrance gate lies on the north side of the main road between Gunjur Project Lodge and Gunjur Beach, and there's a useful Facebook group (**f** *BolongfenyoKunoKafoo (BKK)*) with more information. About 5km further north along the beach, the Katima Delta, which comprises a series of bolongs (creeks) that empty into the sea, is also very rich in birdlife, with huge flocks of terns and white-faced whistling ducks.

Kenye-kenye Jamango Located about 3km south of Gunjur Beach near Nemasu Eco-Lodge, this sacred pilgrimage site, which attracts Islamic scholars and worshippers from all over West Africa, is also known as the Sand Dune Mosque, perched as it is atop a 10m-high dune overlooking the beach. The site is sacred because of a visit there by El Hadj Umar Tall (1797–1864), the founder of the short-lived Toucouleur Empire and influential leader of the Tijaniyya Brotherhood that has since become the largest Sufi order in West Africa. Umar Tall's pilgrimage to Mecca between 1828 and 1831 made him famous (and earned him the title El Hadj), and he went on to challenge the political and social order of the old theocracies, replacing them with a new and more militant brand of Islam. His jihads (holy wars) imposed his authority from Senegal to Nigeria, and attracted thousands of disciples from all over the region, including the Aku (freed slaves of African origin) of Sierra Leone. He visited what is now The Gambia during the latter part of his life when he had turned to a more peaceful philosophy. He stayed in several places in The Gambia, but at this site near Gunjur longer than anywhere else, praying in the shade of trees and large boulders. Everybody is permitted to visit the sacred grounds, and to view the mosque, but only Muslims can enter the building (an architecturally uninteresting concrete construction).

KARTONG AND SURROUNDS

Reputedly founded more than 450 years ago, the agreeable border village of Kartong (also spelt Kartung) is one of the oldest in the country, and known throughout the Senegambia region as the site of a sacred pool called Kartong Folonko. The small town's 5,500 inhabitants are known as Kartonkas, and include a small but distinct community of Balanta immigrants from Guinea-Bissau. The compact town centre lies about 1km inland of the Atlantic coastline and 2km north of the Allahein (or Halahin) River, which flows along the border with Senegal. Kartong is one of the country's most rewarding ornithological destinations, with a checklist of more than 350 species including several recorded nowhere else in the country, and the area's reputation in birdwatching circles has grown hugely since the opening of the Kartong Bird Observatory on the western outskirts of town in 2010. Other attractions include the Kartong Folonko, boat trips on the mangrove-lined Allahein River, Lemonfish Art Gallery and the out-of-town Gambian Reptiles Farm, while the lovely stretch of coast north of town is lined with beach camps and eco-lodges. Tourism here is unusually well organised thanks to the efforts of the Kartong Association for Responsible Tourism (KART), the body responsible for the annual Kartong Festival, which has been running since 2006.

GETTING THERE AND AWAY The occasional gelly-gellys and shared taxis that connect Kartong to Serekunda's Dippa Kunda Station and the central station in Brikama cost around D30. If you can't find direct transport, it will be easiest to catch a vehicle to Gunjur and change there.

Mid-range

 Sandele Eco-Retreat (4 dome lodges & 16 guest rooms) m 7711209/ 9803089; e enquiries@sandele.com; w www.sandele. com. Located 4km north of Kartong opposite the Gambian Reptiles Farm, this award-winning lodge is owned & managed by a British couple with years of hospitality experience in The Gambia & a strong commitment to the development & implementation of sustainable technologies as well as the implementation of eco-principles in 11 local coastal villages. Power is wind- or solar-generated (though there is a back-up generator for emergencies), water comes from a borehole, all toilets are of the compost variety, there is an underground chill room for food storage & it supports a variety of sustainable projects ranging from an innovative solar fruit-drying venture to the creation of a constructed wetland that will recycle grey & black water & a turtle-breeding programme (see box, page 167). The lodge is set in large, densely forested grounds that runs down to a luscious sandy swimming beach as attractive as any in the country & strives for an inclusive family atmosphere with meals being eaten communally. The spacious en-suite guest rooms, made entirely of compressed stabilised earth blocks, all come with king-size beds, walk-in nets, standing fan & private balcony, & there are also more exclusive lodges with vaulted domed roofs & plunge pools. A speciality of the lodge is yoga retreats (there are 2 yoga circles & all guests are welcome to join the complimentary morning or evening sessions) & the grounds also offer rich pickings to birdwatchers. For all its unquestionable merits, Sandele was starting to look in need of some renovation when this guide was researched. Rooms *£35/46/66 sgl/ dbl/trpl, lodges £45/58/75 sgl/dbl/trpl, all rates B&B. Good discounts for groups & longer stays.*

Budget

✳ **Boboi Beach Lodge** (12 rooms) m 3776736; e boboibeachlodge@hotmail. co.uk; w boboibeachlodge.com. Located a few hundred metres west of the main coastal road, this attractive & well-established beach lodge runs down to a sublime tropical beach about 3km north of Kartong & offers the choice of camping (in your own tent), accommodation in a very basic but naturally aerated treehouse (a semi-enclosed stilted platform with a mattress & mosquito net), more spacious beachside bungalow (sleeping up to 4) or 'deluxe' hutted accommodation (a brightly decorated en-suite room with 1 dbl & 1 sgl bed, but no AC or fan). It serves traditional dishes & seafood in the £3.50–4.75 range, & is noted for its friendly staff & varied selection of activities & excursions. Sadly, the lodge was looking a little rundown & in need of some renovation when this guide was researched. *£35 deluxe treehouse/ roundhouse, £50 bungalow, £15 standard treehouse, £9pp camping, all rates B&B.*

 Halahin Lodge (13 rooms) m 7095705/9933193; e boubajaiteh@yahoo. co.uk; w halahin.com. Set in sprawling palm-shaded grounds leading out to one of the most fabulous beaches in The Gambia, this chilled-out beach lodge 2km north of Kartong is (rather confusingly) named for the river that flows several kilometres to its south. Accommodation is in standalone en-suite huts with 1 double & 1 single bed, tiled floor, cane furniture & nets but no fan or AC. A breezy outdoor restaurant serves a varied selection of seafood & other dishes in the £4–5 range. *£25pp B&B.*

 Lemonfish Guesthouse (4 rooms) m 7643948/7728621; e h.stokbroekx@gmail. com; w lemonfish.gm. This likeable Dutch owner-managed art gallery set on a slope a few mins' walk from the town centre offers limited accommodation using shared bathrooms in airy & brightly decorated twin rooms with nets. The delightful & rather bohemian veranda with nothing but the sound of songbirds for company makes this a wonderful retreat for anyone in search of peace & quiet. Set lunches (*around £4pp*) & dinners (*£6*) are available to residents, & it also serves chilled beers & sodas. Boat excursions, birdwatching & fishing trips can also be organised by the relaxed & friendly management, & there are African movie nights. It's a great set-up, one we would recommend unreservedly. *£17pp B&B.*

 Stala Adventures (5 rooms) m 7452553; e leebatarr@yahoo.com; f stalaadventure. Reached along a tidal track through the mangroves, this small locally owned lodge lies on the banks of the Allahein about 5km south of the town centre – quite a trek in the midday heat! Once there, the location is lovely, & the staff can arrange boat &

birding excursions on the river, plus seafood & other Gambian dishes for around £5 per plate. Accommodation is in clean riverside huts with twin beds & en-suite shower & toilet, but no AC or fan. It is a community-based venture, with 30% of profits going to a local clinic. *£17/25 dbl/family B&B.*

🏠 **Tamba Kuruba Equator Lodge** (6 rooms) Apathetically staffed & quite rundown on last inspection, this beach lodge about 2km north of Kartong nevertheless boasts a great location, &

the en-suite thatched huts with net have plenty of potential. *£16.50 dbl.*

Shoestring

🏠 **Blue Mango Lodge and Bar** (4 rooms) m 7335950. The most centrally located option in Kartong is this no-frills lodge with bar attached opposite the Catholic church. The rooms have nets but no fan. *Prices are negotiable but should be around £8.50 dbl or twin.*

WHERE TO EAT AND DRINK *Map, page 158*

Most of the accommodation listed above serves adequate to good food. There are also a few small restaurants and bars in the town centre, with **Sambou's** being the pick of the eateries, and the brightly decorated **Dadaema Bar** the best place to enjoy a chilled beer.

✕ Dudu's Riverside Bar & Restaurant

m 7307217/9984891; e dodousaidy@yahoo. com; ⊕ 07.00–19.00 daily but stays open later for dinner by request. This restaurant is notable for its stilted wooden deck where you can watch terns & gulls skim the surface of the Allahein River & mangroves on the Senegalese shore opposite. It is owned & managed by a friendly chef who learned his craft at one of the country's top package

hotels, & has a varied menu of pizzas, sandwiches, seafood & other mains. Sun is lobster day, & there is usually a stock of chilled beers & sodas. Given the restaurant's location, unless you've time to kill, it might be wise to call in advance so it has time to assemble ingredients & prepare the dish of your choice. Highly recommended. *Meals in the £5.50–6.50 range.*

WHAT TO SEE AND DO Most of the activities listed below can be arranged through the Kartong Association for Responsible Tourism (KART), an admirable organisation that aims to develop a form of tourism that gives maximum benefit to the local community and minimises potentially negative impacts, while also giving visitors the best experience possible in Kartong. Situated next to the chief's house opposite the market and taxi park, the **KART Visitors Centre** (m *7025081/7222726;* w *kartung.org*) is a good place to pick up a local guide – that is, when the stand is open. Your best chance of seeing it manned is during the Christmas and Easter holidays or over the Kartong Festival (first weekend of February).

Folonko Sacred Pool This small green forest-fringed crocodile pool in the heart of town has been sacred ever since Kartong was founded, though its renown today is linked partially to a visit by the eminent mid 19th-century marabout El Hadj Umar Tall (page 163). According to the caretakers, the pool is home to around 20 harmless crocodiles, including one albino whose occasional emergence from the water is said to bring good fortune to those who witness it. However, our understanding is that the pool's one-time crocodilian inhabitants have mostly relocated to the artificial wetlands created by sand mining west of town, and sightings are now very infrequent. Birds, by contrast, are prolific in the substantial forest patch around the pool, which is traditionally protected as a sanctuary and hosts an interesting selection of species including blue-breasted kingfisher, splendid glossy starling and green-headed sunbird.

In common with several other crocodile pools in West Africa, Folonko is an important fertility shrine and pilgrimage site whose presiding spirit is said to be the daughter of Kachikally in Bakau. Barren couples or other individuals seeking divine blessings can bring a gift of kola nuts, candles or money to the pool's elderly female caretakers, who will then pray to the crocodiles on their behalf, a rather strange and eerie ritual that sounds midway between a chant and speaking in tongues. And while this crocodile-whispering routine has clear pagan roots, it seems that most of the pilgrims who visit the site are Muslim, a good example of how traditional beliefs are often integrated into exotic faiths in this part of Africa (and elsewhere, for that matter).

Folonko is still very much an active shrine, attracting far more West African pilgrims that it does tourists. But non-Islamic visitors are welcome, provided they take off their shoes before they approach the pool, treat the shrine with respect, and offer the caretakers a small tip (around D30 per person). The unsignposted site is most easily located by following the main road through Kartong south from the market, then turning west opposite the Catholic church, passing an interesting Creole-style building to your right, and following a footpath through the forest for perhaps 100m to the pool.

Lemonfish Art Gallery (m *7336462/7643948/7728621;* e *h.stokbroekx@gmail. com;* w *lemonfish.gm;* ⊕ *daily*) Situated on the northwest outskirts of town, the Dutch-owned Lemonfish Art Gallery was launched in March 2005 with an exhibition featuring 28 artists from all over West Africa, and it remains one of the best-stocked galleries in the country, with colourful local artworks adorning every spare square inch of wall space. The artists also run workshops. In addition to a fine selection of contemporary African paintings, the gallery also stocks and sells sculptures, jewellery, batiks and fashion items. It is unable to take credit cards, so come with cash if you intend to purchase. Browsers are welcome and the wide veranda is a great spot for a coffee or cold drink.

Balanta village Although the majority of Kartonkas are Mandinka, their numbers also include a small subcommunity of Balanta, who hail from Guinea-Bissau, where they are the most populous ethnic group and were once renowned for their resistance to Portuguese colonisation. Speaking a distinct language which most Gambians can't understand, the Balanta of Kartong live in a cluster of thatched dwellings below a palm plantation in the southeast corner of town, next to the football pitch that doubles as the site of the annual Kartong Festival. These tall fronded trees play an important role in the livelihood of Kartong's Balanta community, as the source of palm oil and wine, which is harvested over January–June. It is possible to arrange demonstrations of the oil-making process; this entails scaling the tall trees to collect the palm nuts, which are boiled in a large pot, then pounded to separate the flesh from the oil, before being cooked some more and finally mixed with water. The oil is then sold to traders in 20-litre containers before bring transported to Serekunda and sold in smaller bottles for around D60 per litre. A visit is best arranged through the KART office, who will also help negotiate a fee with the villagers.

Kartong Festival One of the most prominent festivals in The Gambia has been held in Kartong annually since 2006, usually over the first full weekend in February. The three-day festival takes place in the grounds of St Martin's School and at the nearby football pitch at the southeast end of the village. It is dominated by music and dancing displays, most of it traditional, but it also includes a variety of other events and workshops. For further details, visit their Facebook page (🄵 *KartongFestival*).

The beaches of West Africa have long been a nesting ground for turtles, but in 2015, not a single leatherback turtle was reported in The Gambia for the first time in living memory. In fact, all five of the turtle species found here are now endangered and while there are many natural obstacles to their survival, it's man that brings the biggest threat. Aside from hunters, the turtles must contend with fishermen's nets and plastic waste out at sea, as well as scavenging dogs, monitor lizards, cows on the beach and coastal erosion on the shore.

Turtle SOS Gambia (m *9803089/3647687;* e *tusostg@gmail.com;* f *Turtle-SOS-The-Gambia*) is a collaboration between Sandele Eco-Retreat (page 164) and a number of local and international partners. Since 2014, the project has set up a re-nesting and hatching centre as well as monitoring turtle activity along a 27km stretch of beach. They also help volunteers to raise awareness in local schools and some of the staff have transitioned from hunters to conservationists.

Landing, a former poacher who is now better known as Papa Turtle, explained how as a teacher he earned just D150 a month – less than £3 – with which he had to support not only his wife and children but also his late brother's family. With turtle eggs fetching upwards of D600, it's easy to see why so many poachers carry out this illegal activity. While hunting, Papa Turtle noticed the decline in the population and soon realised that there would be no turtles left if he continued to poach, so when Turtle SOS approached him to work alongside them, it was an easy choice for him.

If you'd like to get involved and help support the project, Turtle SOS Gambia offers basic, full-day or overnight packages (£5/8.50/12pp), allowing guests to visit and observe the hatchery, participate in beach patrols and even enjoy a turtle cocktail (no turtles involved!). Additionally, there are various packages available to adopt a turtle or a nest.

Kartong Bird Observatory/Community Wetland Reserve (m *7003147/ 7332225;* e *kartongbirdobservatory@hotmail.com;* m *kartongbirdobservatory.org*)

The focal point of birding activity on the south coast and only permanent ringing station anywhere in the country, Kartong Bird Observatory was established in 2010 by a team of British birding enthusiasts including resident ringer Colin Cross, who lives on site. It lies on the western edge of town, a couple of minutes' walk from the market, overlooking a large reed-fringed freshwater pool inhabited by an incredible variety of birds. Over 4,000 birds are ringed annually as part of an ongoing international research programme in to bird migration.

With more than 375 bird species recorded in the immediate vicinity, Kartong Bird Observatory is one of the most rewarding sites for aquatic birds anywhere in The Gambia. Among the more alluring regulars are African crake, dwarf bittern, greater painted snipe, Allen's gallinule and pygmy goose, with morning being the best time for bird photography and observing rarities. It is also worth being here in the evening, when around 1,000 herons of eight different species come to roost in the reedbeds, and there is a chance of four-banded sandgrouse, and both long-tailed and standard-winged nightjar. Look out, too, for crocodiles, which are common in the wetlands and grow up to around 4m long. Armitage's skink (see box, page 100) has also been recorded here.

This pool, overlooked by the observatory, forms part of the recently created Kartong Community Wetland Reserve, which extends southward from town across an expanse of reedbeds, open pools and other wetland habitats, most of which are a by-product of the extensive sand mining practised in the area until a few years ago. To explore the community wetland further, the dirt road then runs south from the observatory towards Berracunto and effectively doubles as an elevated causeway offering great views to both sides over several permanent and seasonal pools and other wetland areas. Berracunto is another important sacred site (one regularly visited by former president Jammeh), and while it doesn't really reflect this visually, it can be a very good spot for woodland birds and (at dusk) long-tailed nightjar.

Further afield, the Kartong area is a reliable site for the localised black-crowned crane. It also hosts several species rare or absent elsewhere in the country, and has thrown up a number of firsts for the country in recent years. Among the more unusual species recorded here are an American wigeon, brown noddy, Baillon's crake, little crake, Cassin's honeybird, black-crowned sparrow lark, cuckoo finch and Hudsonian whimbrel. Birders are most welcome to visit the observatory to obtain information about recent sightings at Kartong.

Allahein River Beyond Kartong, the surfaced coastal road carries on southwards for about 3km to a T-junction and immigration post where a left turn leads after about 1km to the north bank of the mangrove-lined Allahein River, which also forms the border with Senegal. Serviced by Dudu's Riverside Bar & Restaurant, this is an excellent place to chill out over a meal or drink, but is also the recognised base for organising boat trips on the river, which usually take in Pelican Island and a nearby oyster factory but can also be tailored towards fishing. The river is rewarding for birds, with various pelicans, kingfishers, gulls, terns and waders likely to be seen. Expect to pay around £12–15 for one or two passengers, to £25–30 for groups of five to eight. Similar trips can also be arranged through Stala Adventures (pages 164–5) for a minimum of around £16.50 for up to five passengers.

Kartong Beach Turn right at the T-junction mentioned above and after about 1.5km you will emerge at Kartong Beach, about 1km north of the mouth of the Allahein River. More of a working beach than a swimming beach, there is a small hamlet and fishing centre here. The beach running southeast towards the river mouth is well worth exploring, whether you are a keen birder or want to sunbathe in a quiet spot. Good birds sometimes spotted include white-fronted plover and great-spotted cuckoo.

Kartong Community Forest Reserve Situated about 3km northeast of the town centre, this 500m² patch of pristine forest was set aside as a community reserve a few years back, but has yet to be properly developed for tourism, though KART hopes to extend its area and to erect a stilted viewing canopy there within the lifespan of this guide. Green, patas and red colobus monkey are reputedly present and it is certain to host a good selection of first birds. To get there, follow the main road north out of town for about 500m past the junction for Boboi Beach Lodge, then turn on to the rough signposted track to your right. The forest lies about 3km along this track, which is very overgrown and should only be attempted either in a 4x4 or on foot.

Gambian Reptiles Farm (m *7004672*; e *paziaud.luc@gmail.com*; ⊕ *08.30–17.30 daily; entrance D250pp*) Relocated from the North Bank a few years back, the

Gambian Reptiles Farm now lies on the east side of the main coastal road about 3km north of Kartong, more-or-less opposite Sandele Eco-Retreat. The brainchild of Frenchman Luc Paziaud, a long-time resident of The Gambia, it provides sanctuary to a wide variety of injured or problem reptiles (in particular venomous snakes that enter houses and need to be removed), most of which are released into the wild when an opportunity presents itself. It doubles as a breeding centre for endangered species and as an educational facility. Indeed, the few thousand Gambian schoolchildren who visit annually are taught that reptiles are not all bad. Most snakes, for instance, are harmless to humans, but help control the numbers of agricultural pests. And crocodiles, by targeting slower and weaker fish as prey, play an important role in curbing the spread of piscine diseases, leading to greater population stability among the riverine fish that form a vital source of protein in the Gambian diet. For tourists, the farm is so unusual and interesting that it is well worth a visit, even if you can't stand snakes (in which case you might want to think of it as therapeutic). The 45-minute tours are led by well-informed guides who will gladly tell you everything you ever wanted to know about snakes but were too scared to ask. In the process, you'll get to see giant monitor lizards, the sluggish Bell's hinged tortoise, chameleons and other lizards, plus a collection of snakes that includes pythons, puff adders and spitting cobras. Unlike most reptile parks in Africa, this is not a tourist trap but a labour of dedication and love, and the income generated by visits helps cover running costs. More adventurously, Luc can also arrange nocturnal river trips to count crocodiles (another facet of his work) for around £40–45 per person.

11

SEND US YOUR SNAPS!

We'd love to follow your adventures using our *The Gambia* guide – why not send us your photos and stories via Twitter (*@BradtGuides*) and Instagram (*@bradtguides*) using the hashtag #thegambia. Alternatively, you can upload your photos directly to the gallery on The Gambia destination page via our website (w *bradtguides.com/thegambia*).

Inland to Brikama and Pirang

The second-largest town in The Gambia, Brikama lies some 15km inland of the Atlantic coastline around Sanyang, and 20km south of the urban conglomerate comprising Banjul, Serekunda and the main coastal resorts. A bustling but somewhat nondescript market town flanking the main South Bank Road to Basse, it rivals Serekunda's Westfield Junction as the main route focus in the coastal hinterland, and feels somewhat transitional in character between the urbanised coast and the underdeveloped country further upriver – a mood epitomised by the down-to-earth livestock market at Abuko and close-to-source handicraft market outside Brikama.

As towns go, Brikama is nothing to shout about. But it does lie at the heart of an area bristling with wildlife-viewing opportunities, all within easy day-tripping distance of the coastal resorts. Foremost among these is Abuko Nature Reserve, the country's largest extant patch of true closed-canopy forest, alive with monkeys, small antelope and colourful forest birds. Other prominent birdwatching sites include community-run forest reserves at Farasuto and Bonto-Pirang, the riverine woodland at Marakissa, the shrimp ponds outside Pirang, and the mangrove-lined creeks around Lamin Lodge. Last but not least, Makasutu Cultural Forest is not only home to the creek-side Mandina Lodges, a superlative upmarket eco-retreat, but also offers day tours that provide a fascinating introduction both to the culture and wildlife of the coastal hinterland.

ABUKO LIVESTOCK MARKET

The small town of Abuko, which straddles the busy Brikama Road around 6km south of Westfield Junction, is the site of one of the country's best-known and busiest livestock markets. It is arguably worth a visit at any time of year, but it becomes a chaotic regional focal point during the build-up to Tobaski, a Gambian variant on the Islamic celebration of Eidal-Adha. Tobaski commemorates the willingness of Abraham to follow a divine instruction to sacrifice his son Ismail (or Isaac) on a mountainside, and it is customary for every family to slaughter a ram. One-third of this ram is eaten by the family, one-third given away to relatives and one-third given to the poor. Over the weeks prior to the festival, breeders and herdsmen from all over the country descend on the market, and the place overflows with rams and people bargaining for them. Tobaski coincides with the end of the annual Hajj (pilgrimage) to Mecca, and falls on 22 August 2018, 12 August 2019 and 31 July 2020. There is plenty of transport to Abuko from Serekunda and Brikama.

ABUKO NATURE RESERVE

Situated on the Brikama Road less than 30 minutes' drive from the northern beach resorts, Abuko Nature Reserve (w *thegambiawildlife.com*; ⊕ *06.30–18.00 daily;*

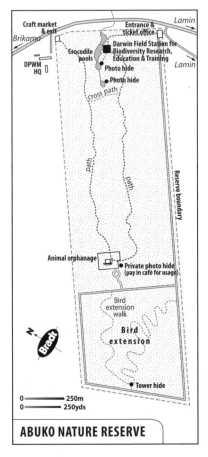

ABUKO NATURE RESERVE

entrance D300), is a popular goal for day trips out of Greater Banjul, particularly with birdwatchers. Extending over a mere 1km², it is the oldest sanctuary in the country, initially set aside in 1916 as a catchment area providing fresh water to Banjul, gazetted as a nature reserve under the supervision of Eddie Brewer, first director of the Wildlife Department of The Gambia, in 1968, and extended to its present size in 1978. The most important habitat in Abuko is the rare remnant patch of pristine gallery forest that hems in the small Lamin River and a few associated pools. This is one of the most northerly projections of the Upper Guinean Forest that extends along much of coastal West Africa from southern Senegal Casamance to western Ghana. Away from the river, the vegetation thins out to become Guinea savannah, which is not as rare as the gallery forest, but still supports plenty of wildlife.

Abuko contains a quite remarkable biodiversity for a reserve of its size, with many thousands of species of fungi, plants, trees, insects and other invertebrates living in and beneath the tall leafy forest canopy. Around 50 mammal species have been recorded, most visibly green monkey, red colobus, bushbuck and Maxwell's duiker. It also supports a varied selection of birds, with some 270 species recorded, and it is perhaps the best site this close to Banjul for forest specialists such as turacos, greenbuls and hornbills. Hides help you to get close to the animals, which are very used to humans and relatively easy to see – indeed, the monkeys in particular virtually ignore human visitors as they go about their daily routines. The least edifying aspect of the reserve is the so-called animal orphanage, a rundown zoo-like set-up that houses a few miserable monkeys and spotted hyenas.

GETTING THERE AND AWAY Abuko Nature Reserve is clearly signposted on the southwest side of the Brikama Road about 7km southeast of Westfield Junction and 1km past the town of Abuko. Public transport running between Serekunda and Brikama can drop you at the entrance. Alternatively, tourist taxis from Kotu, Kololi and the other beach resorts should cost around £15, and standard taxis are even cheaper. In addition, organised excursions to Abuko are offered by most hotels and tour operators in the Greater Banjul region.

AROUND THE RESERVE The ticket office and entrance gate lie at the reserve's southeastern corner, alongside the Brikama Road. In addition to paying the entrance fee here, you have the option of picking up a bird guide, for which there is no charge, but a tip will be expected (in the D60–300 range, depending on how long you spend there). From the gate, a reasonably well-maintained 200m footpath leads through tall gallery forest and across a bridge to the first of Abuko's pools. A quiet vigil here is likely to yield sightings of green monkey, red colobus, bushbuck, Maxwell's duiker, crocodile and Nile monitor, along with water-associated birds such as black-headed night heron, squacco heron, African jacana, African darter and giant kingfisher.

Just past this, on the right, the **Darwin Field Station for Biodiversity Research, Education and Training** (see box, page 179) houses a display about the wildlife in Abuko, while the area around the toilet often yields the localised Ahanta francolin. The centre's upper storey affords a good view of the main crocodile pool, which supports a wonderful variety of birds, including hamerkop, black crake and various herons, kingfishers and birds of prey. At the end of the dry season (March and April), these pools constitute the only fresh water for kilometres around, and thus act as a magnet for larger birds including spoonbills, storks, ospreys and even the odd pelican. As evening turns to night, there is a fantastic display consisting of hundreds of straw-coloured fruit bats that drop by for a drink after leaving their daytime roost at nearby Lamin, but you need special permission to stay on and wait for this.

From the Darwin Field Station, the footpath continues westward through the gallery forest, passing one active and one defunct photo-hide on the way. Among the more conspicuous forest species resident here are such beauties as violet turaco, bearded barbet, common wattle-eye and red-bellied paradise flycatcher. Less easy to observe are several Upper Guinean Forest species at the extreme northern edge of their distribution, among them white-spotted flufftail, green turaco and western bluebill, while other birds uncommon elsewhere in the country include African goshawk, leaflove, grey-headed bristlebill, yellow-breasted apalis, oriole warbler, collared sunbird, yellow-bill, red-shouldered cuckoo-shrike, and green hylia. Heading further east, the forest thins out and you find yourself walking through Guinea savannah with an open canopy allowing you to see the sky.

The footpath then leads to the so-called **animal orphanage**, which was originally established as a refuge for animals that had been orphaned, injured or kept illegally as pets. In its early days, it provided sanctuary to The Gambia's only lions, as well as the orphaned or confiscated chimpanzees that were later released into the River Gambia National Park. Today, the most interesting inhabitants of the orphanage are a few listless spotted hyenas which, like many of the other inmates, were born in captivity and seem destined to die there. The rather cheerless atmosphere is alleviated slightly by a café that serves chilled drinks and not much else. The **café** is also where birders can pay to use a small tin hide overlooking a freshwater pool that's too small to hold many waterbirds, but does tend to attract a steady stream of thirsty forest birds, from turacos and kingfishers to smaller weavers and finches.

Beyond the orphanage, the bird extension walk loops through more savannah to a **tower hide** where you can stand above the level of the treetops. This is a very pleasant walk that takes you through woodland, scrub and open areas. Because of the winding nature of the path you feel as though you have walked through a much larger area than you actually have. Rejoining the main footpath at the orphanage leads you through more savannah until you reach the gallery forest again. The path then takes you to the exit of the reserve. Alternatively, there is a footpath off the return path, about halfway along. It is well signed and will take you back to the first footpath and the entrance via the education centre.

LAMIN

Situated on the Brikama Road about 9km southeast of Serekunda, Lamin is a moderately sized town remarkable only for the large colony of straw-coloured fruit bats that inhabits the mango trees behind the large mosque on the main road. It is also the junction town for Lamin Lodge, a well-known and very enjoyable stilted restaurant on the southern verge of Tanbi Wetland Reserve, about 8km southwest of Banjul as the crow flies. Lamin Lodge is a good place to arrange boats trips into the 45km² reserve, which is one of the country's most important coastal wetlands (indeed, there has been talk over the years of designating it as a national park) and home to an immense variety of birds, along with substantial populations of the hefty marsh mongoose and the secretive West African manatee.

GETTING THERE AND AWAY Lamin lies along the main road between Serekunda and Brikama, and there is plenty of transport there from both towns. Lamin Lodge is 2km east of town, off any transport route, so you must either hire a taxi or walk. Another possibility, popular with birders and fishing enthusiasts, is to come by boat from Denton Bridge (page 91) at the northern end of the Tanbi Wetland Reserve close to Banjul.

WHERE TO STAY AND EAT *Map, page 142*

🏠 **Mandinari River Lodge** (5 rooms) ⊕ N13 18.393 W16 36.318; ☎ (UK) +44 (0)117 9381973; **m** 3394555/7794555; **e** mandinari@ hotmail.co.uk; **w** mrlgambia.com. Set alongside mangrove-lined creeks in the village of Mandinari, 5km from Lamin on a barely paved road, this eco-lodge & restaurant is centred on a little pool area with private bar & BBQ. Bright & airy roundhouses are nicely decorated in earthy hues, & come with en-suite shower, flushing toilets, small kitchenette & garden terrace with hammocks. The Black Pearl restaurant, set on a wooden pirate ship, looks set to open during the lifetime of this edition & will offer fish & seafood dishes. Bike hire is available, & the owners can organise boat & fishing trips & birdwatching excursions in the nearby Tanbi Wetlands, as well as visits to Mandinari village to gain an insight in to local life. Free airport transfers included. *£30pp with reductions for longer stays.*

✗ **Lamin Lodge** ⊕ N13 23.370 W16 37.280; **m** 7784058/9900231; **e** gambiariver@yahoo.com; ⊕ 08.00–17.00 daily (dinners by special request only). Reopened in 2013 after a long period of closure, this venerable & wonderfully rickety stilted 3-storey construction is owned & managed by the same people as Janjanbureh Camp (page 234). It's a great place to enjoy a relaxed lunch in the company of the birds, green monkeys & other wildlife that inhabits the surrounding creeks & mangroves. It serves a good selection of seafood & meat dishes, as well as chilled beers & sodas. It can also arrange dugout trips into the mangroves for around £4/hr for 1 or 2 people, as well as trips further afield to Abuko Nature Reserve, Janjanbureh or the North Bank combination of Juffureh & James Island. It is also the starting point for upriver cruises to Janjanbureh operated by Gambia River Cruises. Overnight accommodation is planned. *Mains mostly in the £4–5.50 range.*

YUNDUM

About 6km southwest of Lamin and 15km from Serekunda, the village of Old Yundum lies close to the junction of the Brikama Road and the newer surfaced road running northwest to Brusubi Junction (for the south coast and Kololi). It is best known as the site of Banjul International Airport, which is the only facility of its type in the country, and carries up to a million passengers annually. Established during World War II as a military airfield, it is where Franklin D Roosevelt became the first serving US president to set foot on African soil during a refuelling stop *en route* to the Casablanca Conference with his British counterpart Winston Churchill in January 1943. The modern airport, designed by the Senegalese architect Pierre Goudiaby, opened in 1997; prior to that it consisted of little more than a few quaint barn-like sheds. The only other points of interest in Yundum are a small but high-quality fruit market by the side of the road, and the adjacent National Bee-keepers Association, which sells an assortment of cheap but very tasty locally produced honey and items made out of natural beeswax, including decorative candles.

If you're heading to the airport and need a stopover, the **Woodpecker Resort** (m *3338880;* e *woodpecker.gambia@gmail.com;* w *woodpecker-resort.com; £21/30 sgl/dbl B&B; map, page 142*) is a decent option, with clean rooms offering free Wi-Fi and restaurant serving fast-food options in the £5–7 range. There's a pool (D100 for non-residents), darts, table tennis and a widescreen TV, and the hotel offers free airport transfers.

BRIKAMA

The administrative headquarters of Western Division, bustling Brikama, though scarcely a metropolis with a population of 80,000, is the second-largest town in The Gambia (a statistic that will give travellers heading upriver some notice of what to expect in terms of urban development). Brikama lies about 22km south of Serekunda, and is reached via the South Bank Road towards Soma and Basse, which bypasses the compact town centre 1km to its south. It is a busy little town, with some historical pedigree, though it has little to show for it unless perhaps you count the small and low-key old town, which runs south from the central market towards the old mosque. Brikama is of interest to travellers primarily for its superb and well-priced craft market, which recently relocated from the centre to an out-of-town site on the Serekunda Road. It is also the main springboard for gelly-gellys and shared taxis heading upriver along the South Bank, and the closest town to a few more rural tourist sites, notably Makasutu Cultural Forest, Marakissa River Camp, and the Pirang Forest Reserve and shrimp pools.

HISTORY According to oral tradition, Brikama was founded in the 13th century by a group of 40 Mandinka exiles from present-day Mali, and its first ruler was one Mansa Kolley. It is said that the site was chosen because it fulfilled a prophecy that the migrants should only settle when they came across a large santang tree (a type of mahogany) whose boughs were hung with the remains of an antelope eaten by a leopard. The town was twice destroyed by Muslim raids (in 1854 and 1874), but in both cases it soon recovered. Today it is well known as the home of one of The Gambia's most famous musical dynasties. This is the Konte family of *jalis* (praise singers) and kora players. The dynasty includes Burama Konte, a well-known composer who was active in the late 19th and early 20th centuries, his son Alhaji Bai Konte (1920–83), who became the first solo kora player to tour the USA when he played at the 1973 Newport Jazz Festival, and his son Dembo Konte (1942–2014), who toured the UK regularly and released several international CDs (often in collaboration with the Senegalese musician Kausu Kuyateh) prior to his recent death at home in Brikama.

GETTING THERE AND AWAY Traffic permitting, Brikama is only about 20 minutes' drive from Serekunda and 30 minutes from Banjul, though it usually takes a bit longer in the regular gelly-gellys and shared taxis that cover both routes for less than D60. Direct roads and regular public transport also link Brikama to Sanyang

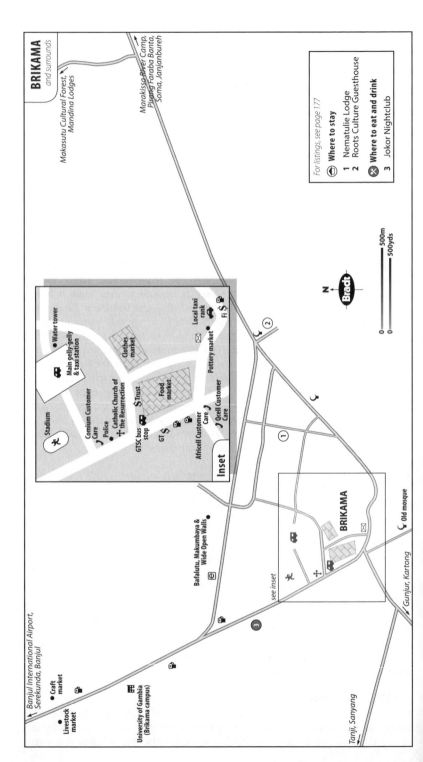

BRIKAMA
and surrounds

Makasutu Cultural Forest,
Mandina Lodges

Marakissa River Camp,
Pirang Taraba Banta,
Soma, Janjanbureh

For listings, see page 177

Where to stay
1 Nematulie Lodge
2 Roots Culture Guesthouse

Where to eat and drink
3 Jokor Nightclub

0 ——— 500m
0 ——— 500yds

N

Inset

Stadium

Water tower

Main gelly-gelly
& taxi station

Comium Customer
Care

Police

Catholic Church of
the Resurrection

Trust

Clothes
market

GTSC bus
stop

GT

Food
market

Africell Customer
Care

Qcell Customer
Care

Pottery market

Local taxi
rank

Fi

Banjul International Airport,
Serekunda, Banjul

Craft
market

Livestock
market

University of Gambia
(Brikama campus)

Bafalutu, Makumbaya &
Wide Open Walls

see inset

BRIKAMA

Old mosque

Gunjur, Kartong

Tanji, Sanyang

13km to the west, and Gunjur 19km to the southwest. For travel upriver, the main station in central Brikama is the best place to pick up gelly-gellys and shared taxis heading to the likes of Tendaba, Soma, Janjanbureh and Basse.

WHERE TO STAY *Map, page 176*

The most popular places to stay in the Brikama area are the exclusive **Mandina Lodges** in the nearby Makasutu Cultural Forest, and more moderately priced **Marakissa Camp** south of town, but these are covered separately later in this chapter. There are also two inexpensive options in town listed below.

Nematulie Lodge (30 rooms) m 7881394. This reasonably central & agreeable cheapie lies in a large compound in the backroads northeast of the market. Accommodation is in small round huts with sgl or dbl bed, net, en-suite shower & toilet but no fan. It can also prepare simple African–European meals (£4.50), which are eaten in a thatched bantaba in the garden. *£6/11 sgl/ dbl, additional £2.50 for B&B.*

Roots Culture Guesthouse (12 rooms) m 7231432. Situated close to the more easterly of the 2 junctions with the bypass road, this scruffy little guesthouse offers hutted accommodation in en-suite dbls with fan, no net, & a notice that a fine will be levied on anybody who 'stains the bed with blood or other stupid things' (you may never look at your fellow hotel guests quite the same way again!). A bar is attached but it serves neither alcohol nor food. *£8.50 dbl.*

WHERE TO EAT AND DRINK *Map, page 176*

There is no shortage of **street food** on offer in and around the central market and bus station, as well as a few undistinguished sit-down eateries. The best-known nightspot, about 200m along the western feeder road from Banjul, is the **Jokor Nightclub**, a lively bar and erratic eatery that hosts occasional live music concerts.

OTHER PRACTICALITIES
Banking and foreign exchange
There don't seem to be too many forex bureaux dotted around Brikama, but there are a few banks, notably the **Trust Bank**, between the market and bus station, which has an ATM accepting Visa cards.

Internet and telephone
The only internet café seems to be on the main bypass road a few hundred metres east of the Jah Oil Filling Station.

SHOPPING
Though not touristy in the slightest, the **central market** in Brikama is one of the largest in the country and a good place to buy groceries, clothes and most other day-to-day goods. There is also a small **pottery market** in the town centre, and the **main craft market** out of town along the Serekunda Road.

AROUND BRIKAMA
Brikama Craft and Livestock markets
Now situated about 2km from the town centre on the north side of the Serekunda Road, this once legendarily chaotic craft market now offers a relatively sedate and orderly buying experience. It is also one of the best places in the country to buy crafts in general and woodcarvings in particular, since its 80-odd stalls cater more to retailers than to tourists, and it is the source of many of the handicraft items sold at inflated prices in the more touristy markets on the coast. Indeed, Brikama is a noted centre for carvers (who produce their best workmanship in the shape of masks or gazelle groups) and you can watch them at work while you browse. For all that, a lot of the stall owners are quite pushy, and it is easy to get sucked in and buy everything in sight, or to get completely fed up with

the hassle and give up before buying anything. Whatever else, try to be both firm and polite with the vendors, telling them you are just looking for the moment, and to maintain a sense of humour at all times. It can be worth the hassle if you find that piece that you really want. Opposite the craft market is a small livestock market that can be quite interesting to wander around when it's busy, and where you are unlikely to receive much hassle – unless of course you are thinking of buying a goat or cow!

MARAKISSA Situated in a well-wooded area about 4km north of the Senegalese border, the village of Marakissa lies about 6km south of Brikama along a dirt road serviced by a regular trickle of bush taxis. It is a popular spot with birdwatchers owing to its proximity to the Allahein River (the same one that forms the border with Senegal near Kartong), which lies about 1km south of town and is serviced by the long-established Marakissa River Camp. The two key birding sites here are the camp itself, which lies 1km south of Marakissa village, sandwiched between a bend in the river and the west side of the road running down the border, and the bridge across the river about 300m further south. The well-wooded section of river flowing past the camp is a good site for giant kingfisher, white-breasted cuckoo-shrike and greater, lesser and spotted honeyguide, while the marshier areas and paddy fields that flank the bridge frequently host large numbers of waterfowl and waders, as well as African jacana, black crake and painted snipe. The camp can also arrange affordable canoe trips along a stretch of river where osprey, long-crested eagle and red-necked falcon are often seen. For non-birders, the area is home to plenty of crocs and giant monitor lizards.

 Where to stay and eat *Map, page 142*

Marakissa River Camp (9 rooms) ⊕ N13 11.375 W16 39.154; m 7779487/9905852; e marakissa@planet.nl; w marakissarivercamp. nl. Boasting a lovely remote riverfront location about 1km south of Marakissa village, this simple, tranquil & well-managed Dutch-owned camp feels a world away from the hectic coastal resorts to its northwest. Accommodation is in round thatched huts with twin beds, nets, en-suite showers & 24hr solar power, while the restaurant serves decent food on a stilted wooden terrace overlooking the river. It's a popular location for birders & guides are available. There are also canoes for hire. Day visitors are welcome. A far more agreeable budget option to staying in Brikama. *Rates on application.*

Kingfisher's Lodge (6 rooms) ⊕ N13 11.400 W16 39.244; m 9824290/7893006; w kingfisherslodge.com. Situated by the river about 1km off the main road, this very friendly lodge has a tranquil bush feel with no electricity available. Solar-powered roundhouses come with dbl bed, en-suite bathroom, separate living area & beautiful garden, & welcoming host Fatou can cook Gambian & European dishes for around £6. A couple of canoes are available to hire (*D250/hr*) & there's an onsite guide with a good knowledge of local flora & fauna who can take you hiking in more remote areas (*D200/hr*). *£7pp B&B.*

MAKASUTU CULTURAL FOREST An exemplary eco-tourism project, Makasutu Cultural Forest (m *6337017*; w *mandinalodges.com/makasutu-forest*) is set alongside the beautiful mangrove-lined Mandina Creek about 5km northeast of Brikama. It is best known perhaps as the site of the exclusive and architecturally innovative Mandina Lodges, but it also offers a selection of worthwhile activities that ensure it's a regular goal for day trips from the coastal resorts. Managed in collaboration with the surrounding communities, the reserve was established in 1993 by two well-travelled British enthusiasts, James English and Lawrence Williams, fulfilling a local legend that two white men would save the forest and make it famous (something they learned after the forest opened). It first opened to clients seven years later, since when it has won many awards, including the National Order of The Gambia in 2012. 'Makasutu' means 'sacred and deep forest' in the local Mandinka language, and the reserve extends over around 10km² of riparian forest, savannah and mangroves, and supports plenty of wildlife, most conspicuously around very habituated 200 Guinea baboons, but also various smaller primates, antelope and carnivores, and aquatic creatures such as crocodile and the occasional West African manatee. The marine and terrestrial birdlife is stunning too.

Makasutu Cultural Forest is highly regarded within The Gambia, not just because of the wildlife found there, but also because it is such a successful blend of different facets. It provides steady employment to more than 100 local people in an area that had seldom seen many visitors in the past: not only workers such as gardeners, drivers, cooks and guides, but also the woodcarvers who utilise the site to sell their wares, and the musicians and dancers who entertain the guests. Visitors, meanwhile, are rewarded with an experience they will long remember and carry home in their hearts. A programme to encourage school visits enables Gambian children to learn about their environment in a fun and positive way. Makasutu, in a nutshell, embodies all that is good about genuine ecotourism.

MAKASUTU WILDLIFE TRUST

The Makasutu Wildlife Trust (MST) is a leading charity that aims to help protect the wildlife and wild habitats of The Gambia, and to encourage a greater awareness about the environment and an appreciation of all aspects of conservation and biodiversity.

The Trust does this by actively involving local people and helping them to understand biodiversity and encouraging its conservation, by promoting education, study and research in the natural sciences and by raising public awareness.

A clear manifestation of this is the successful establishment of a community-based organisation called the Ballabu Conservation Project (BCP). The BCP involves most of the villages in the Kombo East, North and South districts in the West Coast region of The Gambia, whose main activities are promoting general awareness of biodiversity and environmental protection, by creating community forests, and ecotourism.

The MST headquarters are located in the Darwin Field Station inside Abuko Nature Reserve, where it carries out research, education and training on biodiversity, in collaboration with the West African Bird Study Association (WABSA). It conducts bird-study classes at the centre, which has a classroom facility, library, and laboratory, and operates a clinic to rehabilitate injured wild animals and birds and reintroduce them to the wild. It is also able to offer safe, secure and reasonably priced accommodation within Abuko Nature Reserve to visiting research students and volunteers.

The MST has successfully maintained the Gardens For Life programme in 17 schools within the aforementioned districts, and it lobbies for funds to buy seeds and garden implements for them. It has been able to establish a bilateral link with Kembujeh Lower Basic School and Withycombe Primary School in Devon thanks to the management of Makasutu Cultural Forest.

For more information about activities or volunteer work with the MST, it can be contacted at m 8907222/9900460/9900215/7849352 or e laminkuru63@hotmail.com.

Getting there and away Coming from the coast or airport, Makasutu is well signposted on the left side of the main South Bank Road about 2.5km past Brikama. The reception for day visitors lies about 3km along this road, and it is another 1km from there to Mandina Lodges and the arena for the Night Extravaganza (page 181). Overnight stays are usually booked inclusive of transfers from the airport (or wherever you are staying either side). Day trips can be arranged through any local tour operator, with the main specialist being The Gambia Experience (page 46). Plenty of public transport runs from Brikama past the junction, but not along the last 3–4km to the reception and lodges.

Where to stay and eat *Map, page 142*

✳ 🏠 **Mandina Lodges** (9 rooms) 📞 UK +44 845 330 2060; **e** mandina@gambia.co.uk; **w** mandinalodges.com. One of the most inspired & exclusive lodges in the country, Mandina Lodges is spaciously laid out on the south bank of the creek for which it is named. The common area features a large jungle-shaded swimming pool, the imaginative architecture & décor of the tall thatch-roofed dining area & bar, the fine international cuisine, & the wide wooden deck overlooking a mangrove-lined stretch of creek teeming with birdlife. The solar-powered accommodation is all fantastic, & you have the choice of a pagoda-like floating river lodge, a thatch-topped stilted river lodge, or a dbl-storey jungle lodge set a little inland. All rooms come with a framed & netted super king-size bed, high-quality fittings, safe, huge windows offering 180° views, balcony, fan & en-suite shower & compost toilet. All guests have personal guides, who can take them on canoe trips through the mangroves (where there's a good chance of encountering rarities such as white-backed night heron & African finfoot), relaxed walks through the forest, or a range of other activities including fishing & birdwatching. Optional sunset cruises & fishing excursions are extra. The lodge restaurant serves a range of well-presented Gambian dishes, & dinner can be taken alfresco either at one of the tented wooden dining areas or in your lodge., Most people love Mandina Lodges' peaceful bush atmosphere, plentiful birdlife & wide range of outdoor activities – but the lack of AC or Wi-Fi, & remote location, mean it isn't for everybody. Bookings are made directly through The Gambia Experience (page 46). *From £349pp for a 3-night stay HB inc transfers.*

What to see and do The highly worthwhile and enjoyable **day tours** of Makasutu start at around 07.30 (or slightly later if you prefer) in an open clearing below a giant baobab alongside a tall termite hill. You then set out on foot through lush creek-side vegetation encompassing palm forest, mangroves, savannah and dense

---

WIDE OPEN WALLS

The brainchild of Makasutu's Lawrence Williams, this unusual project aims to provide a creative makeover to the 14 villages that comprise the 85km² Ballabu Conservation Project (a buffer zone to Makasutu) and transform them into the subject of an open-air street-art ecotourism circuit. So far, aerosol-brandishing street artists from at least a dozen different countries have helped to decorate four of the villages with a total of around 400 vibrant spray-paint creations, and there are plans to create sculptures in the future. The most accessible of these funkily decorated villages is Galoya. Though not formally open to tourists, anybody can visit the painted village, either in isolation or as an add-on visit to Makasutu, but it is requested that you call Lawrence (**m** *6337017*) in advance, and be prepared to make a donation of around D100, payable to the village. For further details, visit **w** cargocollective.com/wideopenwallsgambia.

forest, looking for baboons, birds and other wildlife, before taking to the water in dugout canoes, then returning to land for another short walk. A Gambian buffet-style lunch is followed by traditional Jola music and dancing. Other cultural interactions include a visit to a local marabout and watching a palm tapper at work. The best numbers for booking day trips are m 7886688/9951547, and the cost is around D1,000 per person.

Since 2014, Makasutu has held the Night Extravaganza every two to three weeks in high season, which starts at 18.00 (when thousands of egrets fly past on the way to their nocturnal roost) in a riverside arena set beneath the stars below a recently constructed four-storey viewing platform. The extravaganza includes a buffet dinner, kora and djembe music, and a climactic performance of traditional masked dancers and fire-breathers. The extravaganzas can be booked through the same number as the day tours and cost around D1,500 per person.

PIRANG AND FARABA BANTA

The villages of Pirang and Faraba Banta (sometimes written Faraba Bantang), situated less than 2km apart some 12km east of Brikama, are about the furthest inland one would normally go from any of the coastal resorts in day-tripping mode. Pirang is well known as the site of a pair of massive silk cotton trees that reputedly once formed part of its fortifications. The larger of the two, standing 43m high and with a girth of more than 50m, is claimed to be the tallest tree in West Africa, and even if this is untrue, it is nevertheless a quite magnificent specimen. Faraba Banta's main claim to fame is, as of 2011, as the site of the Agriculture and Science faculty of the University of The Gambia. Otherwise, the area is of interest mainly to birdwatchers, who have the choice of exploring several worthwhile sites, notably Farasuto Forest near Koloro, Pirang Forest near Bonto, Pirang Pools north of Pirang, and the so-called Bush Track running south from Faraba Banta.

GETTING THERE AND AWAY Pirang lies about 1km north of the main South Bank Road and is serviced by regular bush taxis from Brikama, 12km to its west. To explore the surrounding birding sites, however, you'll either need to charter a taxi from the coast, or else be prepared for a bit of walking and/or hopping around on local transport or donkey- or horse-cart. Directions to the individual sites are given below.

WHERE TO STAY Most people visit as a day trip from the coast, and there seems to be no formal accommodation in the immediate vicinity.

AROUND PIRANG The following sites are described in the sequence you reach them coming from Brikama or the coast.

Farasuto Forest Community Nature Reserve (⊕ N13 17.866 W16 33.915; m 7073623; e mamadouwj@live.co.uk; w farasuto.org) Situated 2km northeast of the South Bank Road where it bisects the village of Kuloro, Farasuto Forest is a 3ha relict patch of closed-canopy forest a short distance inland of the River Gambia. Originally left uncleared by local villagers for use as a ceremonial circumcision site, it was set aside as a community reserve in 2008 at the behest of the Kuloro Bird Club, which comprises around 30 locally based bird guides. Though quite small, Farasuto supports an incredibly diverse birdlife. Around 100 species have been recorded within the forest, and another 200 from the immediate vicinity. It matches Abuko as a site for forest interior specialists, with 11 such species recorded, including

Ahanta francolin, green turaco, spotted honeyguide, grey-headed bristlebill and green hylia, and in July 2013 it yielded what is only the second Gambian record for a wood owl (a secretive species, but presumably resident). Other birds characteristic of Farasuto are violet turaco, sulphur-breasted bush-shrike and several types of greenbul and sunbird. Early morning is the best time to visit to do the very small site justice.

To get to Farasuto, you must first head to the village of Kuloro, which straddles the South Bank Road 8km east of Brikama and 4km west of Pirang (any gelly-gelly headed between these towns can drop you there). The junction for the reserve is on the left coming from Brikama, and although it is no longer signposted, anybody can point you in the right direction. From the junction, a dirt feeder road runs northeast for 2km, passing through the village then open fields, to the entrance gate, which may or may not be manned. Future plans include the construction of toilets and a hide, as well as the reforestation of a plot bordering the reserve.

Pirang Forest Park (✪ *N13 16.898 W16 33.186;* m *6887198/7913305/9887198; entrance D50, guides around D300*) The centrepiece of the Pirang-Bonto Ecotourism Community Project, the 64ha Pirang Forest Park protects The Gambia's second-largest remaining block of moist closed-canopy forest (the largest being Abuko). With a canopy extending to 35m above the ground, Pirang Forest supports more than 200 bird and 80 butterfly species, along with substantial but skittish populations of red colobus, green and patas monkey. It has long been known to birders as the only Gambian site for white-spotted flufftail and wood owl, and while the latter was also recently recorded at nearby Farasuto, Pirang remains the only place where you stand a realistic chance of seeing one, as the guides know the location of a daytime roost. Other good forest birds include Ahanta francolin, red-thighed sparrowhawk, green turaco, swamp greenbul, green crombec and western bluebill.

Situated to the north of the South Bank Road near the village of Bonto, Pirang Forest Park is very accessible but unsignposted and quite difficult to locate. Coming from the coast, you need to follow the South Bank Road for 10km past Brikama until you reach Bonto Junction (✪ *N13 16.675 W16 33.431*) about 2km before Pirang village. At the junction, there is a small sign pointing left towards Bonto village, then after 500m turn right, then after another 300m (after passing a church to your right), left again. The small reception building lies about 150m down this road, and here you can pay the entrance fee, as well as arrange a guide (optional but recommended). Try to time your visit for during the week, as the main path through the forest joins the villages of Pirang and Bonto and there are always plenty of kids at weekends who hassle visitors.

Pirang Pools Extending over about 1km² between Pirang village and the South Bank of the River Gambia, this area formerly hosted about 70 artificial pools that were the site of a shrimp farm but have now been drained (although periodically they do hold water). It is generally listed as the most reliable site in The Gambia for the regal black-crowned crane, but sightings of this unmistakeable tall bird have been infrequent in recent years (although there was a confirmed sighting in 2017 by a local guide). There are also usually good numbers of spoonbills, egrets, kingfishers, waders and other waterbirds, including spur-winged goose and white-faced whistling duck, especially during the wet season. It is possible to see yellow-crowned bishop in the sedges, and crested lark and plain-backed pipit along the bunds. Raptors such as long-crested eagle, western banded snake-eagle and osprey are common during the dry season. The most southerly former pools lie about 600m northeast of the main square in Pirang, and can easily be reached from there on foot.

Faraba Banta Bush Track This informal 3km trail running south from the South Bank Road through an area of relatively open savannah is known as a good site for greyish eagle-owl, a sub-Sahelian endemic recently split from the more widespread spotted eagle-owl. Other good birds associated with the trail are the semi-nocturnal Temminck's and bronze-winged courser, and a host of raptors including ten eagle and snake-eagle species, lizard and grasshopper buzzard, and various goshawks. The track starts in Faraba Banta on the south side of the South Bank Road, almost opposite the signpost for Faraba Kairaba (✪ *N13 14.898 W16 31.492*). You are free to explore independently, but if you want a guide (you will need one to stand a chance of seeing the eagle-owl) and one doesn't find you, then ask around for Abdoulaye, who lives close to the start of the track.

THE GAMBIA ONLINE

For additional online content, articles, photos and more on The Gambia, why not visit **w** bradtguides.com/thegambia.

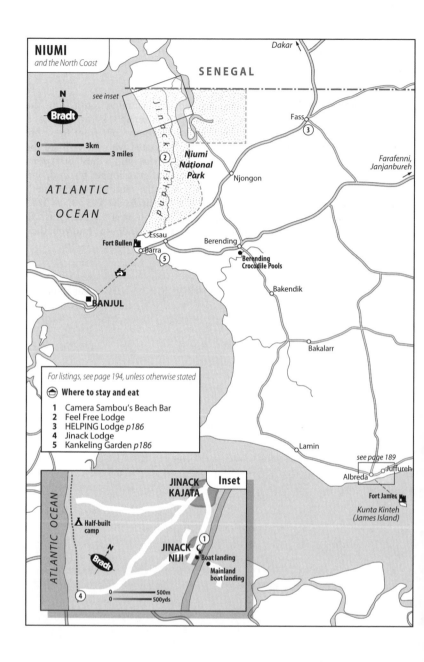

NIUMI
and the North Coast

SENEGAL

Dakar

see inset

N

Bradt

0 ——— 3km
0 ——— 3 miles

Jinack Island

Fass
3

ATLANTIC
OCEAN

Niumi
National
Pàrk

Njongon

Farafenni,
Janjanbureh

Essau

Berending

Fort Bullen
Barra
5

Berending
Crocodile Pools

BANJUL

Bakendik

Bakalarr

For listings, see page 194, unless otherwise stated

Where to stay and eat

1 Camera Sambou's Beach Bar
2 Feel Free Lodge
3 HELPING Lodge *p186*
4 Jinack Lodge
5 Kankeling Garden *p186*

Lamin

see page 189

Albreda

Juffureh

Fort James

Kunta Kinteh
(James Island)

JINACK
KAJATA

Inset

ATLANTIC OCEAN

Half-built
camp

Bradt

N

JINACK
NIJI

1

Boat landing

Mainland
boat landing

4

0 ——— 500m
0 ——— 500yds

184

13

Niumi and the North Coast

Lightly populated by comparison with its southern counterpart, the coastal region of North Bank Division comprises around 10km of bona fide coastline, running up to the Senegalese border from the port of Barra, as well as a long stretch of river frontage running south from Barra towards the venerable port of Albreda. Historically, the north coast and its hinterland formed the Kingdom of Niumi, a centralised Mandinka state that was founded during or before the 15th century, and grew wealthy on the back of the slave trade that dominated the lower river economy into the early 19th century. Today, the old kingdom, which ran inland from the coast as far as Jurunku Bolong, is split into two administrative districts: Lower and Upper Niumi. It also shares its name with Niumi National Park, which protects the coastline north of Barra, an area dominated by Jinack Island, a narrow sandy sliver separated from the mainland by the Niji Bolong in the north and mangroves in the south.

Niumi is relatively undeveloped in terms of tourist accommodation, which is limited to half-a-dozen budget lodges on Jinack Island and around Albreda. Indeed, most tourists who explore the area do so on one of the full-day 'Roots Tours' offered by hotels and operators on the resorts around Banjul. These popular tours focus on the village of Juffureh, which *Roots* author Alex Haley claimed as his ancestral home, and on nearby Albreda and Kunta Kinteh (formerly James) Island, which together host five of the seven structures inscribed in 2003 as the 'Kunta Kinteh Island and Related Sites' UNESCO World Heritage Site' (the other two being Fort Bullen in Barra and the Six-Gun Battery in Banjul). The highlights of Niumi can also be explored independently, crossing from Banjul using the Barra Ferry, and picking up road transport from there.

BARRA AND SURROUNDS

Occupying a westerly prominence on the north side of the 3km-wide strait where the River Gambia empties into the open sea, Barra, with a population of 5,500, is the principal town and main transport hub of the northern coastal hinterland. The town has quite a bustling character, despite its modest size, with the compact market area around the ferry and bus terminals being particularly hectic (and home to a few shady bumster types who habitually try to involve themselves in any transaction involving a tourist). The name Barra is the Portuguese for strait, a reference to the narrowing of the River Gambia at its mouth, and in pre-colonial times it was widely used by Europeans as a synonym for all of Niumi. The only attraction of note in Barra is Fort Bullen, which forms part of a UNESCO World Heritage Site and acquired a museum in 2013.

GETTING THERE AND AWAY Barra is an important public transport hub. It is the northern terminus of the most westerly crossing point along the unbridged River Gambia, the 3km strait between Banjul and Barra, which is serviced both by a public ferry service and by regular private pirogues catering to foot passengers only. Barra is also home to a packed taxi park from where regular road transport heads upriver towards Farafenni and Lamin Koto.

Coming from Banjul, the only option for vehicles is the official Banjul–Barra Ferry, while foot passengers have the choice of the ferry or the motorised pirogues across the Gambia River Mouth. It's not much of a choice, in all honesty. The official ferry service has long been quite unreliable, but in recent years it has deteriorated to the point where it is now the subject of a British Foreign and Commonwealth Office (FCO) (w *www.gov.uk/foreign-travel-advice/gambia*) safety warning. This is due to overcrowding and regular breakdowns that have left it stranded without power mid-crossing on several occasions recently. Lengthy delays are also a problem, and it occasionally stops working altogether. In May 2017, though, it was announced that a new ferry, twice the size of the existing ones, will soon start plying this route raising hopes that the crossing will become faster, safer and more efficient.

The fare is around D200 per vehicle or D25 per foot passenger. The ferry leaves Banjul from the jetty on Liberation Avenue, and both drivers and foot passengers can buy their tickets right there. Coming from the Barra side, however, drivers need to buy their ticket at a poorly signposted office in Essau about 2km from the jetty. The waterborne equivalent of bush taxis, the passenger pirogues that run between Banjul and Barra are, like their terrestrial counterparts, often overloaded. An FCO warning also applies to these boats, which occasionally sink during the crossing (the most recent incident, in which seven people drowned, took place in October 2013). If you do decide to risk it, try to avoid stormy or windy weather, which increases the risk of an incident. The pirogue fare is also D25 per foot passenger, but you pay extra if you want to be carried from the shore to the boat (as most locals do, to keep their clothes dry!).

The main taxi park in Barra lies opposite the police station a couple of hundred metres from the jetty. Here you can pick up the GTSC buses that run five-times daily between Barra and Farafenni (the first one leaves at 07.00, and the last at 17.00), the daily 09.00 GTSC bus to Lamin Koto for Janjanbureh, and regular gelly-gellys to pretty much everywhere on the North Bank, from Albreda and Fass to Farafenni and Kuntaur.

⌂ WHERE TO STAY AND EAT *Map, page 184*

⌂ **HELPING Lodge** (5 rooms) Fass; m 9945174/3607148; e helping-lodge@ helpingcharity.org.uk; w helpingcharity.org.uk/ lodge.html. Run by UK-based charity HELPING (Help for Education & Local Projects IN Gambia), this new guesthouse is in a peaceful location, just south of Fass, that's great for birding. Solar-powered en-suite rooms come with dbls & Wi-Fi, as well as fans built with back-up batteries – good for the nightly power cuts! Transfers from the South Bank & excursions to the sights on the North Bank can be arranged. All profits go towards providing free education for local children & supplies for the local clinic. *£15 dbl B&B.*

⌂ **Kankeling Garden** (3 rooms) Essau; m 9988523/7262009; e shumbaarts@gmail.com; w shumba.org.uk/kinkeling. Situated just east of Essau on the bank of the River Gambia Estuary, this local initiative, run by Kabiro Marong with the help of UK-based Shumba Arts, organises bespoke stays for those who want to learn drumming or dancing during their stay in The Gambia. 'Kankeling' is the Mandinka term for 'as one', & the idea behind the garden was to create a space for both locals & visitors to The Gambia to enjoy the country's music & culture. Their 3-bed bungalow is set among plenty of fruit trees, planted by locals when the garden was first created in 1998, but facilities are fairly basic, with compost toilet & water collected from a nearby tap by donkey cart. Casual visitors are also welcomed, & camping is also available. *From £400pp for 2 weeks, inc FB, drum & dance programme & visits to local cultural events; rooms £20/night, camping £8pp.*

AROUND BARRA

Fort Bullen Museum (🕐 *08.00–18.00 Mon–Sat; entrance D50*) Standing sentinel on Barra Point a few hundred metres west of the ferry jetty, Fort Bullen was the only such structure built on the West African coast with the express purpose of helping eradicate the slave trade. It was constructed on the so-called 'Ceded Mile' granted to the British by King Burungai Sonko of Niumi in 1826 in exchange for an annual subsidy of £100 following negotiations conducted by Sir Charles Bullen, the commander of HMS *Maidstone*. Initially, the fort consisted of little more than the two cannons Bullen took ashore to Barra Point to complement the gun battery at Banjul by covering the northern half of the 3km-wide strait between the two.

Development of the site was stalled when Burungai Sonko tried to revoke the Ceded Mile treaty, a decision that led to the Barra War of August 1831 to January 1832. The present fort, a rectangular laterite structure with a 1,200m² floor area, tall battlements, and a circular bastion in each corner, was built over 1833–34, and its three-gun battery allowed the British to have full control over which ships could enter or leave the river mouth. As a result, the Royal Navy was able to seize more than 1,600 ships and free at least 150,000 captives between then and 1870. During this time, Fort Bullen came under attack only once, when a small force of British troops and civilians had tried to arrest some people in the nearby town of Essau but was fought off with the loss of several lives. The survivors of the force retreated to Fort Bullen, only to abandon it for four months until the following year when the fighting was over.

At the beginning of World War II the Senegalese government sided with the Vichy government in France. This left the British colony surrounded by a potentially hostile enemy, so they modernised the fort and brought in more weapons, namely a four-inch Vickers (which is still there today), and a 12-pounder. After the war, the fort was again abandoned until it was claimed as a National Monument in the 1970s. It was renovated in 1996 for the Roots Homecoming Festival (page 17). In 2003, it was inscribed as part of the 'Kunta Kinteh Island and Related Sites' UNESCO World Heritage Site'. Since early 2013, it has also housed a museum dedicated to the abolition of the slave trade and the fort's role in it, developed with the support of the British High Commission in Bakau.

Berending Crocodile Pools This small village 10km east of Barra is the site of at least four pools linked naturally by a shallow watercourse and surrounded by a small but beautiful patch of forest. The focus of the pool is its population of crocodiles, which are mostly fairly small and seem to be quite shy, though reputedly they do sometimes emerge towards dusk. It is said that when the Mandinka of Berending first arrived in the area, they prayed regularly at the pools, but the practice has dropped away slightly now most of the locals follow Islam. The two main reasons for praying appear to be for a good harvest and to increase fertility for women who have trouble conceiving. Those who pray at the poolside normally bring fish for the crocodiles, but won't swim there. Even if you don't see the crocs, it is a great site for birds, with turacos and robin-chats calling from the lush foliage, broad-billed rollers perched higher in the canopy, and jacanas, crakes and kingfishers active around the reedy shore.

Berending lies on the main North Bank Road about 10km east of the Barra Ferry Terminal and 1km past the junction for Albreda. Inexpensive bush taxis run there regularly from Barra. The pools lie a few hundred metres from the main road, and can be reached by following a sandy track that leads off to the right just before an immense kapok tree.

Fass Situated about 2km south of the border with Senegal, this small town of around 800 inhabitants is known for its large, colourful and lively Wednesday *lumo* (market), which is frequented by both Gambians and Senegalese. If you are in the area, it is worth a visit – there are plenty of bush taxis from Barra, especially on market days. An alternative is horse- and donkey-cart since many local people get to the market using this mode of transport.

ALBREDA, JUFFUREH AND SURROUNDS

Huddled so close together that it's difficult to tell where one ends and the other begins, the historic twin villages of Albreda and Juffureh (also known as Albadarr and Gillifree, or other variants thereof) sit on the North Bank of the River Gambia about 25km upriver of Barra and Banjul. Together with nearby Kunta Kinteh Island, 3km across the water, these villages played a pivotal role in the slave trade that dominated the economy of the lower River Gambia from the late 15th to the early 19th centuries. At various times, the Portuguese, British and French all maintained trading posts in the vicinity, while Kunta Kinteh Island was revived as a strategic British naval base in the abolition era. Today, the area is the focal point of a UNESCO World Heritage Site whose seven components include Fort James on Kunta Kinteh Island and four separate buildings in and around Albreda. Juffureh, meanwhile, leaped to international prominence in 1976 with the publication of Alex Haley's *Roots* (see box, page 191), which claimed it as the place where his ancestor Kunta Kinteh was captured by slave traders. All in all, it's a fascinating area, contrasting with the south coast resorts in almost every conceivable way, and well worth visiting, whether you do so independently or as part of a tour.

GETTING THERE AND AWAY The overwhelming majority of visitors to Albreda, Juffureh and Kunta Kinteh Island join one of the organised Roots Tours offered by most south-coast hotels and ground operators. This is certainly the easiest option, but the area is also accessible to independent travellers who are prepared to put up with the risks and vagaries associated with the ferry from Banjul to Barra (pages 185–8). From Barra it's about 35km by road, first following the surfaced main North Bank Road east for 9km as far as Buniadu, then turning right on to a rather erratic unsurfaced road that heads southwards through Bakendik then veers eastward at Tubo Kolong before entering Albreda. The route is covered by a trickle of shared taxis and gelly-gellys, which take about an hour and cost less than D50, while private taxis should cost around D1,400 but incur a good 2 or 3 hours of waiting time. It's also possible to arrange boat excursions to James Island and Albreda from Lamin Lodge, Tumani Tenda and Berefet on the South Bank.

 **WHERE TO STAY** *Map, page 189*

Kunta Kinteh Roots Camp (36 rooms) m 7904782/9914508; e kuntakintehrootscamp@ gmail.com. Situated in green riverside grounds on the western fringe of Albreda, this pleasant & underutilised camp has a swimming pool, views to the jetty & James Island, food at similar prices to the affiliated Rising Sun Restaurant, & adequate accommodation in spacious en-suite twin rooms

with nets & roof fan, or double rooms with standing fan. Good value. *All rooms £13.50.*

Juffureh Resthouse (14 rooms) m 7054419. Basic but adequately clean rooms with net but no fan can be found at this locally owned lodge opposite the turn-off for the Kunta Kinteh family compound. It seems a pleasant enough place, assuming that the chip-on-shoulder

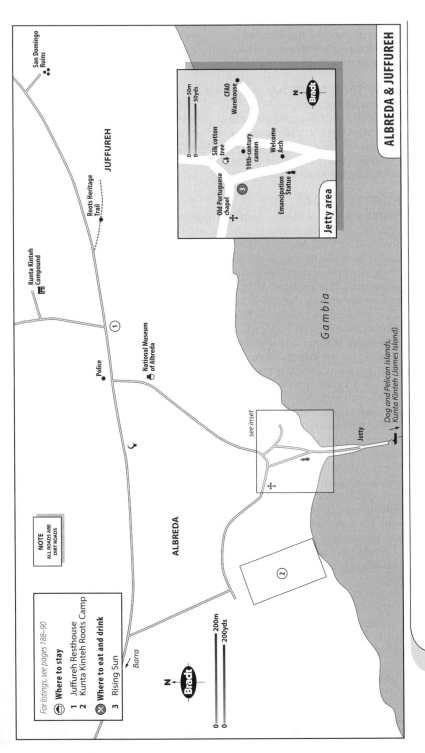

ALBREDA & JUFFUREH

13

For listings, see pages 188–90

Where to stay
1 Juffureh Resthouse
2 Kunta Kinteh Roots Camp

Where to eat and drink
3 Rising Sun

NOTE
ALL ROADS ARE
DIRT ROADS

San Domingo
Ruins

JUFFUREH

Roots Heritage
Trail

Kunta Kinteh
Compound

Police

National Museum
of Albreda

ALBREDA

see inset

Gambia

Jetty

*Dog and Pelican Islands,
Kunta Kinteh (James Island)*

Barra

Jetty area

Old Portuguese
chapel

Silk cotton
tree

19th-century
cannon

Welcome
Arch

Emancipation
Statue

Warehouse

CFAO

0   50m
0   50yds

0   200m
0   200yds

paranoia expressed towards guidebook writers isn't indicative of a generally confrontational management style. It can prepare food, fuller details of which couldn't be disclosed for security reasons, & there is also a shady bantaba. *£5pp with low-season discounts.*

✗ WHERE TO EAT AND DRINK   *Map, page 189*

✗ **Rising Sun Restaurant**   m 7687757; ⏰ 07.00–midnight daily. Situated on the main square behind Albreda Jetty, this friendly open-sided restaurant is an agreeable spot for a tasty, sensibly priced drink or meal, with on-the-ball staff used to pulling out the stops for tour groups. Sandwiches & snacks are available, along with a varied selection of fish, chicken & steak dishes. Portions are generous & a full selection of cold soft drinks & alcoholic drinks is available. *Sandwiches £3.50–5, snacks £1.50–3.*

WHAT TO SEE AND DO

Albreda Rented to French merchants by the King of Niumi in 1681, Albreda was probably the busiest slaving post on the River Gambia until the trade was legally abolished in 1807. Most tour groups arrive at the Albreda Jetty, which extends almost 300m into the river, and leads to the main square via a short footpath flanked by the relatively modern **Welcome Arch** and **Emancipation Statue**. A large shady **silk cotton tree** lies at the heart of the square, and below it is a 19th-century **cannon**, presumably used by the British to bar slaving ships from sailing further upriver. Here, independent visitors will be approached by a representative of the Juffureh–Albreda Development Fund, which was established in 2008 with the dual aims of ensuring that the local community benefits collectively from tourism, and of reducing the hassle to visitors presented by pushy guides and children. All visitors must pay the community fee (D50 per person), which includes the (optional) services of a guide, who will expect a fair tip.

Two buildings inscribed as part of the UNESCO World Heritage Site flank the square. To the left, behind the Rising Sun Restaurant, the substantial ruin of a late 15th-century **Portuguese chapel** is probably the oldest extant structure of its type in West Africa. To the right, reached via a 50m footpath, is the timeworn double-storey **warehouse** once occupied by the Compagnie Française d'Afrique Occidentale (CFAO). The link between the CFAO Building and the slave trade is somewhat tenuous, as it was probably built in 1847, more than a decade after the twin fortifications at Bathurst and Barra closed the river to unwanted traffic. The ground floor, entered through an open arcade, served as a shop and warehouse, while the upper floor comprised the residential quarters of the CFAO management and agents.

A 500m dirt track leads from the right side of the main square to the **National Museum of Albreda** (w *ncac.gm*; ⏰ *08.00–17.00 daily; entrance fee of D96 inc Kunta Kinteh Island*), which is housed in the Maurel Frères Building, a British-built 1840s construction that later served as a warehouse of the eponymous Lebanese trader. Small but harrowing, this well-organised museum has several detailed displays relating to the slave trade out of West Africa and to the harsh treatment meted out to its victims after their arrival in the Americas. It also has a room full of paraphernalia relating to Alex Haley and the *Roots* phenomenon.

Juffureh Bordering Albreda to the east, the tiny Mandinka village of Juffureh is best known for housing the family compound associated with Kunta Kinteh of *Roots* fame (see box, opposite). In fact, there is some dispute among historians as to whether Juffureh could have been the place where Kunta Kinteh actually lived. This is because the village is only 1km from the former slaving emporium

Juffureh achieved global fame in the wake of the 1976 publication of Alex Haley's *Roots*, which purported to trace the author's ancestry back to this otherwise unremarkable village. The hero of Haley's story was his ancestor Toby, a slave bought by a Virginian plantation owner called John Waller. According to Haley, Toby had started life as Kunta Kinteh, born to an Islamic Mandinka family in Juffureh, captured by slavers as a small boy, and then shipped to America on a longboat, where he spent weeks confined below deck with little food or water. Renamed by Waller, Toby passed on the details of his childhood capture to his sons, who in turn recounted them to their sons, and so on, allowing Haley to trace his ancestry back to Kunta Kinteh and Juffureh.

A massive critical and public success, *Roots* sold more than a million copies in its first seven months, spending 22 weeks at the top of *The New York Times* bestseller list, and it earned its author the 1977 Pulitzer Prize. The television series that followed was nominated for 37 Emmy Awards, winning nine, and attracted 130 million viewers in the US alone. It also brought tourism to Juffureh in a big way. At the peak of its popularity, the village was visited by 80% of tourists to The Gambia, and even today it remains something of a pilgrimage site for most US visitors boasting some African ancestry.

In 1993, Alex Haley suffered a fatal heart attack, 17 years after the publication of *Roots*. Within a year of his death, his private papers had exposed much of the *Roots* saga to be invention. It transpired that Toby had been living in America for at least five years before Kunta Kinteh was supposedly shipped there from Juffureh, and that he died almost a decade before the birth of the 'daughter' that supposedly linked his lineage to Haley's. Despite the exposure, however, the Roots Tour to Juffureh and environs remains one of the most popular excursions from the resorts that line the coast south of Banjul. And rightly so. True, there is little doubt that Haley consciously fabricated the genealogical link between himself, Toby and Kunta Kinteh. But there is no denying the deep symbolic truth underlying the *Roots* saga, nor the horrific trade in human lives that formed its inspiration.

of Albreda, whose traders would usually have sourced captives from further afield than what was practically their own doorstep. Whatever the truth, the **Kunta Kinteh Compound** (m *7721233;* ⊕ *daily; entrance D50*) has become something of a pilgrimage site, so much so that in the 1990s it was visited by an estimated 80% of all tourists who came to The Gambia. The family will tell you the oral history of the village and the story of Kunta Kinteh, and pull out a stash of old clippings relating to Alex Haley's visit to the village. Given the tourist traffic the Kunta Kinteh Compound has experienced over the years, it feels very down-to-earth and displays few, if any, trappings of the wealth one might expect. Indeed, it isn't even signposted: to get there from the main road, you need to head north at the junction opposite the Juffureh Resthouse, then turn right after 200m, and enter the first compound to the left.

Back on the main road, about 200m east of the Juffureh Resthouse, a signposted arch to the right marks the start of the **Roots Heritage Trail**, a short nature walk that leads to the waterfront and which is intended as a place of quiet contemplation. Another 400m past this, also to the left, a short footpath leads to the brooding

San Domingo Ruins, set in an overgrown clearing alongside a massive baobab tree. One of the earliest European trade stations founded in West Africa, San Domingo dates to the late 15th century, when it supported a small mercantile community of Portuguese settlers and people of Luso-African descent, who acted as hosts and middlemen to visiting ships. In its prime, the settlement comprised a few large buildings, including one 'of two storeys with courses of mortar running through the laterite rock, plaster tinted pink, a yellow brick arch over one window as well as four rectangular windows beneath a wooden lintel', set in large gardens with a freshwater well. All that remains today is the ruin of one double-storey house, which may or may not be the one described above.

Kunta Kinteh (James) Island

Renamed in honour of Kunta Kinteh in 2011, this small rocky outcrop in the River Gambia, 3km to the southeast of Albreda, was formerly called James Island and is still most widely referred to by that name. It was one of the first landfalls made by the 1456 expedition led by the pioneering Portuguese sailor Luiz de Cadamosto, who named it St Andrew Island after a shipmate they buried on the island. The first fort was built there by Latvians in 1651, only to be seized ten years later by the wonderfully named Royal Adventurers of England, who renamed the island in honour of James, Duke of York. Ideally placed to provide strategic defence for English interests along the river and as a staging post for the shipment of slaves, James Island and Fort James were captured by the French then recaptured by the English several times over subsequent decades.

The location of James Island ensured a clear passage downriver for whichever power controlled it at the time. Hence it was subject to frequent attacks. In 1719, a group of Welsh pirates overran Fort James, and carried off all the goods and slaves. It was attacked less successfully in 1768 by a regiment of 500 Niumi men. In 1779, the French seized the island one last time, without firing a shot, and destroyed the fort. In 1816, Grant also entered into an agreement with the King of Niumi, allowing the British Royal Navy to reoccupy the abandoned fort in exchange for an annual payment of 300 iron bars. Later, however, the British claimed that the king reneged on the deal, so they abandoned their plans for James Island and withdrew, concentrating their future efforts on Banjul. The island was abandoned altogether in 1829.

Almost 200 years later, the extensive ruins of Fort James, centrepiece of a UNESCO World Heritage Site, form the most important relict of the slave trade in this part of The Gambia. Despite its ruinous state, the fort is a poignant site. What remains of the thick stone walls are held together by bulbous baobab roots and scampered across by rats and lizards. The base of the dungeon in which up to 140 slaves were once impounded also survives. A few cannons line the shore, while the beaches are littered by beads, once the main form of currency in this part of Africa. The island is not sinking, as is often stated, but it does require regular maintenance to remedy erosion caused by wave action. However, the eroded shores in fact consist of artificial embankments, built of earth and rock and supported by piled stakes that were created to extend a natural area so small it barely allowed room for anything other than the fort.

Most if not all Roots Tours include a boat trip to James Island. It can also be visited independently by boat from Albreda. This will cost around D800 for a party of up to five, and can be arranged through any of the guides who hang around the main square and jetty. All visitors need to pay the entrance fee of D150, which also allows for entrance to the National Museum of Albreda. An hour is more than enough time to see everything the island has to offer.

Dog and Pelican islands These two small islands lie in the River Gambia just off Dog Island Point. Dog Island, supposedly named after the dog-like barking of the baboons that once inhabited it, was colonised by the British in 1661, who renamed it Charles Island and built a fort on it. However, because the island was vulnerable to attack at low tide when it is possible to walk to it from the mainland (though we have not tried this yet), the fort was abandoned in 1666. The rock that constitutes the island was used to construct both the early fortifications in Banjul and also on James Island. Today there is no sign of Charles Fort. It is possible to hire a boat (from Barra for example) to take you to the island. However, it is very rocky and the landing is far from safe, so perhaps your best bet is to travel there overland.

NIUMI NATIONAL PARK

Effectively a southern extension of Senegal's vast Parc National de Delta du Saloum, the 50km² Niumi National Park is one of the finest and most accessible of The Gambia's protected areas, less than an hour's journey from Banjul, but also one of the most underpublicised. Established in 1986, the park incorporates most of the Gambian coastline north of Barra Point. The dominant feature of the park, its northern tip nudging into Senegal, is narrow, isolated Jinack Island, which is separated from the mainland by the Niji Bolong in the north and shallow mangrove beds (crossable on foot in places when the tide is low) in the south. Jinack is also sometimes known as Paradise or Coconut Island, in reference to the 10km arc of unspoilt sandy beaches along a western coastline whose gradual decline makes for unusually calm swimming conditions. Opposite Jinack, the mainland part of Niumi comprises a large chunk of bush and woodland savannah stretching north from the village of Kanuma, as well as the magnificent Masarinko Bolong and the escarpment above it.

Jinack Island protects a fair amount of wildlife, and it can be very rewarding for birdwatchers. The main attraction for most visitors, however, is the beach, which is serviced by a handful of small camps but otherwise feels quite gloriously underdeveloped by comparison with most of its counterparts south of the River Gambia. Here, you needn't fear being disturbed by the music of ghetto blasters, the thunder of traffic, or the inanities of bumsters. A few other things missing here include pollution, discos and supermarkets. In fact the entire island, populated as it is by a scattering of fishermen, farmers and their families, offers a rewarding, tranquil and unaffected glimpse into rural Gambian life, one particularly suited to keen walkers, whose enjoyment will be enhanced by the absence of motor vehicles on Jinack, and the friendly, welcoming vibe exuded by the villagers.

GETTING THERE AND AWAY Most visitors to the two main beach lodges arrange a boat transfer from Banjul or elsewhere on the south coast when they make a booking. This will cost D1,500 per person one-way and takes around an hour. If you prefer to make your own way there from Barra, a bush taxi to the beach on the mainland opposite Jinack Niji will cost around D800 one-way, then you'll be looking around D50 per person for the boat crossing. Most of the village lodges lie within 5 minutes' walk of Jinack Niji while the ocean-side lodges are only 20 minutes' walk away. The road approaches may be impassable during the rains, but are usually fine in the dry season.

ORIENTATION Jinack Island lies mostly within The Gambia, but the northern part also stretches across the border into Senegal. The small population lives almost

13

entirely in the north, in four villages, of which two lie on the Gambian side. These are Jinack Niji and the more northerly and moderately larger Jinack Kajata, which lie only 500m apart on the island's eastern shore, and can be reached from the mainland by canoe across the narrow mangrove-lined Niji Bolong. Although a few basic lodges are scattered between the two villages, the nicest places to stay, budget permitting, are the smarter and more appealing Jinack Lodge and Madiyana Safari Lodge, which lie on the Atlantic beachfront about 1.5km further west.

WHERE TO STAY *Map, page 184*

Budget

Jinack Lodge (5 rooms)
m (UK) +44 (0)7979 751751, (Gambia) 7778935;
e info@jinacklodge.com; w jinacklodge.com.
Set in sprawling acacia-shaded grounds leading down to an idyllic beach, this friendly British–Gambian venture offers accommodation in colourful solar-powered cottages with a dbl/twin bed, net, outdoor seating & en-suite cold shower & toilet. There's no fans or AC, but the rooms have good natural ventilation. The large common area has a well-stocked bar, restaurant serving daily set menus with meals in the £2.50–3.50 range, & a small library of novels. It is a lovely place to chill, with plenty of relaxed walking opportunities in the vicinity, & it can also arrange day trips by boat to most points of interest in & around Banjul. *£20pp, HB & FB available.*

Feel Free Lodge (4 rooms) m (UK)
+44 (0)7966 510276, (The Gambia) 3430994;
e feelfreelodge@outlook.com; w feelfreegambia. com. Set on a secluded beach south of Jinack, this eco-friendly lodge offers colourful en-suite dbls in peaceful surroundings. The staff can also organise trips to nearby Niumi National Park, plus visits to Jinack village & its school. Beachside BBQs & evening dance shows are also offered. *£17 dbl B&B.*

Shoestring

Camera Sambou's Beach Bar
(4 rooms) m 3055458. Situated in Jinack Niji next to the mosque & alongside the bolong, this owner-managed no-frills set-up offers basic accommodation in small tin-roofed tiled rooms with dbl bed, net & shared baths. The owner can rustle up basic meals. It is a friendly enough set-up & the only place on Jinack that stays open all year, but the village location next to the mangroves isn't great for swimming. *£5pp, with seasonal reductions.*

WHAT TO SEE AND DO For most visitors, the main attraction of Niumi is the **beach** on Jinack, but it is also possible to walk for miles on the island, with the sea on one side and the lush greenness of the bush on the other, accompanied only by small birds wading along the tide's edge or the silhouette of an osprey soaring overhead. Thanks to the Niji Bolon, which separates the island from the mainland, it has never been seriously developed, so it retains a fair variety of wildlife. Indeed, leopard tracks might be encountered just about everywhere on the island – even on the beach – though the animals themselves are extremely shy and are rarely seen. There are also some warthogs, and some of the country's largest crocodiles inhabit the Niji Bolong.

A British bird-ringing group has studied the birdlife here for several years, resulting in a species list that is phenomenal. Especially prevalent are large numbers of Palaearctic migrants that overwinter in the rich coastal scrub or feed themselves up before travelling further south. At Buniadu Point, there are several **lagoons** and a large sand spit that is submerged only at high tide. Here you will find hundreds of gulls, terns and waders, with perhaps a few pelicans or even a greater flamingo. Birds of prey are well represented with dozens of overwintering ospreys along the bolongs and the coast, as well as African fish eagle, shikra, Gabar goshawk, African harrier-hawk and even the massive martial eagle. Uncommon birds recorded here include white-fronted plover, bar-breasted firefinch and European scops owl. The paths running through the interior pass through woodland, shrub and submerged paddies alive with the likes of Senegal coucal, bearded barbet, yellow-crowned gonolek, black-crowned tchagra and various rollers, widows and finches.

A highlight of a visit to Jinack has to be the possibility of **encountering dolphins**, especially around December and January. Bottlenose dolphins can sometimes be seen on the boat trip between Barra and Jinack, cavorting and playing in the waves. Sometimes also a large group of Atlantic hump-backed dolphins will swim along only 100m or so from the shore, giving anyone on the beach an excellent view. This last species is a real speciality as they are found only along the coast of West Africa. There appears to be a group of 20 or so dolphins that spend part of their time off Jinack and the rest of it further north in the Delta du Saloum.

13

Part Four

UPRIVER GAMBIA

Upriver Gambia: An Overview

The River Gambia is the fourth-longest waterway in West Africa at 1,100km. It rises in the moist and mountainous Fouta Djalon region of Guinea (a watershed that also forms the source of the rivers Senegal and Niger), then flows through Senegal's vast Niokolo-Koba National Park and over the Barrakunda Falls, before finally crossing into The Gambia some 300km inland of its mouth as the crow flies, or 450km upstream as the crocodile swims. As it continues its sedate journey towards the Atlantic, this perennial ribbon of greenery and rich source of protein forms the very lifeblood of the Gambian interior. It is also the watery spine that dictates the outline of a serpentine country whose parallel northern and southern borders seldom stray more than 25km from the river's banks as they mimic its worming course.

Below the Barrakunda Falls, the river is flat and sluggish, registering a total altitude drop of around 20m after it crosses into The Gambia. It widens as it approaches the Atlantic, and becomes increasingly saline and tidal past Kuntaur, about 180km from the estuary. Surprisingly, perhaps, not a single bridge spans the Gambian stretch of the river, which remains navigable upstream all the way to the Senegalese border, though no formal passenger boats take advantage of this asset. Instead, all traffic inland must follow one of two parallel land routes, the so-called South Bank and North Bank roads, which both follow a similarly twisting path to the flanking river and Senegalese borders. Several vehicle ferry services link the North and South banks, with the most widely used being the ones that connect Banjul to Barra, Soma to Farafenni, and Janjanbureh to Lamin Koto.

In travel terms, 'Upriver Gambia' embraces anywhere and everywhere significantly inland of Brikama – something like 95% of the country's total surface area. Yet such is the imbalance between coastal and inland tourist development that any excursion upriver should be undertaken in a spirit of adventure and flexibility. True, roads through the interior have registered massive improvements in recent years, with those on the South Bank now surfaced all the way to Basse Santa Su, and the North Bank as far as Lamin Koto. But in most other respects, travel conditions are a throwback to backwater West Africa as it was 20 years ago. Accommodation tends to be quite rudimentary and rundown, water and electricity supplies are erratic, internet access is sporadic, the culinary variety is extremely limited, car breakdowns are commonplace, and the best-laid plans are frequently upset by a general aura of unhurried nonchalance.

For all that, upriver travel offers plenty of rewards, particularly to those willing to engage with West Africa on its own laid-back terms. The humdrum small towns and charming traditional villages of the interior stand in organic contrast to the artificiality of the coastal resorts, and the region also has much to offer in terms of wildlife viewing. And while travel conditions might be on the rough side, Upriver Gambia could hardly be friendlier or safer. If the prospect of independent travel seems daunting, it is easy enough to book on to a guided one- or two-night excursion to the likes of Tendaba Camp, Bintang Bolong or the Chimp Rehabilitation Project

(CRP) in River Gambia National Park. More adventurously, you could rent a self-drive vehicle, or make use of the extensive bus and gelly-gelly network, to travel all the way inland to Basse Santa Su. Either way, no visit to The Gambia would seem complete without an excursion into its rustic interior.

HIGHLIGHTS

TUMANI TENDA This simple but well-run ecotourism camp, only an hour's drive inland from the coastal resorts, offers good birdwatching along with an interesting set of cultural activities. See pages 201–3.

BINTANG BOLONG LODGE Probably the most characterful goal for a budget overnight trip upriver is the stilted lodge with saltwater swimming pool set among the mangroves. See page 205.

TENDABA CAMP The largest upriver camp, Tendaba is a birdwatcher's paradise and the best base for canoe trips into the vast Bao Bolong Wetland Reserve, home to several rare and eagerly sought species. See page 208.

KIANG WEST NATIONAL PARK The country's largest terrestrial reserve protects a little-visited tract of savannah and riverine woodland rich in monkeys, antelope and birds – as well as being home to a few elusive leopards. See pages 210–12.

KER BATCH NATIONAL MONUMENT The less impressive but more off-the-beaten-track of the country's two ancient UNESCO-inscribed stone circle sites is famed for its unique lyre-stone and an adventure to reach. See pages 223–4.

WASSU NATIONAL MONUMENT The most accessible and famous archaeological site in The Gambia, UNESCO-inscribed Wassu comprises 200 megaliths arranged into 11 stone circles. See page 225.

RIVER GAMBIA NATIONAL PARK The top mammal-viewing destination in the interior is home to a renowned Chimp Rehabilitation Project (and excellent clifftop camp). Monkeys and birds are also prolific on boat trips to the islands. See pages 225–30.

JANJANBUREH This small but historic town, set on a forested island in the middle of the River Gambia, is a popular chill-out venue thanks to its many small camps and eateries. See pages 230–9.

KUNKILLING FOREST PARK Monkeys and forest birds are the main attractions of this small community-managed park upriver of Janjanbureh. See page 239.

BASSE SANTA SU The most remote and least Westernised of Gambian towns has an attractive riverside setting and compellingly traditional feel. See pages 241–7.

GETTING AROUND

The River Gambia divides the interior into two halves, which are generally referred to as the North Bank and South Bank, and are connected by several ferry services but no bridges. Both banks are serviced by one main road running inland from the coast in a broadly easterly direction almost as far as the eastern border with Senegal.

The South Bank Road is surfaced all the way from Serekunda and Brikama through Soma to Basse Santa Su (with surfaced feeder roads running north to Tendaba and Janjanbureh), then it continues as a good dirt road as far as Fatoto. The North Bank Road, which starts at Barra, opposite Banjul, then passes through Farafenni, is surfaced as far inland as Lamin Koto (on the riverbank opposite Janjanbureh), but unsurfaced and in poor condition further east. The main north–south road, the so-called Trans-Gambia Highway, is an important through route between northern and southern Senegal, passing through the towns of Farafenni and Soma.

The best road transport is the GTSC bus service that covers the main roads through the North and South Bank, leaving mainly in the morning. The South Bank service runs eight-times daily between Serekunda and Basse Santa Su via Brikama, Soma and Janjanbureh, while the North Bank service runs thrice daily between Barra and Farafenni, with one bus daily continuing on to Lamin Koto (Janjanbureh). In addition, almost all routes are plied by regular private passenger vehicles known as bush taxis or gelly-gellys. These are slightly more expensive than the GTSC buses, and much less comfortable, but they operate far longer hours.

Although several vehicle ferry services connect the North and South banks, they are mostly slow and unreliable, so it is advisable to structure your itinerary in a way that minimises crossings. The busiest service is the Banjul–Barra Ferry across the river mouth, but this has become very unreliable, with waits of several hours being commonplace. The Yelitenda–Bambatenda Ferry, which connects Soma and Farafenni on the Trans-Gambia Highway, is a bit more reliable, but long waits are also often a problem. Further upriver, the short and little-used ferry service between Janjanbureh and Lamin Koto is a far better option both for foot passengers and for self-drivers. There are also ferries further upriver at Basse Santa Su and Fatoto, but these are not recommended unless you have a 4x4 to navigate the poor North Bank Road.

Considering that the River Gambia is navigable all the way to the eastern border with Senegal, it is surprising that the few tours to the interior are mostly road-based. However, one operator that does specialise in water-based expeditions as far upriver as Janjanbureh is **Gambia River Cruises** (w *gambiarivercruise.com*) – see pages 46–7.

OTHER PRACTICALITIES

Upriver travel conditions can come as a shock. Whereas facilities at the coast tend to approximate Western standards (albeit with a touch of Africa at the edges), travel inland is emphatically a back-to-basics experience. There is, for instance, only one ATM in the entire region (at the EcoBank in Farafenni), and foreign-exchange facilities are otherwise limited to a few private forex bureaux in Soma and Basse Santa Su. Internet access is almost as patchy, even using mobile-phone networks, and where cyber cafés do exist, they operate only when there's electricity, which is far from being a given.

In fact, much of the responsibility for the interior's undeveloped feel is attributable to the sparse electricity supply. No upcountry town has a permanent grid supply, and though most are theoretically online from around 18.00 to 02.00, this certainly cannot be relied upon. Since most upriver lodges cannot afford to run generators, or to have solar panels installed, few rooms have functional fans or air conditioning, and are instead dependent on natural ventilation, which can make for long, hot, sticky nights. The lack of electricity also has an impact on things such as the availability of chilled drinks, the quality of lighting in rooms and restaurants, and the standard and variety of food (which cannot be frozen or refrigerated). For some, this simplicity is part of the charm of upriver travel, enhancing the rusticity of the riverside camps and their sense of removal from the coastal resorts. But fair to say it will not appeal to everybody!

Inland to Soma and Farafenni

The most significant north–south road through The Gambia is the 25km strip of well-maintained asphalt that connects the Senegalese border posts at Kerr Ayib and Sénoba. Often referred to as the Trans-Gambia Highway, this interlude along the RN4 between the Senegalese towns of Kaolack and Ziguinchor is probably the busiest road in the Gambian interior (which isn't saying a great deal). And despite its modest length, it is punctuated by two significant towns in the form of Farafenni and Soma, as well as by the vehicle ferry that crosses the River Gambia between Yelitenda and Bambatenda. This chapter covers both the Trans-Gambia Highway and the region to its west, running inland from Brikama and Albreda, and incorporating the larger part of the North Bank, Western and Lower River administrative divisions.

As the closest part of the interior to the coastal resorts, the area featured in this chapter is ideal for those seeking a short escape upriver. The most popular goal for tourists is probably Tendaba Camp, a sprawling riverside lodge bordering two most important conservation areas, namely Kiang West National Park and Baobolong Wetland Reserve. There are also less well-known riverside camps at Tumani Tenda, Berefet and Bintang Bolong, while the small town of Kanilai, birthplace of President Jammeh, hosts the region's only truly tourist-class hotel, as well as a glorified zoo called the Kanilai Game Park. The North Bank town of Farafenni and its South Bank counterpart are respectively the largest and third-largest Gambian towns inland of Brikama, and have decent facilities, but are of limited interest other than as places to break a journey.

THE ROAD EAST TO KALAGI

Kalagi lies 100km east of Brikama along the South Bank Road, immediately before it crosses the Bintang Bolong, a wide tributary of the River Gambia that also marks the border between the Western and Lower River divisions. The freshly surfaced road connecting Brikama to Kalagi runs through a mosaic of tropical wooded habitats, and provides a springboard to several diversions, most of which (the camps at Tumani Tenda, Berefet and Bintang Bolong) are associated with the River Gambia to the north. The road between Brikama and Kalagi also offers access to the presidential village of Kanilai on the southern border with Senegal.

TUMANI TENDA ECOTOURISM PROJECT The Jola village of Tumani Tenda lies on the east bank of the wide mangrove-lined Kafuta Bolong, which merges with the River Gambia about 6km downstream. It is a relatively modern village, having been founded in the 1960s by immigrants from the Casamance, and derives its name from that of a peanut picker called Tumani who once lived there (Tenda means

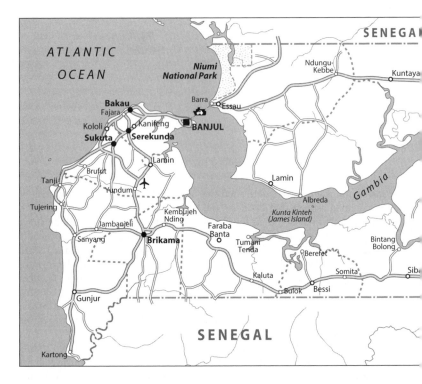

river bank). A strongly Islamic and sustainability-oriented community of 300 individuals split between seven families, it owns around 140ha of land planted with a rich diversity of crops and indigenous plants. In 1999, the village became the site of The Gambia's first ecotourism project, following the construction of a creek-side camp that continues to fund a variety of community projects.

Tumani Tenda is well known to birdwatchers as the best site in The Gambia for observing the brown-necked parrot, a large, handsome and noisy bird that roosts in the mangroves and usually flies across the Kafuta Bolong at around 08.00 and 17.00 *en route* to and from its feeding grounds. Other birds frequently seen in the area include long-crested eagle, stone partridge, long-tailed nightjar, six species of kingfisher, grey-headed bush-shrike and a selection of waders, herons and other waterbirds. Plenty of interesting activities are offered, mostly for less than D60 per person. These include bird walks, boat trips to a bird-rich island on the Kafuta Bolong, tie-dye batik workshops, soap- and salt-making, fishing, oyster collection, farming tours, community forest tours and much more besides (check the website w www.tumanitenda.co.uk for more details). Jola dance and singing performances cost D500. Visitors are asked to dress modestly in keeping with the local Islamic sensibility.

Getting there and away Tumani Tenda lies 2.5km northeast of the South Bank Road along a dirt road signposted to the left about 25km east of Brikama and 2km before the village of Kafuta. Most operators based in and around the coastal resorts can arrange a transfer there. Alternatively, any bush taxi heading to Kafuta or further east can drop you at the junction, from where it is less than 30 minutes' walk to the camp.

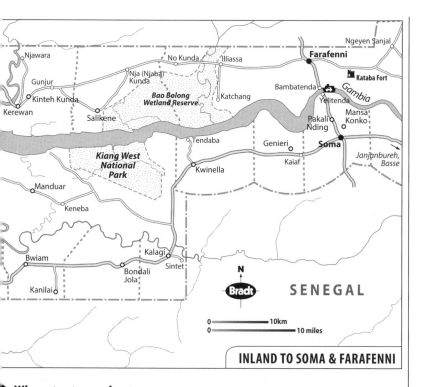

INLAND TO SOMA & FARAFENNI

Where to stay and eat

🏠 **Tumani Tenda Camp** (13 rooms) ⊕ N13 12.982 W16 28.143; **m** 7915080/9903662; **e** tumanitenda@hotmail.com; **w** www. tumanitenda.co.uk. Formerly known as Kachokorr Camp, this well-organised rustic creek-side camp is the focal point of the ecotourism project & all activities can be arranged here, both for day or overnight visitors. Accommodation is in blocks of 2 or 3 simple & rather musty rooms with mud walls, corrugated-iron roofs, twin beds with netting, solar-powered lighting & shared bathrooms & showers. An attractive open-sided restaurant/ bar next to the creek serves decent local meals for around £3.50/plate, as well as a limited selection of drinks. Alongside all the typical excursions including birding & boat trips, you can make soap & go oyster collecting. Every family in the community has at least one member working at the camp, ensuring that they have at least one monthly salary coming in. Good value. *£7pp B&B.*

BEREFET Also known as Brefet, this mixed Mandinka and Jola village of fewer than 400 people stands on the south bank of the Brefet Bolong, a wide creek separated from the River Gambia by the sprawling Sansankoto Island. Berefet lies almost exactly due south of and less than 10km from Kunta Kinteh Island and the North Bank village of Albreda (page 190), and it boasts a similar historical pedigree to them both. The first European trading post was established here in 1664 by a group of British traders known as the 'Gambia Adventurers'. Attached and plundered by rival French traders from Albreda in 1724, Berefet remained dormant for decades prior to 1779, when the Royal Africa Company built a new trading post that would be operated by a succession of individuals prior to being destroyed by the French again in 1820.

Before 1820, the only Africans known to visit the area freely were palm-oil tappers from Casamance. Soon after that, however, a Jola village was established alongside the stone ruins, which provided a useful source of building material.

The Jola were later joined by Mandinka settlers. The village has moved twice since its establishment, as the water from the wells became too salty, and all that remains of the old trading post is a pile of rubble that appears to be the corner of a slave house. But it has a beautiful setting right on the banks of the Brefet Bolong, and is relatively easy to get to. Wildlife in the vicinity includes green monkey, patas monkey, bushbuck, warthog and the usual wealth of birds, including a population of brown-necked parrots that fly across the bolong in the mornings and evenings, giving another good reason to visit. The rumoured presence of the rare Campbell's mona monkey has yet to be reliably confirmed.

Getting there and away Berefet (✦ *N13 14.614 W16 22.817*) lies 6km north of the main South Bank Road along a dirt road signposted to the left at Bessi, almost 40km east of Brikama. The old trading post and Berefet Cultural Camp both lie on the banks of the Brefet Bolong about 1km west of the village itself, while Sankiliba Lodge stands close to the feeder road about halfway between Bessi and Berefet. Several bush taxis run daily from Brikama to Bessi, and any other transport heading between Serekunda and points further east can drop you there. From Bessi, you'll most likely have to walk or hire either a horse- or donkey-cart to get to Berefet.

Where to stay and eat

Sankiliba Lodge (5 rooms)
m 3062207/7251458; e badjiel19@gmail. com; w sankilibalodge.jimdo.com. This owner-managed eco-lodge is set in gardens on the banks of a creek between Bessi & Berefet. Clean whitewashed en-suite rooms have tiled floors, twin or double beds, & cane seating. An open-sided central dining area serves Western & traditional dishes, along with chilled beers & other drinks. Activities include bird walks in the nearby forest & boat trips to Kunta Kinteh Island. Transfers from the airport or coast cost £10pp one-way. *£10/15 sgl/dbl B&B.*

Berefet Cultural Lodge (12 rooms)
Situated in large leafy grounds surrounded by baobabs alongside the creek about 1km west of Berefet, this community-owned lodge offers accommodation in brightly painted round huts connected by 'crazy paving' paths. The rooms are quite poorly ventilated, & could get stuffy at hot times of the year, but the beds do have nets & there is solar lighting. A riverside restaurant serves drinks & meals, & activities include boat trips to Kunta Kinteh Island, Albreda & Juffureh. *£10pp.*

BINTANG BOLONG The largest of the many tributaries that feed the River Gambia, Bintang Bolong rises in southern Senegal and enters The Gambia immediately east of Kalagi (page 207) before meandering westwards for another 50km to its confluence with the main river at Bintang Point. The mangrove-lined creek shares its name with the village of Bintang, which lies on its west bank about 10km upstream of the confluence, and supports a population of around 700. Bintang is best known today as the home of the stilted Bintang Bolong Lodge, one of the longest-serving and most popular upriver camps in The Gambia, situated only 60km from Brikama by road, yet a world away from the coastal resorts in spirit.

Modest though Bintang might be today, its importance as a mercantile port in the earliest days of Luso-African trade is well documented (sometimes under the name Vintang). In 1665, the British explorer Richard Jobson noted that the Royal Africa Company maintained a trade agent there 'chiefly for elephant tusks, wax, honey, etc', and in the early 1680s, the Portuguese explorer Francisco de Lemos Coelho described Bintang as 'the best village on the river, having much trade in hides, as well as wax, ivory and slaves', while the French priest Michel La Courbe noted that it was 'rather a large town ... located on the slope of a hill, with many trees and several Portuguese style houses ... built of earth and covered with palm fronds as large as table cloths'. So far as we are aware, no traces of this long period of European settlement and trade remain, though the hillside location mentioned by La Courbe indicates the site is unchanged.

Getting there and away Bintang (✛ *N13 14.947 W16 12.672*) is connected to the main South Bank Road by a recently surfaced 6km feeder road running north from the tiny village of Killy (which lies about 2km west of the much larger village of Sibanor). Coming from the coast, it's a straightforward 80–90km drive that shouldn't take more than 90 minutes, and organised day and overnight excursions can be arranged through any tour operator. Using public transport, two gelly-gellys run daily from Brikama directly to Bintang, leaving at 10.00 and 15.00. Alternatively, you can pick up one of the more regular vehicles to Sibanor, ask to be dropped at Killy, then take one of the small vehicles that shuttle regularly on to Bintang. Sometimes the lodge's own transport can pick you up if you book in advance.

Where to stay and eat

🏠 **AbCa's Creek Lodge** (18 rooms) ✛ N13 14.709 W16 13.450; m 7994413/4; e abcagambia@hotmail.com; w abcascreeklodge. com. With a feeling of Tarzan's jungle hideaway, this new Dutch–Gambian run lodge has a stunning creekside location just 5 mins' south of Bintang. Funkily decorated rooms are carved from the bush, with solar power & shared bathroom. The owners can rustle up meals for £5–6 using fish caught from the creek & vegetables grown in the garden, & there's a fantastic range of activities on offer, including kayak & boat trips through the mangroves, bike & walking tours, cooking lessons, dance & drum workshops & visits in to the local village & historical sites. Sitting here as the sun rises & the dawn mist evaporates, while monkeys leap from the trees, is just magical. *£29/19.50pp sgl/dbl B&B.*

🏠 **Bintang Bolong Lodge** (6 rooms) ✛ N13 14.570 W16 12.383; m 9929362; e reception@ bintang-bolong.com; w bintang-bolong.com. One of the longest-serving upriver lodges, & slightly deteriorated since its heyday a few years ago, this still has a beautiful mangrove setting & winning rusticity that compensate for the rather basic amenities. Most of the complex is stilted, with raised wooden walkways connecting the main dining area & the rooms, which all come with 1 dbl & 1 sgl bed, a small en-suite shower & private deck overlooking the water. In the early evening, power is drawn from a large generator that also lights up parts of the nearby village. The large & comfortable restaurant/bar serves Gambian & European meals in the £3.50–4.50 range, along with chilled wine, beer & soft drinks. On the nearby riverbank is a small saltwater swimming pool with a hill (a rare thing in The Gambia) that gives a great view over the lodge, the mangroves & the bolong. The lodge arranges boat trips into the surrounding mangroves, further afield to Kunta Kinteh Island, as well as various foot & jeep excursions (check the website for full details). If there are enough guests, dancers & musicians from the village will provide entertainment in the evenings. *£11pp B&B.*

BWIAM Located between the South Bank Road and Bintang Bolong 15km east of Sibanor, Bwiam (✛ *N13 13.449 W16 4.866*) is one of the larger towns in the interior, with a population of around 4,000 and a bustling market that makes few concessions to tourism and is all the more interesting for that. The town has one spurious claim to fame in the form of the so-called *karelo* (cooking pot) that protrudes about 50cm above the ground among a stand of white-flowered silk-cotton trees, just outside of town. There are lots of local tall tales regarding the karelo. One states that this pot is impossible to move. Another more colourful legend claims it has magical powers that make it swivel to point in the direction of an attack – a story probably explained by the fact that the karelo is the base for an artillery piece, although no-one seems to know why or when it was placed there.

Getting there and away Non-express GTSC buses between Serekunda and Soma all stop at Bwiam, but it is probably more efficient to get a bush taxi or gelly-gelly from Brikama. This will cost less than D120.

⌂ Where to stay and eat

⌂ **Bwiam Lodge** (20 rooms)
m 6023254/7799019; **e** bwiamlodge@gmail.com; **w** bwiamlodge.weebly.com. This well-run community-owned lodge, which lies only 200m from the main road, is affiliated to the Ding Ding Bantaba organisation, which helps fight child poverty as well as providing training & employment to local adults. Accommodation is in clean & quiet en-suite rooms with fans, nets & cane chairs, all hung with brightly coloured local fabrics. It caters mainly to the conference & NGO market, but is also one of the more comfortable upriver options, & the staff can arrange birding, fishing, canoeing & cultural excursions, as well as visits to a local batik co-operative. A bar & restaurant is attached, & a generator usually provides power throughout the night. *Around £8.50 dbl.*

KANILAI Abutting the Senegalese border about 15km southeast of Bwiam, Kanilai (✪ *N13 10.318 W16 0.301*) was a rather obscure and unremarkable Jola village prior to the rise to power of its most famous son, former president Yahya Jammeh. Since then, however, it has grown to be one of the most well-known towns in the Gambian interior, thanks largely to the governmental funding behind the construction or installation of street lights, asphalt roads, a relatively reliable electricity supply, a presidential palace, a tourist hotel, a wrestling arena and a game park. The town is also home to Kanilai Farms, an important producer of rice, wheat and other crops owned by the president, and the site of the two-week Kanilai International Cultural Festival, which is usually held over the cusp of May and June every few years. Several events associated with the International Roots Festival (**w** *rootsgambia.gm*), another biennial affair, usually held in early to mid-May of every even year, are staged in Kanilai. Outside of festival times, Kanilai holds little of interest to tourists other than the small game park, though it does boast one of the best hotels anywhere in the interior, and could make for a useful base for exploring most sites between Brikama and Soma, provided that you have your own vehicle.

Getting there and away Kanilai lies about 85km east of Brikama and less than 2 hours' drive from the coastal resorts. Coming from the west, it is connected to the South Bank Road by a surfaced 9km feeder road signposted about 5km east of Bwiam. Using public transport, if you cannot pick up a direct bush taxi in Brikama, take one to Bwiam and change vehicles there.

⌂ Where to stay and eat

⌂ **Sindola Lodge** (40 rooms) ✪ N13 10.354 W16 00.361; **m** 3579085; **e** sindola.rec@gmail.com. The only property in the Gambian interior that might just about scrape a couple of stars in a conventional hotel rating system, Sindola Lodge is set in large, green well-shaded grounds at the northeastern end of Kanilai immediately before the presidential palace. Accommodation is in comfortable modern semi-detached huts with thatched roof, tiled floor, screened windows, queen-size bed, satellite TV, fan, AC & en-suite shower. Facilities include a large & reasonably clean swimming pool, a restaurant with indoor & outdoor seating serving meals in the £4–6 range, a children's playground, & tennis, volleyball & basketball courts. It would be nothing special in any other context, but this sort of comfort is rare indeed this far upriver, even if there isn't a lot to do other than chill out next to the pool. Good value. *£30/40 standard sgl/dbl, £42.50/51 sgl/dbl suite, all rates B&B.*

What to see and do The wrestling arena in Kanilai holds traditional wrestling competitions every few months, and the hotel can arrange performances by local Jola cultural groups. The town also lies within an hour's drive of Bintang Bolong, Kiang West and Tendaba.

KANILAI GAME PARK (⊕ *07.00–20.00 daily; entrance (inc guide) D250pp*) The only permanent attraction in Kanilai is this rather lamentable artificial 10km² reserve, which protects an area of former Guinea savannah once used for farming and for foraging livestock. When it opened a few years back, caged residents included lion, rhino and giraffe translocated from South Africa but these have either all died or escaped in the interim. Other wildlife includes caged hyena and crocodiles, and several semi-free-ranging species not indigenous to The Gambia, for instance zebra, wildebeest, eland and ostrich. There are also naturally occurring troops of patas and green monkey, scrub hare, honey badger and squirrels, together with a good mix of birds including helmeted guineafowl. Visits must be arranged through the reception at Sindola Lodge, and you will need your own vehicle to drive around.

KALAGI This town of around 1,000 inhabitants flanks the South Bank Road some 30km east of Bwiam on the west side of the Bintang Bolong (⊕ *N13 14.509 W15 50.109*), which also forms the boundary between Western and Lower River divisions. The town itself is nothing special, but the adjacent stretch of creek is of interest for the extensive replanted mangroves on the opposite bank, the product of a community project established in 2011, and it also supports a fair selection of wading birds. Boat trips along the bolong can be organised by the Kalagi Riverside Camp, which overlooks the bolong and would be a good place for those using public transport to break up the trip from the coast to points further east.

Getting there and away Although GTSC buses between Serekunda and Soma stop at Kalagi, it is probably more convenient to use a gelly-gelly or bush taxi from Brikama. Either way, the fare is around D120.

Where to stay and eat

🏠 **Kalagi Riverside Camp** (8 rooms) ⊕ N13 15.116 W15 49.931; m 6985565/7843175. This low-key camp has a scenic location on the south side of the main road immediately before the bridge across Bintang Bolong. The small en-suite rooms, set in 1 long block facing the creek, are nothing special, but they do come with lights, standing fan & (according to the management) 24hr electricity & running water. An open-sided restaurant serves fresh fish dishes or chicken yassa for around £3.50/plate, & the management can arrange boat trips on the bolong, 4x4 safaris into Kiang West, & night-time dances. Sadly, on our last visit it was looking quite rundown. *£6.50 dbl.*

TENDABA, KIANG WEST AND BAO BOLONG

Although any one of them can be visited independently of the others, Tendaba Camp, Kiang West and Bao Bolong are conveniently clustered together alongside the River Gambia about 100km upriver of its mouth, and are best treated as a single multi-faceted attraction. The main focal point for tourists, set in the riverside village of Tendaba some 25km north of Kalagi, is Tendaba Camp, which was established in the 1970s by a roving Swedish sea captain, but has long been under local management. Tendaba is probably the most famous and frequented camp in the Gambian interior, and particularly popular with birdwatchers, thanks to the diversity of habitats and species concentrated in the vicinity. That said, it is looking rather rundown these days, and one senses it is trading on its reputation and location as much as anything else, although recent beach developments initiated to prevent erosion to the village have improved things a little.

Although the agricultural land around Tendaba offers some excellent birding opportunities, the most popular activity here is boat trips into the mangrove-lined channels of the vast Bao Bolong Wetland Reserve, a birdwatching magnet that lies on the facing North Bank, but is far more accessible by water than from the landward side. Less commonly visited but equally alluring is Kiang West National Park, which flanks Tendaba immediately to the east. Kiang West is the largest terrestrial protected area in The Gambia, and the last confirmed sanctuary to the likes of leopard and roan antelope, as well as being an important refuge for several species of raptor and other large savannah birds. For planning purposes, one night at Tendaba Camp is just about sufficient to fit in a boat trip into Bao Bolong and some local exploration by foot, but a minimum of two nights is advised if you also want to take a game drive into Kiang West.

GETTING THERE AND AWAY Tendaba Camp is in the village of the same name, around 6km north of the junction town of Kwinella, which lies on the South Bank Road about 120km east of Brikama. The road from the coast to Tendaba is now surfaced in its entirety, so it shouldn't take much more than 2 hours to cover in a private vehicle. The camp is a popular goal for organised overnight excursions from the coast. It is also easily reached by private taxi, and every driver knows where it is. Alternatively, you can catch a GTSC bus from Serekunda or a bush taxi from Brikama and ask to be dropped off at Kwinella, though you may need to walk or hitch the last 6km from there.

Many people visit Kiang West National Park on an organised excursion out of Tendaba Camp, but it is also possible to drive there yourself (pages 210–11).

WHERE TO STAY AND EAT In addition to Tendaba Camp, it is normally permitted to camp at the headquarters of Kiang West, 2km west of Dumbutu, for a small fee. It is also worth stressing that Sindola Lodge in Kanilai, though it lacks the riverside location of Tendaba Camp, offers far superior accommodation, and would be a perfectly feasible base from which to explore this trio of attractions, being less than 60km away on a good surfaced road. Other possible overnight options listed earlier in the chapter would be Kalagi Riverside Camp (only 25km from Tendaba) and Bwiam Lodge (52km away).

Tendaba Camp (83 rooms)
m 9911088; e tendabacampmail@yahoo.com; w tendabacampthegambia.com. This sprawling & well-established camp lies in the heart of the small village of Tendaba, right on the South Bank of the River Gambia. It offers a wide variety of accommodation, ranging from simple en-suite rooms with shower, net & fan to riverside suites with AC, TV & fridge, but it is all looking quite rundown & in need of a good scrub, partly because of the high fuel costs associated with running a generator in an area that has no mains electricity. Other facilities include a swimming pool, a restaurant serving decent buffet lunches & dinners

for D300 & a great little bar perched bar alongside a jetty jutting out into the river, which was closed at the time of updating but due to open during the lifetime of this book. The camp is in the process of building erosion defences with a concrete beach & sunbeds. Activities include guided or unguided bird walks in the surrounding area, boat trips into the Bao Bolong Wetland Reserve (parties of up to 4 pay D1,200, any additional person is D300 extra), & guided jeep safaris into Kiang West (D2,800 for up to 8 people then D350 per additional person, exclusive of park entrance fees). *From £20 en-suite dbl to £45 suite, all rates B&B.*

EXCURSIONS AND ACTIVITIES

Birdwatching around Tendaba There are some excellent birdwatching areas within easy walking distance of Tendaba Camp. Wooded areas immediately around the village support the likes of bearded barbet, Bruce's green pigeon and pygmy sunbird, while the mangrove-lined riverfront is home to various kingfishers and water-associated birds. A particularly worthwhile site is the airfield, which lies about 1km back along, and on the east side of, the feeder road from Kwinella. Terrestrial and woodland species to look out for here include Abyssinian ground hornbill, bateleur, African hawk eagle, four-banded sandgrouse, white-throated bee-eater and the highly endangered brown-necked parrot. The airfield is bordered by a large shallow lake that often supports pink-backed and great white pelican, and a variety of plovers, waders and storks (including the striking but seldom-seen saddle-billed stork). You can explore on your own, but there are usually also a few Gambian birding guides based loosely at the camp who will gladly take you around the area for a small fee.

Bao Bolong Wetland Reserve The normal goal for boat trips out of Tendaba is the Bao Bolong Wetland Reserve, which lies on the opposite side of the river some 2km from the camp. Bao Bolong is the largest of The Gambia's six protected areas, covering 220km², and it was designated as a Ramsar Wetland of International Importance in 1996. It is named after the 140km-long Bao Bolong, which rises near Ferlo in Senegal and empties into the River Gambia about 5km upstream of Tendaba. A number of smaller bolongs flow through the reserve into the main river, and they support some of the country's tallest mangrove forests, because the lower salinity this far upriver exerts a lower osmotic pressure on the trees. The reserve is a very important natural resource for surrounding communities. The mangroves act as a nursery for huge numbers of spawning fish, which form an important source of protein in the local diet. Some of the reserve is also used to grow rice, and thatching materials, building and fencing materials are harvested from within its boundaries.

Boat trips The twice-daily boat excursions into Bao Bolong offered by Tendaba Camp are highly recommended to anybody who fancies a quiet, peaceful trip into the mangroves. The boats follow the labyrinthine Kisi and Tunku bolongs, which are lined with tall mangroves, home to hermit crabs and mudskipper fish, and offer a good opportunity to see interesting mangrove, wetland and other bird species. It is probably the best place in the country to look for African finfoot, a medium-sized waterbird that likes to skulk among the mangrove roots. Also likely to be seen are white-backed night heron, goliath heron (the world's largest heron), hamerkop, martial eagle, blue-breasted kingfisher and mouse-coloured sunbird. Somewhat less frequent are rarities such as white-crested tiger heron, Allen's gallinule, Pel's fishing owl, African swallow-tailed kite, brown-necked parrot, little green woodpecker and African blue flycatcher. Dolphins might stray this far upstream in the dry season, when the water is most saline, while hippos occasionally make an appearance during the rains. Coming by boat, you are unlikely to see any of the other large mammals associated with the reserve, a list that includes spotted hyena, side-striped jackal, red river hog, West African manatee, sitatunga, and African clawless otter.

From the North Bank While the vast majority of visitors to Bao Bolong come by boat from Tendaba Camp, the reserve can also be approached from the North Bank Road. The laterite road leading south from Kontikunda Niji is probably the best option if you have a vehicle or have hired a cart, as this follows the base of the escarpment to the west of Bao Bolong, and is good for wildlife. In addition, dirt tracks lead south into the reserve from the villages of Salikene, Njaba Kunda and Katchang. These tracks are often impassable to vehicles, so you may have to walk or hire a horse- or donkey-cart from one of the villages.

Kiang West National Park (m 6232581; w thegambiawildlife.com; ⊕ 08.00–18.00 daily; entrance D35pp; guide fee D90 per party per hour) Situated 5km downstream of Tendaba, Kiang West National Park is the largest terrestrial reserve in The Gambia, extending across 110km² of dry woodland savannah interspersed with relict forest patches, baobab stands and raffia palm swamp. Established in 1987, it protects an area that has suffered little from human activity, and is probably the country's best remaining example of wilderness, as well as being an important refuge for wildlife. The park incorporates about 12km of river frontage, and associated habitats such as mangrove-lined creeks, salt pans and tidal flats. Its other outstanding geographic feature is a tall laterite escarpment that indicates the past course of the river, and affords some marvellous riverine views and wildlife watching. The best time to visit is towards the end of the dry season, when the vegetation is sparser and you have a far better chance of seeing mammals. However, a visit at any time of the year is sure to produce something of interest.

Fauna Kiang West supports a rich and varied fauna, but seeing most large mammals requires a bit of luck and effort. Most conspicuous are the park's primates, which include Guinea baboon, green monkey, patas monkey and red colobus, along with the nocturnal Senegal bushbaby. Other quite common species include scrub hare, crested porcupine, warthog, roan antelope, bushbuck and duiker. Kiang West hosts the country's most varied selection of terrestrial carnivores, including banded and marsh mongoose, serval, side-striped jackal, caracal, spotted hyena and leopard, but with the exception of mongooses, these creatures are all very shy and good at remaining hidden from watching eyes. The River Gambia is home to West African manatee, African clawless otter and bottlenose dolphin, none of which is seen regularly by visitors. Swampy areas also reputedly provide refuge to the sitatunga, an elusive aquatic antelope about the size of a bushbuck. The river here is usually too saline to support hippo, but the West African crocodile is fairly common.

Kiang West is a superb birding site, with more than 300 species – around half the Gambian total – recorded to date. This includes at least 20 large raptors, notably osprey, African fish eagle, martial eagle, long-crested eagle and the colourful bateleur (the last-named has been adopted as the park's official symbol). You also have a good chance of coming across the Abyssinian ground hornbill, a massive and rather prehistoric-looking bird usually seen stalking about in open country in pairs or small parties. Other Gambian birds that have their stronghold in Kiang West include white-rumped swift, red-winged pytilia, brown-rumped bunting and brown-necked parrot. For more dedicated birders, it is worth searching among the 'little brown jobs' for the plaintive cisticola, which is very local in the more open parts of woodland. Other localised passerines associated with Kiang West include sun lark and chestnut-crowned sparrow-weaver.

Getting there and away The easiest way to visit Kiang West is with one of the affordable jeep safaris offered by Tendaba Camp. If you have your own 4x4, the park can also be visited independently, using one of two approaches. The better of these from most points of view is the same route used by jeep safaris from Tendaba Camp, which starts on the surfaced feeder road from Kwinella on the South Bank

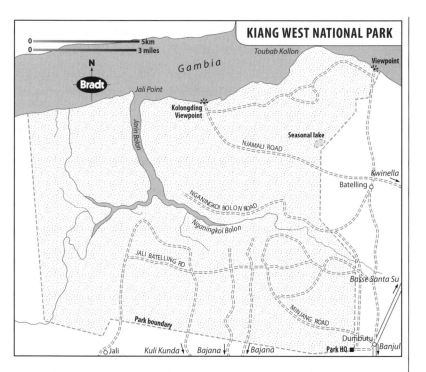

Road. About 2km north of Kwinella or 4km south of Tendaba, turn on to a dirt road running to the west and follow it to the village of Batelling. The village is the most reliable place to pay your entrance fees and arrange a guide (it is also of minor interest for a quartet of rusting cannons set in a copse opposite the mosque, the only relict of European fortifications built in the 18th century). From Batelling it is another 3km north to the entrance gate, which is marked by a disused concrete block on the right.

The other approach is from the village of Dumbutu, which lies on the South Bank Road about 6km before Kwinella coming from the coast. From Dumbutu, an unsurfaced 1.5km road runs west to the park headquarters and what is nominally the main entrance gate. The gate here is frequently untended, however, so you may end up waiting a while to locate somebody to collect your entrance fee and arrange your guide. In addition, it is a long way from the headquarters to the river, and the internal roads are often in poor condition.

Game drives The main game-drive circuit lies to the north of Batelling and can be covered in around 2 hours as a round trip from Tendaba Camp, though birdwatchers in particular will surely want to dedicate at least half a day to it. Wildlife tends to be most active and conspicuous in the first 2 hours after sunrise and last hour before sunset. Ordinarily, we would recommend trying to be there as early as possible in the morning, but given that the park gates only open at 08.00 and you are bound to lose time sorting out paperwork at Batelling or the park headquarters, late afternoon is probably the better option.

Three specific sites of interest lie close to the entrance gate 3km north of Batelling. The first is a palm-fringed seasonal lake overlooked by a low laterite cliff and accessed via a 500m track that branches northeast immediately past the entrance gate. When the lake holds water, it supports plenty of birds and often attracts baboon and warthog. It is also sometimes visited by the handsome roan antelope towards the end of the rainy season.

Better known is Toubab Kollon ('White Man's Well'), which lies on a flat but pretty stretch of mangrove-lined riverbank 2km north of the entrance gate. The site of a long-gone Portuguese trade outpost, Toubab Kollon is also thought to be the most easterly landfall made by the Italian navigator Luiz de Cadamosto when he led the first recorded expedition up the River Gambia on behalf of the Portuguese throne in 1455. At that time, the area was the residence of a Mandinka king called Battimansa, with whom Cadamosto entered into some petty trade. Toubab Kollon now hosts a crumbling picnic site with a view over dense woodland alive with birds but not all that great for mammal-spotting.

Finally, about 3km further west, there is the Kolongding Viewpoint, which can be reached along a signposted sandy track branching west from the road between the entrance gate and Toubab Kollon. Kolongding is set atop a 20m-high, west-facing laterite cliff overlooking a series of shallow pools along the bank of the River Gambia. Wait here quietly either early in the morning or in the hour or so before it gets dark, and you're almost certain to see some wildlife action below.

SOMA AND SURROUNDS

Soma is a busy crossroads town situated where the Trans-Gambia Highway intersects the main South Bank Road around 150km east of Brikama. Despite being the third-largest town in the Gambian interior, supporting a population of around 12,000, it is a rather dusty and amorphous place, possessing all the charm of an overgrown truck stop, and little that might be of interest to travellers except perhaps the large market. Facilities include a couple of small lodges, and it is a good place to buy food, drink and fuel, and to get those punctured tyres repaired. It is also the major public transport hub along the South Bank Road between Brikama and Basse. A few old colonial buildings still stand at Mansa Konko (Mandinka for 'King's Hill'), the former administrative capital about 1.5km north of the modern town centre, while the Soma Wetland, immediately west of town, is the closest place to the coast where the eagerly sought Egyptian plover is regular.

GETTING THERE AND AWAY Coming from the coast or from Basse, the best way to get to Soma is by GTSC bus. Eight such buses run daily in both directions between Kanifing (Serekunda) and Basse, leaving between 06.00 and noon, and stopping at the GTSC station in Soma, which lies a few hundred metres along the Basse Road just before the police station. All these buses also stop at Brikama, Janjanbureh and Bansang. In addition, one GTSC bus runs daily in either direction between Soma and Basse via Janjanbureh, leaving Soma at 07.00 and starting the return trip at around 14.30. There is also one direct GTSC bus between Soma and Kanifing daily, leaving at the same times.

If the GTSC bus timetables don't suit, plenty of bush taxis and gelly-gellys connect Soma to Serekunda, Brikama, Janjanbureh, Basse and most other towns and villages along the South Bank Road, with fares all under D120. They are less comfortable than the GTSC buses, but operate to more flexible hours. On the Trans-Gambia Highway, inexpensive bush taxis (costing less than D60) run north to Pakali Nding and to the Yelitenda Ferry Terminal on the South Bank of the River Gambia, as well as to Sénoba on the border with the Casamance region of Senegal. Most bush taxis and gelly-gellys leave from the main bus station opposite the market.

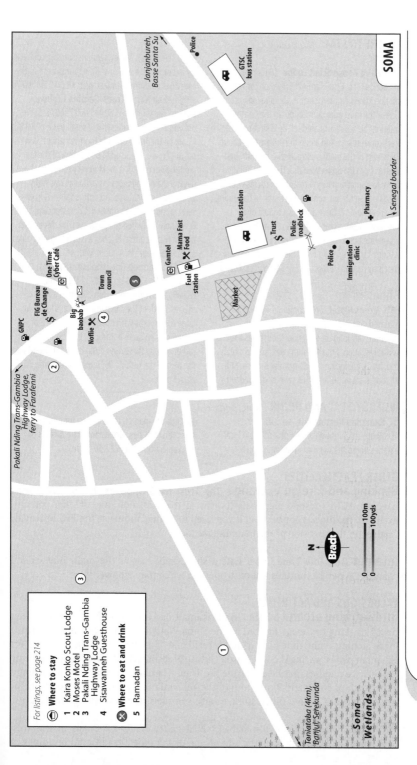

For listings, see page 214

Where to stay

1 Kaira Konko Scout Lodge
2 Moses Motel
3 Pakali Nding Trans-Gambia Highway Lodge
4 Sisawanneh Guesthouse

Where to eat and drink

5 Ramadan

SOMA

⌂ WHERE TO STAY *Map, page 213*
Budget
⌂ **Kaira Konko Scout Lodge** (8 rooms)
m 6655474; **e** kintehlamin200@yahoo.com or
marion.xmas@btinternet.com; **w** kairakonko.com.
One of the most agreeable lodges in the Gambian
interior, this scout-affiliated set-up is situated in a
neat concrete building along the Brikama Rd about
1km west of the main crossroads & a few hundred
metres from the Soma Wetland. The main building
has a few small but airy & clean twin rooms with
tiled floor, net & fan, some using a shared bathroom,
others en suite, & there are also a couple of VIP
rooms with 24hr solar roof fan & private balcony in
a separate building. The self-catering kitchen has
a fridge for the use of guests. The staff will prepare
meals by request. *£10pp, £13pp B&B, £20pp FB.*

Shoestring
⌂ **Moses Motel** (10 rooms) **m** 7069255.
Situated on the northwest side of the main
junction, this long-serving guesthouse has a useful
central location, but the rooms, set around a leafy
courtyard, are looking quite grubby & worn. Still,
all rooms are en suite with a twin or dbl bed with

net & ceiling fan, & they seem reasonably cool. Ask
for a room with a window. New rooms were under
construction during our last visit. *£8.50/12 dbl/VIP.*
⌂ **Pakali Nding Trans-Gambia Highway
Lodge** (33 rooms) **m** 6744598/7796071. Set in
unkempt green grounds in the small town of Pakali
Nding on the Trans-Gambia Highway about 3km
north of town, this used to be the pick of the lodges
around Soma, but it is looking very rundown these
days, & the dining room in particular was filthy
when we last looked in. Accommodation is in en-
suite round huts with dbl bed & net, standing fan
& optional AC (when the power works). Meals are
available by request, & it has a bar. Adequate value.
£5/8.50 en-suite dbl without/with AC.
⌂ **Sisawanneh Guesthouse** (8 rooms)
m 3112595/6263548/7218235/9913064;
e wallyjarjusey@yahoo.com. Situated a few
metres south of the main junction, this lodge has
large tiled rooms with dbl bed & the choice of
a shared or en-suite bathroom, but it is looking
rather grubby these days. Still, it probably ranks as
the best of the rest. *£5 dbl using shared bath, £8.50
en-suite dbl.*

✕ WHERE TO EAT AND DRINK *Map, page 213*
✕ **Ramadan Restaurant** **m** 7782997;
🕘 08.00–midnight daily. The pick of a few local
eateries lining the main road running south

towards the market, this serves a limited but tasty
selection of dishes such as omelette & chips or
chicken & rice. *Around £2.50/plate.*

OTHER PRACTICALITIES
Banking and foreign exchange The **Trust Bank** opposite the **market** doesn't
have an ATM (despite signposts indicating it does), nor does it offer foreign-
exchange facilities. Your best bet if you need to change money is the **FIG Bureau de
Change** on the east side of the main intersection.

Internet The **One Time Cyber Café** a short walk east of the main intersection
charges D6 per 15 minutes but only operates when mains power is on.

EXCURSIONS AND ACTIVITIES
Birdwatching around Soma The Brikama Road immediately west of town lies
on a 1km-long causeway flanked by the Soma Wetland, which can offer rewarding
birdwatching at any time of year, and is rated one of the best sites in the country for
Egyptian plover during the wet season (July to November). Also worth investigating
are the rice paddies that lie alongside the Trans-Gambia Highway past Janoi about
7km north of Soma and 3km south of the Yelitenda Ferry Jetty. It is a good site for
waders, plovers, yellow-billed stork, a variety of raptors, and winding cisticola.

Toniataba The village of Toniataba (⊕ *N13 26.219 W15 34.702*), about 4km west
of Soma as the crow flies, is the site of one of the oldest traditional buildings in

The Gambia, a *murubungu* (roundhouse) with a circumference of around 60m. According to local tradition, the house was originally built around 180 years ago by a marabout called Jimbiti Fatty, who is now buried underneath the floor. The marabout who lives there today – reputedly the seventh in the line – is still regarded to be one of the most important in the Senegambian region, and the house is probably the only surviving example of this type of building. Visitors are welcome, but be warned that you may only view the murubungu from the outside, photography is forbidden, and you will be expected to donate something to the building's upkeep (we were asked the dalasi equivalent of around £165, but settled at a less preposterous figure of around £2). To get there from Soma, follow the Brikama Road west out for 4km, then turn right at the AFET sign and you will reach Toniataba after another 2km.

FARAFENNI

The North Bank counterpart to Soma, Farafenni lies astride the Trans-Gambian Highway about 6km north of the ferry crossing at Bambatenda. It is the most populous upriver urban centre in The Gambia, supporting around 30,000 inhabitants, and the fifth-largest town countrywide. It is also the most important route crossroads north of the river, with a strategic location that attracts plenty of semi-transient traders from Senegal, Guinea and Mauritania to its weekly *lumo* (market), which is held on the northern outskirts of town on Sundays. Though Farafenni is not at all orientated towards tourists, it has above-average facilities, including the few functional ATMs anywhere upriver of Brikama, the APRC General Hospital (one of the country's largest), and a scattering of filling stations, hotels and local eateries.

GETTING THERE AND AWAY Farafenni lies about 115km east of Barra (the North Bank ferry terminus opposite Banjul) and a similar distance west of Lamin Koto (the North Bank ferry terminus opposite Janjanbureh). The road between Barra and Lamin Koto is surfaced in its entirety, and driving non-stop in a private vehicle you can reach Farafenni in well under 2 hours coming in either direction.

Five GTSC buses run daily in either direction between Barra and Farafenni, taking around 4 hours, with the first one leaving at 07.00, and the last at around

---

THE YELITENDA–BAMBATENDA FERRY

A diesel-powered vehicle and passenger ferry crosses the relatively narrow stretch of the River Gambia that breaks up the Trans-Gambia Highway between the South Bank terminus of Yelitenda and its North Bank counterpart Bambatenda. The crossing takes about 10 minutes each way, and there are departures in either direction every 25 to 30 minutes, though long queues often result in significantly longer waits. The first ferry crossing is at 07.00 and it usually keeps running until the last light vehicle has been carried across (typically by around 22.00 and 23.00). The fare for a vehicle is D150, and foot passengers pay a nominal fee (D10). Coming from the south, tickets must be bought at a roadside weighbridge 2km before Yelitenda, while the ticket office on the north side is a few hundred metres before Bambatenda. Plenty of bush taxis ply the 10km road between Yelitenda and Soma and the 5km road between Bambatenda and Farafenni – the fare in both cases is around D25.

17.00. Only one of these buses continues to/from Lamin Koto, leaving Barra at 09.00 and Lamin Koto at 07.00, and taking around 8 hours for the full journey.

Farafenni is serviced by plenty of gelly-gellys and bush taxis. Vehicles heading to Barra and Kerewan leave from the station on the Barra Road before the hospital. Vehicles heading to Kuntaur, Lamin Koto and other points further east leave from a station 100m south of the Kuntaur Road just past the post office. This second station is also where you will find direct gelly-gellys to Serekunda, but since this route involves crossing the River Gambia via the Yelitenda–Bambatenda Ferry, we would recommend travelling to Soma in hops, then picking up transport to Serekunda once you get there. Bush taxis to the Bambatenda ferry terminus and to the Senegalese border post about 3km north of town leave from the main road south of the police station.

🏠 WHERE TO STAY   *Map, page 217*

Budget

🏠 **Eddy's Hotel**   (30 rooms)
m 7676073/7710793. This long-serving & well-known hotel, tucked away on a side road between the market & EcoBank, is centred on a shady courtyard planted with mango & palm trees which double as daytime roosts for the yellow-winged bats that fly around picking off insects after dusk. The rooms are a bit rundown, but still a cut above most upcountry hotels, & the presence of a generator means there is usually power at night, even when the main supply is offline, though this isn't 100% reliable. All rooms are en-suite dbl or twin, & come either with a fan or AC. A limited selection of meals is served, along with chilled beers & soft drinks. There is a protected car park. *£8.50/12.50 dbl with fan/AC.*

Shoestring

🏠 **AMRC**   (11 rooms) m 9909932/7860044. A few mins' walk east of the main crossroads in the centre of Farafenni, this is the best & cleanest option in town. Basic sgl & dbl rooms have shared bathrooms & fan, while the en-suite rooms have AC. Meals are available on request. To find it, look for the side street close to the Medical Research Council compound. If in doubt, ask around – as they say in The Gambia, a man with a mouth is never lost. *£7.50/8.50 standard sgl/dbl, £8.50/10 en-suite sgl/dbl.*

🏠 **Ballanghar Hotel**   (12 rooms) m 9908331. This scruffy hotel in the backroads south of Eddy's has a variety of rooms with shared or en-suite bath. They all come with nets & fans, but are very rundown. *£5 dbl with shared bath, £8.50/10 en-suite sgl/dbl.*

🏠 **Mone-Berre**   (12 rooms)
m 6432172/7433204. A dark but clean & friendly option, with AC rooms. *£6.50/room.*

✗ WHERE TO EAT AND DRINK   *Map, page 217*

Most people who stay at Eddy's also eat there. The food is pretty good though you might wait a while for it to appear, so order it well in advance. For breakfast, there is a good stall serving eggs, bread and coffee on the junction of the Kuntaur Road and the Trans-Gambia Highway, and there's a stand selling good roast chicken sandwiches by the GTSC bus station A local speciality is *bissap* or *wanjo*, a sweet drink made from hibiscus flowers.

✗ **Sunu Yai Fast Food**   m 7627043/9955524; ◷ 07.00–22.00 Mon–Sat. The pick of the local eateries that line the main road, this place is well known for its chicken, served roasted or grilled or yassa-style. No alcohol. *Mains around £2.50.*

♀ **Kerr Makumbo East Time Bar & Restaurant**   ◷ 08.00–late daily. The food here isn't great, but it is a good place for a chilled beer or to watch live Premier League football.

OTHER PRACTICALITIES

Banking and foreign exchange Several banks are dotted around town, the most useful to tourists being the **EcoBank** a few doors down from Eddy's Hotel,

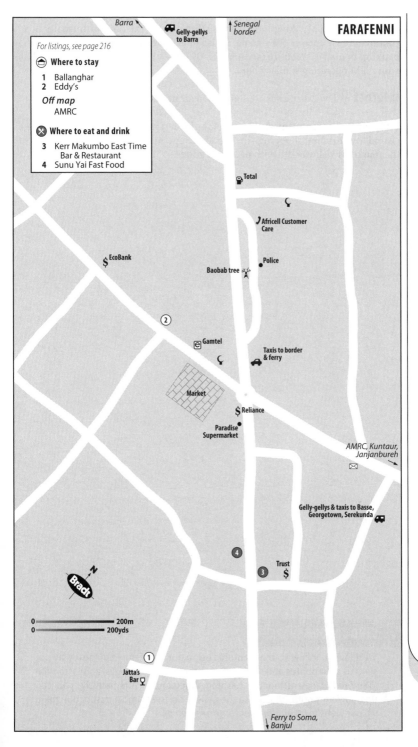

FARAFENNI

Barra ◄

Gelly-gellys to Barra

↑ Senegal border

For listings, see page 216

🛏 **Where to stay**

1 Ballanghar
2 Eddy's

Off map
   AMRC

✖ **Where to eat and drink**

3 Kerr Makumbo East Time Bar & Restaurant
4 Sunu Yai Fast Food

🛢 Total

Ç

♪ Africell Customer Care

● Police

Baobab tree ⚘

$ EcoBank

②

ⓔ Gamtel

Ç

🚗 Taxis to border & ferry

Market

$ Reliance

Paradise ● Supermarket

AMRC, Kuntaur, Janjanbureh →

✉

Gelly-gellys & taxis to Basse, Georgetown, Serekunda 🚌

④

③

Trust $

Bract N

0 ———— 200m
0 ———— 200yds

①

Jatta's Bar 🍷

↓ Ferry to Soma, Banjul

Inland to Soma and Farafenni   FARAFENNI

14

which has an ATM taking international Visa cards – the only such facility in any Gambian town upriver of Brikama. It also offers foreign-exchange facilities during banking hours (⏲ *08.00–16.00 Mon–Fri, 09.00–13.30 Sat*). There's also a **GT Bank** with ATM operating similar hours.

Internet A few **cyber cafés** are signposted around the market area.

Shopping The **central market** is one of the busiest in the country, though not at all geared towards craft shopping. The **Paradise Supermarket** on the main road next to the market is well stocked with packaged goods.

15

Janjanbureh and Central River Division

Running both north and south from the River Gambia to the respective borders with Senegal, Central River Division (CRD) starts about 20km upstream of the Soma–Farafenni Ferry and continues eastward for another 100km or so inland to the border with Upper River Division. As with the rest of the country, the River Gambia is the dominant geographic feature of CRD, and the main tourist focus. However, since salt water from the Atlantic Ocean only intrudes upstream as far as Kau-ur (with some seasonal variation), the riverbanks of CRD are lined not with mangroves but with an altogether more biodiverse and visually appealing mosaic of riparian woodland, gallery forest and freshwater swamp.

The low-key administrative capital of CRD is the old trading town of Janjanbureh, which lies on the north shore of MacCarthy Island about 270km upriver of Banjul. An agreeable and characterful small town, it is studded with timeworn old buildings, and the surrounding riparian woodland offers some good birding and monkey-watching opportunities. Janjanbureh is also the busiest tourist focus in the Gambian interior, serviced by close on a dozen camps and guesthouses, none of which rises much above the budget category. Several worthwhile and reasonably accessible birding sites lie to the east of Janjanbureh, among them a well-known bee-eater colony near Bansang and the underrated Kunkilling Forest Reserve.

The two most compelling attractions in CRD both lie downriver from Janjanbureh. For wildlife lovers, River Gambia National Park, which protects a wide island-studded stretch of jungle-fringed river, is best known for the orphaned chimp communities established on three of its islands, but it also supports hippos and a good variety of monkeys and birds. What's more, the clifftop tented camp operated here by the Chimp Rehabilitation Project easily ranks as the most alluring lodging anywhere upriver of Makasutu. Different altogether are the mysterious medieval stone circles that scatter the North Bank between Farafenni and Janjanbureh. The most famous of these megaliths can be found at Wassu and Ker Batch, both of which are easily accessible and form part of the Stone Circles of Senegambia UNESCO World Heritage Site.

THE SOUTH BANK FROM SOMA TO JANJANBUREH

The now resurfaced 130km road connecting Soma to Janjanbureh can be covered comfortably in under 2 hours. There is little of great interest here apart from a few forest parks and bolongs that sit astride the road, though it might be worth considering a stop at one or two of the places mentioned below. Using public transport, all GTSC buses between Serekunda and Basse stop at Soma and Janjanbureh, but for villages in between you are better off using gelly-gellys or bush taxis. If you are driving from the coast to the Chimp Rehabilitation Project Camp in

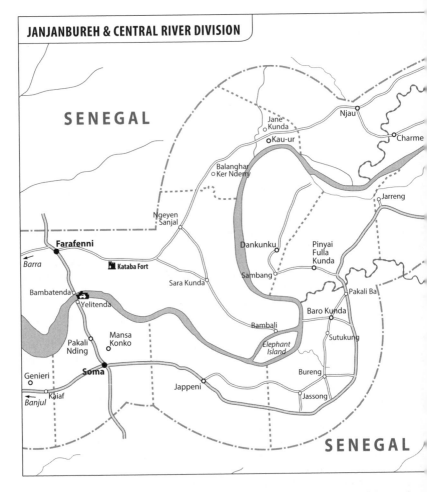

JANJANBUREH & CENTRAL RIVER DIVISION

River Gambia National Park, note that the junction is on the north side of the road at Kudang, around 80km from Soma and 20km past Jarreng.

PAKALI BA This small village lies on the west side of the bridge across the Sofaniama Bolong, a large creek that forms the border between Lower and Central River Division some 45km east of Soma. The wetlands emanating from the bolong can be rewarding for birds, with marabou stork and black-crowned crane among the more interesting species recorded.

JARRENG Situated about 14km northeast of Pakali Ba, this small village is well known for its market, which deals mainly in furniture made from cane and raffia. Some real bargains can be had here, though transporting a cane bed-base on the plane home might be difficult. Still, even if you're not buying, it's very interesting to watch a craftsman at work and to see how the furniture is made. From the village it is only about 2km north to the River Gambia; here it is possible to hire a pirogue and boatman to explore around Poppa Island, where there is a chance of spotting hippos (but don't allow your boatman to go too close to these potentially dangerous creatures).

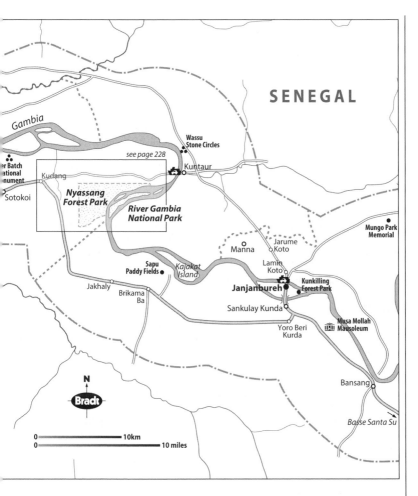

SAPU PADDY FIELDS Running north of the South Bank Road between Jakhaly and Brikama Ba, starting some 35km east of Jarreng, an extensive area of freshwater swamp has been converted to paddy fields, using a tidal irrigation system, to two agricultural schemes that collectively support almost 70 villages and more than 30,000 families. The area is also regarded to be one of *the* birding hotspots in CRD, thanks to a rich mixture of habitats that also includes agricultural land and riverine forest. The area is good for sandpipers and other waders, and interesting species recorded include Pel's fishing owl, pygmy goose, collared pratincole, black coucal, African finfoot and white-backed vulture. About 800m north of Brikama Ba, a copse of mahogany trees on the left side of the Saruja Road (just after a small church) is a reliable roost for the outsized Verreaux's eagle-owl.

There are several road approaches to the paddy fields, the most convenient being the track that branches north from the village of Madina Umfally about halfway between Jakhaly and Brikama Ba. You should reach the most southerly rice fields about 500m along this track, at a T-junction from where a 10km loop road leads past several patches of marsh and forest before returning to the same point. If you are interested to learn more about the agricultural schemes, visit the road for Sapu

Agricultural Station, which lies 3km along a side road signposted to the north about 2km east of Brikama Ba. Using public transport, any vehicle headed between Soma and Janjanbureh can drop you at Brikama Ba from where you can either walk to the paddy fields, or travel in style on a hired horse- or donkey-cart.

THE NORTH BANK FROM FARAFENNI TO JANJANBUREH

The 120km road between Farafenni and Lamin Koto (the North Bank village opposite Janjanbureh) is surfaced in its entirety and, like its South Bank counterpart from Soma, it can be driven comfortably in under 2 hours. The North Bank Road used to be the more popular route to Janjanbureh, but it has fallen out of favour in recent years owing to the resurfacing of the South Bank Road and the increasing unreliability of the ferry between Banjul and Barra. It does, however, offer a lot more of interest to travellers, the main attractions being the ancient stone circle sites at Ker Batch and Wassu (pages 223–4 and 225), which were inscribed as UNESCO World Heritage Sites in 2006, and the opportunity to explore River Gambia National Park by boat from Kuntaur. As with the South Bank Road, the best option for travelling directly between Farafenni and Lamin Koto is the GTSC bus, but plenty of bush taxis also run along the road and can be used to hop between other towns.

KATABA FORT The first point of historical interest along this road, this disused fort at the village of Katabatata was built with British assistance by Sefo Kanni Touré, the King of Kataba (a Wolof kingdom that then covered most of present-day Gambia north of the river) in the early 1840s. Built with laterite boulders and concrete, the site covers about one acre, and was originally enclosed by a stockade of logs and thorns. It was built to fend off the Fula troops enlisted by a neighbouring king who had made several threatening gestures towards the village. All that remains today is a series of overgrown broken foundations on a slight rise just outside the village, and a deep dry well reputedly used by the king only. To get there, follow the North Bank Road for about 10km out of Farafenni, then turn right to Katabatata, a cluster of three villages set about 2km from the main road. Before visiting the ruins, it is advisable to ask permission from the alkalo (chief), who lives in the second village you pass through coming from the main road, and take him a gift of kola nuts.

ELEPHANT ISLAND Almost 5km long and 2.5km wide, the largest island along the River Gambia lies in a transitional area at the farthest point upriver affected by saline water from the Atlantic. Its name dates back at least to the 16th century, when the Portuguese geographer João de Barros noted that roughly halfway upriver to Kuntaur was a landmass 'which our men call the Island of Elephants on account of all the elephants there'. It is also depicted as the Ille Oliphante on a French map dated to 1623. Sadly, the last individual elephant recorded anywhere in The Gambia was shot in the 1920s, but the shallow waters around the island do support the river's most westerly resident hippo population, amounting to around 100 individuals. Also resident are crocodiles and green monkeys, and the plentiful birdlife includes black-crowned crane.

To get to Elephant Island from the main North Bank Road, turn south at Sara Kunda then continue along the bumpy dirt road which leads for 20km to the forested riverbank opposite it and the remote village of Bambali. Most of the road is easy but there are occasional soft spots that require careful navigation unless you have a 4x4. Bush taxis do run from Farafenni to Bambali, but they aren't very frequent. Bambali isn't set up for tourist activities but the alkalo (chief) should be able to arrange lodging in a village compound. Possible trips include a long walk down to the river, or an early-morning or late-afternoon pirogue trip to see the hippos. It's also possible to be taken out at night by a local hunter who will try his best to spot hyena and warthog for you.

KAU-UR The substantial village of Kau-ur (also spelt Kaur), about 40km east of Farafenni, and connected to it by regular bush taxis, is one of two points where the North Bank Road comes close to skirting the River Gambia. It is quite an old town, first documented in 1625 under the name Caur, the 'port of palm trees', by André Donelha, a Luso-African trader from Cape Verde. A few points of interest lie alongside the road west of the village. The first of these coming from Farafenni is Belel Forest Park, which lies on the south side of the road about 5km west of Kau-ur. Belel protects probably the best example of Sudan savannah woodland anywhere on the North Bank, comprising a rich mixture of small trees and bushes with the occasional huge baobab tree dotted among them. Birdlife is phenomenal and includes Savile's bustard, black-headed plover, white-faced scops owl, striped kingfisher and various rollers, bee-eaters, parrots and starlings. The chestnut-crowned sparrow-weaver was first added to the Gambian list in 1994 based on a sighting here.

The first easily found stone circle coming from Farafenni lies about 2km before Kau-ur. Local folklore has it that this stone circle was formed by a wedding party that was turned to stone. To get there, look for the signposted track to Genge Wolof School; follow it north until you pass two small hamlets. The small stone circle lies beneath a tree about 100m past the second hamlet and about 75m east of the track. Back on the main road, about 1km before Kau-ur, the small near-perennial Kau-ur Swamp often hosts a good selection of birds, including little bittern, greater painted snipe, malachite kingfisher, purple swamphen and sometimes even Egyptian plover.

Where to stay and eat

🏠 **Kauren Restaurant & Lodge** (2 rooms) m 3229421/3650047/7171286; e daouda_n@ hotmail.com. This new lodge, built on a high point overlooking the river with panoramic views, has well-built, comfortable rooms. Meals can be arranged for around £5/plate, & guided birding excursions can be organised to local sites. Coming from Farafenni, take the right-hand turn immediately before the police checkpoint, turn left before the school & then take the first right along a rocky track up the hill. *£25/room B&B.*

PANCHANG SWAMP About 25km (15 miles) past Kau-ur, a partially collapsed stone circle comprising eight megaliths lies in an open field 500m north of the village of Nioro. Just past this, the permanent Panchang Swamp, an extension of Nianija Bolong, is focused on a large perennial pool that often hosts a rich birdlife, including a variety of herons and egrets, African jacana, Egyptian plover, Allen's gallinule and a resident population of African pygmy goose.

KER BATCH NATIONAL MONUMENT (⊕ *08.00–18.00 daily; entrance less than D60*) One of four UNESCO-inscribed stone circle sites in Senegambia, Ker Batch, also known as Singhu Demba, is the most important of around 50 such megalithic sites that flank the Nianija Bolong as it winds for 30km from the Senegalese border towards its confluence with the River Gambia. It consists of nine stone circles containing a total of 161 individual megaliths, the tallest of which is around 2.5m high and 1m in diameter. It is best known as the site of the country's only

15

lyre-stone, a tall Y-shaped megalith that was broken in the early 20th century and rather clumsily repaired with concrete by the Anglo-Gambian Stone Circle Expedition of 1965. The symbolic purpose of this unusual megalith is a matter for conjecture, but local legends state that it is where two close relatives that died simultaneously were buried.

Ker Batch is theoretically open from 08.00 to 18.00 daily, though in practice one senses it is more a case of it being open whenever the caretaker is around. The entrance fee includes access to a small, partly roofless and monumentally rundown site museum that provides useful background to Ker Batch and the other Senegambian stone circles, as well as displays relating to contemporary local cultures, and which also doubles as a daytime roost for a colony of slit-faced bats.

Getting there and away Ker Batch (⊕ *N13 45.262 W15 04.113*) lies about 7km from the main North Bank Road and is reached by a sandy dirt road signposted to the south at the largish village of Nyanga Bantang, about 10km east of Panchang. It is well signposted all of the way. For those using public transport, bush taxis do run to Nyanga Bantang from Kau-ur, Kuntaur and Lamin Koto, but from there you must either walk or hire a horse- or donkey-cart. The best time to be in Nyanga Bantang is Sunday, when it is the site of a busy lumo (market) that attracts plenty of traditionally attired Fula women.

KUNTAUR Set on an attractive stretch of the North Bank surrounded by paddy fields, Kuntaur lies about 2km south of the main North Bank Road some 25km past Nyanga Bantang and about 20km before Lamin Koto. Kuntaur is quite a significant town by upriver standards, supporting a population of around 2,500. Its main claim to fame is as the closest town to the Wassu National Monument, which lies back on the main North Bank Road alongside the eponymous junction village. It is also the most normal springboard for visits to River Gambia National Park a few kilometres upriver.

Often transcribed as Cantor, Cantoar or Kantora, Kuntaur is a settlement of some antiquity. Its existence was documented in 1456 by the Portuguese explorer Diogo Gomes, the first European to sail this far upriver, who saw it as the most important market port in the region, with significant commercial links to the then-mysterious gold-trading emporium of Timbuktu (in present-day Mali) and the associated trans-Saharan caravan route to Morocco. Kuntaur also appears in the early 16th-century writings of Duarte Pacheco Pereira as a cluster of four towns, the largest of which supported around 4,000 people and was the site of an important Mandinka livestock market. Then as now, Kuntaur was the last upriver port accessible to ocean-going cargo boats, and while such vessels are now few and far between, a row of rundown riverfront warehouses recalls its long-past colonial-era heyday as a groundnut export centre.

Getting there and away The main transport hub is the junction village of Wassu, which straddles the main North Bank Road about 2km north of Kuntaur. Gelly-gellys to Wassu from Farafenni cost around D90 and those from Lamin Koto cost D30. If you are headed to the Wassu National Monument, it's no more than ten minutes' walk from the taxi park and clearly signposted. To get to Kuntaur, you could walk from Wassu in around 30 minutes, or else charter a donkey-cart for around D60.

Many of the camps at Janjanbureh organise day excursions to Wassu, and it is also possible to travel between Kuntaur and Janjanbureh by boat via River Gambia National Park.

Where to stay and eat

🏠 **Kairoh Garden** (12 rooms) m 2586811; e information@kairohgarden.com; w kairohgarden.com. The only accommodation in Kuntaur is provided by this unpretentious harbour-front affiliate of its namesake in Tanji. Accommodation is in simple & rather sweaty twin rooms with nets & common showers, although there are now 4 rooms with en-suite eco-toilet & showers. An open-sided restaurant serves decent meals in the £2–5 range, as well as beer & other drinks, & offers a great view of the river. There are 2 boats for guests to use, & fishing trips (*D80/hr*) & excursions to Baboon Island (*D2,000*) can be organised. *£6pp room with shared bathroom, £7.50pp room with eco-toilet.*

What to see and do In addition to being the closest town to Wassu, Kuntaur is the best base for day trips around Baboon Island in River Gambia National Park. These can be arranged through Kairoh Garden or any of the boats around the riverfront warehouses, and will cost around D1,800–2,100 per party, excluding entrance fees (see above).

Wassu Stone Circles (⏱ *08.00–18.00 daily; entrance D50*) The best-known and most frequently visited of the four sites that comprise the Stone Circles of Senegambia UNESCO World Heritage Site is Wassu National Monument (⊕ *N13 41.471 W14 52.435*), which boasts the greatest concentration of megaliths anywhere in the country. Altogether, around 200 megaliths, the tallest being about 3m high, are arranged into 11 circles here. In addition, some 200m east of the main site, the quarry where the stones were carved contains several megaliths that broke in transit or before they had been completed. It contains a well laid-out (albeit rather musty and bat-infested) site museum where an array of models, photographs, paintings and other interpretative material help to bring the history of the stone circles to life. The fenced-off site lies about 500m east of the main North Bank Road, perhaps 10 minutes' walk and clearly signposted from the junction village of Wassu.

RIVER GAMBIA NATIONAL PARK

The winding stretch of the River Gambia between Kuntaur and MacCarthy Island has a compelling tropical character, lined as it is with a lush belt of jungle-like riparian forest that evokes the steamy Congo Basin rather than the Sahel. Its centrepiece is the 6km² River Gambia National Park (RGNP), which was gazetted in 1978 to protect Baboon Island and four smaller islets, as well as an adjacent stretch of riverbank, a few kilometres upriver of Kuntaur.

The most publicised attraction of RGNP is the chimpanzees that have been introduced to three of its islands by the Chimpanzee Rehabilitation Project (CRP; see box, page 229), which also operates an excellent tented camp (⏱ *Thu–Sun only*) opposite Baboon Island on the South Bank's Nyassang Forest Park, a state-owned classified forest jointly managed in collaboration with several local communities. Revenue raised by tourist visits to the CRP goes primarily towards the care and welfare of the chimpanzees, though a percentage is used to help fund government conservation programmes and community development projects.

In addition to chimpanzees, RGNP supports healthy populations of several naturally occurring primates, most conspicuously green monkey, red colobus and Guinea baboon, along with a few-dozen hippos, plenty of crocodiles and monitor lizards, warthogs and manatees, and several small antelope and nocturnal carnivore species. The birdlife is fantastic too: the handsome palmnut vulture, African fish eagle and osprey all nest along the river, the secretive African finfoot inhabits

The rivers Gambia and Sine-Saloum (in Senegal) form the southern and northern boundaries of a region scattered with some 30,000 carved stelae arranged into neat circles at several hundred individual megalithic sites. These ancient stone circles, each one reminiscent of a miniaturised Stonehenge, form one of Africa's most enigmatic and intriguing archaeological relicts. And though seldom visited and little known to the outside world, they received an overdue boost when four of the most important individual fields – Wassu and Ker Batch in The Gambia and two others across the border in Senegal – were inscribed as a UNESCO World Heritage Site in 2006.

The stelae of Senegal and Gambia were hand-carved from iron-rich lateritic stones. Most take a simple cuboid or cylindrical shape, but there are also a few impressive lyre-shaped examples, and some are capped with knob-like protrusions that resemble battery terminals. The stones were cut from quarries close to the sites and set vertically into pre-dug pits. Most stones are fairly small, ranging from only 0.75m, but some are much larger at 3m tall.

The number of stones in each circle varies from ten to 24 and the diameter varies from 4m to 7m. Within each stone circle is a slightly domed rise, usually constructed of sand, though a few mounds are topped with lateritic pebbles, presumably to stop erosion. A common feature of many circles is a line of pillars set away on the eastern side. At some sites there are large groups of circles, at others there is only a single circle, while at others still there are no circles at all, only single pillars.

The discovery of large numbers of skeletons buried below some circles, as well as tools, pottery and miscellaneous ornaments, suggests that these sites are essentially vast funerary complexes. Some of the stone circles seem to mark a mass grave containing bodies thrown chaotically into a pit, perhaps after a battle or an epidemic

shaded stretches of riverbank, and it's one of the best places in the country to see forest-associated hornbills, barbets, shrikes, turacos and parrots.

Tourists are forbidden from setting foot on the islands protected within RGNP. This is partly due to the potential danger posed by chimps, who can be quite aggressive toward human intruders. It is also to protect the health of the chimps, which are highly susceptible to human-borne diseases. However, the islands and their inhabitants can be viewed from a boat, ideally with the CRP, which has exclusive access to the channel between Baboon Island and its tented camp. (It can also be arranged through private boat owners in Kuntaur, but this restricts your access to the public channel.) Either way, it is mandatory to be accompanied by a CRP guide on any boat trip running through the park, and an entrance fee of D180 per person is levied.

A NOTE ON ORIENTATION RGNP protects part of an inverted 'S' bend where this typically west-flowing river runs in a broadly northerly direction for about 50km. Furthermore, since the stretch of river that flows around Baboon Island is the central part of the inverted 'S', it actually flows in an easterly direction for around 10km. Rather confusingly, this means that the channel running past what is widely referred to as the South Bank (and past the CRP Camp) lies to the north and west of Baboon Island, while the one running past the nominal North Bank actually flows south and east of the island. Although we draw readers' attention to this apparent paradox, we have opted to stick to the conventional designation of North Bank and South Bank in this section; to do otherwise would be even more confusing.

disease. In other sites it looks as though people were buried alive as sacrifices. Generally the bodies are poorly adorned, often with only a bracelet for decoration and with a weapon, usually a spear, laid beside the body. Sometimes there are also some pottery vessels found by the bodies, usually turned upside-down.

Local oral traditions relating to the erection of the circles are bizarrely inconsistent. While some assert that the stones were set in place at the beginning of time by the gods, others regard them as burial markers left by an ancient race of kings and/or giants, and others still believe they are the petrified remains of disgraced people. Many people also claim that the circles are the home to spirits, whether benign or evil. However, one point on which all oral traditions do concur is that the megaliths have no cultural link with the region's present-day Islamic inhabitants. And this much tallies with the archaeological evidence, which indicates that the stone circles are mostly around 1,000 to 1,500 years old.

But archaeological evidence is also curiously inconclusive about the origin of the megaliths. If they are simply funerary markers, then why do the buried human remains found beneath some circles seem to predate their gravestones by several centuries? What happened to the prosperous and well-organised people responsible for erecting the stone circles over several centuries? Were the constructors, as some archaeologists speculate, associated with the royal city of Cantor, which the Arab chronicler El-Bakri reported as lying somewhere south of the medieval empire of Ghana in AD1067? And is it significant that, while no similar memorials exist elsewhere in West Africa, the southern highlands of Ethiopia, at the opposite end of the Sahel, are studded with megalithic grave markers of a similar size and vintage? We may never know, but part of the fascination of these ancient monuments is the sense of speculation they arouse.

GETTING THERE AND AWAY The closest town to RGNP and normal springboard for visits is Kuntaur, which lies on the North Bank and is readily accessible from the coast by public transport. Kuntaur lies about 20 minutes by boat from the park boundary, and visitors staying overnight at CRP Camp are usually met by prior arrangement at the mooring beach next to Kairoh Garden between noon and 13.00. If you are self-driving, you can leave the vehicle overnight in the grounds of Kairoh Garden for D60.

Though the CRP Camp is usually accessed by boat from the North Bank, it actually lies on the opposite side of the river and is thus accessible by road from the South Bank – a far more attractive prospect than it was a couple of years back, thanks to the recent upgrading of the Serekunda–Basse Road, and the growing unreliability of the Banjul–Barra Ferry. To get there, follow the surfaced South Bank Road east from Serekunda as far as Kudang (about 80km past Soma), where you need to turn left on to a dirt road that may require a 4x4 during and after the rains. Bank on up to 4 hours for the drive to Kudang and around 45 minutes from there to the CRP Camp.

WHERE TO STAY AND EAT *Map, page 228*

☀ 🏠 **CRP Camp** (4 tents, 1 room)
m 6868826/7878827;
e babooonislands@gmail.com; ☒
ChimpanzeeRehabilitationProjectCrpInTheGambia;

⊕ closed Mon–Wed nights. Consisting of just 4 stilted tents set on a tall laterite cliff on the South Bank of the river facing Baboon Island, this is the closest Gambian equivalent to the upmarket bush

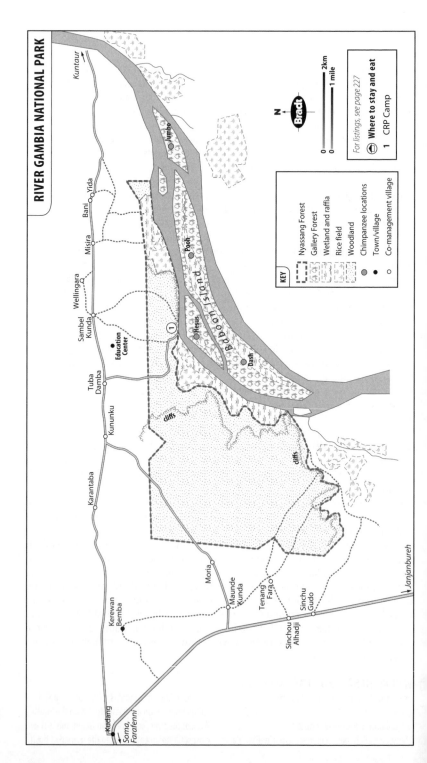

RIVER GAMBIA NATIONAL PARK

KEY

- Nyassang Forest
- Gallery Forest
- Wetland and raffia
- Rice field
- Woodland
- Chimpanzee locations
- Town/village
- Co-management village

For listings, see page 227
- Where to stay and eat
1 CRP Camp

N

0   2km
0   1 mile

Kuntaur

Bradt

Jumbo

Bani Yida

Misira

Wellingara

Sambel Kunda

Education Center

Tuba Damba

Kununku

Karantaba

Pool

Baboon Island

Hesus

Dash

cliffs

cliffs

Moria

Maunde Kunda

Tenang Fara

Sinchu Gudo

Sinchou Alhadji

Kerewan Bemba

Kerdang

Soma, Farafenni

Janjanbureh

camps of eastern & southern Africa. It is also the only truly tourist-class facility inland of AbCa's Creek Lodge in Bintang Bolong, & must rank as the premier goal for a short upriver excursion from the coast. The tents are all set on wooden platforms that look over the canopy to the river, offering great in-house birding (& occasionally primate viewing), as well as good natural ventilation. They come with twin beds protected by solid mosquito nets, a sink at the back, a separate outdoor shower, & plenty of interesting nocturnal animal calls. 2 compost toilets are each shared between 2 of the tents. 1 basic guest room is also available in low season. The other component of the camp is the Waterhouse, which doubles as a dining room, bar, boat jetty, & indoor & outdoor sitting area. Though quite pricey for The Gambia, it is very good value. *£110/120 sgl/dbl, inc all meals, an afternoon boat trip to look for chimpanzees & other wildlife, a morning nature walk, & transfers from Kuntaur.*

ACTIVITIES

Boat trips The highlight of a visit to RGNP is likely to be the 2-hour afternoon boat trips operated by the CRP. These leave at 16.00, a good time to view chimps

CHIMPANZEE REHABILITATION PROJECT

The Gambia's Chimpanzee Rehabilitation Project (CRP) has its roots in the animal orphanage established by Eddie Brewer, then the Director of Forestry, and his daughter Stella at Abuko Nature Reserve in 1968. The first orphaned chimpanzee was taken in there in 1969, and by 1974 they had several, most of them illegally captured and/or orphaned individuals confiscated from traffickers for the international pet trade. These chimps probably originated from Guinea, as there was no trade in these charismatic apes out of Senegal at the time, and they had long been extinct in the wild in The Gambia.

In 1974, Stella decided to release the orphaned chimps into a valley fed by a perennial natural spring in Senegal's Niokolo-Koba National Park. Unfortunately, however, a conflict developed between chimps released by Stella and a wild community living in the same territory. As a result, the survivors, numbering around seven individuals, were relocated to an island in RGNP in early 1979. At around the same time, another group of five orphaned chimps, under the care of the American primatologist Janis Carter, was relocated from Abuko to Baboon Island, followed by a small group from Holland.

In all, over a 25-year period, some 51 chimps were released on to the islands, in many cases after having undergone a retraining course to teach them to forage for wild food, build nests, etc. Only 15 of the chimps released originally survive, but many have gone on to breed successfully, so that there is now a total population of 104 individuals, split between four communities across three of the islands. The rehabilitated animals are quite well adapted to wild living, though the shortage of suitable foraging on the confines of the islands means that their diet needs to be supplemented by fruits and other food sourced from nearby villages.

The primary focus of the CRP today remains the welfare of its chimps, but it also oversees tourism to RGNP, and runs an environmental education programme to raise general awareness about conservation in the surrounding villages. CRP founder Stella Brewer Marsden, awarded an OBE for her work for animal welfare, died in January 2008, aged only 56, and is buried at the CRP Camp, close to the base of the trail up the cliff to the standing tents. Her long-time co-director Janis Carter remains CRP project director, and is also very active in chimpanzee conservation in neighbouring Senegal and Guinea.

15

and other wildlife, and more often than not they yield good close-up sightings of chimps in particular, and excellent photographic opportunities. Other wildlife likely to be seen from the boats includes hippo, green monkey, red colobus, and a good range of forest and aquatic birds. The boat trips are included in the room rate for CRP Camp.

With advance notice, the CRP can also arrange boat trips for day visitors out of Kuntaur between 16.00 and 18.00. These cost around D5,000 per party for up to four people, exclusive of park fees (with an optional lunch for an additional D660 per person). Parties of larger than four pay an extra D1,220 per additional person.

A cheaper option for day visitors – around D240–300 per party – is to take a private boat from Kuntaur. Be warned, however, that the channel between Baboon Island and the South Bank, which usually offers the best chimp viewing, is reserved exclusively for CRP boats. However, you are still quite likely to see chimps from the other channel (which runs north of Baboon Island), as well as hippos, monkeys and a good variety of birds. This rate excludes park fees, which must be paid whichever channel your boat uses.

Another possible boat trip from CRP Camp, usually done in the morning, runs a short way downstream to Sama Boi Konko (Elephant Cliff), said to be the place where the last lonely elephant in The Gambia fell to his death after seeing his reflection in the water below. You can walk to the top of the cliff, which offers stunning views over the river and islands. This boat trip is not included in the overnight rate, but costs an extra D780 per person.

Guided walks The CRP Camp offers an optional free morning walk on the escarpment flanking standing tents. This affords good views over the canopy, which is home to red colobus and green monkey, as well as to colourful forest birds such as bearded barbet and violet turaco. By prior arrangement, and weather permitting, it also offers optional night walks, which come with a good chance of seeing bushbabies, owls, giant fruit bats, and possibly also nocturnal predators such as genet.

Gambia Horse and Donkey Trust (w *gambiahorseanddonkey.org.uk*) Founded in 2002 by the late Stella Brewer Marsden and her sister Heather Armstrong, the Gambia Horse and Donkey Trust (GHDT) is based in the village of Sambel Kunda, one of more than ten villages that belong to the co-management committee of Nyassang Forest Park. In addition to training paravets, harness makers and farriers, the GHDT sponsors local students and provides resources to schools in the area, as well as educating locals to treat their working equines properly, thus improving farming productivity and the welfare of the animals. Formerly affiliated to the CRP, the trust can be visited on foot or by donkey-cart from the tourist camp, and it also welcomes suitable volunteers. There is now a second centre in Makasutu. Visit their website for further details.

JANJANBUREH AND SURROUNDS

Founded by the British in 1823, the port of Janjanbureh (also spelt Janjangbureh), administrative capital of CRD, stands on the North Bank of the 20km² MacCarthy Island about 200km inland of Banjul. Officially known as Georgetown until 1995, it is still often referred to by that name, or as *Makati* (a bastardisation of MacCarthy). A busy and thriving commercial centre throughout the colonial era, it is now quite a sleepy laid-back place with a population of no more than 4,000 and an economy

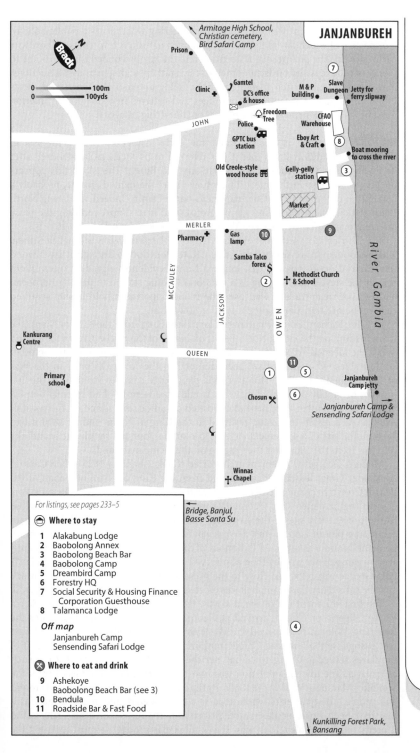

JANJANBUREH

Armitage High School,
Christian cemetery,
Bird Safari Camp

Prison

Clinic

Gamtel

DC's office
& house

Freedom
Tree

Police

GPTC bus
station

Old Creole-style
wood house

M & P
building

Slave
Dungeon

Jetty for
ferry slipway

CFAO
Warehouse

Eboy Art
& Craft

Boat mooring
to cross the river

Gelly-gelly
station

Market

JOHN

MERLER

Pharmacy

Gas
lamp

Samba Talco
forex

Methodist Church
& School

MCCAULEY

JACKSON

OWEN

River Gambia

Kankurang
Centre

QUEEN

Primary
school

Chosun

Janjanbureh
Camp jetty

Janjanbureh Camp &
Sensending Safari Lodge

Winnas
Chapel

Bridge, Banjul,
Basse Santa Su

For listings, see pages 233–5

Where to stay

1 Alakabung Lodge
2 Baobolong Annex
3 Baobolong Beach Bar
4 Baobolong Camp
5 Dreambird Camp
6 Forestry HQ
7 Social Security & Housing Finance
   Corporation Guesthouse
8 Talamanca Lodge

Off map
   Janjanbureh Camp
   Sensending Safari Lodge

Where to eat and drink

9   Ashekoye
    Baobolong Beach Bar (see 3)
10 Bendula
11 Roadside Bar & Fast Food

Kunkilling Forest Park,
Bansang

15

231

so stagnant you might well find yourself wondering whether it's a public holiday, irrespective of which day of the week you happen to visit. A few relics of the town's early days line the picturesque waterfront, and the lushly wooded island is home to plenty of monkeys and birds, but otherwise it is rather lacking in tourist attractions. Nevertheless, Janjanbureh, together with the facing stretch of the North Bank, hosts by far the biggest concentration of lodges and eateries in the Gambian interior, most of which fall firmly into the budget or shoestring category.

HISTORY Not much is known about the early history of MacCarthy Island, though oral tradition states that it was referred to by locals as Janjanbureh after its first settlers, two brothers named Janjang and Bureh. The island first appears on European maps in the late 17th century under the name Lemaine, probably a corruption of the common Gambian men's name Lamin (indeed, the facing North Bank settlement is still called Lamin Koto), and it is almost certainly the place referred to as 'Lame' by the Cape Verdean trader André Donelha in 1625.

The 17th-century settlement in the vicinity of Janjanbureh was Jongkaa Kunda, which stood more-or-less where Lamin Koto does today. Though it lay beyond the reach of ocean-going boats, Jongkaa Kunda evidently played an intermittent role in the slave trade, serving as a temporal trading station to passing European and Luso-African traders, who used the island opposite to hold freshly acquired captives before transporting them further downriver.

In 1785, Richard Bradley purchased Lemaine Island from the King of Niani (the main fiefdom on the facing North Bank) on behalf of the British Crown for around £580. The idea was to convert the island into a small colony for convicts and other 'undesirables' who would have been dumped in the Americas prior to the War of Independence in 1776. However, this plan never came to fruition, as the 200 inmates originally earmarked for what would have been the first colonial outpost on the River Gambia were instead deposited on an oceanic island off the coast of Angola. As a result, the island reverted to the King of Niani, and by 1810 it had become the site of a settlement called Morokunda, founded by Islamic Mandinka refugees from the tribal war then raging on the facing mainland.

Modern Georgetown/Janjanbureh started to take shape in 1823, when Captain Alexander Grant leased Lemaine Island from the King of Niani on behalf of the British Crown to create a settlement for freed slaves. In the same year, the mud Fort George (named after King George IV) was erected by the British, probably close to the present-day site of the Armitage School, and the Reverend John Morgan acquired a plot of land to start a Wesleyan Mission (now the Methodist Church). Lemaine Island was renamed in honour of Sir Charles MacCarthy, an ardent anti-slavery campaigner who by then also served as Governor of Sierra Leone. In 1827, Fort George was relocated close to the present-day commissioner's headquarters, and the subsidiary Fort Campbell was erected on the east side of MacCarthy Island.

The first shipment of 200 freed slaves, mostly Creoles originating from Sierra Leone, Nigeria or Ghana, arrived at Georgetown in 1832. Three years later the Reverend William Fox opened the Wesleyan (now Methodist) School to educate and evangelise the liberated Creole immigrants. By 1837, however, almost half of the slaves settled at Georgetown had perished, mostly from tropical diseases such as malaria. The town's population was boosted by an influx of refugees from the Soninke–Marabout Wars in the 1860s. By the end of that decade, it supported around 400 people, one-quarter of whom died in a cholera epidemic in 1869. Small as it may have been, however, this remote British military outpost on MacCarthy Island is pretty much the sole reason why The Gambia exists today – almost certainly, the river would otherwise have been ceded to the French during territorial negotiations with the British held in 1876.

Georgetown grew rapidly in the early 20th century. The roads were widened in 1905, a post office was opened and a money order system introduced in 1909, and a proper wharf was built in 1917. Over the course of the 1920s, the Bank of British West Africa opened its Georgetown agency, the prestigious Armitage School was established outside town, and a (short-lived) floating bridge was constructed to connect MacCarthy Island to Sankulay Kunda on the South Bank. Georgetown was gazetted as the district and provincial headquarters in 1930, and it remained the second most important administrative centre (and second-largest town in The Gambia in both cases after Bathurst/Banjul) throughout the rest of the colonial era. Post independence, however, Janjanbureh (as the town was renamed in 1995) has suffered a sharp economic decline, largely owing to its remote location and, until recently, the absence of a bridge connecting it to either river bank. Today, though it remains the administrative capital of CRD, Janjanbureh no longer ranks among the country's 20 largest towns, and the widely expressed hope that its economy would be kick-started following the construction of a new permanent bridge to Sankulay Kunda in 2010 has yet to materialise.

GETTING THERE AND AWAY Inaugurated in 2010, the bridge linking the village of Sankulay Kunda to the South Bank of MacCarthy Island now makes it possible to drive to Janjanbureh directly from anywhere on the South Bank without the delay associated with a ferry crossing. By contrast, there is still no bridge connecting Janjanbureh to Lamin Koto on the North Bank; only a motor ferry, which runs between 08.00 and 18.30, costs around D100 per vehicle, and takes around 5 minutes in either direction. Smaller private boats also ferry passengers between Janjanbureh and Lamin Koto for a few dalasi.

By road, Janjanbureh lies around 300km east of Serekunda, 130km from Soma and 60km west of Basse. The best way to travel to Janjanbureh from any of these towns is with the GTSC buses that leave Serekunda for Basse and vice versa throughout the morning. Leaving Janjanbureh, they stop in front of the police station and you should aim to be there before 08.00 for buses headed in the direction of Serekunda and before 09.00 for buses heading to Basse. The fare is around D175 to Serekunda (or D230 for the express bus) and about D60 to Basse. If it doesn't work out with the GTSC bus, gelly-gellys and bush taxis for all these destinations are slightly costlier and run from the station opposite the market throughout the day.

On the North Bank, one GTSC bus runs daily between Barra and Lamin Koto (the ferry terminal opposite Janjanbureh) via Farafenni, Kau-ur and Wassu. It leaves Barra at 09.00 and Lamin Koto at 07.00, and takes around 8 hours in either direction because of the many stops. Gelly-gellys and bush taxis also serve most towns along this route, leaving Lamin Koto from right next to the ferry slipway, and for once these may be quicker than the GTSC bus. The North Bank Road running east towards Basse cannot be recommended; you're advised to use the surfaced South Bank Road instead.

It is also possible to travel between the coast and Janjanbureh by river. A reliable operator offering these boat trips is Gambia River Excursions (m *7784058/9900231; e gambiariver@yahoo.com; w gambiarivercruise.com*), which charges from £190 per person for a one-night trip and £220 for two nights.

⌐ WHERE TO STAY Map, page 231
Janjanbureh offers a choice of many camps and lodges, but none that rise much above the budget category.

Mid-range

⌂ Baobolong Annex (22 rooms) **m** 7773045. Owned by the same family as Baobolong Camp but under entirely separate management, this newish central lodge has a convenient but bland location in a large walled compound on the landward side of Owen Rd. The newer en-suite rooms in Block B are the smartest in Janjanbureh & boast the only AC, though this only works when the mains grid is working (usually from around 18.00 into the early morning, but don't rely on it) & the rooms are quite stuffy when it isn't. The water pressure is also rather fallible. The rooms in Block A are also en suite, & come with a fan, but are older & less smart. It serves a good set b/fast & dinner for £3.50 & £5 respectively, & they can also organise boat trips. *£11/22 sgl/dbl with fan, £25 dbl AC, all rates inc b/fast.*

Budget

✱ ⌂ Janjanbureh Camp (34 rooms) **m** 7784058/9900231. Situated on a forested stretch of the North Bank opposite Janjanbureh town, this pleasant owner-managed camp is commendable for its lush jungle-like gardens running down to the river & spacious but dark thatched en-suite huts with large beds & nets. There is no power, which means no AC or fan, but the rooms are quite well ventilated, & lighting is by kerosene lamp & candle. Wildlife is plentiful, particularly green monkeys & birds. An attractively positioned waterfront restaurant serves à la carte dishes & b/fast, lunch & dinner buffets in the £2–4 range, using meat & other ingredients sourced from the coast. It lies a few hundred metres east of the ferry slipway at Lamin Koto, & a private boat charter from Janjanbureh shouldn't cost more than D120. Good value. *£5/8.50 sgl/dbl, £12.50 2-storey family room (sleeping 4).*

✱ ⌂ Sensending Safari Lodge (18 rooms) **m** 7334408/6911935/6977287; **e** sensendinglodge@gmail.com or ljobarteh32@yahoo.com. Situated right next to Janjanbureh Camp, this riverside lodge has brighter rooms than its neighbour but comparatively unexciting grounds as all the natural vegetation has been cleared, though this may change as it becomes better established. The choice is between large thatched round huts or less attractive tin-roofed square rooms, all with 1 dbl & 1 sgl bed, nets &

en-suite shower. There is no electricity, so no fans or AC, but the round huts seem to be quite well ventilated. B/fast costs around £4, lunch & dinner are around £5. Rooms are fair value. *£12/room.*

⌂ Baobolong Camp (27 rooms) **m** 6865199/7648844/9901667; **e** basirusinyan@yahoo.com; **f** BaobolongGuestHouseRiverView. Probably the pick of the accommodation immediately around Janjanbureh, & popular with tour operators, this long-serving & relatively well-managed camp has a rather bizarre location on the eastern edge of town within view of the riverside but separated from it by an overgrown field. The en-suite rooms are small but clean, & come with a fan & (in theory anyway) 24hr electricity provided by a standby generator when the grid is down. It also serves decent buffet meals, & b/fast, lunch & dinner for £2.50, £4 & £5 respectively. For large groups entertainment is laid on with local dancers & there is a resident fortune teller. Good value. *£10/14/20 sgl/dbl/trpl.*

⌂ Baobolong Beach Bar (3 rooms) **m** 7113238/7648844. Unrelated to its 2 other namesakes in Janjanbureh, this lodge has an unbeatable central location & the small en-suite rooms all come with double bed & fan, but they also look right out on to the riverfront bar, which could make for a noisy night, & feel a bit overpriced for what they are. *£13.50/20 sgl/dbl B&B.*

⌂ Dreambird Camp (4 rooms) **m** 6717386; **e** birdworld6@yahoo.com; **w** dreambird.jimdo.com. This small camp is set in a pleasant green compound tucked away along a footpath leading from opposite Alakabung Lodge down to the riverbank. Accommodation is in spacious but quite scruffy thatched round huts with nets & an en-suite toilet & shower at the back. Meals can be prepared by request, & they can organise boat trips along the river to see hippos. It's one of the more agreeable central options but feels a touch overpriced. *£8.50/13.50 sgl/dbl B&B, camping £2.50pp plus £1.70 for b/fast.*

Shoestring

⌂ Forestry HQ (5 rooms) **m** 7328428/6328428. Set amid giant fromagar trees, this has a lovely forested location overlooking the river. Although cheap, the solar-powered rooms are on the dingy side. There's a kitchen onsite. *£5pp.*

⌂ **Social Security & Housing Finance Corporation Guesthouse** (11 rooms) m 3955733; e flecxy@gmail.com; w sshfc. gm. Although not the catchiest of names, this guesthouse does offer some of the cheapest accommodation around in clean, airy, modern rooms with TV & AC. *£5/10 sgl/dbl.*

Shoestring
⌂ **Alakabung Lodge** (12 rooms) m 7210216/7524247. The pick of the real cheapies, this well-established place is located in the heart of town, & offers accommodation in relatively airy en-suite huts with tiled floor,

standing fan & screened windows. It is set in bright colourful grounds & serves b/fast, lunch & dinner for £3.50, £4 & £4.50 respectively. Good value. *£6.50 dbl.*

⌂ **Talamanca Lodge** (4 rooms) m 7224674/9911100; e talamancalodge@ yahoo.co.uk. Not quite as attractive as the Alakabung, despite its riverfront setting, this simple owner-managed lodge next to the taxi park has small but acceptably clean tiled en-suite rooms with double bed, fan & net. The open-sided restaurant/bar overlooks the river. Pretty good value. *£6.50pp.*

🍴 **WHERE TO EAT AND DRINK** *Map, page 231*

There is no shortage of restaurants and bars in Janjanbureh, none of which could honestly be described as exciting. As is so often the case, the best eateries are often associated with smarter lodgings such as Baobolong Camp. Pride of place probably goes to the riverfront restaurant at Janjanbureh Camp, though eating there if you are staying in town will entail crossing the river twice, either by taking a public boat across to Lamin Koto or chartering a private one directly to the camp's jetty. For meat lovers, given enough notice, local balanta lady, Jonsaba, will prepare delicious warthog pepper soup. Call to arrange delivery (m *2052896*). Other options include the following.

✳🍴 **Bendula Bar and Restaurant** m 3952435/6467367; e bendulajjb@yahoo.com; ⏲ 07.00–midnight daily. Another good choice among several local eateries, this well-run & friendly stalwart on Owen St has indoor seating, a Ficus-shaded courtyard, a reliable stock of chilled beers, & a varied menu including fish & chips or chicken yassa & rice. *Around £3/plate.*

🍴 **Ashekoye** m 9939346/7939310; ⏲ 07.00–14.00 & 18.00–23.00 daily. Pick of the local joints & reckoned by locals to serve the best evening meals. *Snacks are available for £1.50–2.50, whereas mains are around £4.*

🍴 **Bamba's Bar & Restaurant** m 6565449; ⏲ 07.00–02.00 daily. A good place to try local dishes, this small & friendly eatery has a varied menu including fish benachin, chicken yassa,

grilled chicken & vegetarian stew. *Around £3/plate.*

🍴 **Roadside Bar & Fast Food** m 6302629/7748500; ⏲ 08.30–midnight daily. This small restaurant specialises in fish or beef benachin, & it serves beers & other cold drinks. The indoor seating area looks a bit stuffy but you can eat outdoors in the green back garden.

✳🍸 **Baobolong Beach Bar** ⏲ 07.00–late. The top sundowner spot in Janjanbureh, this unpretentious bar has a comfortable riverfront deck from where you can watch the ferry to Lamin Koto plough back & forth, other smaller boats slip past, kids doing somersaults from the jetty, & loads of birds – from hornbills to herons – flying over the river.

OTHER PRACTICALITIES
Banking and foreign exchange
There are no banks in Janjanbureh, and the only **forex bureau** we could locate – **Samba Talco**, next to the Baobolong Annex – evidently doesn't actually change money. Ask at the larger Mauritanian shops to change money, but be warned: they'll only accept pounds sterling or euros.

Internet This is another amenity that seems to be lacking in Janjanbureh, presumably because of the unreliability of mains electricity. It's also often quite

15

Counteracting the steady stream of guides and tour operators from the coast that bring tourists but give little to the local community, JustAct (*Janjanbureh Uniting Sustainable Tourism & Community Training;* m *[UK] +44 (0) 7553 567409/ 6661403/2222446/3297249;* e *jagambia@yahoo.com/jagambiauk@yahoo.com;* w *justactgambia.org*) is a local initiative that aims to provide employment in Janjanbureh. They train and license local residents to become guides specialising in the history, culture, nature and people of the island. Any income generated goes directly back in to the local community and helps to support development initiatives. JustAct can also arrange tours to local sites as well as meetings with local families and opportunities to experience life in the region. Excursions start from half day (*£2.50pp*) to full day including lunch (*£7pp*), and activities include donkey tours (*£5pp*), a palm wine-tapping experience (*£5pp*) and cultural performances such as the Kankurang, drumming, kora and the Kanyelang women's group, with prices starting from £4 per person. Boat trips can be arranged around the island (*£40*) or as far as River Gambia National Park (*£75*), and fishing trips (*£8/hr*) are also available. Finally, for a truly fascinating and local experience, JustAct can arrange homestays either in the town or at a local village.

difficult to pick up a good enough signal for internet browsing on mobile phones using any of the local providers.

Shopping Again, options are limited. The silversmith opposite the Baobolong Beach Bar offers opportunities for watching the traditional methods of these third-generation artisans. The **market** stocks a limited range of fresh and packaged foodstuffs, but a better selection is available at Bansang, about 20km to the southeast.

ACTIVITIES AND EXCURSIONS In addition to the attractions discussed below, Janjanbureh is a useful base from which to visit Wassu National Monument on the North Bank (page 225), and it is also possible to boat here from River Gambia National Park (pages 229–30), though Kuntaur makes for a more convenient starting point for the latter excursion.

Around town A few old buildings of minor interest are dotted around Janjanbureh. Best known among these is the pair of dilapidated **waterfront warehouses** touted as having slave-trade associations according to the local oral history. The roofless and rather fort-like **CFAO Warehouse**, immediately east of what is now the ferry slipway, is often referred to as the Slave Market, though in fact it was constructed in the late 19th century and only ever served as a storage place for legitimate goods. However, it is possible that the same site was used as a camp and assembly point by slave traders in the 16th and 17th centuries. On the opposite side of the ferry slipway, the so-called **Slave Dungeon** – a dank subterranean storeroom adorned with recently added chains and lit by flickering candles to enhance its sinister mood – is also part of a warehouse, built in the late 19th century by the mercantile **Maurel & Prom Company**. Another landmark with tenuous slave trade associations is the **Freedom Tree**, which was planted in front of the police station to replace the 'original' in 2002, and has become the subject of a legend very similar to the one associated with the Freedom Flag at Albreda. Be warned that local guides are adept at guilt-tripping tourists by showing them this trio of spurious sites and then angling for money. Look out for local musician and Janjanbureh institution, Taka Titi, who will set up his drums and chant the town's history to you as he pounds out a beat.

Several less controversial 19th-century architectural landmarks can be seen along Owen Street. A few doors up from the police station, the town's last intact **Creole-style wooden house** was originally built by the Jones family, one of the 200 liberated slaves brought to MacCarthy Island in 1832. The plain rectangular **Methodist Church**, which lies a block further east, is claimed to be the denomination's oldest church in sub-Saharan Africa, having been inaugurated by the Reverend William Fox in 1835 at a site chosen as a Wesleyan Mission 11 years earlier. On the western edge of town, the **Armitage High School** was established as the country's only boarding school in 1923, catering mainly to the progeny of district chiefs, and many of its alumni went on to achieve prominent government positions in the post-independence era. A contender for the country's most underwhelming historical site is the 'last gas lamp' on the corner of Jackson and Meller streets – a relic of a gas lighting system installed in 1905, it is basically just a headless pedestal dwarfed by a 10m-tall concrete pylon right alongside it! **The Kankurang Centre** (m *3840434;* w *ncac.gm; entrance D100*) is a museum set in a large roundhouse on the outskirts of town showcasing the mask traditions of the various tribes of The Gambia.

Birding on MacCarthy Island
Janjanbureh and surrounds offer some superb and undemanding birding opportunities. Indeed, it is possible to see a good selection of forest and aquatic species from the ferry jetty (or the nearby Baobolong Beach Bar) or in the grounds of Janjanbureh Camp on the North Bank opposite town. But the best bird walk on the island is the rough road that leads west from the town centre, past the prison, then passes through a mosaic of woodland, grassland and cultivation, before it reaches the site of the currently abandoned Bird Safari Camp after 3km, where the surrounding riparian forest is particularly rewarding.

FAIRPLAY GAMBIA

Aiming to make use of The Gambia's greatest, woefully under-utilised, asset, while providing training and employment opportunities for the local youth, this social enterprise (m *(UK) +44 (0) 7856670999/315292/3484792/20492;* e *fairplaygambia@hotmail.com;* w *fairplaygambia.org*) specialises in upriver ecotourism. Based in Bansang and Janjanbureh, they work with the local youth group JustAct (see box, opposite) to offer two water-related enterprises. **Kayak Gambia** provides a variety of excursions, including a 2-hour early-bird breakfast trip and 2- or 3-day expeditions staying in local villages or bush camping. Half a day's kayaking around Janjanbureh costs £10 per person while all-inclusive expeditions start at £30 per day. Elsewhere, a solar-powered pirogue, the *Fula Princess*, tours the length of the country with its experienced and friendly crew, who will cook meals using the onboard kitchen or at local lodges. Specialist fishing trips focus on the best sites for the ferocious tiger fish, while birding packages include a full-time guide and use of vehicles and drivers for off-river birding sites, and they can take in Tendaba, Bao Bolong Wetlands, River Gambia National Park, Kunkilling Forest Park and more. Trips start from £45 per person per day.

15

An astonishing seven species of owl (including Verreaux's eagle-owl and the rare Pel's fishing owl) have been recorded in this compact area, along with the likes of violet turaco, Bruce's green pigeon, blue-breasted kingfisher, yellow-throated leaflove, grey-headed bush-shrike, Wilson's indigo-bird and oriole warbler. The jetty at the closed Bird Safari Camp hosts a resident swamp flycatcher, and it's a good place to scan the facing riverbank for the beautiful shining blue kingfisher. You are also likely to see green monkey and possibly red colobus in the vicinity.

Lamin Koto Stone Circle Situated about 1.5km from the North Bank ferry terminus at Lamin Koto, this stone circle stands under a large tree on the east side of the main surfaced road to Farafenni. It doesn't compare with the more impressive megalithic sites at Wassu and Ker Batch, but it is a lot more accessible from Janjanbureh to those with limited time to explore upriver.

Mungo Park Memorial Mungo Park was a Scottish explorer who lived on the North Bank near Karantaba Tenda in 1795 while he learned several local languages in preparation for a trip into the interior to seek the source of the River Niger. He set off with just a few donkeys and servants for company, and had a fascinating journey but failed in his primary goal. When eventually he returned to Britain, he wrote a book entitled *Travels in the interior of Africa*, which was an instant bestseller. In 1801, Park returned to The Gambia and set off again to look for the river's source, this time with a large force of army deserters. Neither he nor any of his men returned alive.

A tall memorial pillar erected to the memory of Mungo Park commemorates the spot from which he set out on his last, ill-fated expedition about 1.5km from Karantaba Tenda and 30km northeast of Janjanbureh. Bush taxis connect Lamin Koto (on the North Bank opposite Janjanbureh) to Karantaba Tenda and cost less than D60. Once there, anybody will be able to guide you to the pillar, which is within walking distance of the village.

Musa Molloh Mausoleum This is the burial place of Musa Molloh Balde, a renowned resistance leader remembered for his prowess both as a warrior and as a skilful diplomat. In 1884, he became the hereditary ruler of the Fulladu Empire, which ran south from the River Gambia into parts of what are now Senegal, Guinea-Conakry and Guinea-Bissau. Originally based at Amdallai on what is now the Senegalese border north of Banjul, Musa Molloh signed a series of contradictory treaties with both the French and British, a deception that led to his being summoned to Saint Louis in 1903 for charges of misconduct by the French administration. Instead, he and his followers crossed into the Gambian part of Fulladu to seek British protection, settling at Kesereh Kunda on the South Bank not far east of Janjanbureh. Tensions between Musa Molloh and the colonial government flared up in 1919, after Governor Sir Edward Cameron received several complaints about the king's brutal mistreatment of local women. As a result, Musa Molloh was exiled to Sierra Leone, and allowed to return to The Gambia only in 1923, stripped of all his traditional powers. He died and was buried in Kesereh Kunda eight years later. In 1971, his tomb was renovated and in 1974 it was declared a national monument. The present tomb was built in 1987 in collaboration with the Government of Senegal. To reach it, follow the main Basse Road east for about 1km from the junction for Janjanbureh to the village of Boraba, where you need to take a turn to the left that brings you to Kesereh Kunda after another 2km or so. You can take a shared taxi from Janjanbureh, walk, or hire a horse- or donkey-cart from local villagers.

Kunkilling Forest Park Situated on the South Bank of the river near the eastern tip of MacCarthy Island, some 5km upstream of Janjanbureh, Kunkilling Forest Park has been set aside by four small villages (including Kesereh Kunda) to protect 2km² of forest- and palm-lined riverfront. Run through by four short eco-trails (none longer than 1km), the forest is home to five primate species, including red colobus, along with warthog, banded mongoose, bushbuck, Gambian sun squirrel, hippopotamus and West African manatee. Mammal viewing is erratic but the birding is outstanding, with more than 150 species recorded. The big special is Adamawa turtle dove, which is common here but scarce elsewhere in The Gambia. Other good birds include Pel's fishing owl, red-footed falcon, marsh owl, Beaudouin's snake-eagle, African finfoot, Senegal parrot, shining-blue kingfisher and lead-coloured flycatcher. Visitors are encouraged to walk at dusk and dawn, when the wildlife is most active.

Visits must be arranged through the Department of Forestry in Janjanbureh. You can either visit their office off Owen Street or call the dedicated forestry guide Haruna Kandeh (m *6418586/9923338*), who will set up your transport and accompany you there. The best way to head there is by boat, which takes about an hour in either direction, allowing for a few birding stops, and costs around D2,400–3,000 per party for the round trip, inclusive of 2–3 hours' waiting time while you explore the forest. By road, you can get to the entrance near Kesereh Kunda in 30–45 minutes. If you don't have your own car, expect to pay around D1,500 for a taxi or D900 for a motorcycle carrying one person only. In addition, there is an entrance fee of D100 per person, and the guide will expect a similar tip. Note that the forestry guide has no pretensions to being a birding guide but he can arrange one if so required. The best time to visit is early morning (leaving Janjanbureh at around 06.00) or later afternoon (leaving at around 15.30).

Kajakat Island About 5km long and up to 2km wide, this large island lies in the middle of the River Gambia about 6km downstream of MacCarthy Island and a similar distance upstream of the eastern boundary of River Gambia National Park. Also known as Kai Hai (the name of the nearest North Bank village), the island is said locally to be haunted by various sprits, including a man-eating dragon-like creature that might well reflect a folk memory of an outsized killer crocodile. As a result of its taboo status, the island remains uninhabited, and the cover of dense natural forest is largely intact. Hippos and crocodiles are resident in the surrounding waters, and the island itself supports a similar selection of forest and aquatic birds to the nearby national park, including a large flock of knob-billed ducks that sometimes roost off the south side.

From MacCarthy Island it is easy to take a boat trip to Kajakat. This can be arranged with any local guide or more reliably perhaps with most of the lodges, including Janjanbureh or Baobolong Camp. Expect to pay around D2,400–3,000 per party to rent a boat for a 2–3-hour round trip. With private transport, it would also be possible to visit the island from Kai Hai, which lies about 2km from the riverbank and is the site of several megalithic circles. If you are in the area, a more esoteric national monument is the birthplace of Sir D K Jawara (the first president of independent Gambia) at the village of Barajali about 8km west of Kai Hai.

BANSANG

Perched on the South Bank of the River Gambia about 20km southeast of Janjanbureh, Bansang is a significantly larger and less moribund town, with a population of around 7,500, a bustling market, and the country's largest inland hospital. For all that, it is a quite unremarkable place, with the only point of local interest being a well-established colony of dashing red-throated bee-eaters that nests in a nearby quarry, in a mud bank overlooking a small pool that also hosts plenty of nesting weavers, bishops and other small passerines in breeding season.

GETTING THERE AND AWAY Bansang lies about 20km from Janjanbureh, immediately north of the South Bank main road heading east towards Basse. Several bush taxis run back and forth between the two daily, costing less than D60, and a hand-pull ferry connects the town to villages on the North Bank. If you are heading to the quarry where the bee-eaters nest (⊕ *N13 26.225 W14 39.944*), continue along the Basse Road for about 600m past the main feeder road into Bansang, then after crossing a small rise take the first track to your right, which leads to the nesting site after another 500m.

WHERE TO STAY AND EAT Most people who visit Bansang for the bee-eater colony do so either as a day trip from Janjanbureh or *en route* to Basse. However, there is one adequate shoestring lodge in Bansang.

Bintou's Paradise Hotel (16 rooms)
m 7552465/6235490; e saikoufatty52@yahoo. com. Boasting a breezy riverside location in the town centre, this hotel displays quite a contrast between the genuinely attractive & characterful deck overlooking a forested stretch of river, & the warren-like interior, whose gloominess is amplified when the main electricity is offline. The tiled en-suite rooms are quite spacious & acceptably clean, & come with a standing fan & lights, or in some cases AC, all of which depend on an electricity supply that is usually (but not always) forthcoming from 18.00 to 02.00. It also serves b/fast for £2 & lunch or dinner for £3.50. *£6 /15 dbl fan/AC.*

UPDATES WEBSITE

Go to w bradtupdates.com/thegambia for the latest on-the-ground travel news, trip reports and factual updates. Keep up to date with the latest posts by following Philip on Twitter (🐦 *@philipbriggs*) and via Facebook: f fb.me/ pb.travel.updates. And, if you have any comments, queries, grumbles, insights, news or other feedback, you're invited to post them directly on the website, or to email them to Philip (e *philip.briggs@bradtguides.com*) for inclusion.

16

Basse and Upper River Division

Basse Santa Su, more normally abbreviated to Basse, is set on the South Bank of the River Gambia about 370km inland of Banjul. The administrative capital of Upper River Division, it is also the largest Gambian town east of Farafenni, having witnessed a huge population surge in recent decades, from around 5,000 inhabitants in 1983 to 20,000 today. Basse once must have been a river port of some significance, at least judging by the decaying Victorian buildings that dot its small timeworn waterfront. And it still serves as a transport depot for the local peanut and cotton trade, but these days it is, above all, a market town – indeed, the sprawl of narrow streets that comprises the town centre comes across as one vast chaotic bazaar, spilling over with shops and stalls laden with all manner of imported goods and local wares.

Basse has a strikingly different character from any other Gambian town, thanks to its isolation from the coast and strong cross-border trade links, not only with Senegal, which encloses it on three sides, but also to a lesser extent with Guinea, Mali and Mauritania. From a visitor's perspective, it feels far less Westernised than any other comparably sized Gambian town – traditional smocks and straw hats are still very much *de rigueur* here – yet it also has a rather cosmopolitan atmosphere, albeit one that mainly reflects its diversity of West African influences. True, Basse lacks for overt tourist attractions, but for those whose travels in the region are otherwise confined to coastal Gambia, a visit to this busy, noisy, thriving and emphatically African town will be a genuine eye-opener.

Though Basse is refreshingly free of bumsters and touts, a visit there will push many travellers outside their normal comfort zones. The town's roads are dusty, pot-holed and uncomfortably narrow, public services such as electricity and running water are erratic even by upriver standards, and hotels and restaurants are all on the rudimentary side. Sadly, in this last respect, Basse has gone backwards in recent years, thanks to the closure of several relatively alluring tourist amenities established around the turn of the millennium. The main reason for this decline is probably that the gradual deterioration of upcountry roads after the 1990s meant fewer and fewer tourists were prepared to drive all the way to Basse from the coast. If that is the case, it is to be hoped that the recent resurfacing of the South Bank Road from Serekunda will generate renewed interest in visiting the country's most remote large town.

Away from the urban hustle of Basse, Upper River Division exudes an aura of peace and timeless traditionalism. True, most houses are now roofed with corrugated iron rather than thatch, and misshapen TV aerials protrude skywards in the most remote places. Of course, there are modern amenities such as schools and health clinics. But despite this, many aspects of day-to-day life have changed little in hundreds of years. Women work out in the fields and cook food over open wood fires. Men still go out to hunt with ancient guns, or sit and chat beneath the bantaba. And because few toubabs set foot in the area, people tend to be extremely welcoming to and curious

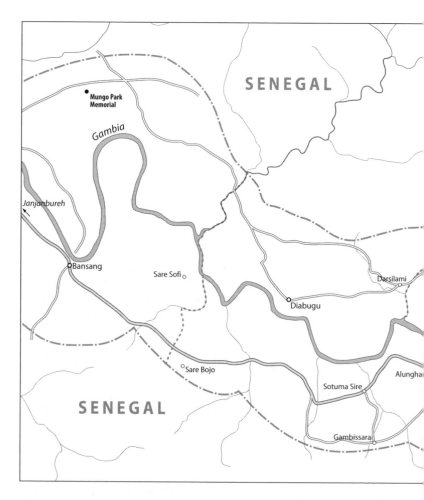

about visitors, though English as a spoken language is less common than elsewhere. As is the case with its administrative capital, Upper River Division is short on bespoke tourist attractions, but it can be very rewarding to those who want to experience an Africa that remains largely undistorted by the trappings of the tourist industry.

GETTING THERE AND AWAY

Basse is about 370km inland of the coast by road. Coming from Banjul or Serekunda, the best route is the South Bank Road via Brikama and Soma, which is now surfaced almost in its entirety, and should take under 5 hours in a decent private vehicle. It is also possible to drive to Basse via the North Bank, but this will require two ferry crossings, and the road east of Janjanbureh is in very poor condition, so it cannot be recommended unless you have a specific reason (birders, for instance, regard the North Bank of Upper River Division to be the best place to seek the localised sun lark and rufous scrub robin).

Using public transport, your most comfortable option is the eight GTSC buses that run in either direction between Kanifing (Serekunda) and Basse daily, stopping

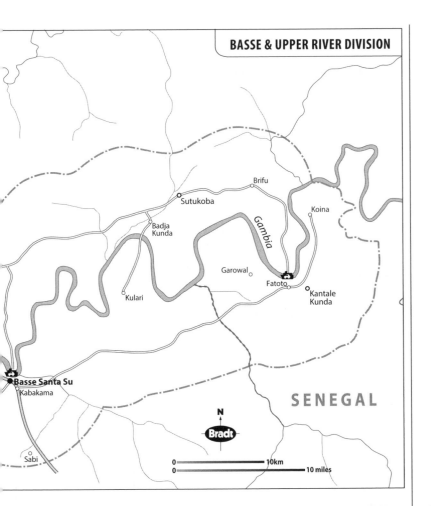

Brifu

Sutukoba

Koina

Badja
Kunda

Gambia

Garowal

Fatoto

Kulari

Kantale
Kunda

Basse Santa Su

Kabakama

SENEGAL

N

Bradt

| 0 | | 10km |

| 0 | | 10 miles |

Sabi

en route at Soma and Janjanbureh. The buses all leave between 06.00 and noon, with the best option being the air-conditioned express service that leaves at 08.00 in either direction. Tickets cost around D350/425 for a regular/air-conditioned bus and the trip usually takes 7–8 hours, depending on the frequency and duration of stops. The express service is marginally more expensive but an hour or two quicker. If the GTSC buses are full, or you need to travel in the afternoon, regular gelly-gellys and shared taxis connect Basse to Janjanbureh, Soma, Serekunda and elsewhere on the South Bank for D290, but the vehicles are more uncomfortable and less reliable.

An inexpensive motor and passenger ferry links Basse to the facing North Bank. It operates from 08.00 to 18.00, but will cross the river only when enough vehicles have arrived. If you are on foot and want to get across quickly, there is a busy trade in small boats that ply the same route, though you may have to share it with a motorbike or two.

ORIENTATION

Basse is quite a spaced-out town. The town centre and market area form a compact warren of busy roads lined with several budget hotels, bars and eateries, as well as

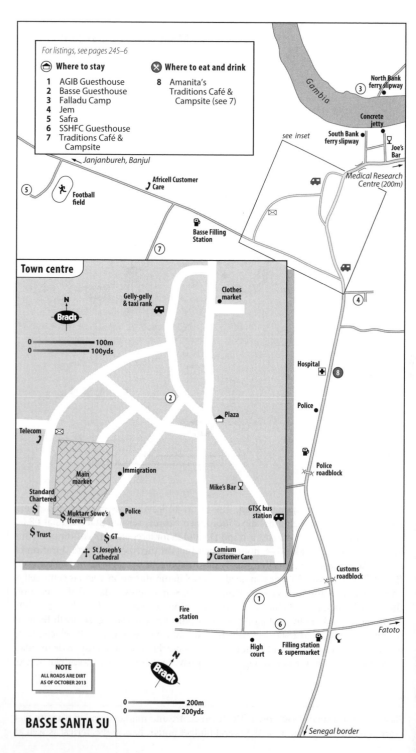

For listings, see pages 245–6

Where to stay
1. AGIB Guesthouse
2. Basse Guesthouse
3. Falladu Camp
4. Jem
5. Safra
6. SSHFC Guesthouse
7. Traditions Café & Campsite

Where to eat and drink
8. Amanita's Traditions Café & Campsite (see 7)

← Janjanbureh, Banjul

Gambia

North Bank ferry slipway ③

Concrete jetty

South Bank ferry slipway

Joe's Bar

Medical Research Centre (200m)

see inset

Africell Customer Care

Football field ⑤

Basse Filling Station

⑦

Town centre

N
Bradt

0 ————— 100m
0 ————— 100yds

Gelly-gelly & taxi rank

Clothes market

④

Hospital ⊞ ⑧

②

Plaza

Police ●

Telecom ✉

Main market

● Immigration

Police ▣

Police roadblock ✕

Standard Chartered $

$ Muktarr Sowe's (forex)

● Police

Mike's Bar ♀

GTSC bus station

$ Trust

$ GT

✝ St Joseph's Cathedral

Camium Customer Care

Customs roadblock ✕

①

Fire ● station

⑥

Fatoto →

High ● court

Filling station & supermarket

NOTE
ALL ROADS ARE DIRT
AS OF OCTOBER 2013

N
Bradt

0 ————— 200m
0 ————— 200yds

BASSE SANTA SU

↙ Senegal border

the main gelly-gelly park and GTSC bus station. The riverfront, jetty and ferry to the North Bank lie about 150m further north, and are reached by crossing a small bridge adjacent to the gelly-gelly park. About 1km southeast of the town centre, and separated from it by a small open area, the relatively smart suburb of Basse Mansajang is the site of the better hotels, several administrative buildings, and the main intersection of the roads running east to Fatoto and south to The Gambia's most-used eastern border crossing into Senegal.

WHERE TO STAY   *Map, page 244*

Basse has limited accommodation options and nothing catering specifically to tourists, the one exception being Falladu Camp which recently reopened.

Budget

🏠 **AGIB Guesthouse**   (30 rooms) m 3361888/3665995. Set in a shadeless concrete compound in Mansajang, this unsignposted hotel is named after the Islamic bank that owns it. Although something of a study in soullessness, it offers far & away the best accommodation in Basse, with the added advantage of having a back-up generator which usually kicks in during the night if the mains power fails. The spacious tiled dbl rooms come with AC, fan, fridge & satellite TV, & are in pristine condition. Alcohol is forbidden (along with 'use of prohibited drugs, gambling & acts of sodomy') & there is no restaurant, but meals can be prepared by arrangement. *£8.50/12 dbl with shared bath/en suite, £20 VIP with 2 dbl rooms & sitting room.*

🏠 **Falladu Camp**   (48 rooms) ✆ 5668743; m 9906791. Located on the riverside facing the town, 100m from the ferry jetty, this is set in spacious gardens, although these are starting to look a little overgrown. Rooms are in very basic thatched roundhouses, & decent meals are served. It has a tiny boat that ferries guests across the River Gambia for free, & pirogue trips can be organised. *Rates should not be more than £20 dbl.*

🏠 **SSHFC Guesthouse**   (19 rooms) ✆ 6784952; m 7267788/3955734. This former government guesthouse in Mansajang lies in agreeably shady grounds around the corner from the AGIB Guesthouse. Comfortable in an old-fashioned way, rooms come with AC & fan, fridge & bathroom. *£10/room.*

Shoestring

🏠 **Basse Guesthouse**   (8 rooms) m 7189913. This long-serving 1st-floor guesthouse has a conveniently central location on a junction halfway between the GTSC & gelly-gelly parks. The rooms are quite rundown & scruffy, but spacious enough, & come with a dbl bed & standing fan. You can almost forgive the grubbiness of the shared bathroom because of the enthusiasm & friendliness of Soury, the owner-manager. Fair value. *£4 dbl.*

🏠 **Jem Hotel**   (8 rooms) m 7735620. This long-serving hotel (now known as the London Night Club) on the backroads east of the hospital is looking pretty tired these days, its lackadaisical aura epitomised by the non-functional state of the advertised bar & restaurant. The rooms, which come with a fan but not much else & share a bathroom, are worth considering only if the other options in this range are full. *£5/room.*

🏠 **Safra Hotel**   (22 rooms) m 9810066. Situated off the Serekunda Rd about 1km west of the market, this 3-storey hotel has acceptably clean but slightly musty rooms with dbl bed &, in some cases, a standing fan. There is no restaurant but you can eat at nearby Traditions or Solid Properties. *£5/room.*

Camping

⛺ **Traditions Café & Campsite**   Situated about 200m south of the Serekunda Rd, this family-run café (page 246) has space for campers to erect their own tent in the small banana garden. *£3.50/tent.*

WHERE TO EAT AND DRINK   *Map, page 244*

In addition to the sit-down eateries listed below, Basse is pretty good for inexpensive street food, a local speciality being tangy *ful* sandwiches made with fresh tapalapa rolls – try the stall in front of Amanita's. Of the handful of drinking holes dotted around town, the riverside **Joe's Bar** has the more attractive location, but **Mike's Bar** is more central.

✕ **Amanita's Restaurant** m 7719215/ 9952150; ⏱ 07.00–midnight Mon–Sat, 16.00– midnight Sun. Tucked away behind a courtyard opposite the hospital on the road to Mansajang, this popular eatery has a Senegalese owner & chef. It usually serves a selection of 3–4 tasty local dishes. Great value. The beers are cold & cheap too. *Around £1–2/plate at lunch & dinner.*

✕ **Traditions Café & Campsite** m 7335562; e sulaymanjallowtradition62@yahoo.com; ⏱ 07.00–midnight daily. It's not often you have the chance to dine with a bona fide king. The owner's brother, who is also a traditional

healer, will eagerly prove his royal credentials. Though less convenient than it used to be since its relocation in 2012, this long-serving café remains a friendly set-up serving a good selection of local & international dishes, best ordered at least an hour or 2 in advance. Soft drinks are served, but no alcohol. It also arranges boat trips on the river close to town for around D600/hr, as well as excursions further afield such as to Senegal's Niokolo-Koba National Park. As well as hosting & feeding guests, the management plant trees locally in an effort to stop forest fires. *Mains £4, snacks/sandwiches £2.50.*

OTHER PRACTICALITIES

BANKING AND FOREIGN EXCHANGE Basse's sole ATM can be found at **GT Bank**, close to the market. The **Trust Bank** and **Standard Chartered Bank** have branches opposite each other adjacent to the central market, but neither has an ATM nor forex facilities. Likewise, several of the private **forex bureaux** dotted around town seem unwilling to change any foreign currency into dalasi. The one exception we're aware of is **Muktarr Sowe's** (*Shop #8;* ⏱ *08.00–18.00 daily*), in the row of small shops in front of the market, which changes US dollars at a similar rate to the one offered in Banjul.

INTERNET There are a couple of internet cafés in Basse.

SHOPPING Though the **central market** doesn't cater specifically to tourists, quite a few local handicrafts are on offer, generally at cheaper prices than you'll get on the coast. For serious batik-buyers, **Traditions Café** has a good relationship with several local tie-and-dye artists as well as other local craftspeople, and can arrange viewing sessions by request.

ACTIVITIES AND EXCURSIONS

AROUND TOWN The town itself lacks any obvious tourist focus other than the sprawling market, which is great fun to explore, as are the surrounding side roads. That aside, the main attraction is the riverfront, renowned in ornithological circles as the most reliable Gambian site for the localised Egyptian plover or crocodile bird. This colourful and eagerly sought wader is often seen picking along the muddy riverfront between Joe's Bar and the ferry jetty, with sightings being most regular in the early morning between September and December, but unusual from March to May.

Also worth a look, and difficult to miss on account of its incessant chirruping, is the colony of Gambian epauletted fruit bats that roosts in the hospital grounds about 300m along the road towards Mansajang. These rank among the largest bats found on the African mainland, with a 1m-long wingspan, and are most impressive at dusk, when columns of several dozen can be seen flapping heavy-winged over the town centre and the hotels in Mansajang.

RIVER TRIPS The best way to see wildlife around Basse is to charter one of the small private passenger boats docked next to the ferry jetty to take you further along the river. You should see plenty of green monkeys in the riverine forest, and might also encounter a few outsized monitor lizards. And the birding can be superb, not only improving the odds of your seeing an Egyptian plover, but also offering a good chance of several species that appear to be less common further west, notably a trio of stunning bee-eaters – northern carmine, red-throated and little green – that breed in the mud banks. Even if birding isn't your thing, it is a peaceful and enjoyable river trip, one that could be extended downriver as far as Tambasensan, where hippos are quite often encountered, though this is not guaranteed.

Rates are flexible, but expect to pay at least D120–180 per party per hour. If you don't feel like negotiating directly, the folk at Traditions Café can set up a boat trip for a fixed rate. For birders, afternoon is probably the best time to do the trip, ideally departing at around 16.00. If you are thinking of boating as far as Tambasensan, an earlier start is recommended.

SOTUMA SIRE Flanking the main South Bank Road about 12km west of Basse, the village of Sotuma Sire is known locally for its small pottery industry. The products made here are characterised by their earthen colour and white enamel patterns, and include some relatively original and unusual items, including enamelled candlesticks. The potters are easy to find as you will see a batch of various pots placed next to the road, and there are also a couple of roadside kilns. If they are not around, a nearby store owner will negotiate a price on their behalf. Any gelly-gelly or bush taxi travelling between Basse and Janjanbureh can drop you there.

FATOTO Set in a relatively hilly area about 40km past Basse, the scattered port of Fatoto is the most inland settlement in The Gambia, situated only 10km east of the Senegalese border. More of an overgrown village than a small town, it supports a population of around 2,000, and has absolutely no tourist facilities. Nevertheless, birdwatchers might want to drive through from Basse, since it offers an opportunity to see several species rare elsewhere in The Gambia, including Adamawa turtle dove, northern carmine bee-eater, and African swallow-tailed kite, the last-named a dainty tern-like bird of prey that hovers effortlessly overhead while it hunts for insects. Otherwise, the main reason you'd be likely to visit Fatoto is for the sense of completion associated with travelling all the way across the country, in which case you may as well aim to do so on a Sunday, when it livens up slightly for the weekly market. The road from Basse is unsurfaced at the time of writing and most private vehicles will get through in around an hour. A few inexpensive bush taxis run between Basse and Fatoto daily costing around D50, but they are not that frequent, though the volume is highest on market day.

SARE NGAI The Monday market at this small village 30km north of Basse is one of the best in Upper River Division. It stocks many products that cannot be found in Basse market, and is particularly known for its beautiful cloth. Even if you're not buying, the livestock section is well worth spending some time at. You will need to cross the ferry to the North Bank to get there.

Appendix 1

LANGUAGE

English is the official language. Most people around the coast and other tourist areas speak it to some degree, and many are very fluent. As a rule, however, the further you go upriver, the fewer people speak English. This is where learning a few words in a local language will come in handy. The trouble comes in deciding which language to learn, since several are in everyday use. Mandinka makes most sense as the majority of the population is Mandinka. But Wolof, Jola or Fula people respond well if you can greet them in their own language so we have also added the commonest greetings. It feels good to know that someone has gone to the trouble of learning a few phrases in your language and just a few words will make many people happy.

Note that the foreign words given below are spelt phonetically, ie: as they are pronounced.

UNIVERSAL GREETING The importance of greetings in The Gambia cannot be overemphasised. Everybody greets one another, either verbally or through handshakes, and this can sometimes take several minutes. It's just another manifestation of the friendliness of the Gambian people. Even people who are too far away to talk or to shake hands will clasp their own hands above their head to greet you at a distance. The universal greeting is in Arabic because most of the population are Muslims. The greeting is: *Salam malekum* (loosely translated as 'Peace be with you'), to which the response is: *Malekum salam* ('Peace returns to you').

BASIC MANDINKA WORDS AND PHRASES

Good morning	*Esama*
Good afternoon	*Etinyang*
Good evening	*Ewulara*
How are you?	*Kori tanante?* (response: *Tanante*, which means 'I am fine')
How is your family?	*Sumoole?* (response: *Ebebeje*, which means 'they are fine')
How is your wife/husband?	*Ila muso/kemo le?* (response: *Ebebeje*)
How are your children?	*Ding ding olule?* (response: *Ebebeje*)
How is your work?	*Do kwo be nadi?* (response is normally: *Domanding, domanding*, which means 'slowly, slowly')
No	*Hani*
Yes	*Haa*
Thank you	*Abaraca*
Thank you very much	*Abaraca bake*
Good	*Abetiata*

Very good	*Abetiata bake*
Water	*Jio*
What is your name?	*Etondi?*
My name is ...	*Nto mu ... le ti*
Where do you come from?	*Ebota minto le?*
I come from ...	*Nbota ... le*
How much (money)?	*Jelu lemu?*
Where is ...?	*... le?*
White man	*Toubab*
Black man or child	*Mofingo*
Go away!	*Acha!*

WOLOF GREETINGS

Good morning	*Naka subasi*
Good afternoon	*Naka bekeck*
Good evening	*Naka ngosi*
How are you?	*Naka nga def?* (response: *Jamarek*, which means 'I am/they are fine')
How is your family?	*Naka wa kerrgi?* (response: *Jamarek*)
Thank you	*Jere jef*

JOLA GREETINGS

| How are you? | *Kassumay?* (response: *Kassumay kep*, which means 'I am fine') |
| How are you? | *Katabo?* (response: *Kocobo*, which means 'I am fine') |

FULA GREETINGS

| How are you? | *Nambata?* (response: *Jamtan*, which means 'I am fine') |

SERER GREETINGS

| How are you? | *Nafio?* (response: *Memehen* or *Jamarek*, which means 'I am fine') |

MANDINKA NUMBERS

1	*kiling*	21, 22, etc	*muwang ning kiling* (literally twenty and one), *muwang ning fula*, etc
2	*fula*		
3	*saba*		
4	*nani*		
5	*lulu*	30	*tang-saba*
6	*woro*	40	*tang-nani*
7	*worowula*	50	*tang-lulu*
8	*sei*	60	*tang-woro*
9	*kononto*	70	*tang-worowula*
10	*tang*	80	*tang-sei*
11, 12, etc	*tang ning kiling* (literally ten and one), *tang ning fula*, etc	90	*tang-kononto*
		100	*keme*
20	*muwang*	1,000	*wili kiling*

Appendix 2

GLOSSARY

Here follows a glossary of terms and names used in this book and/or in The Gambia itself.

AC	air conditioning
adobe	mud building
afra	grilled meat
alkalo	chief of village
APRC	Alliance for Patriotic Reorientation and Construction (ruling party under President Jammeh 1996–2017)
attava	bitter green tea
ba	big (often forms part of place names)
balafon	traditional xylophone
bantaba	covered meeting place in centre of village (or in lodge/hotel gardens). It is the origin of the word 'banter'.
baobab	large, distinctive trees
Barrow, Adama	President of The Gambia since 2017
Bathurst	colonial-era name for Banjul
Baye Fall	Gambian and Senegalese disciples of a Sufi Islamic sect founded by Cheik Bamba, who protested against French colonialism
benachin	red, tangy, sometimes very spicy, rice dish cooked with vegetables and/or meat
bengula	meeting place
bissap (aka wanjo)	sweet drink
bolong (or bolon)	creek
bumsters	young guys who make their living on the fringes of the tourist industry, often through harassment
bush taxi	minibus or larger vehicle used as public transport
butut	cent-like subdivision of dalasi
café touba	spiced sweet coffee
cowry	small white shell used as currency in pre-colonial times
dalasi	local unit of currency
djembe	traditional drum
domoda	stew made with groundnut sauce
DSTV	South African multi-channel satellite television service
endemic	unique to a specific area
en suite	room with private toilet and shower attached
exotic	not indigenous, eg: pine plantations
forest	wooded area with closed canopy
forex bureau	bureau de change
Fula	pastoralist ethnic group also living in Mali and Senegal

Gamou	Islamic gathering involving a night of praying and chanting with a *marabout*
gelly-gelly	as bush taxi
griot	oral historians and praise singers of the ancient West African empires that tell the histories of families at ceremonies. They are known as *jeli* in Mandinka.
gris-gris	protective talisman worn around the body (pronounced 'gree-gree'. Usually a piece of Arabic scroll wrapped and sewn up in leather. Also known as *ju-ju* or *amulet*.
GTSC	Gambian Transport Service Corporation, a recently privatised bus service
guesthouse	cheap local hotel
harmattan	dry dusty wind blowing across West Africa from the Sahara in the dry season
indigenous	occurring in a place naturally
insh'allah	'God willing' in Arabic and an all-round useful phrase ('Will you give me money?' 'Tomorrow, insh'allah')
Jammeh, Yahya	President of The Gambia since 1994
Jawara, Sir Dawda	Prime Minister then President of The Gambia from independence in 1962 until 1994
Jola	predominant ethnic group in southern Gambian and Senegalese interior
Julbrew	local lager-like beer
July 22 Coup	Bloodless 1994 coup that effectively transferred power from President Jawara to President Jammeh
kankurang	mystical masked creature that accompanies boys during Mandinka initiation ceremonies, or terrorises villages as a form of social control, depending upon your view
kola nuts	bitter and mildly narcotic nuts chewed throughout West Africa
kora	traditional harp-like instrument
Koriteh	local name for Eid al-Fitr, the feast marking the end of Ramadan
koumpo	Jola dancer covered in green reeds that becomes possessed by a spirit and spins out of control
Lamin	name commonly given to first-born sons
lorry	term used occasionally for any large passenger vehicle
lumo	weekly market
mamapara	masked stilted dancer from the Mandinka tribe, known as *chakaba* in Wolof
marabout	Islamic mystic leader
Mbalax	aggressive and percussive Senegalese pop music, using *sabar* and *tama* drums, popularised internationally by Senegalese singer, Youssou N'Dour
murubungu	mud house
nding	small (often forms part of place names)
nyankotan	basic rice dish
palasas	meat and spinach stew thickened with peanut butter
panga	local equivalent of a machete
PPP	People's Progressive Party (ruling party under former President Jawara)
Ramadan	the holy month of Islam, commemorating when the Koran was revealed to Muhammad, during which fasting takes place from dawn till dusk

riparian woodland	strip of forest or lush woodland following a watercourse, often rich in fig trees
riverine woodland	as riparian woodland
sabar	traditional drum
Sahel	dry savannah belt dividing the forested coast of West Africa from the Sahara
savannah	grassland with some trees
Serahule	ethnic group with historic links to the Mali Empire (also called Soninke)
Serer	ethnic group whose main population centre is in northern Senegal and The Gambia
seyfo	district chief
shared taxi	form of public transport carrying a full quota of passengers between two fixed places
shawarmas	Lebanese-style take-away comprising grilled meat and salad in pita bread
station	as taxi park
superkanja	okra soup
surfaced road	road sealed with asphalt or similar
tapalapa	heavy Gambian-style bread
taxi park	terminus for shared taxis and gelly-gellys
Tobaski	also called Eid al-Adha, this commemorates Abraham's readiness to sacrifice his son on God's command and the last-minute substitution of a ram. Every Islamic family that has the means will purchase a ram, of which they eat one third, give one third to their friends and donate the final third to the poor.
toubab	non-derogatory term for white person or Westerner – urban legend says it derives from boys asking colonials for 'two bob' coins
town taxi	charter taxi, as in Europe (but not metered) used for a 'town trip'
West Sudanese	architectural style using mud and wood typical of mosques of the Sahel
Wolof	dominant ethnic group on the coast south of the River Gambia
woodland	wooded area lacking closed canopy
yassa	chicken or fish stewed or marinated in onion and lemon

Appendix 3

FURTHER INFORMATION

BOOKS

Food Until Ida Cham (see page 149) writes her Gambian cook book, probably the best guide to the cuisine of the region is from Senegalese chef, Pierre Thiam. Not simply a cook book, but a full-colour exploration of Senegal's culinary culture – equally at home on the coffee table as in the kitchen. Two volumes, *Senegal: Modern Senegalese Recipes from the source to the bowl* (2015) and *Yolele! Recipes from the Heart of Senegal* (2008) are available from Lake Isle Press.

History and culture Faal, Dawda *A History of The Gambia – AD1000 to 1965* Edward Francis Small Printing Press, 1997. This is quite a detailed and easy-to-find local publication relating the history of the country and dealing with it from the perspective of a West African.

Haley, Alex *Roots: The Saga of an American Family* Doubleday, 1976. Many of the specifics have been discredited since Haley's death, but this Pulitzer-winning tome, set partly in The Gambia, still provides a highly readable novelistic introduction to the slave trade and the impact on its victims.

M'Bai, Pa Nderry *The Gambia: The Untold Dictator Yahya Jammeh's Story* iUniverse, 2012. Written by a highly regarded Gambian investigative journalist now living in the USA, this is probably the most balanced available account of the achievements, failings and peculiarities of President Yahya Jammeh.

Meagher, Allen (Editor) *Historic Sites of The Gambia – An Official Guide to the Monuments and Sites of The Gambia* National Council for Arts and Culture and International, 1998. This is an excellent little book that is very readable and contains lots of information not only on historic sites but also on the culture of the country.

Park, Mungo *Travels in the Interior of Africa* 1858. The extraordinary account of Scottish explorer Mungo Park's journey from The Gambia as he traced the course of the Niger, during which he encountered African despots, was taken captive by a Moorish chief and robbed and stripped naked by Fulani bandits.

Sonko-Godwin, Patience *Ethnic Groups of the Senegambia: A Brief History* Sunrise Publishers, 1985. Widely available in the country, this provides a useful and quite readable overview of the country's main cultural groups.

Thomas, Hugh *The Slave Trade: History of the Atlantic Slave Trade, 1440–1870* Phoenix, 2006. Weighing in at a daunting 900 pages, this is probably the most authoritative recent history of the trade that trafficked an estimated ten million Africans into a life of bondage in the Americas between the 15th and 19th centuries.

Language There are a few Wolof- and Mandinka-language dictionaries and primers available on Amazon, but to get started, an eminently worthwhile resource is the Live Lingua Project (**w** *livelingua.com/peace-corps-language-courses.php*), which offers a free archive of downloadable Peace Corps language lessons including Wolof, Jola, Fula, Mandinka and others.

Natural history

Barlow, Clive, Wacher, Tim and Disley, Tony *A Field Guide to Birds of The Gambia and Senegal* Christopher Helm Publishers, 2nd edition, 2005. This out-of-print book used to be *the* field guide to the birds of The Gambia and Senegal. It has been supplanted as first choice by the same publisher's more recent Borrow and Demey guide listed below. Still, it is a very good book, and can safely be recommended as a supplementary field guide to anybody sufficiently dedicated to carry two.

Barnett, Linda, Emms, Craig and Santoni, Christina *The Herpetofauna of Abuko Nature Reserve, The Gambia* Bulletin of the British Herpetological Society, No 77 Autumn, 2001. This short paper covers all the amphibians and reptiles that have been found in this species-rich nature reserve.

Borrow, Nik and Demey, Roy *Helm Field Guide to the Birds of Senegal and The Gambia* Christopher Helm Publishers, 2012. This superb field guide is well laid out, with informative text, good illustrations and detailed distribution maps, and very up-to-date and thorough both for The Gambia and Senegal. A must for all birdwatchers.

Borrow, Nik and Demey, Roy *Helm Field Guide to the Birds of Western Africa* Christopher Helm Publishers, 2004. To the same high standard as the same authors' guide to Senegal and The Gambia, this is less useful to those sticking to these two countries, but a better bet for those travelling more widely in the region.

Edberg, Etienne *A Naturalist's Guide to The Gambia* J G Sanders, 1982 (English edition). Original edition in Swedish. Although quite dated now, this is still the best of the guides available for naturalists who are visiting The Gambia. It includes an introduction to the country, places to visit and a section on common animals and plants. This is a gem of a book with some very good black-and-white illustrations. Worth getting hold of.

Gosney, Dave *Finding Birds in The Gambia* Easybirder, 2011. Useful and compact guide to some of the most popular birding sites in the country, with handy hand-drawn maps too.

Kasper, Phyllis *Some Common Flora of The Gambia* Stiftung Walderhaltung in Afrika, 1999. This is a very useful illustrated guide to the common plants found throughout the country.

Kingdon, Jonathan *The Kingdon Guide to African Mammals* Academic Press, 1997. This is undoubtedly the best and most thorough field guide on terrestrial African mammals, but not really aimed at a casual one-off visitor. All the known land species are covered with the most up-to-date classification. Colour illustrations throughout and easy to use.

Kingdon, Jonathan *The Kingdon Pocket Guide to African Mammals* Princeton Pocket Guides, 2005. This condensed version of the full guide listed above will be sufficient for most visitors, and it is far cheaper and more portable.

Larsen, Torben *Butterflies of West Africa – Origins, Natural History, Diversity, Conservation* Apollo Books, 2005. A monumental achievement by the author, who has spent many years amassing a great deal of data for the region. If you're into butterflies, and aren't put off by the hefty price tag, this will be a must.

Penney, David *Common Spiders and Other Arachnids of The Gambia* Siri Scientific Press, 2009. One for specialists, this enjoyable field guide to the country's spiders, harvestmen, ticks, scorpions and allies has 170 photos.

Penney, David *Field Guide to Butterflies of The Gambia, West Africa* Siri Scientific Press, 2009. Though only 80 pages long, this is a useful field guide to the country's rich variety of butterflies, and illustrated with 230 photographs.

Penney, David *Field Guide to Wildlife of The Gambia* Siri Scientific Press, 2nd edition, 2012. This is a very portable and current paperback primer to the country's wildlife, with plenty of details on invertebrates and plants, but also some useful information on larger species (though coverage of birds is limited). Almost 800 pictures are packed into its 160 pages.

Health

Wilson-Howarth, Dr Jane *The Essential Guide To Travel Health: Don't let Bugs, Bites and Bowels Spoil Your Trip* Cadogan Guides, 2009. A guide to healthy travel for adults.

Wilson-Howarth, Dr Jane and Ellis, Dr Matthew *Your Child Abroad: A Travel Health Guide* Bradt Travel Guides, 2014

Travelogues

Fenton, Simon *Squirting Milk at Chameleons* (Eye Books, 2015) and *Chasing Hornbills* (Eye Books, 2016). In turn amusing and harrowing, these easy-to-read memoirs by the late updater of this guide offer a fascinating insight in to life among the Jola people in a village near the border of The Gambia and Senegal.

Long, Rosemary *Under the Baobab tree* (Eric Dobby Publishing, 1993) and *Together under the Baobab tree* (Eric Dobby Publishing, 1994). Collections of newspaper articles by a Glaswegian journalist who married a Gambian and attempted to set up a beach bar some years ago, although little seems to have changed.

Other West Africa guides For the full list of Bradt's Africa guides, see w bradtguides.com/shop.

Briggs, Philip *Ghana* Bradt Travel Guides, 2016.

Connolly, Sean *Senegal* Bradt Travel Guides, 2015.

Manson, Katrina and Knight, James *Burkina Faso* Bradt Travel Guides, 2012.

Manson, Katrina and Knight, James *Sierra Leone* Bradt Travel Guides, 2017.

Sykes, Tom *Ivory Coast* Bradt Travel Guides, 2016.

Velton, Ross *Mali* Bradt Travel Guides, 2009.

WEBSITES

w **accessgambia.com** Excellent resource for information on travel, accommodation, tours, news and current affairs in The Gambia.

w **fatbirder.com** Twitchers should visit Fatbirder for news on the latest bird sightings.

w **gov.uk/foreign-travel-advice/gambia** Up-to-date travel and safety advice from the UK Foreign Office.

w **travel.state.gov/content/passports/en/country/the-gambia.html** Up-to-date travel and safety advice from the US State Department.

w **visitthegambia.gm** Official website of the Gambia Tourism Board.

Index

INDEX OF ADVERTISERS